Penguin Books
KATHERINE MANSFIELD
The Woman and the Writer

Born in Rotorua, a town so detested by Katherine Mansfield, Gillian Boddy now lives in Wellington, New Zealand. She graduated from Auckland University at nineteen and has taught in England and New Zealand. Her research into Katherine Mansfield has taken her to Britain, Europe, Noumea and Australia.

The mother of two children, Gillian Boddy has also been a television panellist, and is a freelance journalist, a senior counsellor and teacher of English at Queen Margaret College, Wellington, and a university tutor in New Zealand literature. With two other women, she formed a film company to make a television documentary on the life of Katherine Mansfield which was shown at the Cannes Film Festival and is to be screened internationally. She has been commissioned to arrange an exhibition of Katherine Mansfield photographs and invited to speak at a number of conferences in 1988.

Katherine Mansfield

The Woman and the Writer

Gillian Boddy

Penguin Books

Penguin Books Australia Ltd
487 Maroondah Highway, PO Box 257
Ringwood, Victoria, 3134, Australia
Penguin Books Ltd
Harmondsworth, Middlesex, England
Viking Penguin Inc.
40 West 23rd Street, New York, NY 10010, USA
Penguin Books Canada Limited
2801 John Street, Markham, Ontario, Canada,
L3R 1B4
Penguin Books (N.Z.) Ltd
182-190 Wairau Road, Auckland 10, New Zealand

First published by Penguin Books Australia, 1988

Typeset in Times by Computype Creative Typography
Made and printed in Australia by Globe Press
Designed by Josie Semmler

CIP

Boddy, Gill, 1944-
Katherine Mansfield, the woman and the writer.

ISBN 0 14 008632 3.

1. Mansfield, Katherine, 1888-1923 – Biography.
2. Mansfield, Katherine, 1888-1923 – Diaries.
3. Authors – New Zealand – 20th century –
Biography.
4. Women authors – Biography.
I. Mansfield, Katherine, 1888-1923.
II. Title.

NZ 823' .2

Contents

Illustrations

Preface

When I was fifteen my English teacher read us Katherine Mansfield's famous story 'The Garden Party'. I did not enjoy this first introduction to 'the one peacock in New Zealand's literary garden', and as a result I avoided her writing throughout my school and university studies.

My *real* meeting with Katherine Mansfield, the woman and the writer, occurred years later when I was faced with the task of introducing her work to students in her native Wellington. I began by reading John Middleton Murry's editions of her letters, scrapbook and journal. Soon I discovered not only a gifted writer whose short stories have been translated into at least twenty languages, including Japanese and Chinese, but a remarkable woman.

Having read the collection of her papers, letters and notebooks in the Alexander Turnbull Library, I continued my research, in London, Europe and in parts of New Zealand I had never known before. From all this she emerged not as the ethereal tragic figure of the Mansfield myth but as an enigmatic woman who was so many things – rebel, dreamer, musician, mimic and so much more; a woman who loved Beethoven and Charlie Chaplin.

And so I helped my students to share a little of what I had experienced. Their response was enthusiastic and has remained so. This book began as a thirty-page illustrated pamphlet for other students. On others' advice it expanded.

I have included brief extracts from her letters, notes and diaries, poems and reviews. Although these are fragmentary and at time unreliably dated, they, with the many illustrations, will give some insight into her mercurial character, at times cruel, harshly intolerant, at times warm, loving and generous and above all, defiantly alive. I have also included selected stories that I hope will appeal to readers meeting her work for the first time so that they will go on to read others which I would very much have liked to include. I have also given a list of books and articles which I have consulted as they could provide a useful source for readers. One particularly helpful resource would be Nelson Wattie's *Bibliography of Katherine Mansfield References 1970–84*. I have not, however, included a bibliography of Katherine Mansfield's work as a full bibliography, compiled by Brownlee Kirkpatrick, is to be published soon.

Over the years that I have worked on this project, the Mansfield industry, or 'Mansfield mania' as critics have wryly described the phenomenal interest in this writer, has mushroomed: biographies, criticism, radio, film, stage and television interpretations of her work, and life. Those who have enjoyed her work for years must be pleased at this revival of interest even if they do not always agree with the modern interpretations which have largely destroyed the myth. Like many others I have been faced with the difficult question of nomenclature! Mansfield, Katherine Mansfield, Katherine? Finally I decided to use Kathleen and Kass as she was known to her family and friends until, at Queen's College she herself adopted her first two initials as her professional name. Not long after she would advise an Australian editor that she wished to be known simply as K. Mansfield or K.M., and so, in her own words, 'Let me take the case of K.M. ....'

Katherine Mansfield: The Woman and the Writer is intended then as an introduction, not a definitive study. I hope that this collection of notes, poems, illustrations, letters and stories, with a linking commentary, will help to bring K.M. alive for others; to enable them to enjoy her and her work, to feel something of what she felt – 'a kind of freedom – a sense of *living* – not enduring – not existing – but being alive'.

Acknowledgements

I should like to thank the many people who helped me in my research, in particular Mrs F. Ball, Miss G. Beauchamp, Mrs G. Beauchamp, Mrs A. Bennett, Monsieur J. Borel, Mr and Mrs Cockburn, the late Mr B. Coster, Mr H. Cullerne, the late Mrs E. Dobson, Miss Stephanie Fierz, the late Miss Ruth Herrick, Mrs R. Ingrams, Mr H. G. Lawrence, Dr Frank McKay, Mr James Moore, Mrs Jeanne Renshaw, Signor Flavio Parrini, the late Mrs E. Robison, Monsieur and Madame Simon Rey, Dr C. K. Stead, Mrs D. Stephenson. My special thanks are due to Mrs Margaret Scott for her assistance and encouragement.

Thanks are also due to Mrs Barbara Angus, Professor Antony Alpers, Professor Jacqueline Bardolph, Mr Noel Carrington, Mr Peter Day, Dr Cherry Hankin, Mr Michael Harlow, Miss Brownlee Kirkpatrick, Miss Katherine Middleton Murry, Mr Colin Middleton Murry, Professor Vincent O'Sullivan, and Mrs Claire Tomalin for their interest and assistance.

I am grateful to Monsieur Michel de Salzmann, Mme Jeanne de Salzmann, Monsieur Henri Tracol and Mr James Moore for assisting with my research and allowing me to include illustrations of George Ivanovich Gurdjieff and his followers at the Institute for the Harmonious Development of Man; and to Mrs Julian Vinogradoff for permission to include illustrations from *Lady Ottoline's Album*. In my research regarding Katherine Mansfield's stay in Wörishofen, I am indebted to the late Professor Schäfer to Herr and Frau Kreuzer, Herr Lothar Burghardt and Herr and Frau Repka.

The following institutions and organisations have kindly allowed me to use materials in their possession: the Bibliothèque Nationale, Paris; the British Library, London; the Harry Ransom Humanities Research Centre, University of Texas at Austin; the Karori Historical Society; the Mitchell Library, Sydney; the Mills Memorial Library, McMaster University; the National Library of New Zealand; the Newberry Library, Chicago; Radio New Zealand Archives; the Rotorua Museum; the Wellington Public Library. I am especially grateful to Mr James Traue and the staff of the Alexander Turnbull Library, Wellington for their unfailing and invaluable assistance, and for permission to include illustrations and manuscript materials from its unique collection.

Every effort has been made to acquire copyright permission. I apologise sincerely for any omissions, and regret concerning proprietorial rights that in a few cases I have been unable to locate holders of material.

I am grateful to the following for permission to quote: © 1988 the Estate of Katherine Mansfield for previously unpublished material and the Society of Authors as the literary representative of the Estate of Katherine Mansfield and the Estate of John Middleton Murry; Laurence Pollinger Ltd and the Estate of H. E. Bates for an extract from *The Modern Short Story* published by Michael Joseph Ltd; Laurence Pollinger Ltd and the Estate of Mrs Frieda Lawrence Ravagli for extracts from *Frieda Lawrence: The Memoirs and Correspondence* and *The Collected Letters of D. H. Lawrence* published by William Heinemann Ltd; Viking Penguin Inc., Angelo Ravagli and C. Montague Weekley, Executors of the Estate of D. H. Lawrence for permission to quote from *The Collected Letters of D. H. Lawrence* edited by Harry T. Moore; Curtis Brown Ltd and the Estate of the Hon. Dorothy Ann Brett for extracts from *Lawrence and Brett: a Friendship*; the Sophie Partridge Trust, Jonathan Cape Ltd, and Holt, Rinehart and Winston for extracts from *Carrington: Letters and Extracts from her Diaries* edited by David Garnett; the Literary Estate of Leonard Woolf and the Hogarth Press and Harcourt Brace Jovanovich, Inc. for extracts from *Beginning Again*; the Literary Estate of Virginia Woolf and the Hogarth Press and Harcourt Brace Jovanovich, Inc. for extracts from *The Common Reader, the Diary of Virginia Woolf* edited by Anne Olivier Bell and *The Letters of Virginia Woolf* edited by Nigel Nicolson. Acknowledgements are also due to Mrs Laura Huxley, and Chatto and Windus for extracts from the *Letters of Aldous Huxley,* Mr John Carswell for extracts from Catherine Carswell's *The Savage Pilgrimage* published by Secker and Warburg; Mr Peter Day for references to Ida Baker's *The Memories of L.M.* published by Michael Joseph Ltd and illustrations of L.M.; Pierre Sichel for an extract from *Modigliani* published by E. P. Dutton & Co.; Michael Holroyd and William Heinemann Ltd for an extract from *Lytton Strachey*; William Heinemann Ltd for a brief extract from *An Autobiography* by Enid Bagnold; Jeffrey Meyers and Hamish Hamilton for a reference to *Katherine Mansfield*; Christopher Hassall and Longman for an extract from *Edward Marsh: A Biography*; Price Milburn Ltd for an extract from *New Zealand Short Stories* by Joan Stevens. Thanks are also due to A. D. Peters and Co Ltd for permission to quote from the *The Life of Bertrand Russell* by Ronald Clark published by Jonathon Cape and Weidenfeld and Nicolson; Constable & Co. for extracts from *Today we will only gossip* by Lady Beatrice Glenavy; Granada Publishing Ltd for extracts from *Mark Gertler: Selected Letters* edited by Noel Carrington; Faber and Faber Ltd for extracts from *Ottoline at Garsington* by Robert Gathorne Hardy; Cassell Ltd for an extract from William Orton's *The Last Romantic*; the Oxford University Press for an extract from *The Modest Art: A Survey of the Short Story* by T. O. Beachcroft; the Yale University Press for an extract from *Katherine Mansfield: A Critical Study* by Sylvia Berkman; John Johnson Ltd for extracts from *Katherine Mansfield* by Antony Alpers published by Jonathon Cape and *The Life of Katherine Mansfield* by Antony Alpers published by Jonathon Cape Ltd and Viking Penguin Inc.; Methuen and Co. Ltd for extracts from F. A. Lea's *John Middleton Murry*; Routledge and Kegan Paul Ltd and Harcourt Brace Jovanovich, Inc. for a brief extract from *In Search of the Miraculous* by P. D. Ouspensky; the Marsden School Old Girls' Association for extracts from *Marsden: The History of a New Zealand School for Girls*; Farrar, Straus and Giroux, Inc. for permission to reprint a photograph from *The Intelligent Heart* by Harry T. Moore, and Miron Grindea for extracts from Adam International Review; St Martins Press and Macmillan Press, London and Basingstoke, for permission to quote from *Katherine Mansfield* by Clare Hansen and Andrew Gurr, and Macmillan Press for permission also to quote from *Katherine Mansfield and Her Confessional Stories* by C. A. Hankin.

I would also like to thank the BBC Halton Picture Library for permission to include a photograph of Lady Ottoline Morrell, and the Photo Source for an illustration of George Ivanovich Gurdjieff, the Hogarth Press for an illustration of Leonard and Virginia Woolf.

Very real thanks are also due to my family and friends who have helped me in so many ways. I must also express my thanks to Michael MacDonald, Lindsay Missen, Deborah Coddington and Alister Taylor.

Finally I would like to thank the editors and designers for Penguin Australia in Melbourne who have succeeded in making my long-term wish become a reality.

Author's note

When transcribing from manuscripts I have tried to retain Katherine Mansfield's paragraphing and punctuation, including her use of the ampersand and her frequently omitted apostrophe. I have, however, added the apostrophe where its omission would hamper the reader's immediate understanding as in, for example, 'He'll'. The retention of the ampersand and much of the original punctuation will, I hope, help to convey something of the actual impression given by the original text.

A particular difficulty in reading the manuscripts has been to distinguish between Katherine Mansfield's use of commas and dashes, but I have tried to be as accurate as possible. For reasons of space I have had to cut many quotations; . . . indicates such an omission. Where she herself used . . . as punctuation, this is indicated by -- to avoid confusion.

A variant or questionable interpretation of a word has been indicated in square brackets and in a very few cases I have corrected an accidental omission or error for the sake of complete sense. Katherine Mansfield used both Katie and Katy, Lesley and Leslie, Sidney and Sydney which may also explain some apparent inconsistencies. Although many of her letters were dated, others, especially those to her husband, were not, and the dating of her notebooks and journals except when writing in an actual diary, was erratic and spasmodic. In general I have used the dates given by J. Middleton Murry.

G.B.

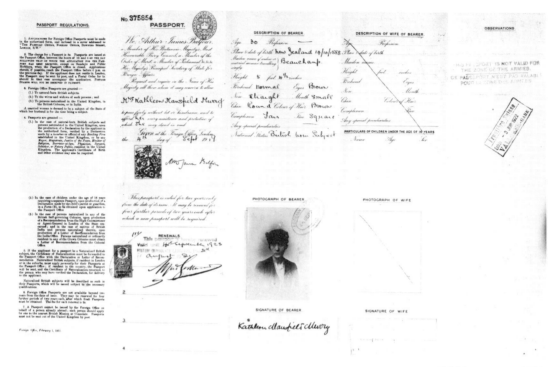

K.M.'s passport, 1922

1 'From a little land
with no history'

Beginnings

Wellington, the colonial capital of New Zealand, was a small town in 1888. The *Evening Post* for Monday 15 October carried only two simple birth notices, one of which read: 'Beauchamp – On 14th October, the wife of Mr Harold Beauchamp of a daughter.'

Kathleen Mansfield Beauchamp was born on that Sunday morning in Tinakori Road, in a simple wooden house built by her father above a deep bush-covered gully.

There were to be six children in the Beauchamp family – Vera, Charlotte, Kathleen, Gwendoline, Jeanne and Leslie, the youngest and the only son. Their mother, Annie Dyer, was a finely beautiful, sensitive and fastidious woman whose love of life was hampered by frequent illness. Her husband, Harold Beauchamp, was an

It's a small town, planted at the edge of a fine deep harbour like a lake. Behind it, on either side there are hills. The houses are built of light painted wood. They have iron roofs coloured red. And there are big dark plumy trees massed together . . .
'Daphne', 1921

Wellington in the 1880s. The Beauchamps' is the large square white house with two chimneys.

1

Kezia had been born in that room. She had come forth squealing out of a reluctant mother in the teeth of a 'Southerly Buster'. The Grandmother, shaking her before the window, had seen the sea rise in green moutains and sweep the esplanade. The little house was like a shell to its loud booming. Down in the gully the wild trees lashed together and big gulls wheeling and crying skimmed past the misty window.
'The Aloe'

25 Tinakori Road

ambitious successful man. He was soon to become part owner in the old importing firm Bannatyne & Co. which he had joined at eighteen. He would also rise rapidly in Wellington's commercial world, gaining status and wealth, becoming a member of the Wellington Harbour Board, director of several important companies, a Justice of the Peace and in 1901 chairman of the Bank of New Zealand. Although a controversial figure, because of his humble goldfield origins and independent views, he was to be knighted in 1923 for his service to his country in financial and commercial matters.

Conventional, respectable and respected, Harold Beauchamp epitomised much that Kathleen, or Kass as she was often called, was later to reject. Nevertheless, it was he who arranged for the publication of her first stories. He himself appeared in many of them, portrayed at first harshly, but later often sympathetically and perceptively. In 1915 she wrote:

father was a self-made man and the price he had to pay for everything was so huge and so painful . . . He was young and sensitive still. He still wondered whether, in the deepest sense he got his money's worth. He still had hours when he walked up and down in the moonlight half deciding to chuck this confounded rushing to the office every day – and clear out . . .

Many of her early childhood memories of her father were fondly affectionate – carrying her from the house during an earthquake; or as a train laughingly chugging around the tennis court, his children clinging to his back until they steamed 'majestically' into the nursery for breakfast. It was he too who told the children the family anecdotes about their great-grandfather, John. A Cheapside silversmith with a love of hunting and poetry, he was the family's 'original pa-man'.

In a kind of verbal shorthand that was part of the Beauchamp's private code of family expressions, Kathleen and others in the family perpetuated his memory by the frequent use of this phrase to describe a certain kind of character or quality. It seems to have been used to suggest a cheerful, somewhat extravagant, recklessly unsettled approach to life, combined with an ability to laugh at oneself, and all of this tinged with a slight touch of pomposity.

Great-grandfather John had once been known as 'The Poet of Hornsey Lane' and the family were taught to remember him and their grandfather, Arthur, who came to New Zealand from Australia through the rhyme:

I'm the last of the old Hornsey Laners
the last of the Beauchamp campaigners,
The last of the eight it's sad to relate,
I'm the last of the old Hornsey Laners!

Grandma's birthday . . . and one day I must write about Grandma at length, especially of her beauty in her bath – when she was about sixty. Wiping herself with the towel. I remember now how lovely she seemed to me. And her fine linen her throat her scent. I have never really described her yet . . .
'Journal', 21 January 1922

Back row: Vera, Jeanne, K.M., Mrs Beauchamp.
Front: Chaddie, Mrs Dyer, Leslie

The person to whom Kathleen turned most frequently for love and understanding was her grandmother, Grannie Dyer – formerly Miss Margaret Isabella Mansfield. With her daughters Belle and Kitty she had lived with the Beauchamps from the early days of their marriage. It was she who gently admonished the children, ran the house and cared for them.

Annie Beauchamp had been born in Upper Fort Street, Sydney, not far from the wharves beneath where the harbour bridge now stands and Harold had been born in the Victorian goldfields. Nevertheless for them, as they rose in Wellington society, as for other colonial New Zealanders, it was England that was to be seen as the mother country. So it was that Grannie Dyer became particularly important to the Beauchamp children when their parents returned 'home' to England in 1889 and 1898. It was not surprising that Kathleen remembered her grandmother all her life with warm affection.

Gwendoline was born in October 1890 but died three months later. The last daughter, Jeanne, was born in 1892.

When Kathleen was four her father, now the owner of Bannatyne's which he had developed into a very successful business, leased a large home in the country area of Karori:

In the days of our childhood we lived in a great old rambling house planted lonesomely in the midst of huge gardens, orchards and paddocks. We had few toys, but – far better – plenty of good, strong mud and a flight of concrete steps that grew hot in the heat of the sun and became dreams of ovens.

With her sisters she attended the local Karori school. A plump,

plain, bespectacled and moody child, she apparently shone in arithmetic but, ironically, proved to be an erratic speller. Later on the happy memories of this period, a time of roaming and exploring in fields and gardens, would be reshaped into some of her finest stories including 'Prelude' and 'The Doll's House'.

In 1898 the family moved back to town, to a spacious white house in Tinakori Road, later the setting for 'The Garden Party'.

Our house in Tinakori Road stood far back from the road. It was a big, white painted square house with a slender pillared verandah and balcony running all the way round. In the front from the verandah edge the garden sloped away in terraces & flights of concrete steps – down – until you reached the stone wall covered with nasturtiums that had three gates let into it – the visitors' gate, the Tradesmen's gate, and a huge pair of old iron gates that were never used and clashed and clamoured when Bogey & I tried to swing on them.

For the fact was, the school the Burnell children went to was not at all the kind of place their parents would have chosen if there had been any choice. But there was none . . . the consequence was all the children of the neighbourhood, the Judge's little girls, the doctor's daughters, the storekeeper's children, the milkman's were forced to mix together.
'The Doll's House'

Karori School

Earlier in 1898 the three oldest Beauchamp girls were enrolled for Term II at Wellington High School in Thorndon. It was here that the nine-year-old Kathleen's first published story appeared in the *High School Reporter*, with the schoolgirl editor's comment: 'This story, written by one of the girls who have lately entered the school shows promise of great merit. We shall always be pleased to receive contributions from members of the lower forms.'

The school magazine published a second story in 1899 and she followed in her sister Vera's footsteps by winning a prize for Eng-

I think of our house our garden us children – the lawn – the gate & Mother coming in. Children! Children! I really only ask for time to write it all – time to write my books. Then I don't mind dying I live to write ... let me finish it without hurrying – leaving all as fair as I can ...
'Journal', 19 May 1919

On the steps at 75 Tinakori Road 1898. Back row: Mr and Mrs Beauchamp, Mrs John Ruddick. Centre: Jeanne, Marion Ruddick, Belle Dyer. Front: K.M., Leslie, Chaddie

a wooden building jutting out into the sea. Over the entrance was a square tower and inside were the dressing rooms opening off the galleries . . . we were put one by one into a harness while the instructor held the reins and propelled us from the gallery through the deep water . . . Kathleen made hard work of it.
Marion Ruddick

The Thorndon Baths

lish, as well as French and arithmetic. Like her sisters she played in the school croquet tournament. Charlotte and Kathleen also entertained the girls with songs and recitations at concerts in the large, dark hall of the old wooden building. Obviously for Kathleen it was not as unhappy or as unproductive a childhood as it has often been painted. Her young Canadian schoolfriend Marion Ruddick with whom she explored Thorndon and swam in the Thorndon Baths later remembered her as plump, bespectacled, inky fingered and capable of violent likes and dislikes. She remembered too her feeling of awe at the visit of Richard Seddon, the premier and a close friend of the Beauchamps. Clearly by then the family had gained considerable social status and wealth.

In 1899 Vera, Charlotte and Kathleen left the high school for nearby Miss Swainson's, a private school requiring fees of four guineas a term. One of her teachers, Mrs Henry Smith, found her 'a surly sort of girl' who was 'imaginative to the point of untruth', whose written work was 'too prolific, poorly written, poorly spelled and careless' and – worse still – was one who 'put herself in too much'. One contemporary remembers her as one of a threesome, 'We were all fat . . . We used to walk arm in arm at playtime . . . Kass learnt the cello. She was fond of music.'

Another teacher, Eva Butts, remembered her as enjoying playing tricks on teachers – on one occasion challenging her: 'I've been reading a lot about Free Love. What do *you* think?' Nevertheless her rebellion was a quiet one. She was 'dumpy' and 'biddable', her work was 'exceedingly lacking in grammar, style and finish . . . smeary, blotted with ink. No subject she was *asked* to write on interested her.'

Although some found her difficult, she became very close to the young part-Maori princess, Maata Mahupuku. Kathleen was soon a member of the school's A.R. club, a select group comprising the

Outside Miss Swainson's Second to back row: Kathleen Beauchamp 5th from right; third row: Vera Beauchamp 2nd from left; front row standing: Jeanne Beauchamp 3rd from left; front row: Charlotte Beauchamp 1st on left, Martha Grace (Maata Mahupuku) 2nd from left

school's best writers and speakers, which met secretly in a room at the top of the back stairs and put out a school magazine called the *Comet*. She appeared with Charlotte as Tweedledum and Tweedledee in a production of *Alice in Wonderland* and her clever impersonations showed that she had inherited Grandfather Arthur Beauchamp's flair as an entertainer. A later journal entry gives a glimpse of those school days:

Why can't I change my hair ribbon on Wednesday afternoon. All the other girls are allowed to . . . But 'No', says Mother. You may put on your thread work pinafore, but you may not put on your blue satin hair ribbon. Your ordinary brown velvet one is perfectly neat, suitable and unobtrusive as it is. (Mother loves sentences like this.) I cant help what *all the other* girls do. Have you got your thimble. 'Yes Mother in my pocket.' 'Show it me, dear' 'I said Mother it was in my pocket.' 'Well show it to me so that I can be perfectly sure.' 'Oh Mother why do you treat me like a baby? You always seem to forget on purpose that I'm in my teens. None of the other girls' mothers . . .' Oh well, I'll take my blue satin hair ribbon in my pocket & change when I get to school. It serves Mother right. I don't want to deceive her, but she makes me deceive her, & she doesn't really care a bit – she only wants to show her power . . .

Everything is different on Wednesdays . . . The ink pots are put away by the monitors, the desks pushed against the wall . . . the chairs are arranged in little groups – the windows are opened wide . . . the camellias are white & red in the bright sun. We are making [cheap] flannelette chemises for the Maori Mission. They are as long as night-dresses, very full with huge armholes & a plain band around the neck – not even a lace edging. Those poor Maoris – they can't all be as fat as these chemises! . . . it is very quiet & when the Headmistress reads Dickens aloud there is something so fascinating in her voice I could listen for years & years . . . The headmistress herself is exactly like one of those illustrations – so tiny so spry . . . What does she remind me of – she reminds me of a bird and a donkey mixed.

The Kathleen Beauchamp of these years was often awkward and rebellious. In the same spirit of rebellion she was later to reject Wellington for its brashness and emptiness, but there can be no doubt that it also provided her with vivid memories that she cherished for the rest of her life. Summer holidays at Island Bay and Day's Bay; ferry trips across Cook Strait to visit her grand-parents and great-uncle and aunt:

A rough sea journey is a strange conglomeration of sensations & I in a moment seem conquered by a thousand memories – am a child again sitting on the deck in my Grandmother's lap.

The little town of Picton, the wild beauty of the Sounds, the family property at Anakiwa, her grandfather's articulate humour and grandmother's hymn singing at the piano were an integral part of her childhood. There are still many Beauchamp descendants in the area today. One recently expressed her regret about the many 'lies about Kathleen' wishing that she could be left in peace; remarking that her later 'antics' would have gone unnoticed in our modern permissive society!

The colourful beauty of the sea, the golden hills of Wellington and the wind, even the life of the colonial Edwardian society she soon came to despise, had already become part of her soul. Many years later its place in the pattern of her life would be acknowledged, even to her father:

The longer I live the more I turn to New Zealand. I thank God I was born in New Zealand. A young country is a real heritage, though it takes one time to recognise it. But New Zealand is in my very bones.

Harold Beauchamp was not only a successful businessman, and owner of several properties. He was also a man who, like his wife, enjoyed music and poetry. In his opinion this 'young country' did not offer sufficient cultural stimulus for his daughters. Moreover, their English cousins were attending Queen's College in London.

Father is a Tolstoi character. He has just the point of vision of a Tolstoi character. I always felt that Stepan in Anna Karenina reminded me of someone.
May 1917

Harold Beauchamp about 1890

I have a very soft corner in my heart for the 'Niwaru' . . . Do you remember how Mother used to enjoy the triangular shaped pieces of toast for tea? Awfully good they were too, on a cold afternoon in the vicinity of The Horn. How I should love to make a long sea voyage again one of these days. But I always connect such experiences with a vision of Mother in her little sealskin jacket with the collar turned up. I can see her as I write.
to Sir Harold Beauchamp, 26 June 1922

The Beauchamp family, Las Palmas, 1903. Back row: K.M., Harold Beauchamp, W. Crow, B. J. Dyer, Vera. Front: Chaddie, Annie Beauchamp, Leslie, Captain Fishwick, Jeanne, Belle Dyer

In truly 'pa-man' style he booked the entire passenger accommodation of the cargo ship *s.s. Niwaru* and the family embarked for England – complete with a clavichord and a canary in a cage.

After forty-two days they arrived. Vera, Chaddie and Kathleen, in black velour hats and sailor coats with brass buttons, walked up the wide front steps of Queen's College in Harley Street. For the next three years Miss Clara Wood's boarding hostel next door would be their home. The Beauchamps, knowing the girls would be well cared for by their aunt, Belle Dyer, who later became Miss Wood's assistant, returned to Wellington in November.

Queen's College was a progressive school for its time, run on the lecture system. Girls could attend or not, as they wished, although they were required to write papers as evidence of their studies. Kathleen may have gained comparatively little formal education but it was a rich and colourful experience for her:

Nobody saw it, I felt as I did. My mind was just like a squirrel. I gathered & gathered & hid away, for that long 'winter' when I should rediscover all this treasure – and if anybody came close I scuttled up the tallest, darkest, tree & hid in the branches.

But someone did get close; it was at Queen's College that she formed one of the important relationships of her life, with the quiet and musical Ida Baker. Together they planned their future musical careers and even decided on the professional names that would lead them to fame. Ida chose her mother's name, Katherine Moore, but her forceful friend, having already decided on Kath-

erine for herself, convinced the pliable Ida to take Leslie instead
– the name of Kathleen's young brother. So Ida Baker became
Leslie Moore and Kathleen Beauchamp, taking her grandmother's
maiden name, became Katherine Mansfield. The friendship of
K.M. and L.M. was a strange one, but it was to last a lifetime.

Years later Vera remarked that L.M. was her sister's 'walking
shadow' and that she and her sisters felt they had to allow K.M.
'a loose rein . . . our lives did not run on parallel lines, there was
a very wide divergence. I felt she'd chosen a bohemian way of life,
mine was much more conventional.'

Ruth Herrick, another friend at Queen's College, described K.M.
at that time as a girl of great vitality, impulsive and strong willed.
Some girls apparently disliked her intensely because she was moody
and somehow 'different'. Nevertheless they all apparently found
her greatly entertaining with her vivid imagination, flair for mimicry and ingenious sense of mischief. On one occasion, dressed as
a prospective parent she interviewed the unwitting principal on
behalf of her daughter! Apparently she and the other colonials at
the school came as something of a shock to the system. Already
the young New Zealander was an enigma – 'If she wanted you to
like her she could be utterly charming, that was part of the enormous vitality, she could be great fun to be with. On the other
hand, she could be moody and morose for days on end.'

Much of her early writing and letters and personal notes reflect
this adolescent moodiness, but life was certainly not all rebellion.
The school's 1906 magazine describes an auction on the last day
of the bazaar:

*I need you & I rely on you. I
lean hard on you – yet I can't
thank you or give you
anything in return – except
my love. You have that
always.*
April 1920

Ida Baker (L.M.)

All the stalls sent their various produce to be sold by the hammer, generally at ridiculously low figures, though Katherine Beauchamp, who next
took the hammer, occasionally succeeded by her determined and most
professional air in really doubling the price of some things, the Colonial
jams especially going at prices far exceeding what had been asked for
them at the stalls . . . enquiries were anxiously made, when at last everything had been disposed of, after the voices of the two brave auctioneers,
who showed that womens' inferiority is not extended to that branch of
professionalism in any case.

She was not a businessman's daughter for nothing. She partici-
pated in debates wryly described as 'a great outlet' by her sisters,
in the elegant high-ceilinged waiting room, and in school concerts,
on one occasion playing 'an artistic and beautiful rendering of
Tchaikovsky's "Chanson Triste"' on her cello. Not always the
rebel, she took part in at least some of the school's activities:
tennis, croquet, and cricket in Regent's Park, swimming competitions at the Marylebone Baths, tea in the park kiosk and visits

She had been as yet utterly idle at school, drifted through her classes, picked up a quantity of heterogeneous knowledge, and all the pleading & protestations of her teachers could not induce her to learn that which did not appeal to her.
'Juliet'

Queen's College pupils, Regent's Park, Summer term 1905. K.M. is on the far left, back row. Chaddie is immediately in front, Vera is fourth from left in the back row. Belle Dyer is on the far right in the centre row

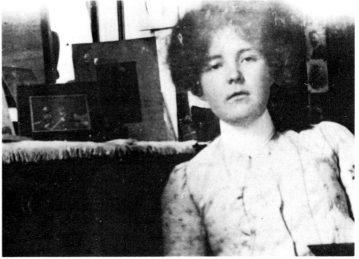

Juliet looked around her room curiously. So this is where she was to spend the next three years.
'Juliet'

K.M. in her room, Queen's College

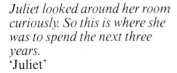

to the theatre. She attended the Royal Academy of Music and many concerts, visited art galleries and spent stimulating evenings at the homes of her friends and teachers.

Despite an increasing tendency to stay away from class, her work was generally considered 'very good', although today's students might gain some comfort from learning that one of the world's great short story writers was once considered 'unsatisfactory' in English language and 'disappointing' in English literature.

K.M. wrote five stories for the school magazine and eventually became its editor. Most of those stories are vivid recollections of a happy childhood. One, 'Die Einsame', is intriguingly different. A turgidly romantic Wildean tale, it indicates – in its subject and exaggerated style – the direction in which she was already beginning to look for inspiration. There are hints of the features that would later characterise her writing – the spontaneous joy in living things; the image of the sea – vast and mysterious; the moments of joy and disillusionment. Already these contrasts were part of the fabric of her life and of her writing.

Although she loved London's theatre, concerts and art galleries, there must have been moments when, gazing across the cobbled mews below her bedroom window, she remembered a very different view.

In September 1905 the three Beauchamp girls were demurely decorative bridesmaids in white silk and chiffon at their Aunt Belle's wedding to Mr Harry Trinder at St Marylebone Parish Church followed by a reception given by Miss Wood.

There could be no greater contrast between such reminders of her childhood world and the sophisticated cynicism of the writing of Oscar Wilde, Walter Pater and other 'decadents'. She was introduced to their heady ideas at this time by the school German professor, Walter Rippmann, during stimulating evenings at his home; their beliefs were to become her credo. She came to believe in Wilde's dictum 'the only way to get rid of temptation is to yield to it.'

K.M. was already in love with Tom Trowell, a young cellist whom she had known in Wellington. In 1903 this gifted musician (whose professional name was Arnold) and his brother Garnet had been sponsored by a group of Wellingtonians, including Harold Beauchamp, to continue their studies, at the Brussels Conservatoire. In the spring of 1906, after a visit to Paris, Aunt Belle had taken the girls to Brussels. K.M. revelled in her first taste of Europe and the romantically bohemian existence of the Trowell brothers and their friend Rudolf. There was even, she told Ida, a memorable incident when she had swum naked at a secluded beach.

In April, after her return to London, the Trowells arrived to give their first recitals. Despite the arrival of her parents to take their daughters home, now their education had been completed, K.M., seventeen, vibrantly alive and in love, felt herself on the threshold of great adventures. There was a renewal too of her friendship with Maata. She certainly did not wish to return just then to New Zealand.

Nevertheless, K.M. began to suspect that 'Caesar', Tom Trowell, did not really reciprocate her ardent feelings, so during the time the family spent together in London she poured her passion and confusion into her unfinished novel *Juliet*. She also discovered that:

Father is greatly opposed to my wish to be a professional cellist . . . so my hope for a musical career is absolutely gone – It was a fearful disappointment . . . so in the future I shall give *all* my time to writing.

I love her very much indeed.
to Sylvia Payne,
4 March 1908

Ida Baker, left and Gwen Rowse, Queen's College

He must always be everything to me the one man whom I can call Master and Lover too and though I know I shall have many fascinating connections in my life none will be like this – so lasting – so deep – so everything, because he poured into my virgin soul the life essence of Music.
June 1907

Tom (Arnold) Trowell

The inevitable return could not be escaped. In October, the Beauchamps sailed on the *Corinthic* via South Africa. From K.M.'s point of view the trip home was not a success. Her journal reveals an egotistical preoccupation with herself and her own emotions. Experience, it seemed, should not consist merely of one man or woman but of 'the whole octave of the sex'.

Her passionate shipboard infatuation with a young MCC cricketer, 'Adonis', with 'the face of a statue' is described in truly purple prose:

When I am with him a preposterous desire seizes me, I want to be badly hurt by him. I should like to be strangled by his strong hands. He smokes cigarettes frequently & exquisitely fastidiously ... We exchanged a long look and his glance inflamed me like the scent of a gardenia ... Oh, I want to push it as far as it will go. Tomorrow night there is to be a ball ...

Indeed, the influence of Oscar Wilde had been an intoxicating one.

She complained that her parents were, 'prying & curious ... My father spoke of my returning as damned rot said "look here he wouldnt have me fooling around in dark corners with fellows".' This perhaps was not a surprising attitude for an Edwardian father accompanying an eighteen-year-old daughter on a ship carrying the MCC cricket team. Nothing they could do was right. Her feelings of rebellion were exacerbated by small details. Angrily she wrote of her father and mother:

His hands covered with long sandy hair are absolutely cruel hands. A physically revolted feeling seizes me ... She is constantly suspicious, constantly overbearing tyrannous ... they are a constant offence to me ...

Already she knew with the arrogant certainty of youth:

I shall never be able to live at home – I can plainly see that. There would be constant friction. For more than a quarter of an hour they are quite unbearable – & so absolutely my [mental] inferiors.

A few weeks after K.M.'s return to 75 Tinakori Road her grandmother, whom she had not found time to visit, died suddenly:

My Grandmother died on New Years Eve – my first experience of a personal loss – it horrified me – the whole thing. Death never seemed revolting before – this place – steals your Youth that is just what it does – I feel years and years older and sadder.

She was saddened by the death of her grandmother, trapped by her family and horrified by the provincialism and ugliness of her home town with its 'narrow, sodden, mean, draggled wooden houses, colourless save for the dull coarse red of the roof – and

the long line of grey hills, impassable, spectral like.' K.M. felt that life in New Zealand was unbearable, as she wrote to her cousin, Sylvia Payne:

I feel absolutely *ill* with grief and sadness here – it is a nightmare . . . Life here's impossible – I can't see how it can drag on – I have not one friend – and no prospect of one. My dear – I know nobody – and nobody cares to know me – There is nothing on earth to do – nothing to see – and my heart keeps flying off – Oxford Circus – Westminster Bridge . . . my old room . . . and a corner in the Library. It haunts me all so much – and I feel it must come back soon – How people ever wish to live here I cannot think.

Dear – I can't write anything. Tonight I feel too utterly hopelessly full of *Heimweh* [homesickness].

Harold Beauchamp became Chairman of the Bank of New Zealand in April 1907 and the family moved to fashionable Fitzherbert Terrace, to a large house with a ballroom, croquet lawns and gardens, now the site of the United States Chancellery. They were frequently bewildered by K.M., by her intense unconventional relationships, her bitter rejection of them and their life. Even after the dance held to celebrate her nineteenth birthday and their initial agreement to her plans to return to England, she wrote:

Damn my family. O heavens – what bores they are – I detest them all . . . Even when I am alone in a room, they come outside the door and call to each other – discuss the butchers orders or the soiled linen and I feel – wreck my life . . .

She poured out her frustration in letters to L.M., to her sister Vera and in 'huge complaining diaries'. Many of these notebooks were later destroyed but some, together with her letters, exist.

If I do once go back, she thought, all will be over. It is stagnation, desolation that stares [me] in the face. I shall be lonely. I shall be thousands of miles from all that I care for.
'Juliet'

K.M., 75 Tinakori Road

They have been making havoc of our pine avenue – cutting down some of the trees ... horrible crashing tearing sound.
to Vera Mackintosh Bell,
19 June 1908

47 Fitzherbert Terrace

I pass down the central walks towards the entrance gates. The men and women and children are crowding the pathway, looking, reverently, admiringly, at the carpet bedding, spelling aloud the Latin names of the flowers. Here is laughter and movement and bright sunlight – but behind me – is it near, or miles and miles away? – the bush lies hidden in the shadow.
'In the Botanical Gardens',
2 December 1907

The Botanical Gardens in the early 1900s

They reveal that it was a dual existence. Although closeted alone in her book-lined room she may at times have yearned for England and her friends, her life in Wellington was not always quite as unbearable as she and others have described it. She studied the cello with Mr Trowell and played each week in a trio with another friend, Millie Parker. There were walks in the Botanical Gardens and days at Island Bay watching the fishermen as they hauled in their nets in the sunlight, the gaunt golden mountains stretching out to sea behind them.

Harold Beauchamp obtained a General Assembly Library reader's ticket for K.M. This enabled her to spend many pleasant afternoons there. Her reading apparently included Henry James, Shaw, Maeterlinck, Ibsen, Heine and Nietzsche and Marie Bashkirtseff. Later her work was to be frequently compared to that of

Chekhov so it's unfortunate that it is impossible now to discover if she also read the library's collection of Chekhov. One librarian recollected that she read the Jacobean and Elizabethan dramatists, de Maupassant and Flaubert. Her formal education may have been completed but her intellectual curiosity knew no bounds. She was practical enough to enrol eventually in typing and book-keeping classes at the Technical College.

She found time too to join in the tennis parties, croquet afternoons, balls and plays which were part of fashionable Wellington society's way of life. To Vera she wrote:

Here is a little news – don't call me conceited – I think I am [more] popular than almost any girl here at dances – Isnt it funny – It makes me glad – in a way – but it's a little trying. Shall I tell you the men who like me – too much . . .

There were moments of glee such as when she counted her suitors for her cousin: '*five* men have asked me to marry them'. There was even a three-week engagement to a young Englishman 'because his figure was so beautiful'. One of the Beauchamps' guests dryly remarked years later that the girls often spoke French to each other thinking that the guests at their parties would not understand.

John Parker, a school friend of Leslie's, remembered K.M. as 'surly, moody, unpopular, bad tempered'. As a boy he had been startled when, on seeing him pass below her window in Fitzherbert Terrace, she poked her tongue out at him. Jeanne, by contrast, recalled that she was 'a child among the children', delighting in giving a young cousin, who visited frequently, piggy back rides round the tennis court. Despite K.M.'s moody irritability which was 'not just directed at father', K.M.'s sisters felt it had been a happy, warm home and 'there were many days when she thoroughly enjoyed it all.'

Nevertheless the darker, more restless side of her nature, finding little real satisfaction in such social events, was reflected in some of her less conventional behaviour and partly revealed in a notebook, begun in July 1906. The carefully copied quotations from Oscar Wilde and others, included a certain 'A.W.' – A Woman – presumably K.M. herself:

'to have the courage of your excess – to find the limit of yourself!' – A.W.
'Big people have always entirely followed their own inclinations. Why should one remember the names of people who do what everyone else does? To break the law with success is to be illustrious.' – A.W.

Reflecting her chaotic confused thoughts, much of her writing during those Wellington days was intense, elaborate, fanciful and egotistical, for she found herself 'colossally interesting'. The recurring phrase 'not one man or woman but the complete octave of sex' and her diary entries show quite clearly that she defied convention in her sexual relationships. She seems to have believed implicitly in Oscar Wilde's words which she had noted:

Realise your Youth while you have it. Don't squander the gold of your days listening to the tedious . . . Live! Live the wonderful life that is in you. Let nothing be lost upon you. Be always reaching for new sensations . . . Be afraid of nothing.

Her early school stories and journal notes suggested that there were deeper motives for her behaviour. Despite her sisters' assertion that their parents were warmly loving, since childhood she had clearly felt, as she herself wrote, 'the odd man out'. She was never entirely sure of her parents' love and a very real need for warm unquestioning love seems to have been the basis for many of her dreams and fantasies and for many of her actions, stories, and that picture of her family which her sisters saw as 'extraordinary' and 'completely wrong'.

A warm, passionate creature by nature, now on the edge of womanhood, aware of her own body, her own feelings and like so many others confused by them, K.M. was eager to experiment, to know life. How much of her reaching for new sensation was reality, how much fantasy, is difficult to determine. Certainly she herself found it difficult to draw the line in her writing between fact and fiction. One would frequently merge with the other. One Sunday in June at Day's Bay she described her feelings about her companion:

I am here almost dead with cold . . . I feel that to be with my head on her breast – is to feel what Life can hold – all my troubles, my wretched fears are swept away. Gone are the recollections of Caesar & Adonis.

The entry continues, however:

I am in love with rainbows & crystal glasses – the rainbow fades – & the glass is splintered into 1000 diamond fragments. Where are they scattered – in the immensity of the sky to the four winds of heaven – gone . . . In my life so much Love in imagination, in reality 18 barren years – never pure spontaneous affectionate impulse. Adonis was, dare I seek into the heart of me – nothing but a pose. And now she comes and pillowed against her clinging to her hands, her face against mine – I am child woman and more than half man. Outside the sea is washing fully with the sound of perfect harmony . . . I cannot sleep shall not sleep again. This is madness – I know – but it is too real for sanity, it is too swiftly incredible to be doubted – Once again I must bear this changing of the tide – my life is a

Rosary of fierce combats for two – each bound together with the powerful, magnetic chain of sex, and at the end – the emblem of the crucified hangs surely . . . I feel I cannot continue my hard course of loving – and being unloved – of giving . . . What is the next move I wonder my death, my resignation . . . I snap my fingers at Fate I will not dance to the Music of the Marionettes. Damn it all!

Menaced by 'night terrors' since infancy K.M. instinctively and consciously explored her darker side. At such times these strangely morbid elements of suicide, fulfilment through death, were to haunt her all her life becoming a sombre, recurrent motif in her writing which was not always masked by the humour and optimism.

After a description of the moonlit yard filled with terrifying shapes, the notebook continues:

Somehow silently she woke – & came over to me – took me again into the shelter of her arms – We lay down together still silently . . . her hands round my body, stroking me lovingly – warming me – moving to give me more life again. Then her voice whispering 'Better now Darling?' I could not answer with words . . . I drew close to her warm sweet body, – happier than I had ever been, than I could ever have imagined being – the Past once more buried, – clinging to her – & wishing that this darkness might last for ever . . .

It was perhaps not surprising that she should wonder 'O Oscar! Am I peculiarly susceptible to sexual impulse?'

Of another relationship however, K.M. remarked, 'No Im glad about the whole affair. I shall pervert it . . . make it fascinating.' Where then did the truth end and the fascinating elaborations begin? Some weeks later, after the end of that 'frantically maudlin relationship & one better ended . . . ' with her friend Edie Bendall, she expressed her bewilderment at her own conflicting emotions:

Do other people of my own age feel as I do I wonder so absolutely powerful *licentious*, so almost physically ill I alone in this silent clock filled room have become powerfully. I want Maata I want her as – I have had her – terribly – this is unclean I know but true. What an extraordinary thing. I feel savagely crude – and almost powerfully enamoured of the child I had thought that a thing of the Past – Heigh HO!!!!!!!!!!! My mind is like a Russian novel.

It seems, despite the humour here, that she never fully resolved these feelings of guilt about her bisexuality.

Edie Bendall had just returned from Art School in Sydney when she met K.M., nine years her junior. Over seventy-five years later, and a great-great-grandmother, she remembered their loving friendship with gentle nostalgia:

We would meet every evening at five o'clock and go for long walks . . .

and have great chats . . . about everything. We had lovely days there [Day's Bay]. We went over in the ferry . . . She had her own style, she was very funny . . . a very good actress . . . her voice was beautiful, low. She adored her brother but I only remember Katherine. Moody? yes . . . but she never really changed. I always thought she would really like to come back here . . . I was devoted to her. I loved her . . . and I think she loved me.'

At the same time K.M. was still dreaming of her 'other self', Tom Trowell, her Caesar, confiding to her diary:

To me you are man, lover, artist, husband, friend – giving me all – & I surrendering you all – everything and so this loneliness is not so terrible to me, because in reality my outer life is but a phantom life – a world of intangible, meaningless grey shadow. My inner life pulsates with sunshine and Music & Happiness . . . But whatever happens – tho you marry another – tho we never meet again – I belong to you, we belong to each other . . . Each night I go to sleep with your letters under my pillow & in the darkness I stretch out my hands – & clasp the thin envelope close to my body so that it lies there warmly & I smile in the darkness and sometimes, my body aches as though with fatigue – but I understand.

This then was the relationship later lightly dismissed by Vera as a 'childish crush'.

Neither the fantasy nor the reality was enough, the call of life was too strong. She could not bear to 'look ahead into the long unutterable grey vastness of misty Future years . . .' When Arnold's father, her cello teacher and friend, left New Zealand she felt she had been completely deserted. Disillusioned by accounts Ida had sent her of Arnold's activities in London she declared, 'I do not care at all for men, but *London*, it is Life . . .' She had determined to 'fight, *for Life*', to convince her father finally of her need to return.

To a young man she had used 'merely for copy' and her family and friends she may have appeared sophisticated, assured, reserved – but it was, as so often, a facade:

I am always so supremely afraid of appearing ridiculous – the feeling is fostered by Oscar, who was so absolutely the essence of savoir faire. I like to appear in any society – entirely at my ease – conscious of my own importance, which in my estimation is unlimited, affable and very receptive. I like to appear slightly condescending, very much of le grand monde – & to be the centre of interest – Yes – but quelque fois to my unutterable chagrin inimitable shyness seizes me – isn't it ludicrous – I become conscious of using my hands and slightly inclined to blush.

K.M. had determined on her return to New Zealand that she would become a writer. Her resolution was strengthened by the literary success of her father's cousin Elizabeth, and the encouragement of her father's acquaintance, journalist Tom Mills, who was impressed by the 'sweetness' of her poems, though taken aback by her 'sexy writings', vignettes he advised her to send to the Australian *Native Companion*. She soon instructed its editor that she desired to be known only as K. Mansfield or K.M.

In the meantime she continued to write:

In a year to have lived so much! . . . I have been reading . . . writing and lately have been [to] a great many Balls and loved them . . .

Chaddie & I – with our maid – are living alone at this little cottage built on the rocks – It has only three rooms – two bedrooms fitted with bunks and a wide living room. We had both been feeling wretchedly ill and bored with Wellington – oh the tedium vitae of 19 years! so have come here – where we bathe and row and walk in the bush or by the sea – and read – and I write. One could not be lonesome here. I seem to love it more each day as the sea is a continually new sensation with me. Our life is absolutely free . . .

Much has been written of K.M.'s unhappiness in Wellington and the bitter conflict with her family, particularly her father. Inevitably, as her letters and notes show, there were rebellious arguments. K.M. longed for London and the life she had barely begun to experience. She fought vehemently for her ambitions and for her freedom. She felt alone among the New Zealand 'philistines', misunderstood and frustrated. Her father, not surprisingly, felt the need to curb her strong will and to guide her in her search for independence. As a result there were moments of painful misunderstanding between them but there were also times of family closeness. K.M.'s later writing shows that she was well aware, even at this difficult time, of another side to the eminently successful businessman; the 'pa-man' whom she railed against and ridiculed.

The sea sounded sturdy – resolute full . . . It seemed to call upon her to live a boundless, free glorious life . . . The cottage stood upon a great ledge of brown rock that stretched out to sea.

The Cottage, Day's Bay

She spent much of her time with the babies of the family, Leslie, whom everyone adored, and Jeanne, who remembers this time as a happy one, asserting that K.M.'s relationship with her father is the most misunderstood thing about her. In Jeanne's opinion he loved all his children deeply and demonstratively. Convinced by K.M.'s arguments, by the successful publication of her vignettes and, in his daughter Jeanne's words, by the painful awareness 'that you cannot own a person', he eventually agreed to allow K.M. to return to London.

In November 1907 she began a camping tour with friends through the wilder parts of the central North Island and discovered for the first time the harsh beauty of her country that she had not known before. She momentarily forgot the sophistication of London life, even the difficulties of the last few months, as she met and responded warmly to the Maori people and absorbed the wild beauty of the bush and the barren open spaces of the plains. All that she saw was noted in careful, if sometimes illegible, detail in a small black notebook.

During the journey they met another small travelling party which included a young boy who, owing to bizarre circumstances, had been disguised as a young deaf and dumb Maori. As an elderly man, he recalled the meeting with delight. Apparently feeling sorry for him, K.M. had persuaded him through sign language to go 'skinny-dipping' in a nearby stream, exhorting him, 'don't be shy'! Later he and the local Maori children watched intrigued as she fashioned a moustache from horse's hair to entertain them.

Rotorua, a mecca for tourists even then, was not however a success:

After brief snatches of terribly unrefreshing sleep I woke – and found the grey dawn slipping into the tent – I was hot & tired and full of discomfort – the frightful buzzing of the mosquitoes – the slow breathing of the others seemed to weigh upon my brain for a moment and then I found that the air was alive with birds' song.
'Journal', November 1907

Camping, Eskdale, K.M. in hat, back to wagon

*And across the paddock a
number of little boys come
straggling along – from the
age of twelve to three – out at
elbow – barefooted . . . some of
them almost beautiful . . .
Give me the Maori and the
tourist but nothing between.*
Notebook, November 1907

The camping party at Te Whaiti,
with some of the local Maori
people. K.M. is standing, second
from left

*A party of us went a round trip
to the Hamurana Spring – the
Okere Falls, across Lake
Rotoiti to Tikitere.*
Notebook, November 1907

Tourists at Tikitere

I confess, frankly, that I hate going trips with a party of tourists – they spoil half my pleasure – don't they yours? You know one lady who is the wit of the day and is 'flirty', and the inevitable old man who becomes disgusted with everything, and the honeymoon couples – Rotorua is a happy hunting ground for these. We came back in the evening grey with dust – hair and eyes and clothing – so I went and soaked in the Rachael bath . . .

To retrace that Urewera journey today, as far as it is possible, is still an experience. The strange, powerful, brooding spirit of the country can still be felt and one is constantly reminded of what a fit, vigorous, intrepid and confident young woman K.M. must have been. To reach the Tarawera Baths where having 'bathed in our nakeds' they returned to camp, feeling 'inwardly and outwardly like velvet', is a risky enough venture in broad daylight and wearing sensible boots. K.M. managed that precipitous path in her long skirt at night, guided only by a flickering candle in a tin carried by an 'aged', toothless man.

The last note made on the journey described not just the return to Wellington on the train, but an abrupt, and typical, change in K.M. herself:

In the train – December 17th
Has there ever been a hotter day – the land is parched – golden with the heat. The sheep are sheltering in the shadow of the rocks – in the distance the hills are shimmering in the heat. M & I sitting opposite each other. I look perfectly charming.

In January 1908 she wrote 'The Education of Audrey', typed by her father's secretary and published by Wellington's *Evening Post* the following January. She had already written to her, in purple ink on purple paper, of her resolute intention to return to London:

Castles have been tumbling about my ears since Father came home. Do not mention, I pray you, my London prospects to him – he feels very sensitive – but willy nilly: I GO, I'm determined.

On 23 January 1908 she sat outside the Wellington Town Hall writing a letter in German to 'mein lieber Freund', Tom Trowell. In this unposted letter she declared, 'I am coming to England early in March. I hate Wellington'. Before she could leave, however, a dramatic event took place which nearly caused her bewildered parents to change their minds. The usual explanations of this incident are based on L.M.'s rather vague recollections of a letter from K.M. which described her parents' shocked reaction to her colourful journal account of an incident during a ball.

Another possible explanation for her parents' concern could lie in a story told years later by Tom Mills who said that after moving to Feilding in 1907, he had received his one and only letter from K.M. In this she had explained that she was being blackmailed and that her father had advised her to write to Mills for help as he knew the Wellington police well, through his time as a reporter with the *Evening Post*. Mills apparently travelled down to Wellington and intervened by speaking to the police. Soon after, as a result of some unofficial pressure, a certain 'anonymous young man' sailed from Wellington.

Whatever the reason, her fate swung in the balance and her sprawling erratic notes are feverishly confused. 'I shall end of course – by killing myself.' By March the situation seemed little better:

I purchase my brilliance with my life – It were better that I were dead really – I am unlike others because I have experienced all that there is to experience. But there is no-one to help me. Of course Oscars Dorian Gray has brought this S.S. to pass.

I try & make family life so gorgeous – not hatred and cold linoleum – but warmth & hydrangeas.
to Anne Estelle Rice, January 1921

Jeanne, K.M. and Leslie

In May she wrote:

O, Kathleen do not weave anymore of these fearful meshes – you have been so loathsomely unwise. Do take wisdom from all that you have and must still suffer. I really know that you *can't* stay as you are now – be good – for the love of God – be good & brave, and do tell the truth more & live a better life – I am tired of all this deceit – and the moon still shines – and the stars are still there. You'd better go & see the Doctor tomorrow about your heart – and then try to solve all the silly, drivelling problems. Go anywhere. Don't stay here – accept work – fight against people . . .

Social scandal was apparently averted. In a more tranquil mood she wrote to Vera:

I do not think that the dice is thrown haphazard – I was not *ready* for London or for an independent life, when the Trowells went, so it is better to have waited and *thought*.

Whatever had worried her parents, the secret, darker side remained hidden. There was a series of farewell parties including a progressive bridge party, and a tea party given by the daughter of the Prime Minister, Sir Joseph Ward:

There was a pig-drawing competition . . . beautiful records of Melba and Tettrezini were heard, and a fortune teller was kept busy . . . Miss K. Beauchamp wore a dark brown coat and skirt, and black fox furs.

In July 1908 K.M. left Wellington with its 'singular charm and barrenness' for the last time. Her parents travelled with her to Lyttelton from where she sailed on the *Papanui* for England in order, as the *New Zealand Free Lance* put it 'to continue her literary studies'. It was an indication of her father's status in this young country that she was one of only three saloon class passengers and her ticket was complimentary.

The Restless Years

When K.M. arrived in London, intent on a literary career, she was nineteen, with an allowance of one hundred pounds a year from her father. He had arranged that she stay at Beauchamp Lodge, a hostel in Paddington for music students. Her arrival marked the beginning of a confused, frenetic period of her life. A later comment in a book review perhaps offers the best explanation:

We are the children of an ungracious and a greedy age. Perhaps it is not so much that we are difficult to amuse, but we are quickly tired. Repetition – the charm of knowing what is coming, of beating the tune and being ready with the smile and the laugh at just the right moment, no longer has the power to soothe and distract us. It wakes in us a demon of restlessness, a fever to break out of the circle of the tune, however brilliant the tune may be.

Later she was to see this as a wasted, shabby period, but to the capricious K.M. this 'Life', this erratic, bohemian existence, was all she had ever dreamed of those thousands of miles away, in the little cottage caught on the rocks between the bush and the sea. She remained an enigma to her friends – by turns vital, enthusiastic, cold, remote and cruel. It was certainly a very different world from the one she had just left where partners for bridge and supper had been chosen in 'a novel' way by matching characters from Shakespeare and Dickens.

Despite the lack of order in her life at this time, there were moments when she could be unexpectedly fastidious and particular. One can imagine, for example, the surprise experienced by friends of Aleister Crowley, the prince of the occult, when one evening, after smoking hashish, the unconventional colonial, who was expected to do something wildly uninhibited, instead sat quietly arranging matches in patterns on the floor. K.M. herself described coming down to earth from a rosy haze, with the incredible realisation that all the bookshelves were lined with hundreds of parcels identically labelled 'Jesus Wept'.

K.M. had gone to London determined to be a writer, yet only one poem and one story were published in the fifteen months after her arrival. She used her other talents to supplement her allowance by performing witty and entertaining skits at fashionable parties. Her love affair with Tom Trowell was over, but within three weeks of arriving in England she had fallen deeply in love with his violinist twin brother, Garnet. For a brief happy time she stayed with the family at Carlton Hill, St John's Wood. Writing to a friend years later her affectionate memories stretched this short interval into a longer period:

I lived there in Carlton Hill for a long time when I was young and very very happy. I used to walk about there at night – late – walking and talking on nights in Spring with two brothers. Our house had a real garden, too, with trees and all the rooms were good – the top rooms lovely.

There is still some doubt about the exact order of events at this confused time in her life. From mid-September Garnet was touring northern England and Scotland with the Moody Manners Opera Company. Her many letters to 'my husband' and the gently evocative poem 'Sleeping Together' convey something of the tender closeness she knew with this young musician. Other poems which she sent to him in November in Hull emphasise the ingenuous nature of this love affair which seemed to promise a better, sweeter

world, a world somehow free from 'the drunken, bestial, hiccough-
ing voice of London.'

SLEEPING TOGETHER

SLEEPING together . . . how tired you were! . . .
How warm our room . . . how the firelight
    spread
On walls and ceiling and great white bed!
We spoke in whispers as children do,
And now it was I – and then it was you
Slept a moment, to wake – "My dear,
I'm not at all sleepy," one of us said. . . .

Was it a thousand years ago?
I woke in your arms – you were sound
    asleep –
And heard the pattering sound of sheep.
Softly I slipped to the floor and crept
To the curtained window, then, while you
    slept,
I watched the sheep pass by in the snow.

O flock of thoughts with their shepherd Fear
Shivering, desolate, out in the cold,
That entered into my heart to fold!
A thousand years . . . was it yesterday
When we, two children of far away,
Clinging close in the darkness, lay
Sleeping together? . . . How tired you
    were! . . .

But it was not to last. The story that K.M. left Garnet because
the way he ate his boiled eggs offended her fastidious nature has
become legendary. What is more certain is that his parents came
to disapprove of the relationship. Her unfinished novel *Maata*
begun in 1913 suggests that the Trowell disapproval was based on
the discovery that Garnet and K.M. had been lovers during her
stay at Carlton Hill. She found herself alone at Beauchamp Lodge,
and even, in what must have been a moment of empty despair,
sold her cello for £2.

About this time she met George Bowden, a music teacher, at a

A SAD TRUTH

We were so hungry, he and I
We knew not what to do
And so we bought a sugar cake
Oh, quite enough for two –

We ate it slowly, bit by bit
And not a crumb was wasted
It was the very best, we said
That we had ever tasted –

But all this happened years ago
Now we are rich and old
Yet we cannot buy such sugar cake
With our united gold.

dinner party in St John's Wood. Although he was ten years older, they shared a similar sense of humour and an interest in music. It was to be unfortunate for both of them that this was not the end of their relationship. Unexpectedly they announced their engagement. K.M. introduced Bowden to her guardian in London and her parents were duly notified. Bowden found her a witty, stimulating companion, but unpredictable. He soon discovered that her changes in mood and appearance were almost a complete change of personality. At her suggestion the marriage date was suddenly moved forward, presumably to forestall any intervention by the alarmed Beauchamps. On 2 March 1909 they were married in the Paddington Registry Office with L.M., perturbed and worried, as the sole witness and K.M. herself dressed in black. A typical touch of irony perhaps?

Had the stylish clothes of white silk, coral pink and red that she had worn to those Wellington bridge parties only eight months before met the same fate as the cello? Was Bowden right then, to insist later that the suit was chosen not for its funereal colour, but because it was the only fashionable outfit K.M. possessed? Whatever the reason, the ceremony was certainly very different from the elegant society wedding in Wellington's Cathedral late that year, when her sister Vera married James Mackintosh Bell, a Canadian mining engineer and all the ships in Wellington harbour wore bunting to mark the occasion.

Although K.M. had warned him not to expect too much from their marriage, saying that they 'would meet at the casual roadside camp fire rather than share the life of the open road together', Bowden was certainly not prepared for her completely unresponsive attitude on the marriage night; nor for her subsequent immediate disappearance. She was to remain his wife for the next nine years, trapped in a travesty of marriage. Why then had she married him at all? Was he quite simply the only solution, as suggested in her story 'The Swing of the Pendulum'? Was it a desperate gamble for security; the result of an impetuous whim; the need to experiment with yet another new experience; or was it perhaps intended as proof of her heterosexuality, as a desperate letter about 'my secret' written at this time would suggest? Could she have suspected she might be pregnant or was she retaliating against the Trowells' rejection? It was, in Bowden's own words, 'an insoluble mystery'.

Shortly after she travelled with Garnet on tour, to Glasgow and Liverpool apparently as part of the company chorus. In April she returned to London. Whatever the reason for her marriage she was now alone again, except for the faithful L.M. who helped her as she endured the bleak days and nights. The 'night terrors' – the fear of something dark and unknown – which had plagued her since childhood, drove her in her depression to an increasing dependence on the sedative Veronal. Her journal and diary entries are chaotic and confused. She was clearly haunted by the memory of 'this man I love with all my heart the other I do not even care about.'

By the end of April she knew she was pregnant with Garnet's child. Easter was spent miserably in Brussels. Even taking into account her flair for self dramatisation it was certainly a restless, bitterly unhappy period in her life:

29 April – In this room. Almost before this is written I shall read it from another room and such is Life. Packed again I leave for London, shall I ever be a happy woman again? . . . Sick at heart, till I am physically sick, with no home, no place in which I can hang up my hat & say here I belong – for there is no such place in the wide world for me. But attendez – you must not eat & you had better not sleep! No good *looking* 'fit' & *feeling* dead . . . I wonder when I shall sit & read aloud to my little son.

It was less than a year since she had sailed from New Zealand – she had found 'Life' and encountered experience – but at what cost. Years later writing in her journal on a stormy night in Italy, she would remember, 'I cannot sleep. I lie *retracing* my steps – going over all the old life before –– the baby of Garnets love.'

Her mother, alarmed by what she had heard about K.M.'s life and her sudden marriage, was due to arrive in England at the end of May. K.M., trying valiantly to set her world to rights, found a respectable flat and, bravely armed with a new hat, set out to meet her. The hat was apparently not a success. Her fragile independence shattered before her watching relatives, K.M. was whisked off to her mother's hotel.

K.M.'s presence on the station platform was ignored by her relatives, and at first by her mother until she remarked, 'Why child! What are you wearing? You look like an old woman in that. As if you were going to a funeral!'

According to L.M. and others, it seems unlikely that Annie Beauchamp knew of her daughter's pregnancy but she was alarmed about her behaviour, particularly about the possibly 'unnatural' nature of her relationship with L.M. In order to separate them, and to avoid further scandal, she escorted K.M. to Bavaria early in June. L.M., quite bemused, was similarly despatched – to the Canary Islands with her sister. Though some of K.M.'s relation-

There are no trees in the 'Luft Bad'. It boasts a collection of plain wooden cells, a bath shelter, two swings . . . And there in all weathers we take the air – walking or sitting.
'The Luft Bad'
Postcard of Bad Wörishofen

On the appointed day the married ladies sailed about the pension dressed like upholstered chairs . . .
'The Modern Soul'

The Pension Müller, one of several places where K.M. stayed in Wörishofen. Today much altered it remains as the Allgäuer Hof, its best room named after K.M.

ships with women friends did involve a physical relationship it seems that in this particular case Annie Beauchamp's reaction was unjustified. Nevertheless, having settled her wayward daughter in Wörishofen, she returned to London. On 10 June she sailed to New Zealand where she cut K.M. out of her will. This seems, even for those times, a harsh punishment for an unsuccessful marriage compounded by unproven suspicions about the relationship with L.M. Did Annie Beauchamp know after all of K.M.'s pregnancy, now probably at least three and a half months advanced?

K.M. moved several times in Wörishofen, a small, pretty town set in the pine forest near Munich, and famous for Pastor Kneipp's cold water therapy, which she was to describe in her stories with some humour: 'I was soaped and smacked and sprayed and thrown in a cold water tank.' Years later she would remember standing outside the library, 'spring-lilac-rain-books in black bindings'. It was a desolate time:

I am ill . . . it is the pain that makes me shiver . . .

The only adorable thing I can imagine is for my Grandmother to put me to bed & bring me a bowl of hot bread & milk & standing, her hands folded – the left thumb over the right – and say in her adorable voice: – There, darling, isn't that nice. Oh, what a miracle of happiness that would be . . .

Some day when I am asked –
'Mother, where was I born' and I answer – 'in Bavaria, dear,' I shall feel again I think this coldness – physical, mental – heart coldness, hand coldness, soul coldness. Beloved – I am not so sad tonight – it is only that I feel desperately the need of speech – the conviction that you are *present* . . .

Her memories of Garnet in 'Glasgow-Liverpool-Carlton Hill-*Our Home*' were of little comfort. On a day of 'steady, persistent rain that seems to drift one from one memory to the other' she described the endless night in which she had just fought another stage in her battle against Veronal:

Now I know what it is to fight a drug. Veronal was on the table by my bed – oblivion – deep sleep – think of it! but I did not take any . . .

The joy of that small triumph would not have lasted long; the 'terrible confusion' in her body, the pain that 'seems to diminish and grow worse again' were presumably not, as she thought, because of a chill but the initial stages of the miscarriage that occurred soon after. In an attempt to counter her empty despair L.M. sent a small London boy, convalescing from pleurisy, to holiday with her. For some time she cared for him but it was not

. . . this old Arabian shawl!
Bind it about your head and
throat,
. . . What strange sweet
charm
Lingers about the Arabian
shawl . . .
Let that other life
Fold us like the Arabian
shawl.
'The Arabian Shawl'

K.M. Rottingdean 1910

a permanent solution to K.M.'s problems. She found the Germans incompatible; the whole experience seemed a nightmare come true. Despite a few friendships, in particular a close relationship with a young Pole, Floryan Sobieniowski, who tried to persuade her to join him, it was a bleak empty time. Her misery and revulsion crystallised in the cruelly satirical, bitterly humorous short stories published soon after her return to England. Most of them were later included in the collection entitled *In a German Pension*.

One consequence of K.M.'s stay in Bavaria, where she had possibly been introduced to the writings of Chekhov, was a lifelong admiration for all things Russian which strongly influenced both her writing and her lifestyle. This was illustrated for a time by her style of dress, her later occasional adoption of a Russian variation of her name, Katharina, and close involvement in the translation of Russian literature into English.

On her return to London in January 1910 she moved, with the help of L.M., to the Strand Palace Hotel at eleven shillings a night. Her husband was away at a country house party when the butler brought him a succession of telegrams peremptorily demanding his return to London. They were signed, 'Your wife'. Bewildered, Bowden returned immediately to live with K.M. for a brief and unsatisfactory period in his flat in Gloucester Place. Although she visited his studio in Bond Street and gave a recital of her sketches at one of his concerts, their worlds were far apart. Their time together finally came to an end when K.M. became ill. After an operation for peritonitis she was rescued by L.M. from the nursing home where she felt 'the surgeon was displaying an unprofessional interest in her body'. Her medical expenses paid, at her request,

*She looked a dreamer but her
dreams were big with life . . .*
'Juliet'

K.M. about 1913

by Harold Beauchamp, K.M. convalesced at Rottingdean under
L.M.'s careful supervision before returning to London and a flat
in Cheyne Walk, Chelsea.

   The exact nature of this operation and an ensuing illness which
apparently affected her ability to bear children was not made clear
to K.M. for some years. During those years she suffered from
severe pains, her 'rheumatiz'. It seems those were, in fact, a symp-
tom of an untreated sexually transmitted disease.

At Bowden's suggestion she had met A. R. Orage, the editor of the *New Age*, a weekly review of literature, politics, art and religion. Orage and his mistress and co-editor Beatrice Hastings subsequently became friendly with K.M. and she began to write for the magazine. Perhaps because of the influence of these new friends, or possibly because of the traumatic experiences she had so recently endured, her writing at this time was frequently cruelly malicious, sarcastic and spiteful. Her search for 'Life' – for new sensations – for something she knew existed but could not find, continued. Her life became increasingly erratic. There were many parties, new acquaintances and always new experiences. Much of her life was dominated by Beatrice Hastings, a fiercely possessive, vituperative woman with a cruel gift for satire and innuendo.

Some of K.M.'s happier times were spent with a young teacher, William Orton, whom she met at a Hampstead tennis party on an early autumn day in 1910. In his autobiographical novel *The Last Romantic*, the story of Michael, he draws a picture of his 'Catherine' when they were both twenty-one. She was, he felt, tense, passionate and totally dedicated to her work. Beneath her restless vivid gaiety she was deeply shaken by the collapse of her marriage, but still urged on by a deep insatiable need for new experiences. Several men, including her former teacher Walter Rippmann, were attracted to her and she became seriously involved with one, the son of a well-known publishing family. L.M. described them as happy and in love, until his family's disapproval brought the affair to an end. It was, perhaps, too late.

From her rooms in Cheyne Walk, overlooking the plane trees and the river, she moved to Clovelly Mansions in Gray's Inn Road early in 1911 and possibly shortly after realised that she was again pregnant. Despite the inability or unwillingness of the father to commit himself to her, L.M. has described K.M.'s mood at this time as one of contentment. In April 1911, having ensured that K.M. was provided with sufficient money for the baby, L.M. sailed to visit her father in Rhodesia. When she next saw K.M. the money had disappeared – and the baby was never mentioned.

A later story, 'This Flower' begun in January 1920 during a difficult time when she seemed almost haunted by her past, may provide a clue. Originally (and coincidentally) entitled 'Late Spring', it is about a young woman's discovering of her pregnancy. With the help of a shady doctor she conceals the diagnosis from her charming lover who is, of course, greatly relieved.

Certainly, with her family due to arrive in May, K.M. would not have wished to be pregnant. It is perhaps strangely ironic that K.M. subtitled the story with the lines: 'But I tell you, my lord fool, out of this nettle, danger, we pluck this flower, safety.' They would later be used in very different circumstances.

It is perhaps not surprising that K.M. later wrote of her destructive years:

I've *acted* my sins, & then excused them or put them away with 'it doesn't do to think about these things' or (more often) it was all experience. But it hasn't *all* been experience. There is waste – destruction, too.

There is no clear evidence of what exactly happened, but it is possible that Beatrice Hastings arranged an abortion for her young protegée. This is suggested by Pierre Sichel in his biography of Modigliani, as well as by L.M. and others. Antony Alpers, however, cites medical evidence which indicates that it is unlikely, because of her earlier operation and the infection she had already contracted, that K.M. could have become pregnant at this time. It was, however, still possible.

In May K.M. returned to write for the *New Age* and in the same month her family, except for her father, arrived in London for the Coronation. During the following months she spent much of her time with the family; none of whom, it seems, had any idea of her recent trauma. During this visit she had the opportunity to renew her close friendship with her seventeen-year-old brother Leslie, or Chummie, as the family called him. Unfortunately she also developed pleurisy which necessitated her going to Europe to recuperate. She travelled from Bruges to Geneva, was eventually met by L.M. and in September they returned together to London. In the autumn of 1911 her collected short stories were published under the title *In a German Pension*. Reviewers spoke of 'acute insight' and 'unquenchable humour'. Her former friends from the *New Age* made the comment, 'When Miss Mansfield gets quite clear of the lachrymose sentimentality as so often goes with the satirical gift, she will be a very amusing and refreshing writer'.

The *Spectator's* review must also have aroused rather mixed feelings in the young author:

. . . a series of sketches of German life, written with humour and insight, which remind the reader of 'Elizabeth and her German Garden'. Unfortunately, however, they have not the same freedom from offence against good morals and good taste that distinguish the work of the elder author.

In a 1933 article, written to defend Sir Harold Beauchamp from criticism of his role in K.M.'s life, Tom Mills made the comment that these stories were in fact commissioned by the *New Age* whose editors had sent K.M. to the continent to study certain 'European health resorts'. Was this perhaps the official New Zealand version of that tragic Bavarian interlude?

During this difficult year she continued her friendship with William Orton. They each led their own erratic lives but were bound together by love and understanding and the search for some kind of spiritual peace. Some of the entries in his autobiographical book, *The Last Romantic*, were apparently written by K.M. and are therefore included in the 1954 edition of her *Journal*. Sometimes again it is difficult to distinguish between reality and fantasy in the confused entries:

Michael [Orton] came yesterday afternoon and asked me for Black Opal [a ring she had given him which they shared as a sort of talisman] . . . He was dressed in pale grey with that delightful vivid tie. I promised to meet him later at Queen's Hall . . . When the bells were striking five the Man came to see me. He gathered me up in his arms and carried me to the Black Bed . . . It grew dark. I crouched against him like a wild cat. Quite impersonally I admired my silver stockings . . . my yellow suède shoes . . . How vicious I looked! We made love to each other like two wild beasts. Very late at night we sat under a tree in the Park. The moon shone under the branches of fast-withering trees. The grass smelled of earth. In deep shadows lovers lay entwined. But all about me was Michael. He came towards me . . .

It is little wonder that a later entry that same evening continues with empty weariness, 'I want to begin another life; this one is worn to tearing point.'

Her poetry written at this time also reflected an urgent desire to escape from 'this ugly scramble', 'Catherine and Michael's' fragile dream world could not last. Her last entry in their joint notebook was made in April 1912:

Dear: the evening is slipping away . . . My life has been sad lately – unreal and turbulent. You know the absurd unreality of reality and the sense of chaotic grief that overpowers us when we attempt to fuse ourselves . . . So – blind I have been lately and deaf and frightened. But now I am utterly happy. I am at home again here . . . a silk shawl wrapped round my body, sandals on my feet. I lie on the floor smoking and *listening* . . . Yes, the poems – I cannot forget them, and I understand them far better. Many other poems I know – especially poems about rain and fitful winds and stars in dark pools of water. I think of you more often than you think of me. You are always in my heart – even when my heart – my beloved and my dear – has been most like the sand castle and nearest the waves – you have been safe and secret and treasured I shall always love you. One day perhaps we shall smile again to each other and I shall take your head in my hands and kiss you tenderly. Perhaps and perhaps. Goodnight. It is Easter Eve. Christ be with you Catherine.

I am more & more impressed with the uniqueness of her genius. Her infallible vision is something apart in this age of spoof. I don't think there's much chance of her being really recognised for what she is.
J.M. Murry

K.M. and John Middleton Murry, October 1913. Chaucer Mansions

K.M. began submitting stories to *Rhythm*, a new avant-garde quarterly edited by John Middleton Murry. After rejecting her first offering, Murry, who was intrigued by her work which seemed to echo his own bitter 'revulsion from life', accepted 'The Woman at the Store' for publication. They first met at the writer W. L. George's in December 1911, after which he visited her several times at Clovelly Mansions. She persuaded him to leave Oxford to work in the 'real' world and arranged to let him the second sitting room in her flat. This was the Buddha room, with its grand piano, black covered couches and the stone Buddha which once belonged to L.M.'s father. By mid-April 1912 Murry had become K.M.'s lodger at 7s.6d. a week. On his first morning he found a note in the kitchen: 'This is your egg. You must boil it. K.M.'.

In *Rhythm* they found a common bond. Designed by Murry and his friends for those who welcomed the recent Post-Impressionist Exhibition in London, its intention was 'to seek out the strong things of life . . . Both in its purity and brutality it shall be real.' Interestingly *Rhythm* was also the first magazine in England to include Picasso's drawings.

K.M. became Murry's assistant and for some time their relationship remained platonic. Each night they shook hands at the top of the stairs before going their separate ways to bed. He was an extraordinarily handsome young man while she was vital, strikingly attractive and vivacious. Both were sensitive and vulnerable. K.M. had been deeply shaken by the chaotic experiences of the past three years and Murry, for his part, was still suffering from the memory of an unfortunate love affair in Paris. In his misery he had tried to find forgetfulness in a brief sexual encounter but, to his utter mortification, the only result was a painful venereal infection.

Inevitably the friendship between K.M. and Murry deepened. He knew very little of her earlier erratic life and his naive innocence and bashful diffidence were strangely appealing. One evening as they sat talking beside the fire she challenged him – 'Why don't you make me your mistress?' Not long after, despite his earlier misgivings that such a relationship might destroy their friendship, they became lovers. When George Bowden heard of the relationship he called on them at Clovelly Mansions. It was a pleasant visit during which K.M. asked him to sing for them, but the matter of a divorce was not mentioned until he was just about to leave. Neither seemed particularly eager to pursue legal proceedings. In May 1912 he received a friendly letter from K.M. discussing an American divorce, 'in every way the wisest plan for us both'. He stated quite unequivocally that when the idea was dropped because of legal difficulties, neither K.M. nor Murry ever asked him again to institute legal proceedings – despite later suggestions by Murry and others that he had refused to co-operate. Not sur-

It is like winter already. This morning there was a fog & I am sitting by a fire with michaelmas daisies and chrysanthemums in the room.
to Jeanne, October 1913

K.M., Chaucer Mansions

prisingly Bowden did not enjoy being cast as the involuntary villain of the piece and there may be some truth in his wry suggestion that in some way it may have suited K.M. to appear to be tied to an unfeeling husband who would not relinquish her. Certainly in the early years she may have seen herself as yet another in the line of liberated women writers such as George Sand, or used her marriage as an excuse to evade any other final commitment. Possibly she may also have feared her family's reaction to the stigma of divorce.

In spite of a deep love for each other, Murry and K.M's life together was to be stormy and restless. Each was to demand far more than the other could give. Even at the beginning there were difficulties. Once Murry's mother and aunt invaded Clovelly Mansions to persuade him to abandon his life of sin, and Enid Bagnold remembered a stormy K.M. in Dan Rider's bookshop. ' "Tell him I've *left!*" she cried out slamming down the key... She looked like a white-faced cat with a tiger in its eyes.'

On the whole, however, the first two years together were happy times. The Two Tigers, as they were known, spent evenings in Chelsea pubs and made new friends among the varied figures of literary and artistic London. Besides their work together they shared an enthusiasm for music halls, Tottenham-Hotspurs, the Russian ballet and post-impressionism. In June 1912, Murry rashly changed the paper to a monthly. K.M. collaborated in the editorial work and wrote book reviews. Their contributors came to include W. W. Gibson, James Stephens, Walter de la Mare, John Drinkwater, Rupert Brooke and H. G. Wells. There were stimulating luncheons with fellow writers at the Café Royal and Treviglio's in Soho. In September 1912 they moved into a little cottage at Runcton where they were visited by K.M.'s old friend Floryan Sobieniowski and, more happily, by Eddie Marsh, Rupert Brooke and Frederick Goodyear.

In November this idyllic rural existence came to an abrupt end. *Rhythm* had been entrusted to K.M.'s publisher, Stephen Swift. Swift found himself faced with charges of bigamy and with inevitable bankruptcy and so elected to disappear, leaving K.M. and Murry with large debts. They returned to London. K.M.'s allowance was pledged to pay the debt, a hopelessly impractical solution but, with the assistance of Eddie Marsh and others, *Rhythm* was temporarily rescued. Increasingly, however, Murry found himself unable to cope. In May 1913 *Rhythm* became the *Blue Review*, but even with contributors like D. H. Lawrence, James Elroy Flecker, Max Beerbohm and Hugh Walpole, it was doomed. It collapsed finally in July. By then K.M. and Murry were renting a cottage in Buckinghamshire and so spent much time apart. Their letters spoke of frustration and loneliness.

At the end of 1913 K.M. and Murry, in an attempt to solve their massive problems, decided to try their luck in Paris where they had friends and happy memories from their visits the year before. They took a large flat at 31 Rue de Tournon which K.M. decorated. She had a gift for creating a home out of very little. Nevertheless, their finances were still in a precarious position.

Tea, the chemist & marmalade —
Far indeed today Ive strayed,
Through paths untrodden shops unbeaten
And now the bloody stuff is eaten.
The chemist, the marmalade & tea,
Lord how nice & cheap they be!

There were gay excursions with Murry's old bohemian friend, the writer Francis Carco. Together they explored the *bals musette* and the cafés of Montmartre and wandered through narrow streets and boulevards till dawn. It was a happy romantic interlude, something of which K.M. captured in the moving story 'Something Childish but Very Natural', written in that Paris flat but unpublished until 1924. Murry's hope for work in Paris did not eventuate and K.M.'s allowance was needed to cover their living expenses. As a result the monthly payments to their creditors ceased.

'To K M M & J M M of a flat 31 Rue de Tournon – still born.' This cryptic entry in her notebook revealed the inevitable end of their Paris idyll. It was as if, 'God opened his hand and let you dance on it a little and then shut it up tight – so tight that you could not even cry.'

Murry was recalled to England to face bankruptcy proceedings and their few possessions were sold. Weary, but 'unbeaten', K.M. surveyed the chaos:

Everything is packed of ours – the book-packer is here now and we are waiting for the man to come and take away the furniture. Grimy and draughty and smelling of dust, tea-leaves and senna-leaves and match-ends in the sink, cigarette ash on the floor, you never saw an uglier place – now – or a more desolate. The clock (sold, too) is ticking desperately, and doesn't believe it's going yet, and yet is hopeless. Jack, in a moment of desperation, has sold even the bedding . . . Yes, I *am* tired, my dear, a little, but it's mostly mental. I'm tired of this disgusting atmosphere of eating hard boiled eggs out of my hand and drinking milk out of a bottle. It's a gay day outside.

In answer to K.M.'s desperate call L.M. sent them some money, but for safety's sake she ripped the notes in two and sent them in two separate envelopes. K.M., receiving them in different posts, was totally bewildered. They returned to London to a friend's flat

Have I ruined her happy life?
'Journal', March 1914

L.M., Rhodesia 1914

in Beaufort Mansions, off King's Road, and while Murry in his new role as art critic for the *Westminster Gazette* explored the galleries, K.M. searched through a succession of dingy flats.

Although L.M. still visited K.M. during these early years with Murry, she felt there was now very little room for her in K.M.'s life. Formerly it had been their parents who had separated them because of what they had felt to be an unwise, unhealthy relationship. Wörishofen's cold water cure had very possibly been a rather drastic attempt on Mrs Beauchamp's part to control her wayward daughter's sexual proclivities – a fashionable version of the cold shower treatment long recommended for young men. L.M. once related the story of Harold Beauchamp's bank manager taking her to lunch to enquire if she shared a lesbian relationship with K.M. Mystified, she had returned to ask an amused K.M. what he had meant. This time, however, it was L.M. herself who had decided to leave England to visit her family.

In March 1914, L.M. sailed for Rhodesia. The opening two chapters of K.M.'s unfinished novel *Maata*, which were completed in November 1913, and her diary entries at this time show that K.M. had realised – despite her characteristic preoccupation with herself – that L.M.'s feelings for her were all-consuming. The confused ambivalence of her own emotions was also inescapable:

Have I ruined her happy life – am I to blame? When I see her pale and so tired that she shuffles her feet as she walks when she comes to me – drenched after tears – when I see the buttons hanging off her coats & her skirt torn – why do I call myself to account for all this, & feel that I am responsible for her. She gave me the gift of herself. 'Take me Katie. I am yours. I will serve you & walk in your ways, Katie' I ought to have made a happy being of her. I ought to have 'answered her prayers' – they cost me so little & they were so humble – I ought to have [proved] my own worthiness of a disciple . . . Yes, I am altogether to blame. Sometimes, I excuse myself. 'We were too much of an age. I was experimenting & being hurt when she leaned upon me – I couldn't have stopped the sacrifice if I'd wanted to – but it's all prevarication. Tonight – I saw her all drawn up with pain, & I came from Jack's room to see her crouched by my fire like a little animal. So I helped her to bed on the sofa & made her a hot drink & brought her some rugs & my dark eiderdown. And as I tucked her up, she was so touching – her long fair hair – so familiar, remembered for so long, drawn back from her face that it was easy to stoop & kiss her, not as I usually do one little half kiss, but quick loving kisses such as one delights to give a tired child. 'Oh' she sighed 'I have dreamed of this' (All the while I was faintly revolted) . . . Good God! I must be at ordinary times a callous brute. It is the first time in all these years that I have leaned to her & kissed her like that. I don't know why I always shrink ever so faintly from her touch. I could not kiss her lips. Ah, how I long to talk about it, sometimes – not for a moment but until I am tired out and I have got rid of the burden of memory. It is ridiculous in me to expect Jack to understand or to sympathise and yet when he does not & is bored or hums I am dreadfully wretched – mainly perhaps because of my own inability to enchant him . . .

This uncertainty about her relationship with Murry continued. In April she wrote that he was:

far too absorbed in his own affairs . . . he doesn't consider the people within his reach, psychologically speaking. As long as ones mood isn't directed towards or against him, he's quite unconscious and unsuspicious. Very sane, but lonely and difficult for me to understand.

There were still financial difficulties; they moved to one miserable flat in April, to another in July and even her writing was unsatisfying:

Nothing that isn't satirical is really true for me to write just now. If I try to find things lovely I turn pretty pretty, and at the same time I am so frightened of writing mockery for satire that my pen hovers and wont settle.

I have nothing to say to 'charming' women I feel like a cat among tigers.
'Journal', 26 March 1914
K.M. 1914

She already knew that the social round of 'pretty rooms, pretty people' was no longer for her.

On one such occasion Murry and K.M., together with D. H. Lawrence and Frieda Weekley, went to visit Catherine Carswell and Ivy Litvinov in Hampstead. K.M., suddenly confronted by the ecstatic, colourfully dressed Ivy Litvinov, turned and fled into the Hampstead tube station, a startled Murry in pursuit and the remaining four looking on in astonishment.

Murry and K.M. had met Lawrence and Frieda in 1913 and in July 1914 were witnesses at their wedding in the Kensington Registry Office. On the way Lawrence stopped the taxi, ran into a jeweller's and emerged with a wedding ring for Frieda. Taking off the ring she had worn for the fourteen years of her marriage to Ernest Weekley, she gave it to K.M. The friendship between the Lawrences and the Murrys was extraordinarily intense and complicated. Later there were quarrels, misunderstandings and deep bitterness, but nonetheless K.M. wore that ring for the rest of her life – much to Frieda's apparent surprise.

K.M. and Murry continued to move frequently, in London and in the country. By Murry's estimate they lived in no fewer than thirteen houses in two years. In August war was declared. Like so many others they had little inkling of what this would mean. In October 1914 they moved to Rose Tree Cottage in Buckinghamshire, not far from the Lawrences and the Cannans. For Murry it was a time of friendship with Lawrence and Gordon Campbell

It is a pity that all things must pass and how strange, it is, how in spite of everything, there are certain people like Lawrence, who remain in ones life for ever, and others who are forever shadowy.
to Koteliansky, December 1921

D.H. Lawrence, K.M., Frieda and J.M. Murry 1913

but K.M., restless and unhappy in the small damp cottage, was bored by the men's endless intellectual theorising and soul searching. In December she confided to her diary her certain feeling that the relationship with Murry must end:

What we have got each to kill – is my *you* and your *me*. That's all. Let's do it nicely and go to the funeral in the same carriage, and hold hands hard over the new grave, and smile and wish each other luck. I can. And so can you. Yes, I have already said adieu to you now. Darling it has been lovely.

A telling incident occurred during a Christmas party at the Cannans', when a play was devised, loosely based on K.M. and Murry's relationship. Their young artist friend, Mark Gertler, was cast in the role of the 'other man'. He and K.M. enjoyed their roles so much that the play ended not with K.M. returning to Murry as the script demanded, but remaining with Gertler who described the incident to Lytton Strachey:

The second party, I got so drunk that I made violent love to Katherine Mansfield! She returned it, also being drunk. I ended the evening by weeping bitterly at having kissed another man's woman and everybody trying to console me. Drink has curious and various effects on me.

The Lawrences, also at the party, were shocked – despite their own frequent violent quarrels. To their bewilderment, Murry seemed quite unmoved.

On New Year's Day K.M. resolved, 'this year I have two wishes to write to make money . . . It is only poverty that holds us so tightly'. She was also determined to sort out her confused emotional life. Her diary entries about her relationship with Murry at this time were frequently baldly matter of fact:

we were lovers & at 12 o'clock I was dead tired . . .

Four days later:

Jack and I were lovers after supper in my room. I nearly 'cut across his line of male' by talking of Francis . . . went to bed wretched with myself.

On 9 January she wrote:

Jack & I lay in bed, deeply in love, strangely in love . . . We gave each other our freedom in a strange way.

Part of this freedom involved the continuing and intense correspondence with Francis Carco which had begun the previous November. When an unexpected letter from him had arrived 'it seemed quite inevitable – the writing – the way the letters were made, his confidence and his warm sensational life'.

Murry seemed to refuse to take the correspondence seriously, perhaps because he was himself 'a terribly innocent lover'. Despite this, his letters were often frank with longing:

Even now that I begin to imagine our caresses, my head snuggling against your wonderful breasts, my lips feeling slowly over them till I kiss – it is all so true. Do you understand what I mean. The word is funny. But I mean it's not just desire, or wickedness, or excitement, but the being of two good souls and bodies together & making suddenly a better thing.

In the beginning K.M. had loved Murry partly for his inexperience as a lover, but that had palled. By the end of January she wrote: 'This sad place is killing me. I live upon old, made up dreams – but they do not deceive either of us'.

On 3 February her brother arrived in England for his military training. It is possible that she borrowed money from him for her escape from England, but a recently published letter from Leslie suggests he was unaware of K.M.'s intentions:

I ran up to London with Uncle Harry and went straight to the Bank . . . On coming out of Kays room . . . who should I run into but Kathleen who had come to draw her money! Considering that she had had the 'flu . . . I thought she was looking wonderfully fit . . . We went off to lunch together and picture her happiness at seeing one of the family, not having the faintest idea that I was coming over. She is more in love than ever with J. M. Murray . . . They are going over to Paris at the end of this week to collect materials for the new job. I do not expect to see K. again for some time.

From Paris, K.M. made an incredible journey by train to the front where she joined Carco at Gray. It was a brief interlude, snatched recklessly on the very edge of the battlefield – that alone would have appealed to K.M.'s innate sense of drama.

I don't really love him now I know him – but he is so rich and so careless – that I love. We spent a queer night . . . The little lamp, the wooden ceiling . . . And F. quite naked making up the fire with a tiny brass poker – so natural and so beautiful. F. again dressing en petit soldat . . . Washing & brushing his hair with my ivory hair-brush & then just for a moment I saw him passing the window – then he was gone. That is a terrible moment for a woman.

In a letter the day she left England Murry had commented that he was not sad or miserable, only 'vaguely uncomfortable'. Nevertheless he had hurried to the Lawrences for support, and later described this episode with Carco as a stupid and disappointing affair. Like so much in her life the adventure was to become 'copy' – the basis for her story 'An Indiscreet Journey'. She also used Carco later as the model for the detestable narrator of 'Je ne parle

. . . we lay like 2 old people coughing faintly under the eiderdown and laughing at each other . . . we went to India, to South America, to Marseilles . . . & then we came to Paris & somehow I lost him in a crowd of people & it was dark . . . then he was in my arms again & we were kissing.
'Journal', 20 February 1915

Francis Carco, revisiting the Quai aux Fleurs in 1933. The flat he lent K.M. is on the second floor in the building behind

pas français' while he, for his part, turned her into Winnie in his novel *Les Innocents*.

Ten days after her departure for Paris, she returned to England and Murry. Rose Tree Cottage was bleak and cold; she was ill and confined to bed. Paris seemed to offer life, vitality, all those elements which she felt to be so essential to her stultified creative spirit, as she wrote to her friend Koteliansky:

It is very cold here. It is winter and the sky from my window looks like ashes . . . My God, what poverty! So I write about hot weather and happy love and broad bands of sunlight and cafés – all the things that make life to me. Yes, you are quite right. I *am* wicked. Would it be very rude if I asked you to send me a few cigarettes? If it would – do not send them.

After a brief visit to the Lawrences, K.M. moved to London. Finding it impossible to work there she returned to Paris in March and again in May. Although Murry knew he would miss her, he understood her need to work and they corresponded daily.

Murry may have felt she had been disillusioned by her brief encounter with Francis Carco, but she certainly had no qualms about staying in his empty apartment on the Quai aux Fleurs, near Notre Dame. In fact, they continued to correspond, presumably without Murry's knowledge. A letter to K.M. from Carco, though signed with a pseudonym 'Marguerite Bombard', dated 26 March 1915, thanked her for her letter and suggested another visit to Gray. There is no trace of her reply, nor of any other later correspondence between them. K.M. did, however, remember his vital delight in 'the detail of life, the *life* of life. Carco feels that too – but nobody else. Perhaps in a negative way, Lesley does.'

L.M., however, was still in Rhodesia and K.M. was in Paris to work on a novel, *The Aloe*, later reworked and completed as *Prelude*. Her letters, written from her room overlooking the Seine and the trees of the Ile Saint Louis, or in nearby cafés, were vivid with life. She responded wholly to the colour and vibrancy of Paris.

There had also been brief forays into bohemian, artistic and literary circles of Paris with her old friend Beatrice Hastings. Beatrice, involved in a violently stormy affair with Modigliani, had apparently 'dismissed Dado [Modigliani] & transferred her virgin heart to Picasso – who lives close by – strange and really beautiful though she is still . . . she is ruined . . .'

The next day she described a party at Beatrice's flat, in the Rue Norvins, Monmartre

there arrived 'du monde' including a very lovely young woman, married & *curious* – blonde – passionate. We danced together . . .

The evening ended in an angry argument when K.M. refused to

She was a small, slim woman, pleasant but distant, her large dark eyes looked everywhere at once . . . She hardly looked the type to suit Milord, neither her make up nor her shoes were those of the young women of Paris. It upset him. He noticed moreover that her coat, though stylishly cut, was decorated with symmetical rows of round nickel buttons. translated from 'Les Innocents' by Francis Carco

K.M. 1915

I fell into the open arms of my first novel . . . Its queer stuff. Its the spring makes me write like this . . . I shut up shop & went for a long walk along the quai – very far. It was dusk when I started, but dark when I got home. The lights came out as I walked – & the boats danced by. Leaning over the bridge I suddenly discovered that one of those boats was exactly what I want my novel to be –– with people rather dark and seen strangely as they move in the sharp light and shadow and I want bright shivering lights in it and the sound of water. (This, my lad, by way of uplift.)
to J.M. Murry, 25 March 1915

Notre Dame and the Seine

stay the night. It was the end of the friendship. Empty drunken destructive evenings were not what K.M. wanted from life:

I walked on today and came to a garden behind Notre Dame. The pink and white flowering trees were so lovely that I sat down on a bench . . . little staggering babies with spades and buckets made mud pies or filled their baskets with fallen chestnut flowers or threw their grandfathers caps on the forbidden grass plot. And then there came a chinese nurse trailing 2 babies. Oh, she was a funny little thing in her green trousers and black tunic . . . But after I had watched a long time I realised I was in the middle of a dream. Why haven't I got a real 'home' – a real life – Why haven't I got a chinese nurse with green trousers and two babies who rush at me and clasp my knees – I'm not a girl – I'm a woman. I *want* things. Shall I ever have them? To write all the morning and then to get lunch over quickly and to write again in the afternoon & have supper and *one* cigarette together and then to be alone again until bedtime – and all this love and joy that fights for outlet – and all this life drying up, like milk, in an old breast. Oh, I want life. I want friends and people and a house I want to give and to spend (the P.O. savings bank apart, Darling).

Murry's letters from Elgin Crescent echoed many of those longings:

I wish we had hundreds and hundreds of pounds and that I was there with you . . . Tiggle – why aren't you in my arms in my big bed to-night?

He too felt, 'I want to take life into my arms – to walk, run, scamper hand in hand with you.'

In the summer, after her return to London, K.M. and Murry moved to St John's Wood not far from the Lawrences in Hampstead. Murry and Lawrence planned a new review to be called the *Signature*, and the house at 5 Acacia Road became a centre for their friends, for work and discussion. For K.M. it was also a place of peace. In Murry's words, 'The "aspegs" as Katherine called them were excellent.'

Her relationship with her brother Leslie was later described by her sister Jeanne as the only true love affair of her life. At Acacia Road they would spend hours together in her room or in the garden at dusk, recreating their home and childhood as she described in her journal:

They are walking up and down the garden in Acacia Road. It is dusky; the Michaelmas daisies are bright as feathers. From the old fruit-tree at the bottom of the garden – the slender tree rather like a poplar – there falls a little round pear, hard as a stone.
'Did you hear that, Katie? Can you find it? . . . Do you remember . . . We shall go back there one day when its all over.'
Their shadows on the grass are long & strange . . . a puff of strange wind whispers in the ivy and the old moon touches them with silver . . .

Writing to their parents Leslie described his visit:

I had a most comfortable roost at Kathleen's dear little house in Acacia Road St John's Wood, Jack Murray is a kind quiet soul and he and K. are perfectly sweet to each other – in fact I was awfully glad to see how smoothly things were running. They pay £52 per year for the house and it is the acme of comfort *and* cleanliness. Marvellously cheap, don't you think?

In early October, shortly after arriving in France, Leslie was killed demonstrating grenades at Ploegsteert Wood. Only three days before 'The Wind Blows', a hauntingly evocative memory of a shared childhood incident, appeared in the *Signature* under the title 'Autumn II'.

At first K.M. tried to hide her overwhelming grief. There were parties and gatherings and many of her friends did not even guess what had happened. Dorothy Brett, describing a chaotic party at this time, tells of K.M.

sitting on the sofa clasped in some man's arms; Koteliansky is singing on the balcony; Gertler and Carrington are squabbling as usual. While I, distraught, play the pianola fast and furiously . . . it ends in the early hours of the morning . . . we are propping a very amiable, completely drunk Murry up against the wall . . .

He puts his arm round her . . . & the ivy walls of the garden glitter like metal . . . She leans against his shoulder. The moonlight deepens. Now they are facing the back of the house. A square of light shows in the window.
Give me your hand. You know I shall always be a stranger here.
'Journal', October 1915

Acacia Road

Manuscript of 'Sanary'

By November K.M. could no longer play charades. Desperately unhappy, she fled with Murry to Marseilles. Unable to cope with her feelings or his own bitter resentment at her total preoccupation with her grief, Murry soon returned to London alone, leaving K.M. in the Hotel Beau Rivage, overlooking the sea in the small town of Bandol.

'Do you remember, Katie?' I hear his voice in trees and flowers, in scents and light and shadow. Have people, apart from these far away people, ever existed for me? ... Supposing I were to die, as I sit at this table, playing with my indian paper knife, what would be the difference – No difference at all. Then why don't I commit suicide? Because I feel I have a duty to perform to the lovely time when we were both alive. I want to write about it and he wanted me to. We talked it over in my little top room in London . . .

Leslie's death was to be a turning point in her life, as Lawrence, understanding her empty loneliness, gently predicted in a letter written in December 1915:

Do not be sad. It is one life which is passing away from us, one 'I' is dying; but there is another coming into being, which is the happy, creative you. I knew you would have to die with your brother; you also, go down into death, and be extinguished. But for us there is a rising from the grave, there is a resurrection, and a clean life to begin from the start, new, and happy. Don't be afraid, don't doubt it, it is so.

Gradually the sun and the sea began to work their healing magic. There were walks into the hills and along the coast to Sanary.

SANARY

Her little hot room looked over the bay
Through a stiff palisade of glinting palms,
And there she would lie in the heat of the day,
Her dark head resting upon her arms,
So quiet, so still, she did not seem
To think, to feel, or even to dream.

The shimmering, blinding web of sea
Hung from the sky, and the spider sun
With busy frightening cruelty
Crawled over the sky and spun and spun.
She could see it still when she shut her eyes,
And the little boats caught in a web like flies.

Down below at this idle hour
Nobody walked in the dusty street;
A scent of dying mimosa flower.

*On the mantlepiece in my
room stands my brother's
photograph. I never see
anything that I like, or hear
anything, without the longing
that he should see and hear,
too – I had a letter from his
friend again. He told me that
after it happened he said over
and over 'God forgive me for
all I have done' and just
before he died he said 'lift my
head Katy I can't breathe' –
To tell you the truth these
things that I have heard about
him blind me to all that is
happening here . . .*
to Koteliansky, Marseilles,
19 November 1915

Leslie Beauchamp

Soon there was enough of the old spirit for her to enjoy a chance
encounter and the opportunity to smile at herself:

So, feeling extremely solitary and romantic I sat me down upon a stone
& watched the red sun which looked horribly like a morsel of tinned
apricot sink into a sea like a huge junket. I began, feebly, but certainly
perceptibly to harp: 'Alone between sea & sky' etc. But suddenly I saw a
minute speck on the bar coming towards me – It grew, it granded. It
turned into a young officer in dark blue, slim, with an olive skin, fine
eyebrows, long black eyes, a fine silky moustache. 'You are alone,
M[adame?]
'Alone, M[onsieur.]'

'You are living at the hotel, M[adame?]'
'At the Hotel, M[onsieur.]'
'Ah, I have noticed you walking alone several times'.
'It is possible M[onsieur.]'
He blushed put his hand to his cap.
'I am very indiscreet, M[adame.]'
'Very indiscreet, M[onsieur.]'

As her grief became bearable, K.M. began to realise how dependent she was on Murry for her happiness:

I have loved you before for 3 years with my heart and my mind but it seems to me that I have never loved you *avec mon âme* as I do now. I love you with all our future life – our life together which seems only now to have taken root and be alive and growing up in the sun. *I* do not love you, but Love possesses me utterly . . . I have never felt anything like it before. In fact I did not comprehend the possibility of such a thing. I seem to have only played on the fringe of love . . . Is it too late . . . You are *really* coming?

Overjoyed at the news of Murry's impending visit she had arranged to rent a small villa:

I have found a tiny villa for us, which seems to me almost perfect in its way . . . It has a stone verandah & a little round table where we can sit & eat or work . . . It is very private & stands high on the top of a hill. It is called the Villa Pauline.
to J.M. Murry, 29 December 1915

The Villa Pauline

Now I am just waiting. I have ordered the little stores and the wine and the wood. All the windows are open – all the doors – the linen is airing. I went to the flower market and stood among the buyers and bought wholesale you know, at the auction in a state of lively terrified joy, 3 dozen rosebuds and 6 bunches of violets.

For three months K.M. and Murry knew real happiness at the Villa Pauline. They would sit together working or reading at the round table on the stone verandah. Sometimes they would walk over the cliffs to a favourite spot they called Cape Sixpence and in the evenings write verses for each other in the tiny warm kitchen:

We might be fifty we might be five,
So snug so compact so wise are we!
Under the kitchen table leg
My knee is pressing against Jack's knee . . .

While Murry concentrated on what was to be his first major work, a critical study of Dostoevsky, K.M. tried to recreate the early golden days in her own distant 'undiscovered country'. For weeks she remained frustrated, unable to transform her memories into the stories she so desperately wanted to write. Then one day she found and re-read the uncompleted manuscript of *The Aloe* and, realising it was 'right', set to work to complete it.

In the meantime D. H. Lawrence had written frequently, suggesting despite earlier occasional disagreements, that they should all live together somewhere in Cornwall. Eventually he found what he considered would be the ideal spot, at Zennor. Accordingly in April they returned, to Cornwall, and the Lawrences, K.M. with reluctance. Lawrence had teasingly rebuked her for her queasy misgivings, but they were to prove more accurate than his dreams of *bludbruderschaft* and summer happiness.

K.M. confided her feelings to her Russian friend S. S. Koteliansky, whom she had met through Lawrence and whose friendship she was to treasure for the rest of her life.

I cannot stand the situation between those two, for one thing. It is degrading – it offends ones soul beyond words. I don't know which disgusts me worse, when they are very loving and playing with each other or when they are roaring at each other and he is pulling out Frieda's hair and saying 'I'll cut your bloody throat, you bitch' and Frieda is running up and down the road screaming for 'Jack' to save her . . .

Life near the Lawrences was like 'sitting on a railway station with Lawrence's temper like a big black engine puffing and snorting'. Six years later she wrote to Sydney Schiff:

I should like to have friends, I confess. I do not suppose I ever shall. But

I call it already Katherine's house, Katherine's tower. There is something very attractive about it. It is very old, native to the earth, like rock, yet dry and all in the light of the hills and the sea. It is only twelve strides from our house to yours: we can talk from the windows; and besides us, only the gorse, and the fields, and the lambs skipping and hopping like anything and seagulls fighting with the ravens, and sometimes a fox and a ship on the sea.

You must come, and we will live there a long, long time, very cheaply. You see, we must live somewhere, and it is so free and beautiful, and it will cost us so very little. And don't talk any more of treacheries and so on. Henceforward let us take each other on trust . . .

D.H. Lawrence to J.M. Murry and K.M., 8 March 1916

'Katherine's tower', Zennor, Cornwall

there have been moments when I have realised what friendship might be. Rare moments – but never forgotten. I remember once talking it over with Lawrence and he said 'We must swear a solemn pact of friendship. Friendship is as binding, as solemn as marriage. We take each other for life, through everything – for ever . . . We must *swear*.' At the time I was impatient with him.

At this time, however, K.M. found the frequent scenes of violence distasteful, and neither she nor Murry could cope with Lawrence's desire for a blood brotherhood. In his misery Lawrence wanted more than they could either give or understand. They shared his deep hatred of the war, the realisation that it had brought the end of the world as they had known it, but they were bewildered by the intensity of his feelings, his mystical doctrine of 'love-and-hate'.

K.M. found occasional days of peace and quiet in Cornwall, but they were not sufficient:

Except for my little maid (whose *ankles* I can hear stumping about the kitchen) Im alone, for Murry & Lawrence have plunged off to St Ives with rucksacks on their backs & Frieda is in her cottage looking at the childrens photographs, I suppose. Its very quiet in the house except for the wind and the rain & the fire that roars very hoarse and fierce. I feel as though I and the Cornish Pasty had drifted out to sea – and would never be seen again. But I love such days – rare, lonely days. I love above all things, my dear, to be alone. Then I lie down and smoke and look at the fire and begin to think out an EXTRAORDINARILY good story about Marseille. Ive reread my novel today too and now I cant believe I wrote it. . . . I want to talk about the Ls. but if I do don't tell Kot and Gertler for then it will get back to Lawrence & I will be literally murdered . . .

I hate games where people lose their tempers in this way – Its so witless. In fact they are not my kind at all. I cannot discuss blood affinity to beasts for instance if I have to keep ducking to avoid the flat irons and the saucepans.

K.M. was further irritated by what she regarded as Lawrence's phallic obsession:

. . . I shall *never* see sex in trees, sex in the running brooks, sex in stones & sex in everything. The number of things that are really phallic from fountain pen fillers onwards! But I shall have my revenge one of these days — I suggested to Lawrence that he should call his cottage The Phallus & Frieda thought it was a very good idea . . .

Frieda's recollections were somewhat different:

We had great times doing things together, like making potpourri with dried rose leaves and herbs and spices, or painting wooden boxes and having those deliciously female walks and talks. She trusted me, I was older and she told me much of her life . . . She had a Dickensish kind of way to give small events a funny kind of twist, and sharp and quick she pounced on anything funny that happened and gave you a swift look, the rest of her face innocent . . .

If I had to describe her in one word I would choose the word *exquisite* . . . soft fine shiny brown hair and delicately grained skin, not tall and not small and not thin nor stout . . . When we went bathing I thought her pretty as a statuette.

After two months K.M. and Murry moved to Mylor, thirty miles away on the south Cornish coast. In explaining why they had broken their lease, Lawrence remarked that at times K.M. seemed 'out of joint' with herself and everybody else.

The friendship never quite recovered. Nevertheless some of the letters written by both K.M. and Lawrence after this time were affectionate. She later remarked that she was more like Lawrence than anyone else. He too felt a kind of kinship with her; an awareness of what Frieda described as 'the terrible gift of nearness, she can come so close.' Although Frieda herself did not trust K.M., she seemed to understand her. 'But I do love her, if she tells lies, she also knows more about truth than other people.'

Certainly in September that year K.M. still cared enough for Lawrence to defend him in a now famous incident at the Café Royal. She, Gertler and Koteliansky were seated near two men and a woman who were loudly criticising a volume of Lawrence's poems. Katherine, smiling sweetly, asked them to lend her the book for a moment then, to their confusion, calmly walked out of the café, book in hand, followed by Gertler and Koteliansky.

When they had the little cottage at Mylor, K.M. and Murry

spent much of their time in London and at Garsington Manor near Oxford as guests of the striking, eccentric and aristocratic Lady Ottoline Morrell. Murry had met her through Lawrence in 1915 and she had become one cause of arguments between the couples. At Garsington, a Jacobean manor house furnished in a romantic if somewhat whimsical style, Lady Ottoline, a well-known hostess in literary and artistic circles, gathered a group of artists and writers around her including Aldous Huxley, Siegfried Sassoon, T. S. Eliot, Mark Gertler and Lytton Strachey. It was on Lady Ottoline that Lawrence based the character of Hermione in *Women in Love* in which K.M. and Murry also appeared, much to their surprise, as Gudrun and Gerald.

Mark Gertler, the painter with whom K.M. had previously shocked Lawrence at the 1914 Christmas party, also appeared in that novel as Loerke, the artist for whom Gudrun abandons her husband. That, however, was to remain fiction. Although K.M. was again finding her relationship with Murry unsatisfactory and they were frequently apart during 1916 and 1917, she failed to keep a planned meeting with Gertler at Garsington and that relationship developed no further – except in Lawrence's imagination.

It was at Garsington too that K.M. met Dorothy Brett again and established the beginnings of a long friendship. Many of K.M.'s letters to Brett are lively, spontaneous and amusing. Brett, although handicapped by deafness, was an artist and one with whom K.M. felt a close affinity and sympathy although at one stage suspecting she was in love with Murry.

K.M. spent many evenings as Lady Ottoline's guest. At times she appeared reserved, remote, perhaps unsure of herself in the company of the other guests who were frequently well-known members of the so-called Bloomsbury set. On other visits she entertained the household with her impersonations, ragtime skits and folk songs. There were evenings of long intellectual discussions, dancing on the lawn in the moonlight and moments of quiet intimacy picking the flowers in the twilight garden.

In spite of the warning of her lover Bertrand Russell, that K.M. was not to be entirely trusted, Lady Ottoline and K.M. achieved a kind of friendship. At one stage though, K.M.'s letters became remote and cool. Puzzled, Lady Ottoline insisted on knowing the reasons. To her apparent bewilderment she discovered that Murry had told K.M. that he thought Lady Ottoline was in love with him. It was in fact Murry who wrote to Lady Ottoline in September 1916, declaring that he suspected he was in love with her. Bloomsbury gossip thrived on the ensuing complications. Although K.M. and Lady Ottoline managed to salvage their friendship so that some of K.M.'s most affectionate letters were written to Lady Ottoline, an element of mistrust remained.

Of course I fully & absolutely accept your statement. It was a typical idiotic London rumour. As such I told it John – I never dreamed he'd retell it or I'd rather done anything than start a grimy snowball – But let's stop it please. *The odious affairs are too horrid will you come and have tea with me one afternoon & tell me what you told them about Cezanne's pictures . . . Kamerad! Kamerad!*
to Mark Gertler, n.d.

Mark Gertler

Regardless of the many poses and changing moods, and her irritation at K.M.'s belief – shared by Murry – that they belonged to an artistic élite quite apart from the world of ordinary mortals, Lady Ottoline seems to have understood much about K.M.

I should love to have known this beautiful, secretive but impulsive and emotional woman before she had been hurt and bruised by life, and perhaps before the ambition of being an artist and a great writer, and of using people for that end had become such an absorbing game . . . She is brilliant, witty in describing people and is certainly not kind or charitable. She and Lytton got on very well together and he enjoyed her witty talk; but I love her vivid awareness of the trembling beauty of life.

Much of the detail of the period between the move to Mylor in June 1916 and late 1917 is uncertain. Murry was likely to be called up to join a labour battalion unless he could find a war job of 'national importance'. Accordingly he spent much time in London seeking such a position, while K.M. remained trapped in what she now saw as the 'ugly little house' at Mylor or visited Garsington. Both were haunted by the possibility of Murry's conscription, and the war with its toll of 400 000 soldiers dying in the Battle of the Somme between July and November was a constant, fright-

She's a queer study – she's early sixteenth century really & I think she suffers very much in trying to accommodate herself to today . . .
to Violet Schiff,
4 November 1920

Lady Ottoline Morrell

ening shadow. Murry's friend Frederick Goodyear, who had been so strongly attracted to K.M., died horribly in May 1917. It was a dark period for them both, in many ways, and this was further exacerbated by misunderstandings and lack of money. Nevertheless, despite her seemingly erratic feelings for him, she was still able in May 1917 to write of her love for him:

Last night there was a moment before you got into bed. You stood, quite naked, bending forward a little – talking. It was only for an instant. I saw you – I loved you so, loved your body with rich tenderness. Ah, my dear! And I am not thinking now of 'passion'. No, of that other thing . . .

Clearly much of the time was spent at Garsington – Gertler, in a letter written in June 1916 to Koteliansky, referred to K.M. as having returned to Cornwall and Murry before his own arrival at Garsington. Both that letter and Koteliansky's reply hint at difficulties between K.M. and Murry.

She was at Garsington again in July and August. In September Dora Carrington, another Garsington guest, told Lytton Strachey that K.M. and Murry 'have been here for weeks' and gave a rather uncharacteristic glimpse of 'even Katherine knitting woollen counterpanes'.

During that September visit it was arranged that K.M. and Murry would stay with Brett and Carrington at Maynard Keynes's house in Gower Street, Bloomsbury. Carrington, a bright, vivacious, young woman, loved K.M. for her sense of fun and gaiety. In a letter to Strachey, who had found K.M. alluring yet impassive, she wrote:

I loved her so much that her writing to me was and remains one of the non-important manifestations of her being. It is her being, what she was, the aroma of her being, that I love. She could do things which I disliked intensely, exaggerate and tell untruths, yet the way she did it was so admirable, unique, that I did not trouble at all about what she spoke
. . .

S. S. Koteliansky to Sydney Waterlow, 21 June 1927

K.M. and S. S. Koteliansky, 1916

We acted a play. Katherine sang some songs and danced ragtimes. We talked late into the night together after it was all over in bed.
What fun we will have in Gower Street. She will play all the games I love best. Pretending to be other people and dressing up and parties!

In the same month, they moved in to Gower Street, Murry having taken a position in the War Office. Christmas was spent at Garsington with Bertrand Russell, Carrington, Lytton Strachey, Aldous Huxley, Maria Nys and, of course, Lady Ottoline and her husband Philip. These few days at Garsington when the time was spent in walking, talking and festivity, seemed to produce a Bloomsbury hothouse atmosphere in which intrigue and gossip continued to flourish. In the midst of all this K.M. found time to write a play which was performed with great success on the last night, with the elegant Lytton Strachey as a grandfather in a red woollen beard!

An amusing Xmas party here. Murry, Katherine Mansfield, Lytton Strachey, Brett and Carrington, Bertrand Russell and Maria Nys. We performed a superb play invented by Katherine, improvising as we went along. It was a huge success, with Murry as a Dostoevsky character and Lytton as an incredibly wicked old grandfather.
Aldous Huxley to Julian Huxley, 29 December 1916

Garsington Manor

Since November 1916 K.M. had been meeting and correspond-
ing with Bertrand Russell, no longer Lady Ottoline's lover. From
her letters she seems to have admired Russell and been attracted
to him, so that by early December she could write 'You have
already, in this little time, given me so much – more than I have
given you.'

He in turn admired her mind and searching curiosity, but later
made it quite clear that theirs was not a sexual relationship, as
others have suggested and as the letters themselves could be seen
to imply. They did, however, spend evenings together at dinner
and sitting in front of the fire at Gower Street. Much of their time
was spent discussing the manuscripts they exchanged and their
work. Clearly K.M. felt she knew him well enough, by February
1917, to criticise his article 'The World After the War' which he
had sent her. She thought it:

admirable until – may I be quite frank? – I came to the last sentence . . .
Were you getting your philosophic own back on us all – or – – I really
don't know even now. But very many thanks all the same. I hope you do
not think me too rude.

I am a recluse at present & do nothing but write & read & read &
write . . .

The story promised to him in that letter was never completed
and it seems from her remote tone that the friendship which had
once so excited her was now 'over the brim of the world'. Writing
to Lady Ottoline three months later she remarked only that she
had seen him 'once', so giving Lady Ottoline no hint of the amount
of time they had in fact spent together.

Some of K.M.'s time in January 1917 was spent working as a
film extra, which she described to Bertrand Russell:

My last day with the 'movies' – walking about a big bare studio in what
the American producer calls 'slap up evening dress' has laid me low ever
since. But I shall be quite well by Tuesday.

A naturally talented actress, this was not her first involvement
in films. In a 1915 journal she had referred to 'a woman who had
been in the cinema with me'. This earlier reference gives some
basis for a story told by Anne Estelle Rice, whom K.M. had first
met in May 1912. Meeting K.M. carrying a pile of books which
she had just reviewed and was about to sell, Anne expressed some
surprise at her 'strangely different' appearance. K.M. replied that
she had just jumped off the Battersea Bridge in order to be rescued
by the hero of a film. If this extraordinary story was true – keeping
in mind K.M.'s liking for colourful drama – it was as well that she
had spent so many hours in the Thorndon Baths and had become
an extremely good swimmer.

In writing to Russell about her film work in January 1917 she had commented: 'I hope to move at the end of next week, but my cough is so disastrous in this khaki weather that I can hardly conceive of leaving Gower Street except feet foremost.' Soon after, Carrington was dismayed on returning from the 'Woolves' at Asheham to find K.M. :

in a sad plight yesterday sitting fully dressed in outdoor clothes on a bed, with a gas fire roaring in a tiny room, remains of 12 days' meals, for she hadn't left the room for that number of days! Her face was pale grey with deep red rims round her eyes. She admitted all the females in the house were now raving lunatics and she likewise insane.

Early in February K.M. took a studio flat at 141a Church Street, Chelsea, while Murry rented rooms at 17 Redcliffe Road. He continued his work at the War Office and visited her in the evenings. Their separation was apparently caused by their inability to find a suitable flat because they were unmarried and therefore undesirable tenants. Divorce proceedings would also have made it unwise for them to live together at this stage.

It seems certain too that their relationship was once again under considerable strain. Her notebooks were still strangely devoid of details of her life. One, headed '141a Church St', began optimistically: 'In these notes – so help me Lord I shall be open and above board.' It contains some delightfully witty notes including one on *Howard's End*.

E.M. Forster never gets any further than warming the tea pot. He's a rare fine hand at that. Feel this teapot. Is it not beautifully warm? Yes, but there aint going to be no tea. And I can never be perfectly certain whether Helen was got with child by Leonard Bast or by his fatal forgotten umbrella. All things considered I think it must have been the umbrella.

It had been nearly a year since K.M. and Murry had returned to Cornwall from Bandol. In that time, apart from working on *The Aloe* and various fragments, she had completed nothing. Now her life seemed to have been sufficiently settled for her to be able to work at her writing once again. 'To be alive and to be a "writer" is enough ... there is *nothing* like it.' Another notebook entry contains fragments, ideas for stories but little more, while a third begun in 1916 has carefully detailed notes, one headed 'Lecture III, on fractures and anatomy', followed by notes on books by both K.M. and Murry.

L.M., who had returned from Rhodesia late in 1916, eventually joined K.M. at Church Street. Often exhausted from her work at the munitions factory, L.M. would sleep in the curtained gallery above the main room. Generally this was a reasonably harmonious arrangement, with L.M. trying to keep out of the way when a visitor or Murry called. One visitor at least was nevertheless surprised by her hidden presence, as Aldous Huxley described in a letter from Eton College:

Last Sunday I looked in on Katherine in her curious little kennel in Chelsea; all very mysterious, particularly when she suddenly gave a shout in the middle of our conversation and was answered by the sleepy voice of somebody who was in bed behind a curtain and whose presence I had never realised.

Early in 1917, apparently without Murry's knowledge, K.M. renewed her contact with the *New Age* which in May published the first of a number of pieces which appeared in quick succession. These included 'The Common Round' based on her film experiences and 'Mr Reginald Peacock's Day'.

During the summer she worked to reshape *The Aloe* into *Prelude*, completing it in August to send to Virginia and Leonard Woolf for publishing by their new Hogarth Press.

About this time too she was visited by an old friend from New Zealand, the Canadian Marion Ruddick. As they sat in the large room with its makeshift furniture, and later in a little restaurant in Greek Street, she watched K.M. smoke continuous cigarettes, her eyes dark in the pale oval face, and wondered how much happiness the intervening years had really brought her friend. Ironically, that year, 1917, was to be the last in which K.M. was to know anything even approaching normal health.

If she seemed weary and changed to her old friend, how did she appear to others now meeting her for the first time? In her diary entry for Thursday 11 October, Virginia Woolf wrote:

We could both wish that ones first impression of K.M. was not that she stinks like a – well civet cat that had taken to street walking. In truth, I'm a little shocked by her commonness at first sight; lines so hard & cheap. However, when this diminishes, she is so intelligent & inscrutable that she repays friendship.

For Dorothy Brett, the artist, the early impressions had been very different:

small, her sleek dark hair brushed close to her head, her fringe sleeked down over her white forehead; she dresses nearly always in black with a touch of white or scarlet or a rich, deep purple ... Her movements are quaintly restricted; controlled, small, reserved gestures. The dark eyes glance about much like a bird's, the pale face is a quiet mask, full of hidden laughter, wit, and gaiety. But she is cautious, a bit suspicious – and on her guard.

Looking back years later at their friendship she recollected:

She had daring, courage and a tremendous sense of humour. She was like a sparkling brook – like quick silver. Her changes of mood were rapid and disconcerting; a laughing joyous moment would suddenly turn through some inadequate remark into biting anger . . . Katherine had a tongue like a knife, she could cut the very heart out of one with it, and repent of her brilliant cruelty the next moment. She could be cruel. She had no tolerance of the stupid or the slow. Her mind was quick, so clear, so ahead of the thoughts and conversation of others, that if they lagged behind she became impatient, bored and finally angry . . . Katherine would take on jobs – strange jobs – just for the experience. She would have strange relationships with people for the same purpose. Her great delight was a game she played of being someone else . . . riding in a bus or eating in a Soho café . . . She would act the part completely until she even got herself mixed up as to who and what she was.

These rapid changes of role were recognised and remarked on by many who knew her, people as different as George Bowden, Virginia Woolf and Koteliansky. To Aldous Huxley, 'She was an unhappy woman, capable of acting any number of parts but uncertain of who, essentially, she was . . .'

Leonard Woolf remembered that although she seemed on guard against a hostile world:

By nature, I think, she was gay, cynical, amoral, ribald, witty. When we first knew her, she was extraordinarily amusing. I don't think anyone has ever made me laugh more than she did in those days. She would sit very upright on the edge of a chair or sofa and tell at immense length a kind of saga, of her experiences as an actress . . . There was not the shadow of a gleam of a smile . . . and the extraordinary funniness of the story was increased by the flashes of her astringent wit.

As the year went on there were further visits to Garsington, and to the 'Woolves' at Asheham after which she assured Virginia:

dont let THEM ever persuade you that I spend any of my precious time swapping hats or committing adultery. I'm far too arrogant & proud. However, let them think what they like.

In November, after visiting Murry at Garsington while he was ill, she developed a bad cold which turned into pleurisy. Her doctor advised her to leave England to seek the sun in the south. Delightedly she planned to return to Bandol.

Although I am still snapping up fishes like a sealion, steaks like a landlion, milk like a snake (or is that only a 'tale'?) and eggs . . . they seem to go to a sort of Dead Letter Office. . . . Of course I feel now that I've only to get into the sun and I'll simply burst into leaf and flower again.

Murry too was still far from well – Aldous Huxley in fact described him as having suffered 'a most hideous breakdown', an incident he himself later referred to as 'that six weeks' so-called breakdown at Garsington'.

K.M.'s journey was a nightmare under war-time conditions. When she reached Bandol, the little town had changed; the Hotel Beau Rivage was under new management and its prices had soared. Their favourite pâtisserie was boarded up, the tobacconist had no cigarettes – only cigars. She was eager for their marriage in May and a real life together at last, but even the longed for letters from Murry were delayed. Instead of the blue golden days she remem-

And then came our little home in sight. I went on, though I don't know how, pushing open the Allègres singing gate, walked over those crunching round stones. The outer door of our villa was open. When I reached the stone verandah, and looked again upon the almond tree, the little garden, the round stone table, the seat scooped out of stone, the steps leading down to the cave, and then looked up at our pink house, with the swags of shells painted over the windows & the strange blue grey shutters I thought I had never, in my happiest memories, realised all its beauty . . . finally I came away & leaned a long time on the wall at the bottom of our little road looking at the violet sea that beat up, high and loud against those strange dark clots of seaweed. As I came down your beautiful narrow steps — it began to rain. Big soft reluctant drops fell on my hands & face. The light was flashing through the dusk from the light house and a swarm of black soldiers was kicking something about on the sand among the palm trees – a dead dog perhaps or a little tied up kitten.
to J. M. Murry, 18 January 1918

The Villa Pauline

bered, there seemed to be only cold, grey wind and heavy mist. Despite her depression and rapidly deteriorating health K.M. worked on one of her best-known stories, 'Je ne parle pas français', recalling her days in Paris with Murry and Carco.

'My work excites me so tremendously that I feel almost insane at night', she wrote to Murry and, working at a feverish pace as the large sprawling writing shows, she completed the story within six days. In the same burst of activity she wrote 'Sun and Moon', a New Zealand story about a young boy's moment of disillusionment and 'Bliss', set in a very different sophisticated milieu. She also revisited the Villa Pauline where she and Murry had been so happy.

Alarmed at her illness and with the best of intentions – although unasked – L.M. made the difficult journey to Bandol. K.M., frustrated by her separation from Murry and resenting the loss of her independence, greeted her and her squashed *babas au rhum* from Paris with withering scorn. A week later, on 19 February, after bounding back to bed in the early morning sunshine, K.M. began to cough:

bright red blood ... Oh, yes, of course I am frightened. But for two reasons only. I don't want to be ill, I mean 'seriously', away from Jack. Jack is the 1st thought. 2nd I don't want to find this is real consumption, perhaps its going to gallop – who knows – and I shan't have my work written. *Thats what matters.* How unbearable it would be to die – leave 'scraps', 'bits' ... nothing real finished.

Writing to Murry on the same day she was resolutely cheerful, joking to him about her lungs, nicknaming them her 'wings'.

Bogey, this is NOT serious does NOT keep me in bed is absolutely curable, but I have been spitting a bit of blood ... This is a silly old letter all about my wings. Forgive it, my love.

This time the fishermen mending their nets and the colourful bustle of the market place beneath the fountain had lost their magic. These things were no longer enough. Her bright spirit faltered and she wanted only to return to England and Murry.

With L.M. she arrived in Paris on 22 March.

This has been a bad day – looking for an hotel all day – with 'do let us take a taxi Katie' and strange desires on L.M.s part to go to hotels at about £1,000 a bed and £500 petit dejeuner. Finally, late this afternoon I was passing along the Boulevard St. Michel & saw this – at the end – next door to the Sorbonne. It is very quiet – trees outside, you know, and an extremely pleasant chiming clock on the Sorbonne même ... The hotel seems just what is wanted. Six francs for my room with dejeuner – a big square room with 2 windows a writing table . . . But this is a fine room to work in . . . until they let me come home I shall stay here and write.

For three weeks, the two women were trapped by bureaucratic red tape. There were difficulties over K.M.'s permit and as the German army advanced, Paris officials did not view the travel plans of two English women as a high priority. It was a frightening time. Desperately short of money, K.M. was apparently forced to spend the money her mother had sent her for her wedding and very possibly to borrow from Carco or Beatrice Hastings. Helplessly she watched as the city she loved was gradually destroyed by the bombardment from the Germans' new giant cannon, which some wartime wit was jokingly to dub 'Big Bertha'. Eventually K.M. gave up seeking the crowded safety of the hotel cellar, preferring instead to remain in her darkened room overlooking the roofs of the Sorbonne. Finally she reached Redcliffe Road and Murry. She described the homecoming to L.M. She no longer regarded her as a travelling incubus, but with affection, even reverting to her nickname 'Jones':

'Home' looked lovely . . . I never want to go out again . . . But Jones – one's own fire – and lighting the gas & making the tea – and oh! the hot bath which really was hot – & Jack & Jack and Jack . . .

Somehow her relationship with L.M. had been rescued from the bitterness of Bandol, for the letter continued:

Does it gleam to you, too – like a little jewel beyond price – those hours on the boat that you sat on the floor in a draught and I sat on the lounge & we put the red on the black & wanted a seven? I was so happy . . . were you? Try & forget that sad sick Katie whose back ached in her brain or whose brain ached in her back . . . I would like to turn to you & say 'Oh Jones, we are quite all right, you know' . . .

For the moment at least K.M. had no desire to move:

If I had my way I should stay in the Redcliffe Road until after the war. It suits me. Whatever faults it has it is not at all bourgeois. There is 'something a bit queer' about all the people . . . The charwomen, blown old flies, buzz down each other's basements . . . No 50 'ad a party last night. You never seen anything like the stite of 'is room this morning . . .
. . . 'Igh time 'e did get married, I say. 'Is fiangse spends the night with 'im already – E says she 'as 'is bed and 'e sleeps on the table – You don't tell me a great stick of a fellow like im sleeps on is table!'? But do you like this sort of talk?

On 3 May K.M. and Murry were married. Two stone lighter, she was now very ill and the event she had looked forward to with such longing proved sad and empty. She was to write soon after:

Our marriage. You cannot imagine what that was to have meant to me . . .
And it really was only part of the nightmare, after all. You never once
held me in your arms & called me your wife. In fact the whole affair was
like my silly birthday. I had to keep on making you remember it . . .

'One ought to face facts'

Her tuberculosis was confirmed. Murry, now chief censor for the
War Office, sent K.M. only a fortnight later and against her will,
to Looe in Cornwall, in the care of Anne Estelle Rice. There her
moods vacillated between violent despair and desperate hope. In
one letter she would encourage Murry to rent the house they had
seen together in Hampstead, in another she would try to dissuade
him. Helplessly she tried to explain:

A very dark obscure frightening thing seems to rise up in my soul . . . I
am enveloped and powerless to withstand it. So please try & understand
. . .

Fate even provided her with a constant reminder of her illness:

The man in the room next to mine has the same complaint as I. When I
wake in the night I hear him turning. And then he coughs. And I cough.
And after a silence I cough. And he coughs again. This goes on for a long
time. Until I feel we are like two roosters calling to each other at false
dawn. From far away hidden farms.

K.M. responded with joy to the rugged beauty of the Cornish
coast, but for her fellow guests and the hotel's pervading odour of
'roast mutting', she could feel only revulsion. She was confused
about her own feelings, uncertain of Murry's love and their future
together.

Of course L.M. will keep us one remove from each other; she'll be a 'help'
that way – Did you realise that when you were so anxious to keep her.
For of course as you know, I'd have chucked her finally after the Gwynne
night if it hadn't been for your eagerness.

On this occasion she was particularly angry that L.M. had had
the temerity to discuss her friend's health with her employer, Mr
Gwynne. He had aggravated the situation by suggesting to L.M.
that K.M. should enter a sanatorium.

Her letters to L.M. and to Murry were at times cruelly sarcastic,
at others poignant with her frustrated love, 'I want nothing but
you – and by you I mean our home our child our trees and fruit
. . .' It seemed instead of such a calm, happy, 'normal' existence
that she was doomed to move from hotel to hotel, 'wandering

eternally in rooms papered with birds, chrysanthemums in urns and bunches of ribbons, and furnished with fumed oak and lace curtains.'

There were times too when she longed for that distant country which must have seemed a lifetime away. '11 500 miles are so many – too many by 11 449¼ for me.' Murry, for his part was also frequently bewildered, hurt and depressed, and occasionally, like her, exhilarated.

After a brief time together in Looe they returned to London. *Prelude* and 'Bliss' were published amid preparations for the new house and a furore over Murry's review of Siegfried Sassoon's poems. Then, K.M. received the news of her mother's death. It came as a severe blow, 'I feel – do you know what I mean – the *silence* of it so. She was more alive than anyone I have ever known . . .'

To Dorothy Brett she wrote:

She *lived* every moment of life more fully and completely than anyone I've ever known – and her gaiety wasn't any less real for being *high courage* – courage to meet anything with.

Ever since I heard of her death my memories of her come flying back into my heart – and there are moments when it's unbearable to receive them. But it has made me realise more than ever that I love *courage*-spirit-poise (do you know what I mean, all these words are too little) more than anything.

Clearly she would have been unaware of her mother's letter to a friend written in May on receiving the news of K.M.'s illness:

This was a great grief & shock to us as you may imagine . . . I wired them authority for any extra special expenditure for the dear child, & I know everything will be done for her that is possible, for she has been taken in to Belle's and Dora's fold by Chad long ago & is quite a pet with them all. Chaddie has been marvellously good to her ever since she arrived in England, & Kass has so enjoyed the attention of this loving & generous sister, but it seems that nothing much can be done for her now but make the remainder of her life as happy & comfy as possible. Of course if it was possible I should go home to her by the next steamer, for I know she would love to see me again, for she has at last learnt to love her Mother & Father, & has written us adoring & adorable letters lately, & so sweetly & quaintly put, poor poor darling she has missed so much in life, but it was quite her own choosing, fortunately she was the last to see Leslie off to France, & she has never forgotten this privilege for she simply worshipped her only brother & he had such loving compassion for her always through all her misdeeds.

The Murrys were on the move again. This time they set up

In spite of her frailty and delicate hold on Life – one really felt that she was an undying soul. She was such a part of Life – especially these last few years. She seemed to live in everything . . . it was so extraordinary how close *she kept to her children. Her last letters especially were quite uncanny. We seemed to be thinking the same thoughts . . . I wish we had not all lived so scattered.*
to Clara Palmer,
30 December 1918

Annie Burnell Beauchamp

house at 2 Portland Villas, Hampstead with L.M. as housekeeper and two servants. It was a tall, grey building which they nick-named 'The Elephant'. It was also time to meet Koteliansky and Lawrence again, to renew old friendships, to heal the rifts of the past.

The war ended, but the longed-for peace could not bring a miracle. For K.M. the preparations for festivity were 'odious'. It seemed no lesson had been learned from the waste and destruction.

Oh, why is the world so ugly – so corrupt and stupid? When I heard the drunks passing the house on Monday night, singing the good old pre-war drunken rubbish, I felt cold with horror. They are not changed . . .

Nevertheless, Christmas was a merry affair; Murry 'seemed to wear a paper hat (a large red and yellow butterfly) from Xmas Eve until after Boxing Day'. They gave a party with charades, stockings, a tree, decorations and Christmas crackers shared with Koteliansky, Mark Gertler, the Campbells and others:

I wanted to say to everybody – Let us stay forever just as we are – Don't let us ever wake up and find it is all over.

A New Year's celebration with Anne Estelle Rice Drey had, however, to be cancelled.

Since then Ive been
(Pulse one sixteen
Temperature one 0 three)
Lying in bed
With a wandering head
And a weak, weak cup of tea.
Injections, chère
In my derrière
Driven into a muscular wad
With a needle thick
As a walking stick –

Early in 1919 Murry became editor of the *Athenaeum*, to which K.M. contributed several book reviews a week. She felt, however, that she and Murry were far apart; L.M.'s ever present solicitous care, on the other hand, she found claustrophobic. Frustrated by

Yes, Brett is a brick I feel impatient with her sometimes because she will think it necessary to write to me about what Koteliansky used to call 'extremely serious questions'. And somehow those 'questions' ring a little false from Brett. They are not what one wants from her. But I do appreciate my wickedness.
to Sydney Waterlow, March 1921

Dorothy Brett and K.M. Hampstead Heath

her own illness, she was frequently unreasonable and impatient with L.M.'s inefficiency. It was at this time she forced L.M. to burn the letters she had written her from New Zealand and during L.M.'s visit to Rhodesia. It is not surprising that an elderly neighbour who knew nothing of Katherine Mansfield, the writer, remembered only a dark, ill, bad-tempered woman who went for long walks with another unhappy woman but never with her husband.

The many visitors included Lawrence, Walter de la Mare, Koteliansky, her cousin, Countess Elizabeth Russell, Lady Ottoline and most frequently, her brother-in-law Richard Murry, and Dorothy Brett. Particularly important at this time was her friendship with Virginia Woolf. Although Virginia had first considered K.M. 'an unpleasant but forcible and utterly unscrupulous character' and one who seemed 'to have gone every sort of hog since she was 17, which is interesting' she had come to regard her as 'the very best of women writers – always of course passing over one fine but very modest example'. She was astute enough to realise, as on one occasion when K.M. was hurt at not being asked to one of Roger Fry's parties, that her brittle composure was only a superficial facade. The Woolfs had accepted *Prelude* for publication because Virginia felt it had a certain quality of beauty and life. 'Bliss', published in the *English Review* in August 1918, she had condemned for its 'superficial smartness ... And the effect was, as I say, to give me an impression of her callousness & hardness as a human being.'

Nevertheless, by the end of 1918 Virginia was visiting K.M. once a week. Her diary contains a bleak picture of K.M. at Portland Villas:

... husky & feeble, crawling about the room like an old woman ... Illness, she said, breaks down one's privacy so that one can't write – The long story she has written breathes nothing but hate. Murry & the Monster [L.M.] watch & wait on her, till she hates them both; she trusts no one; she finds no 'reality'.

Although there were moments of coolness and inexplicable silence on K.M.'s side, so that Virginia felt that their friendship 'was almost entirely founded on quicksand', she admitted a fondness for K.M. Certainly K.M. felt that they shared a passion for writing and, for a time at any rate, returned Virginia's affection:

You are immensely important in my world, Virginia. I didn't say a quarter that I wanted to yesterday – but it will keep.

This mutual affection, however, did not entirely preclude a certain amount of professional jealousy between the two writers but

I wonder if you know what your visits were to me – or how much I miss them. You are the only woman with whom I long to talk work. *There will never be another ... Farewell, dear friend (May I call you that).*
to Virginia Woolf, 27 December 1920

Virginia and Leonard Woolf

even so, after K.M.'s death, Virginia was to admit to Dorothy Brett, 'she gave me something no one else can'. In her diary she went even further in her regret that she had allowed gossip and small lies to weaken their friendship:

Did she care for me? Sometimes she would say so – would kiss me – would look at me as if (is this sentiment?) her eyes would like always to be faithful. She would promise never never to forget. That was what we said at the end of our last talk ... I have the feeling that I shall think of her at intervals all through life. Probably we had something in common which I shall never find in anyone else.

K.M., on the other hand, envied Virginia her happiness and the security of her husband's constant love. She seemed unaware of Virginia's intermittent but terrifying battle against insanity which led finally to her suicide in 1941:

How I envy Virginia; no wonder she can write. There is always in her writing a calm freedom of expression as though she were at peace – her roof over her, her own possessions round her, and her man somewhere within call. Boge what have *I* done that I should have *all* the handicaps – plus a disease and an enemy.

Portland Villas! – it sounds like one of those houses where a 'few guests are taken slightly mental not objected to. Firm home-like treatment.' But inside it is going to be a vision – a sort of spring perpetual.
to Lady Ottoline Morrell,
22 July 1918

At this time the *Athenaeum* was publishing K.M.'s reviews, her poetry under the pseudonym Elizabeth Stanley, and the translation of Chekhov's letters in which she had collaborated with Koteliansky. Certainly in Hampstead there were times of peace and contentment: 'A husband, a home, a great many books and a passion for writing – are very nice things to possess all at once.'

And there were times of wry nostalgic introspection:

& that tall back of the house with the windows open & the coloured curtains flying – is her house. She is a stranger – an alien. She is nothing but a little girl sitting on the Tinakori hills & dreaming: 'I went to London and married an englishman & we lived in a tall grave house with red geraniums & white daisies in the garden at the back.

The Hampstead winter of 1918 had not improved her health and K.M. realised all too well that the coming winter would drive her away once again from the home she had come to love; the near normalcy of concerts, walks and friends that she had been able to enjoy so briefly. Nevertheless, despite the feverish pain caused by a new course of injections, her spirit survived. Enthusiastically she looked forward to a visit from her father, their first meeting for years:

... my plans are still rather en l'air until I have seen him. Why, I don't know. But he seems to me a kind of vast symbolic chapeau out of which I shall draw the little piece of paper that will decide my Fate. But that is absurd.

The visit was a mixed success. While K.M. enjoyed her father's lively enthusiasm and humour, she felt disappointed that Murry on meeting his father-in-law for the first time made little effort. There was not much Harold Beauchamp could do anyway to change the course of events. Supported by her doctor, Sorapure, in whom she had great faith, K.M. had once again refused to enter a sanatorium, despite specialist opinion that such treatment was her only chance. Although she had briefly toyed with the possibility of a 'sanatorium until next April', she rejected it on the grounds that she would be unable to write, and that for her would have been a kind of living death.

In September 1919 K.M., Murry and L.M. travelled to San Remo in southern Italy. The hotel was pleasant but they were soon forced, by the guests' alarmed complaints, to leave and to pay for the fumigation of her room.

This, for one as fastidious as K.M., must have been a final humiliation. They moved to the Casetta Deerholm, a small villa surrounded by wild olives and figs, high above the sea at Ospedaletti. At first, even after Murry's return to London, it seemed ideal. Despite the cough which still left her 'short of puff', her health improved. She could wander on the terraced hillside and explore the nearby town. The warm air was vibrant with the buzz of cicadas, the distant sound of the sea below, the flickering light and shadow of the trees. Again, however, the dream fell apart. The Italian villagers were unfriendly, the gardener was a swindler and his wife's hiss was like 'steel spittle'. Day after day passed without a letter from Murry; she became obsessed by the hollow roar of the sea.

A visit from her father, her cousin Connie Beauchamp and a friend was a brief happy respite:

Father suggested a run into San Remo which we took – I was – I am, just a little corrupted Bogey darling. That big soft purring motor, the rugs & cushions – the warmth the delicacy – all the uglies so far away. We 'ran' long past San Remo . . . I didn't dare to speak hardly because it was so wonderful & people laughing & silly Pa talking Maori down the whistle to the chauffeur . . . Pa & I talked & the sun streamed into the car & he said we were like a couple of hothouse plants ripening . . .

Father at the last, was wonderfully dear to me. I mean – to be held & kissed & called my precious child was almost too much. To feel someones arms around me & someone saying, 'Get better you little wonder. You're your mother over again' – Its not being called a wonder – its having love present close warm to be felt, and returned . . .

I *fed* them & Pa left me five 3 castles cigarettes!!! He made the running, talking french – telling stories – producing spectacles (he had four pairs of them – Connie had three & Jinnie had three). At one moment they were all trying each others on – in this little room – it was like a dream. [A drawing of many pairs of spectacles] And here on the table are five daisies & an orchid that Pa picked for me & tied with a bit of grass & handed me – If I had much to forgive him I would forgive him much for this little bunch of flowers. What have they to do with it all?

The euphoria of the visit soon passed. She was ill and frustrated, her depression returned. She wanted only Murry and felt trapped by L.M., who was struggling with the cottage's primitive plumbing and cooking facilities. Her clumsy inadequacy exacerbated the violent swings of mood which were symptomatic of K.M.'s tuberculosis. The relationship between the two women was corroded by a blind irrational hatred she felt powerless to control:

My black fit is on me . . . Christ! to *hate* like I do . . . My deadly deadly enemy has got me today and I'm simply a blind force of hatred. Hate is the *other* passion. It has all the opposite effects of Love . . . it makes you feel hideous degraded and old, it makes you long to *destroy* . . . Its like being under a curse . . . Her great fat arms, her tiny blind breasts, her baby mouth, the underlip always wet and a crumb or two or a chocolate stain at the corners – her eyes fixed on me – fixed . . .

She increasingly felt that it was 'madness to love & live apart' but Murry, feeling committed to his work and the need to earn a living for them both, was unsure of what to do. He wrote each day but his letters were frequently delayed. At times he must have felt beaten and bewildered. In November, for example, he fantasised about:

. . . your wonderful body beneath mine again, of kissing . . . The nights come when my physical love for you is unbearable.

She replied sadly:

Your Saturday letter when you spoke of us being lovers – was like a credo I believe to me. It seemed to bring the future, near and warm and *human* . . . It is all memories now – radiant, marvellous faraway memories of happiness . . . Let us live on memories then . . .

The remainder of the letter was more optimistic, but nevertheless it is hard to imagine the despair they must both have felt at that time – and she had only just turned thirty-one.

Her letters varied in tone, at times determinedly cheerful and hopeful, at others hopeless and depressed. Her bitter poem 'The New Husband' finally decided Murry, though she then wrote reassuringly, telling him not to come, reminding him:

I dont *fret* darling. Fretting always seems to me tearing at the frayed edge of a feeling. I tear the whole feeling into great black bits.

But Murry disregarded her telegrams and travelled to Ospedaletti for Christmas. The visit was not a success. They played cards and their old stone game of Cape Sixpence which they had played so happily in Bandol and Cornwall, but there were strange moments of emptiness.

After Murry's return to London K.M. seemed to reach the absolute limit of her endurance, as the entries in her small red leather diary show:

January 8 BLACK . . . A day spent in Hell. Unable to do anything. Took brandy – determined not to weep – wept . . .

11 . . . I love him but he rejects my *living* love . . . These are the worst days of my whole life.

12 . . . I cannot sleep. I lie *retracing* my steps – going over all the old life before – – the baby of Garnets love.

She had finished and posted 'The Man Without a Temperament' – a subtle yet sharply uncompromising picture of the bleakly empty relationship between an invalid and her husband. Feeling perhaps that Murry had failed her, she came to reconcile herself to her need, after all, for L.M. and to realise the invidious position in which she had placed her irritating but long-suffering friend:

I look back and think how she tried to run the house for us. She failed – but *how* she tried! . . . Who else would have done it? Nobody on earth . . . In Hampstead she was in a false position . . .

The villa was isolated and after one scare from intruders she had slept with a revolver beside her volume of Shakespeare on the bedside table. A postal strike was the final blow. Determined to escape the isolation she crossed the border – home to her beloved South of France.

In Menton she realised that the period she had just endured had brought her perilously close to madness. Despite the two doctors at the L'Hermitage clinic – 'an ass and an ass' – she felt she would recover. She was still, however, plagued by misunderstandings and doubts about Murry, who seemed to have neither the money nor the understanding she needed:

Goodbye. I am bitterly disappointed with the answer to my letter but I *must* bear it. You say you are not ashamed. I dont want you to be ashamed. And then you say you sent the £20 the moment you had it. February 1 came too late. Damn the £20. I suppose from that you look upon yourself as a man who is being bled – *you* did all in your power, but FATE and your wife would not wait. Its *utterly* false. I wanted love & sympathy and understanding – were you cleaned out of those until February 1st? It is a nightmare that you wont understand.

Certainly Murry seems to have been remarkably matter-of-fact and lacking in sensitivity and intuitiveness at this time when K.M. was in a panic over her increased expenses. In answer to her request that he should contribute £10 a month towards her expenses in Menton, he replied that though things were 'tight' he would send her £20 if she would repay him on publication of her forthcoming book. At times, though, the harsh scorn or absolute depression which his letters provoked seemed unjustified and irrational – Murry clearly thought so, even as late as 1948. Her reactions are, however, hardly surprising. Since childhood K.M. had been a creature of wildly fluctuating moods; Antony Alpers has also suggested that tension, associated with what is now known as the 'menstrual syndrome' could have aggravated those extremes. Certainly she had never been a particularly calm or equable woman. Her enforced separation from Murry, her isolation from her London life and friends and, brave though she was, her illness must have been hard to bear with constant equanimity.

Still, there seems little doubt from Murry's letters that he loved her, wanted her to be well, wished her to be with him, and as well as working hard was searching for a country home which would suit her health. On the other hand, he seemed often to be strange about money; he also was unable to understand completely the nature of her illness or its effects on her. He therefore failed to gauge the effect of casually thoughtless remarks. He was, as his brother remarked years later, 'without radar'.

A letter from Lawrence living in Capri depressed and angered her even further. He wrote: 'I loathe you. You revolt me stewing in your consumption.' At this point Lawrence seems to have been possessed by a blind hatred of the Murrys as illustrated in later letters:

The *Nation* said K's book was the best short story book that could be or had been written. Spit on her for me . . . I hear from London the *Athenaeum* lost £5000 a year under our friend, I know in whose pockets I should look . . .

They were, he said later, 'Two mud-worms . . . playing into each other's long mud bellies'. Lawrence's antagonism to the Murrys

I am longing to be home. It is a great strain to live away from ones own tribe, with people who, however dear they are, are not artists. These people's minds are about 1894 – not a day later. to J. M. Murry, March 1920

K.M. (front right) on the steps of the Villa Flora, Menton, Miss Connie Beauchamp in front and Miss Fullerton behind

was presumably not entirely shared by Frieda. During a visit to Germany in 1924 she and Murry admitted to feeling a strong mutual attraction. Loyalty to 'Lorenzo' meant, however, that the physical fulfilment of this was not achieved until Lawrence's death in 1930. Of this brief affair Murry was to write, 'for the first time in my life I knew what fulfilment in love really meant.' A lasting friendship developed – but all this lay in the unknown future.

In Menton K.M. was rescued by her cousin Connie Beauchamp and Jinnie Fullerton and taken to their large comfortable house, the Villa Flora. No longer needed, L.M. worked at a nearby nursing home, visiting her friend occasionally. There were visits from other friends too, including recent acquaintance Sydney Schiff (whose novel, *Richard Kurt*, written under the pseudonym Stephen Hudson, K.M. had reviewed in November) and his wife Violet.

She revelled in the bright clear air, the long drives along the coast or high into the hills. It was a period of peace and happiness when K.M. seemed, for a time at least, to have regained her fragile equilibrium

Describing the colour and life of Menton to Richard Murry, she continued:

I can't help seeing all the evil and pain in the world: it must be faced and recognised, and I can't bear your sentimentalist or silly optimist. I know it all: I feel it all. And there is *cruelty* for instance – cruelty to children – how are you going to explain that? and, as you say, the beauty – yes, the beauty that lurks in ugliness, that is even outside the pub in the gesture

Yesterday we went to La Turbie (I can't spell it and am ashamed to ask). Its up up high high on the tops of the mountains. Its a tiny ancient roman town – incredibly ancient! With old bits with pillars & capitals . . . I kept seeing it all – for you – wishing for you – longing for you.
to J. M. Murry, 4 March 1920

Menton is a lovely little town, small and unreal like all these places are, but even here there are real spots. The colour and movement everywhere make you continually happy. It's all ruled by the sun; the sun is King and Queen and Prime Minister . . .
to Richard Murry, February 1920

Menton

of the drinking woman. I can't explain it. I wish I could believe in a God. I can't. Science seems to make it *im*possible. And if you are to believe in a God it must be a good God and no good God could allow his children to suffer so. No, Life is a mystery to me. It is made up of Love and pains. One loves and one suffers, one suffers and one has to love . . . I don't mean a personal love – you know – but – the big thing.

By April, however, she was restless again, longing to be alone with her own kind. She and Murry had discussed for some time the possibility of taking a house in the country. After some investigation Murry had negotiated to buy 'Broomies', a cottage in Chailey, Sussex. With pleasure she envisaged summers spent there and at Portland Villas, and winters in the South of France. In fact she was never to stay in this cottage around which they built so many fantasies.

At the end of the month she returned with L.M. to Hampstead and Murry, and what was to be her last full summer in England:

I am writing in a little top room. The sun shines, faint reluctant. But its pleasant here – so still. If only one can get ones stories written – if only one is allowed time enough!

In April the *Athenaeum* published the translations of Chekhov's diary in which she had collaborated with Koteliansky. From June until December, her stories as well as her reviews appeared regularly. But behind the pleasure she must have gained from the growing recognition of her work, visits from friends and the enjoyment of her home, there was a darkening shadow. Not only did she feel she was running out of time but her uncertainty of Murry's love had become an insidious nagging fear. Even Brett could no longer be trusted:

Brett in her letters to Murry is unbalanced. This morning when she wrote how she wanted to rush into the cornfield – *horrified* me. And then he must *smack* her hand and she threatens to cry over him until he's all wet. Poor wretch! She's 37, hysterical, unbalanced, with a ghastly family tradition – and he has 'awakened' her. Her face is entirely changed: the mouth hangs open, the eyes are very wide: there is something silly and meaning in her smile which makes me cold . . . Whatever he may feel about it now the truth is she flattered him and got him! She listened and didn't criticise & sat at his feet and worshipped and asked for the prophet's help and he told her the old old tragedy. If Murry hadn't met me which would have won? His vanity & self absorption would have delivered him into the arms of countless INFERIOR females (its always the 5th rate who play this 'game') At the same time his honesty and his faith in Art might have saved him. It would have been a rare toss up. Look what happened last winter, for example while I was away. X 'thought him very distinguished' Y 'said she was frightened' of him – and so forth. He was puffed up tremenjous – and wouldn't hear one single word contrary to his opinions. I'll never forget it. He was *furious* at a sign of criticism. I wonder if the whole thing will be repeated this winter. I suppose so . . .

Murry omitted this entry in his edition of her journal. A ringed note in his writing explains the omission: 'Not used because of B. & J.M.M. a little'.

K.M. mistrusted Murry's intention to take rooms at Brett's house in Thurlow Road instead of remaining at The Elephant for the winter when she returned to Menton:

Was their relationship friendship? Oh, no! He kissed her and held her arm and they were certainly conscious of a dash of something far more dangerous than *l'amitié pure* . . . He said 'doesn't Gertler live there, too?' But Gertler never had the very beginnings of such a relationship with Brett – – as Murry knows . . . This is what I must remember when I am away. Murry thinks no more of me than of anybody else.

K.M. returned to this entry several times. These postscripts reveal the changing feelings she was to experience regarding this relationship between one of her closest friends and her husband.

They also suggest this gradual process of disengagement caused by her illness, her work and her insecurity about Murry. At Menton in December 1920 she noted:

I wouldn't mind a straw if he went & lived at Thurlow Road . . . I don't love him less, but I do love him differently. I don't aspire to a *personal* life . . .

In June the following year in Montana she added:

it seemed to me very stupid and strange that we should have hidden from each other. By stupid I mean of course stupid in me to write such stuff.

The final postcript six weeks later was bleakly terse: 'neither stupid nor strange. We both failed.'

This perhaps resulted from confirmation of her suspicions that Murry and Brett had had a brief affair after her return to Menton. It seems very probable that if her suspicions were not realised then, they were after her death.

Murry was, she felt, repelled by her illness:

I cough and cough and at each breath a dragging boiling bubbling sound is heard . . . Life is – getting a new breath, nothing else counts And Murry is silent, hangs his head, hides his face with his fingers AS THOUGH it were unendurable – This is what she is doing to me! Every fresh sound makes MY nerves wince. I know he can't help these feelings. But oh God! how wrong they are. If he could only, for a minute, serve me, help me, give HIMSELF up! . . . I feel I never could get well with him. Its like having a cannon ball tied to one's feet when one is trying not to drown. It is just like that.

When the willows turned to gold it was time to leave once more. Her cousin in Menton had moved to another large house and already K.M. had arranged to rent the little Villa Isola Bella at the bottom of the garden. Accompanied by the patient and indispensable L.M., she returned to Menton in September.

Shortly after their arrival, K.M. was confronted by an unpleasant reminder of those earlier restless years. The Pole from Bavaria, Floryan Sobieniowski, who had later renewed their acquaintance in Chelsea and at Runcton, was attempting to blackmail her with letters she 'would give any money to recover'. With quiet anger she asked Murry to end the business by obtaining a sworn statement and the letters Sobieniowski possessed, in exchange for £40 payment borrowed from L.M.

Her collection, *Bliss and Other Stories*, which contained both recent and earlier work, was published by Constable in December. Encouraged by the generally favourable opinions and despite her illness she achieved an incredible amount of work at Menton,

If you were here you'd know what I mean. Its a kind of freedom – a sense of living – not enduring – not existing – but being alive. I feel I could have children here for about a farthing each & dress them in little bits cut off ones own clothes.
to J. M. Murry, 22 October 1920

K.M. at the Villa Isola Bella

including her weekly book reviews and some of her best-known stories such as 'Miss Brill'. One, 'The Daughters of the Late Colonel', had possessed her so entirely for the short period of its composition that she and L.M. celebrated its completion with tea, in the early morning light of her room. As she explored the tangled garden or stood, dressed only in a black paper fan to dry at her open window high above the shimmering sea, K.M. rediscovered a kind of quiet, simple happiness. She responded with a deep intensity to the beauty around her.

There were, of course, moments of rebellion – her illness persisted:

I am stuck in bed – by my old doctor . . . I hate bed. I shall never go to bed in Heaven . . . If a cherubim and a seraphim come winging their way towards me with some toast and jelly I shall pop like a chestnut into Hell and be roasted.

Murry joined her there several times – there were moments of the longed-for shared happiness:

Murry is here for Christmas. The weather is superb & champagne only 30 francs a bottle. There is always un feu d'enfer in my chambre à coucher. The secret is, chère (Oh, I can only say these things to YOU!) we are continually suggesting to Marie she should go to Vespers, Bénediction, la messe. The poor old creature can't understand this mania de la pousser vers l'église. Its a mystery! But what is one to do? The house is so small. I send her to market, to the poste – out to see her friends – anywhere . . .

Red. Nov. 1

to Isabelle

Re your journey

city own love

while I think of it: would it worry you very much to bring your big suit case (registered) with clothes in it? Things to wear

This little place is and always will be for me – the one and only place, I feel. My heart beats for it like it beats for Karori.
to J.M. Murry, 10 November 1920

Drawing from letter, 5 November 1920

Champagne in this air & this sun is unsafe for all people under – say ninety-nine! Queer it is. I believe if I lived in England I could be a eunuch quite cheerfully but – – there's something in the air of France – – which is very *restorative* . . .

Nevertheless, there were irritating frustrations and difficulties, culminating in the discovery of the extent of Murry's relationship with Princess Elizabeth Bibesco. The wife of Prince Antoine Bibesco, she was the daughter of the ex-prime minister, Mr Asquith. Although K.M. had steadily maintained that she and Murry were two free, independent beings and was aware of his acquaintance with Princess Elizabeth, she felt betrayed but resolved to overcome the pain this caused:

. . . suffering must become Love. This is the mystery. This is what I must do. I must pass from personal love which has failed me to greater love. I must give to the whole of Life what I gave to him. This present agony will pass – if it doesn't kill. It wont last . . .

The fearful pain of these letters – of the knowledge that Jack wishes me dead and of his killing me will fade. I must turn to work. I must put my agony into something, change it – 'Sorrow shall be changed into Joy'.

It is to lose oneself more utterly – to love more deeply – to feel oneself part of Life – not separate.

Oh Life! accept me – make me worthy – teach me – I write that. I look up. The leaves move in the garden – the sky is pale & I catch myself weeping. It is hard – it is hard to make a good death! And the horrible vulgar letters of this woman . . . and his *cruel* insulting letter about 'no *physical attraction*' (!!) 'I think she is in love with me' and so on – were they necessary? He now claims his right not to suffer on my account any more – Oh God! How *base* in its selfishness . . . *no*. I must not blame him any more and I must not go back . . .

To live – to live – that is all.

To Murry she wrote, 'and please darling dont tell me about Madame la Princesse.'

When Murry arrived for his first visit at Christmas she had tried to accept the 'mysterious fitness' of their relationship:

We are, as I said yesterday, the two sides of the medal – separate, distinct and yet making one. I do not feel that I need another to fulfil my being and yet having Jack I possess something that without him I would lack. In fact we are – apart from everything else – each other's *critic* in that he 'sees' me . . .

In March she wrote to L.M. in exasperation:

Elizabeth Bibesco has shown signs of life again. A letter yesterday begging him to resist Katherine 'You have withstood her so gallantly so far how can you give way now.' And 'you swore nothing on earth should ever come between us.' From the letter I feel they are wonderfully suited & I hope he will go on with the affair. *He wants to.* 'How can I exist without your literary advice' she asks. That is a very fascinating question I shall write to the silly little creature & tell her that I have no desire to come between them only she must not make love to him while he is living with me, because that is undignified. He'll never break off these affairs tho' and I don't see why he should! I wish he'd take one *on* really seriously & leave me. Every day I long more to be alone . . .

To Princess Elizabeth she wrote a bravely haughty letter a few days later instructing her to stop writing 'little love letters to my husband'.

In his journal years later, Murry tried to explain these relation-ships with Brett and Princess Elizabeth, which he felt K.M. had so misunderstood. He was, he explained, 'starving for some fem-inine warmth and tenderness' having 'spent years tending and anxious for a sick wife.' It was, 'a little hard. While she was well, I had to be the companion of her "innocent" self; and when she was ill, I had to be "the man without a temperament".' He ended the relationship with Princess Elizabeth with the explanation that he loved K.M. and would therefore do as she wished. Perhaps K.M. would have gained some slight comfort if she had read Virginia Woolf's description of the princess as, 'pasty & podgy, with the eyes of currant bun, suddenly protruding with animation. But her animation is the product of a highly trained mind . . . '

There were other more minor irritations, frequently financial, but somehow the relationship between Murry and K.M. still survived although her original delight in the little Isola Bella did not:

We are both frozen, we shiver all day. I get up from 11–5.30 and turn the clock round so as to get back to bed more quickly. I've been spitting blood since Tuesday too – which is horrid. It makes one feel that while one sits at the window the house is on fire. And the servants have gone mad or bad or both. One has completely disappeared, only her feather duster

Menton seems to hold years of life. How hard it is to escape from places. However carefully one goes they hold you – you leave little bits of yourself fluttering on the fences – little rags and shreds of your very life. But a queer thing is – this is personal – however painful a thing has been when I look back it is no longer painful, or no more painful than music is. In fact it is just that. Now when I hear the sea at the Casetta its unbearably beautiful.
I must begin working. I'll never be a wealthy woman. I write like this because I write at such a pace. Here is some money. Be well! Be happy! Eat! Sleep! Yours ever K.M.
to L.M., 7 March 1922

K.M., Villa Isola Bella, Menton 1920

remains. She wasn't a little one either. But I expect we shall come across her one day. I have a fancy she is in one of the chimneys.

Again inevitable disillusionment had followed joy – it was time to move on once more, this time to try the well-known Spahlinger treatment in Switzerland.

Although Murry gained details of Swiss cures from Sydney Waterlow, he was no longer considered by K.M. to be 'a person to consult, or to expect from or to count on'. In May he returned to England to deliver his lectures on 'The Problems of Style' at Oxford. His letters were warm with love which K.M. seemed to reciprocate. She travelled with L.M. to Switzerland, around the lake from Geneva through Clarens to Baugy. There she posed as 'a lady with a weak heart & lungs of Spanish leather' in order to avoid the humiliation of San Remo.

The cleanliness of Switzerland! Darling it is frightening. The chastity of my lily-white bed! . . . Every daisy, in the grass below has a starched frill – the very bird droppings are dazzling.

From there she moved to the Chateau Belle Vue at Sierre. After Murry's arrival in June they moved again, up to the Chalet des Sapins at Montana sur Sierre, not far from her cousin Elizabeth at Randogne.

They shared a relatively happy, peaceful six months during

We have taken a small – not very small – chalet here for two years. It is quite remote – in a forest clearing . . . The air feels wonderful but smells more wonderful still . . . there are little glades and groves full of flowers . . .
M and I live like two small timetables. We work all the morning and from tea to supper. After supper we read aloud and smoke; in the afternoon he goes walking and I crawling . . . And though the chalet is so arcadian it has *got a bathroom with hot water and central heating for the winter and a piano and thick carpets and sunblinds I am too old not to rejoice in these creature comforts as well.*
to Lady Ottoline Morrell,
24 July 1921

The Chalet des Sapins,
Montana sur Sierre

which she wrote some of her greatest stories, including 'At the Bay', 'The Garden Party' and 'The Doll's House'.

I think I really judge a place by how vividly I can recall the past one lives in the Past – or I do. And here it is living.

High on her open balcony looking across the peaceful valley to the great snow-covered mountains, she remembered the very different beauty of her childhood – the sun catching the drops of dew which hung heavy on the feathery *toi toi*; the two ragamuffin children of a Karori washerwoman sharing one fleeting moment of beauty. From the luminous clarity of those memories she recreated those glimpses of a beauty which she knew existed beyond the bounds of time or place.

But even for K.M., living in the past could become 'cold comfort. I want to live in the past, present and future all at one and the same time'. For a little while she seemed almost to succeed. Murry skated on the frozen lake while K.M. worked on her balcony or went for long drives through the quiet forest. There was, after all, something to be said for 'married pairs'.

I confess, for my part I believe in marriage. It seems to me the only possible relation that really is satisfying . . . Does this sound hopelessly old fashioned? I suppose it does. But there it is – to make jam with J.M.M. to look for the flowers . . . to talk, to grow things, even to watch J.M.M. darning his socks over a *lemon* . . .

It was indeed a relatively calm, harmonious ménage. The household cleaning and cooking were entrusted to a gentle, if erratic Swiss, Ernestine. L.M. spent her evenings at the chalet but lodged in a rented room 'about two miles away'. For a time she worked in a nearby clinic but must have felt reassured, if bewildered, by K.M.'s letter in November asking her to move in with them as 'permanently part of the scheme', for £10–£12 a month. Even Wingly, K.M.'s adored cat retrieved by L.M. from London in August, had 'quite settled down, reads Shakespeare with us every night . . . He's like a little anchor here'.

Eventually, to Murry's dismay, even Switzerland lost its charm for her:

It's all scenery . . . I suppose the snow is very good for one. But it's horrid stuff to take and there's far too much of it. Immense fringes of icicles hang at our windows. Awful looking things like teeth . . .

Instead she longed for spring and its promise of new life. Determined to find that final elusive cure which would enable her to live life, rather than merely to exist, she asked Koteliansky for details about the new X-ray treatment that the Russian Manoukhin was giving in Paris.

She wished also to see a dentist:

I want to put my head into the jaws of a really good painless modern man
. . . They have very large wooden buns here for tea with nails in them and
powdered glass on the top, exprès pour les anglais. I defy anyone to grind
them to powder without an accident!

Accompanied by L.M. and armed with a list of hotels and 'teeth
snatchers' provided by her friend Anne Estelle Rice, she travelled
to Paris for a preliminary examination by Manoukhin. It was
decided that treatment would begin immediately. After the inevitable misunderstandings, Murry decided to join her in Paris after
all. L.M. returned to Switzerland to cope once again with tidying
up their household affairs.

With the publication of her latest collection, *The Garden Party
and Other Stories* and commissions for further stories, she knew
that her work was finally gaining wide recognition, but still she
felt, 'That regret for what one has not seen and felt – for what has
passed by – unheeded. Life is only given once and then I *waste* it.'

Drawing on her final slender reserves of strength and the old
irrepressible humour, she endured the exhaustingly painful treatment:

After five doses of XRays one is hotted up inside like a furnace and one's
very bones seem to be melting. I suppose this is the moment when real
martyrs break into song but I can think of nothing but fern grots, cuc-
umbers and fans and they won't mix in a story. However this stage does
not last.

Many long hours passed in enforced isolation in her hotel room
playing chess and cribbage with Murry. There were painful afternoons 'in a tight bony dentist's chair while a dreadfully callous
American gentleman with an electric light on his forehead . . .
angled with devilish patience for the lurking nerves.'

She dreamed of a visit to New Zealand with Murry, of giving
readings of her stories as Charles Dickens had done, and she completed her final great story, 'The Fly'. As the agonising effects of
the treatment lessened she became caught up in a round of lunches
and social engagements but they held little appeal:

Cities are too detestable. I should never write anything if I lived in them.
I feel bare and distracted. And all those dreadful parties – Oh how odious
they are. How I hate the word 'chic'. C'est pas chic, moins chic, pas chic,
très chic. French women haven't another note to sing on. And the heat!

The first stage of treatment over, though with nagging doubts
about its success, the Murrys willingly returned to Switzerland to
Randogne, to a hotel which was not quite as L.M. had described.

'Good God! whatever made you tell such bangers', K.M. wrote indignantly to L.M. who was now in London, dismissed it seemed by K.M., and sadly planning to set up a teashop with a friend. A few days later came a letter asking her to rejoin K.M. and planning an elaborate deception of Murry:

I want you if you can come to me. But *like this*. We should have to deceive Jack . . . He helps me all he can but he can't help me really & the result is I spend all my energy – every bit – in keeping going. I have none left for work . . . Jack can *never* understand . . . It would have to come entirely

I am the only guest left in this big, empty, dim hotel. It is awfully nice here, my dearest friend. It is full summer. The grasshoppers ring their tiny tambourines and down below the gardener is raking the paths.
to Koteliansky, 4 July 1922

Chateau Belle Vue, Sierre

from you. I'll draft a letter . . . if you agree, write it to me. It's not wrong to do this. It is right. I have been wanting to for a long time. I feel I cannot live without you. But of course we'll have to try and live differently.

K.M. was also turning in another new direction. While at Montana sur Sierre she had read *Cosmic Anatomy*, a theosophical text which she felt helped her to understand the 'relation of things'. Murry disagreed, condemning it as 'occultism'. This led to a major rift between them that was frustrating and painful for them both.

At the end of June K.M. and L.M. moved down the mountain to Sierre, to the quiet, gracious Chateau Belle Vue. Murry remained at Randogne with K.M.'s cousin, Countess Russell, but visited K.M. frequently. Dorothy Brett, apparently forgiven, arrived too. There were quiet warm afternoons in the pleasant garden and entertaining evenings of billiards, a game K.M. remembered from her New Zealand childhood. In August she wrote her will, in which she remembered so many of her friends including, despite the long silence, D. H. Lawrence. Strangely enough, on the very day that she remembered him his ship had called briefly at Wellington where, in memory of what they had once shared, he sent her a postcard with the one word 'Ricordi' – remember.

'The Canary', her final attempt in fiction to reconcile those paradoxes in life which she herself had known so well, was completed in Sierre. It had never been easy to resign herself to the limitations imposed on her and Murry by her illness, but now she knew:

. . . perhaps the truth is some people live in cages and some are free. One had better accept one's cage and say no more about it. I *can* – I will . . . My trouble is John. He ought to divorce me, marry a really gay young healthy creature, have children and ask me to be godmother. He needs a wife beyond everything. I shall never be a wife and I feel such a fraud when he still believes that one day I shall turn into one.

She had realised too the need to accept the realities in life which are so often unwanted but inevitable:

I *do* believe one ought to face facts. If you don't they get behind you & they become terrors, nightmares, giants, horrors. As long as one faces them then one is top-dog. The trouble is . . . to face them calmly, easily – to have the habit of facing them. I say this because I think nearly all my falsity has come from *not* facing facts . . .

On her return to London she stayed with Dorothy Brett in Hampstead where she was encouraged by Orage to attend lectures given by Ouspensky, the disciple of Gurdjieff, the Eastern mystic whose ideas seemed to her to be linked with those of *Cosmic*

J. M. Murry and K.M. Chateau Belle Vue, Sierre

For a long time she said she did not want to change anything in him, and she meant it. Yet she hated things in him & wished they were otherwise. Then she said she did not want to change anything in him and she meant it . . . But now she loved him so that even the dark things she loved, too.
'Journal', December 1920

Anatomy. Alarmed, and in despair at the direction in which her thoughts were now taking her, a direction which he quite simply could not follow, Murry left the house next door where he had been staying to join his friend Locke Ellis in the country.

At this time there were several meetings with her father and sisters and visits to Sorapure and another doctor whose treatment was similar to Manoukhin's. She was delighted to be in 'a *private* house again with . . . no strange foreign gentleman staring at your letters in the letter rack.' Despite everything she remained dissatisfied. The journal entries during these last few weeks in London are mostly an uncharacteristically terse list of appointments:

It frightens me. When Im with people I feel rather like an unfortunate without a racquet standing on the tennis court while a thrashing game is being played by the other three.

Having advised her father that she was drawing her allowance in advance she returned quietly to Paris with L.M., ostensibly to continue with Manoukhin's treatment. Already, however, she felt that despite her gain in weight the treatment was straining her heart. She had become convinced, in the face of Murry's uncompromising disapproval, that the fault in all medical treatment lay in trying to cure the body, not the soul.

All her life K.M. had been a creature of extremes, and without any clear religious conviction. In 1918 she had written to Lady Ottoline Morrell of the need for some kind of inner belief:

You see, I cannot help it. My secret belief – the innermost 'credo' by which I live is – that *although* Life is loathsomely ugly and people are terribly often vile and cruel and base, nevertheless there is something at the back of it all – which if only I were great enough to understand would make *everything*, everything, indescribably beautiful. One just has glimpses . . .

K.M. now felt the need for more than mere 'glimpses'. She sought some kind of harmony and balance, a spiritual peace. It was not surprising, therefore, that what she had heard of the teaching of Gurdjieff appealed to her. A Caucasian Greek, Gurdjieff had travelled widely through France, Afghanistan and Europe, acquiring and teaching the principles of his complex psycho-philosophical system. Although he was a charlatan to some, to his followers he offered hope of a new life through his doctrine that man's full potential can be achieved only through harmonious balance of the three interacting centres – physical, emotional and intellectual. This harmony of the soul could be gained only through conscious self-knowledge and work, which included manual work, meditation and physical exercise. This exercise in turn involved dance exercises modelled on ritualistic temple dances he had seen in the East. His teaching had a considerable following in America; in London, through Ouspensky; and in France where he had established his Institute for the Harmonious Development of Man, at Avon near Fontainebleau.

K.M. returned to the Select Hotel in Paris:

I can see your eyes laughing at the name of my hotel. What a name. One can only breathe it. Never mind. If only you knew how glad I am to be in it after our chase round Paris last night . . . I remembered this hotel where I stayed during the bombardment. Still here. Still the same. I have a funny room . . . that looks over the roofs of the Sorbonne. Large grave gentlemen in marble bathgowns are dotted on the roof. Some hold up a finger; some are only wise.

There on her thirty-fourth birthday, she had tried to clarify her conflicting thoughts. A note to Murry explained:

These pages from my journal. Dont let them distress you. The story *has* a happy ending – really & truly.

They were never posted.

... I cannot work ... My spirit is nearly dead. My spring of life is so starved that its just not dry. Nearly all my improved health is pretence-acting. What does it amount to? Can I walk? Only creep ... It is the existence of a parasite ... Do I believe in medicine alone? No. Never. In science alone? No. Never. It seems to me childish and ridiculous to suppose one can be cured like a cow *if one is not a cow* ... I have heard of Gurdjieff who seems not only to agree but to know infinitely more about it. Why hesitate?

Fear. Fear of what. Doesn't it come down to fear of losing Bogey? I believe it does. But good heavens! Face things. What have you of him now! What is your relationship. He talks to you – sometimes – and then goes off. He thinks of you tenderly. He dreams of a life with you SOMEDAY when the miracle has happened. You are important to him as a dream. Not as a living reality. For you are not one. What do you share? Almost nothing. Yet, there is a deep sweet tender flooding of feeling in my heart which is love for him and longing for him. But what is the good of it as things stand? Life together, with me ill is simply torture with happy moments. But its not life. I have tried through my illness (with one or two disastrous exceptions) to prevent him facing wholly what was happening. I ought to have tried to get him to face them. But I couldn't. The result is he doesn't know me. He only knows wig-who-is-going-to-be-better-someday. No. You do know that Bogey and you are only a kind of dream of what might be. And that might be never never can be true unless you are well. And you won't get well by 'imagining' or 'waiting' or trying to bring off that miracle yourself.

Therefore if the Grand Lhama of Tibet promised to help you – how can you hesitate! Risk! Risk anything! ... Do the hardest thing on earth for you. Act for yourself. Face the truth ...

By now it was not just 'health' in its narrow sense that she wanted but:

... the power to live a full, adult, living breathing life in close contact with what I love ... to lose all that is superficial and acquired in me and to become a conscious, direct human being. I want, by understanding myself to understand others. I want to be all that I am capable of becoming so that I may be – (and here I have stopped and waited & waited and its no good – there's only one phrase that will do) a *child of the sun* ...

Then I want to WORK. At what? I want so to live that I work with my hands and my feeling and my brain. I want a garden, a small house, grass, animals, books, pictures, music. And out of this the expression of this I want to be writing (though I may write about cabmen. Thats no matter).

BUT – warm, eager living life – to be rooted in life – to learn, to desire to know, to feel to think, to act. That is what I want. And nothing less. That is what I must try for. I wrote this for myself. I shall now risk sending it to Bogey. He may do with it what he likes. He must see how much I love him. And when I say 'I fear' – don't let it disturb you, dearest heart. We all fear when we are in waiting rooms. Yet we must pass beyond them and if the other can keep calm it is all the help we can give each other . . .

And this all sounds very strenuous and serious. But now that I have wrestled with it its no longer so. I feel happy – deep down. May you be happy, too . . .

I'm going to Fontainebleau on Monday . . .

Dissatisfied with her work and even more with her life, K.M. had made her decision. Reluctantly, L.M. accompanied her friend to Avon, to The Institute for the Harmonious Development of Man, an old monastery set in acres of land. Here some sixty people of varied nationalities and backgrounds lived together in a colourful, exotic community following the frequently eccentric directives of Gurdjieff. L.M.'s diary described their second evening at Fontainebleau: 'Last evening spent in the salon before an enormous fire . . . Atmosphere intensely alive.' After a day in Paris she returned for dinner. 'Dreadfully depressed & self conscious. Spent evening upstairs alone. K. came up radiant her eyes shining. She is staying for a fortnight "under observation".'

The next few entries speak of L.M.'s acute sense of loss.

Friday 20
came away for last time – absolutely dazed . . .
Saturday 21
I feel as if I had come from a funeral of one who has meant the world & Life to me – indeed I have said Goodbye to Katherine.

Writing from her large airy room overlooking the park, K.M. tried to explain her decision to Murry:

. . . in the deepest sense Ive always been disunited . . . I really cant go on pretending to be one person and being another any more, Boge. It is a living death. So I have decided to make a clean sweep of all that was 'superficial' in my past life and start again to see if I can get into that real living simple truthful *full* life I dream of . . .

According to Ouspensky she felt as they talked one evening in the garden that she had gone some way in her spiritual search:

I have long since looked upon all of us without exception as people who have suffered shipwreck upon an uninhabited island, but who do not yet know of it. But these people here know it. The others, there, in life, still

Mr Gurdjieff is not in the least like what I expected. He's what one wants to find him really. But I do feel absolutely confident he can put me on the right track in every way, bodily and t'other governor. I haven't talked money to Mr Gurdjieff yet
to J.M. Murry, October 1922

George Ivanovich Gurdjieff

think that a steamer will come for them to-morrow and that everything will go on in the old way. These already know that there will be no more of the old way. I am so glad that I can be here.

She had determined on entering the Institute that she would not write for three months: 'I am at an end of my source for the time. Life has brought me no FLOW. I want to write, but differently – far more steadily.'

To her old friend Orage she had remarked earlier of her stories, 'There is not one that I dare show to God.'

As they sat together one evening she apparently showed him fragments of stories, then tore them up, explaining that they must be different – as she would be. She endured her rigorous unorthodox treatment stoically – peeling onions and potatoes, cleaning the salon in the icy midnight cold, tramping round the muddy pigsty and inhaling the vapours from 'Mrs Murry's cows' in a colourfully painted loft above the barn. Unlike her beloved Chekhov, whose last letters she had just read, K.M. had not given up hope: 'I am learning to live. But I have not "disappeared" . . . I am far less disappeared than ever I was.' The restless confusion of her life had led her here, to the conclusion that 'the whole

At 34 I am beginning my education
to J.M. Murry, November 1922

Gurdjieff, K.M., Mme Julia Ostrowska (Gurdjieff's wife)

difficulty in life is to find the *way* between extremes ... to get a hold of the pendulum.' All her life she seems to have sought to become integrated – through so many relationships, experiences of all kinds, and her work. This was to be her final desperate attempt.

How far K.M. succeeded in finding that new life of which she dreamed is uncertain. There was to be so little time. Despite the miserable room to which she was moved for a period and the intense cold, she responded with joy to the strange energetic life of the Institute – the incredible Christmas festivities with the pudding for sixty mixed in a baby's bath, the strange rhythms and movements of the dancing, the warmth of the people she met. She had reassured L.M.:

I am not dead though you persist in pretending I am. And of course I shall not be here all my life. 'Connected' with this work & these ideas, yes, but that is different.

By January she had:

... moods when I simply pine for the S. of France or somewhere like Majorka. *When* this time is over I shall make for the South or East and

The dancing here has given me quite a different approach to writing ... There is one which takes about 7 minutes and it contains the whole life of woman ... it gave me more of woman's life than any book or poem.
to J.M. Murry, 12 November 1922

Dancing at the Institute

I am looking for signs of Spring already.
Unposted letter to L.M., January 1923

The Institute.
K.M.'s room has the shutters open

never go North again . . . Write and tell me how you are will you? dear Ida?

Her last gentle letters to L.M. and Murry seemed to have something of that calm steady acceptance she had sought for so long. That 'queer finality' she herself had recognised. When Murry visited her on 9 January 1923, he found her radiantly happy yet serene. In the evening as they climbed the stairs to her room she began to cough. Within half an hour she was dead. Murry, shocked and grieving, faced the task of telling her family and friends:

We had been very happy together – and I had seen something of what she understood & lived by here in Le Prieuré. And she died.

There's nothing to say, Sydney. I know you loved her – in a strange way perhaps she didn't always understand as well as I did. I don't know. No, she understood far more than I. She had found happiness here – that is undoubted.

She was buried at Avon, Fontainebleau. Her sister Chaddie wrote to Vera:

That Friday was such a beautiful day . . . after lunch we drove to the little Protestant church . . . The coffin was first covered with K's beautiful black shawl and then beautiful flowers were placed on it, all so beautifully arranged by dear Ida . . .

The service was in French and the little Church was quite crowded . . . After the service we drove to the cemetery, a very long way, and it was bitterly cold & almost dark by the time we reached there.

On an evening in Bandol years before, K.M. had copied lines from *Henry IV* into a small notebook. Later she had chosen them for the title page of *Bliss and Other Stories* and, on a black day in Ospedaletti, noted them yet again for that sadly defiant story, 'This Flower'. Now, in choosing those words for her gravestone, John Middleton Murry showed an intuitive understanding that he had too often lacked:

But I tell you, my Lord fool, out of this nettle danger, we pluck this flower, safety.

KATHERINE MANSFIELD
WIFE OF
JOHN MIDDLETON MURRY
1888 - 1923
BORN AT WELLINGTON
NEW ZEALAND
DIED AT AVON

Let me take the case of K.M. She has led, ever since she can remember, a very typically false life. Yet, through it all, there have been moments, instants, gleams, when she has felt the possibility of something quite other.

VILLA ISOLA BELLA

GARAVAN

MENTON A/M.

viii
1921

My precious darling,

I shall never forget your
beautiful gesture in handing me that
letter. I read it and I drove home
with you and you are still here. You
have been in every moment of the day;
it is as though you had gone up to
the mountains for a long afternoon.
I have never loved you so. No, my
precious, until now I did not know
what it was to love like _this_. This
peace and this wonderful certainty are
quite new.
          Take care of yourself.

2 Letters and journals

Looking back, I imagine I was always writing. Twaddle it was too. But better far write twaddle or anything, anything than nothing at all.

*I*n a will dated 14 August and apparently written and witnessed on that day at the Chateau Belle Vue in Sierre in 1922, Katherine Mansfield bequeathed 'all manuscripts notebooks papers letters' to her husband:

I should like him to publish as little as possible and tear up and burn as much as possible. He will understand that I desire to leave as few traces of my camping grounds as possible.

In a letter a week earlier, to be handed to him after her death, she had written:

All my manuscripts I leave entirely to you to do what you like with. Go through them one day, dear love, and destroy all you do not use. Please destroy all letters you do not use. Please destroy all letters you do not wish to keep & all papers. You know my love of tidiness. Have a clean sweep Bogey, and leave all fair – will you?

Less than two weeks after her death, Chaddie informed Vera that Murry was intending to publish two more collections of stories

& as soon as he can at least five volumes of her letters and poems, he says he has a most unique and fascinating collection . . .' Constable will take anything he can give them of K's they all think she is a genius & no modern woman like her.

K.M. herself frequently destroyed many of her own letters and notes, even forcing a reluctant L.M. to incinerate the voluminous pile of letters written during her isolated years amongst the New Zealand 'philistines' and those written to L.M. in Rhodesia. It was

In spite of everything how happy we have been.
to J.M. Murry, 7 August 1922

K.M. and J.M. Murry, Isola Bella 1920

with some glee that she remarked on another occasion that mice had made a nest in another bundle of letters to L.M. The night before leaving the Chalet des Sapins, a year before her death, she noted:

Tidied all my papers. Tore up and ruthlessly destroyed much. This is always a great satisfaction. Whenever I prepare for a journey I prepare as though for Death. Should I never return all is in order. This is what Life has taught me.

The huge 'complaining diaries', as she had jokingly described her notes from earlier restless years, had also met with a similar fate.

Nevertheless, John Middleton Murry felt it his duty to collect as many letters and notes as possible for publication:

Her letters are essential to a real understanding of her work. They form a single whole with her stories . . . there were moments when it seemed to me that her letters more completely expressed the nature of her genius than even the most remarkable of her stories.

Many would disagree about the literary value while others, particularly those who were closest to her, regarded his action as a kind of unjustifiable betrayal. Over the following years he published almost everything she had ever written – at first by including pieces in the *Adelphi* and then in collective volumes: the *Poems* in 1923; the *Journal of Katherine Mansfield* in 1927; in 1928 a two-volume edition of *The Letters of Katherine Mansfield*; in 1930 *Novels and Novelists*, which contained her *Athenaeum* reviews and a note on Lawrence; and in 1939 *The Scrapbook of Katherine Mansfield*. In 1951 he published a 700-page volume, *Katherine Mansfield's Letters to John Middleton Murry* – and in 1954 an enlarged 'Definitive Edition' of the *Journal*.

D. H. Lawrence and others condemned what they saw as a kind of posthumous exploitation. His intention, Murry maintained until he died in 1957, and there is little doubt that he believed it sincerely, was to demonstrate and establish what he considered the unique quality of her genius. While he had loved the woman of unique spirit he had also admired the writer of rare perception. Nor was he so insensitive as not to note the irony of the situation when the house which he bought to share with his second wife was paid for by £1000 of K.M.'s royalties. Similarly when he bought the farm where he and his fourth wife were to live he remarked, 'It is Katherine who has bought this farm for us'.

Readers of K.M. have much to thank John Middleton Murry for: his location of material, the painstaking transcriptions of her difficult writing, and the sensitive editing and compiling of her papers into volumes which gave a moving picture of her as a woman and a writer. In fact, so moving was the picture of K.M. which they projected that a kind of Mansfield myth evolved. Already in 1923 she was being described as the 'saintliest of women'. K.M. herself would surely have found such a description amusing.

Gradually a kind of cult developed which idolised her as a courageous, tragic figure but ignored her very human weaknesses. Even Virginia Woolf was devastated when she read the private grief and fears of the woman she had always considered to be so 'inscrutable'. Lytton Strachey's reaction to the *Journal* was very different:

> . . . quite shocking and incomprehensible. I see Murry lets out that it was written for publication – which no doubt explains a good deal. But why that foul-mouthed, virulent, brazen-faced broomstick of a creature should have got herself up as a pad of rose-scented cotton wool is beyond me.

Very little, in fact, had been written with publication in mind and such attempts were usually abandoned.

Koteliansky, who had so loved the vibrant life in her, 'the greatest talent for being a human being' that he had ever known, felt that Murry had cut out all the jokes when he edited her letters.

No published text, of course, can quite convey the feeling of immediacy which is gained from the actual letters and notebooks, the many pages of varied size and colour. The writing alone conveys so much – at times neat, controlled, at others large, erratic, scrawling across the page in feverish haste. Through these pages we can glimpse her paradoxical character; her feelings and aspirations. There is pain, beauty and irrepressible humour.

Murry himself took pains to point out that the *Journal* and *The Scrapbook* were not two carefully kept books, as such, but had been compiled by him from a number of sources such as diaries, notebooks, story outlines, letters, jottings and fragments of all kinds. Many notebooks were undated, or begun at front and back; and often several were used at the same time. K.M. may have described herself to Orage as 'a selective camera' but it was even more true of Murry, the selection being determined, of course, by his own attitude. He invented nothing. He ordered and dated the material as well as he could but he too was an artist and one with a particular image to project. As a result he found it necessary to give greater form or coherence to many passages, particularly the untidier ones; by use of punctuation, paragraphing and the occasional alteration of tense he attempted to give shape and sense to what was often an uninterrupted flow of words. Often these alterations changed K.M.'s own emphasis and lessened the spontaneity of the original.

In a letter sent in May 1917, K.M. wrote: 'Last night there was

a moment before you got into bed. You stood, quite naked . . . '
In his printed version it appears in a more grammatical if less
spontaneous and effective form: 'Last night, before you got into
bed, you stood, quite naked . . . ' In another, her comment 'are
you fair in punishing me so horribly?' became for some reason
'are you justified . . . '

It is harder to explain the difference between the printed text of
an early letter's postcript 'PLEASE SEND ME NO MONEY' and
the original's 'PLEASE SEND ME MONEY'.

He also felt it necessary to omit passages which might reveal
too much of the rebellious, restless side of her nature. Others who
had known her were also protected by omissions or by use of
initials only. Some of her comments about her friends and even
Murry himself which he did not include would certainly have been
hurtful to those concerned. Unflattering references to T. S. Eliot,
their friend Sullivan and others were omitted by Murry. The most
frequent omissions were references to Dorothy Brett. In a letter to
Murry written in March 1920, for example, her name and one
sentence are omitted:

Poor Brett! she asks me to forgive her. Of course, I forgive her – but she
ought to take herself in hand. She cant afford to drift. And one cant fall
drunk 'into a Lav' & then talk of the beauty of Cinnamon & Angelica
[Murry's book] . . . Well I cannot afford to judge.

To Brett though she wrote only ten days later:

Don't feel bitter! We must not. Do let us ignore the people who aren't real
and live deeply, the little time we have here. It really does seem that the
world has reached a pitch of *degradation* that could never have been
imagined – but we know it – we are not deceived.

Despite this avowed closeness she wrote angrily to Murry:

Thank you, my precious for sending me Bretts [letter] to you. As a matter
of fact I do resent it most deeply – the peeping into your shirt and the
threat to be severe with you – I cant say how hateful that was to me . . .

But Bogey don't let her come near! Forgive me – dont let her touch you.
I've no earthly right to interfere and yet – there it is . . . Is Gertler really
ill? . . . Its like all Bretts friends having *spotty lungs*. I'm very sorry but I
cant forgive these things . . . Theres a kind of agitation in Bretts atmosphere that repels me.

Among the recipients of some of her warmest, most trusting
letters were her friends Violet and Sydney Schiff, whom she had
met in Menton. Nevertheless she wrote to Murry:

I dont like the world. Its a horrid place. When I think of the Schiffs
Sunday lunch – I feel there is no place for us except Beyond the Blue
Mountains.

A fortnight later in another letter Murry omitted not only their name but the first paragraph in which she was highly critical of them.

Another case of deliberate omission is particularly interesting because of the well-known members of the Bloomsbury set involved. In November 1919 Murry wrote to K.M. that he had had tea with Vanessa Bell:

I liked Vanessa . . . We talked a lot about you. Nice things . . . she couldn't make up her mind about *Night & Day* . . . I think that Virginia & Vanessa however much we disagree with them – and, as I said, I think that we are profoundly at cross purposes with Virginia, at least – are the two women with whom you & I have most in common (except, perhaps, Brett) . . . They don't make that continual, ghastly, enervating *personal* claim on your attention that other women do . . . There's something hard & definite & self-contained about them.

He continued by saying that Virginia had called him 'the most intellectual of all modern critics' which he denied, and that he felt Virginia was fascinated 'by unessentials':

She sees only the apparatus never the essentials . . . it's quite impossible for her to have any *notion at all* of what you and I are up to.

In publishing K.M.'s reply in 1951 he tactfully omitted the sisters' names and a reference to Vanessa's painting:

Yes, I agree about Virginia. I have only met the sister once. Id like to know her tho' I confess as a painter I think shes *awfully bad*. But she sounds very attractive.

In a letter to Murry from Paris in 1915, K.M. had strongly denounced Frieda Lawrence as 'a great fat sod' – an understandable omission! In another she discussed an acquaintance's 'millionaire husband' who 'has just floated the British Cellulose Company – with 2 millions of treasury money to help him.' Libellous gossip?

So although the publisher's note to the 1951 edition of her letters states that 'he (Mr Murry) has restored all the passages omitted from her letters on their first appearance in 1928', this was not entirely accurate. (He did, however, improve her erratic French.) The Oxford University Press five-volume collection of her letters, edited by Vincent O'Sullivan and Margaret Scott will be invaluable as the first complete definitive publication of her fascinating letters.

Although the 1951 edition of *Katherine Mansfield's Letters to John Middleton Murry* corrected some errors in dating and made other alterations, some required further revision. Some letters in the 1928 edition were incomplete; others, including those to L.M.,

Bertrand Russell and Princess Elizabeth Bibesco, have only more recently become available. Inevitably many remain unlocated, possibly destroyed, such as those to Francis Carco, Lytton Strachey and others. Some are not yet cleared for publication.

The writing itself presented vast problems in transcription and in some cases, Murry explained, his omissions were caused by illegibility. At times, however, this was certainly only one of the reasons for the omission of certain passages; some are marked with the note 'omitted this deliberately'. In some cases there is no indication in the published journal or letters that a certain section has been omitted or transposed. In the earlier quoted entry for December 1920 on 'suffering', for example, he omits the bitter comment, 'the knowledge that Jack wishes me dead'.

Some of the entries, such as those journal entries concerning his relationship with Princess Elizabeth Bibesco, certainly have been altered in sequence and Murry's arrangement and dating certainly help the reader to see him in a more favourable light. It is, of course, possible to understand Murry's reasons for presenting his selective picture – his desire to protect others, at times even to protect himself, and above all to protect the image of the woman he had loved. As a serious scholar and editor he would have been wiser to indicate that there were omissions, but nonetheless some of the criticism that has been levelled at him is unfair.

There may have been omissions and transpositions but there was no ground for Lawrence's charge, 'I hear he *inserts* the most poignant passages himself. Ottoline declares that in the letters to her, large pieces are inserted, most movingly.'

The publication in 1983 of Murry's letters to K.M., selected and edited by C. A. Hankin, helped balance what had been a fairly one-sided picture of the relationship.

K.M. used over twenty different names and pseudonyms in her personal and professional life. Even to those who knew her well she was an enigma, a woman of many moods; chameleon-like she could adapt to her surroundings, consciously adopting the pose she felt necessary for that moment. At other times her moods or attitudes were entirely spontaneous. As she herself remarked in notes for a book review:

if one was true to oneself . . . True to oneself! Which self? Which of my many – well, really, thats what it looks like coming to – hundreds of selves. For what with complexes and suppressions, and reactions and vibrations and reflections – there are moments when I feel I am nothing but the small clerk of some hotel without a proprietor who has all his work cut out to enter the names and hand the keys to the wilful guests. Nevertheless, there are signs that we are intent as never before on trying to puzzle out, to live by, our own particular self . . .

In more serious moods she realised the inevitable dangers of such a divided being.

Somehow too she managed to keep the various threads of her life separate; some of her friends never, or seldom, met each other. They even knew her by different names: Kathleen, Katherine, Katie, Kass. To each of them she appeared in a different role – and for some she had an incredible vitality, to others she seemed reserved and cool. One acquaintance, Mary Cannan, remarked that K.M. always gave people what they wanted, implying that she could be sufficiently insincere – and sufficiently clever – to assume whatever role people expected. Even her closest friends like Koteliansky at times wearied of her poses. Virginia Woolf, on the other hand, recognised that part of K.M.'s fascination might even lie in her feeling that she was expected to say absurd things. Few were allowed to glimpse the real K.M. She was an intensely private person, 'a secretive creature to my last bones', who frequently longed to be alone and then, inevitably, wished she were not.

K.M.'s letters and papers are an intimate revelation of her fluctuating moods. They are also immensely valuable for the insight they give into the relationship between a writer and her work; her deliberate uncompromising determination to perfect her craft. Even more remarkably they are imbued with a strange quality of life. It is almost as if she herself were there, speaking in that strangely deep resonant voice that so many remembered – the reader cannot help but feel warm with her gaiety, bewildered with her despair, impatient with her unreasonable intolerance and yet compassion for the courage of one who refused to join in the 'marionette dance of fate'.

Certainly for one who complained letters 'are fumbling things' and 'I can't write letters any more', her correspondence was remarkable for its enormous volume alone. Thanking her friend, Sylvia Lynd, for a letter she continued:

It really is a heavenly gift to be able to put yourself, jasmine, summer grass, a kingfisher, a poet, the pony, an excursion and the new sponge bag & bedroom slippers all into an envelope. How does one return thanks for a piece of somebody's life? When I am depressed by the superiority of men I comfort myself with the thought that they can't write letters like that. You make me feel, too, that whatever star they were born under it wasn't the dancing one.

The gift she described was one she herself possessed. By comparison Murry's letters, though sincere, are lacklustre, for as he himself remarked, 'The more I try to make my letters live, the less I seem able to.' Sadly too he was right when he apologised wryly, 'I can't think of anyone who is so dead certain to hit the wrong note as I am.'

There is room in these pages to show only a little of the nature of the writing contained in the many notebooks and thousands of letters written by K.M. In looking at extracts which show the ideas which preoccupied her, the way in which she wrote to, and of, the people who were part of her life, we can glimpse something of the woman behind the biographical facts.

Fascinated by life and the detail of life, K.M. had a superb sense of the ridiculous. At times her humour was sharp, scornful and mocking and sometimes gently ironic. Keenly perceptive, K.M. was able to see not only what others often most wanted to hide, but also some of her own moments of frailty. 'It is of immense importance to learn to *laugh at ourselves'.* Even in the endless succession of doctors and waiting rooms there could be moments of humour.

Sometimes the humour was in an unexpected word or image as in the old woman whose one tooth was 'a sort of monument to all the 31 departed ones.' Sometimes it came merely from a deliberately comic mis-spelling or doggerel.

TEDIOUS BRIEF ADVENTURE OF K.M.
A doctor who came from Jamaica
Said: 'This time I'll mend her or break her
I'll plug her with serum
And if she can't bear 'em
I'll call in the next undertaker . . .

The patient, who hailed from New Zealing
Said: 'Pray don't consider my feeling
Provided you're certain
'Twill not go on hurtin'
I'll lie here and smile at the ceiling.'

There were moments, too, of mimicry:

'You are always an invalid – nein?' says Bobone . . .
'Vot is your age – dirty-five?'
'No,' I said – 'dirty-one'.
'Zo.'

At other times the humour relied on exaggeration or irony. Describing Murry and L.M.'s well-meaning attempts to nurse her she wrote:

Light refreshments, bouillon raw eggs and orange juice were served on the journey. Jack M. came in, fell over the screen went out again, came back, dropped a candle, groaned, said 'Oh God does my love for you matter tuppence?' & went again and the Faithful One changed the hot water bottles so marvellously often that you never had a hot water bottle at all. It was always being taken or brought back.

In a later letter to Anne Estelle Rice Drey, with a drawing of 'me among the pallums' in Menton, she remarked:

my heart is not a boxers heart & I'll never be able to climb trees or run or swim again. Isn't that a bit steep of Almighty God. Im always praising him too, but there you are – Im terribly happy all the same and I don't *think* the world has lost an athlete, darling – do you?

K.M.'s satire in her early stories was often cruelly malicious. There were moments of maliciousness in her letters and journals too, but more often the satire was light and mockingly irreverent.

Frieda writes me that there is a 'rumpus' between me and – them I suppose. I see this 'rumpus' – don't you? A very large prancing, imaginary animal being led by Frieda – as Una led the Lion. It is evidently bearing down on me with Frieda for a Lady Godiva on its back. But I refuse to have anything to do with it. I have not the room now-a-days for rumpuses. My garden is too small and they eat up all one's plants – roots and all.

A great admirer of the artists of the music hall, K.M. herself had the same innate sense of timing and the ability to combine several kinds of humour. Condemned as she was to spend much of her life in a succession of hotels, dining opposite a white serviette, and eating 'tough rissoles and . . . watery gooseberries', the 'uglies' whom she met were a frequent target for her acerbic wit:

. . . the symbol of Switzerland is that large middleclass female *behind*. It is the most respectable thing in the world. It is Matchless. Everyone has one in this hotel; some of the elderly ladies have two.

The strain of 'perpetual radiance' was frequently too great and sometimes her humour betrayed signs of a grim desperation:

If I were there you'd spend 10 minutes with me – give me those ten minutes here. *Help me, help me.* If I veep I getta de fever and I am veeping strong!!

From Looe in 1918 she wrote about a doctor who:

was a New Zealand boy. That explains my feeling of confidence . . . He said: Yes there is no doubt I have definitely got consumption. He appreciated that a sanatorium would kill me *much* faster than cure me. (Its a 2nd lunatic asylum to me) . . . Must live in a summer house (find the summer) eat & drink milk and not get excited or run or leap about or worry about anything . . .

There were times when even her sense of humour could not save her. Instead there was only utter emptiness and despair. At such moments reading her journals seems almost an intrusion into a terribly private grief.

Her letters and notes tell the story of a restless, confused search for many things, but through it all her love of beauty, in all things, was constant, profound and genuine. As a result there is a lyrical beauty in some of K.M.'s letters and notes which is equal to anything in her finest stories:

Some one brings in wood from the dark lamp stained yard – the evening meal is prepared – the charcoal is broken, the dishes are clattered, there is a soft movement on the stairs . . . In dusky rooms where the shutters are closed the women, grave & quiet turn down the beds.

Even in Ospedaletti where the mosquitoes roared like lions and where she had known the deepest misery, she could capture moments of beauty and peace with the clarity of an impressionist painting:

. . . the roses hang heavy . . . Aged men in pale blue trousers are sweeping up the dead leaves & there is a succession of bonfires – puffs of white fine smoke with the old figures moving in it, sweeping & bending.

She needed only a few lines to paint a picture:

The wind died down at sunset. Half a ring of moon hangs in the hollow air. It is very quiet. Somewhere I can hear a woman crooning a song. Perhaps she is crouched before the stove in the corridor, for it is the kind of song that a woman sings before a fire – brooding, warm, sleepy and safe.

There was the same minute observation, the same delight in detail, in a description of a park in Paris:

This evening I went walking in a park. Big drops splashed from the leaves and on the paths there lay a drift of pink and white chestnut flowers. In the fountain basin there was a great deal of mixed bathing going on among some sparrows. A little boy stood just outside the park. He thrust one hand through the railing among the ivy leaves and pulled out some tiny snails, arranging them in a neat row on the stone wall. 'V'la! mes escargots!' but *I* was rather frightened, that, being french, hed take a pin out of his jacket and begin eating them! And then they locked the park up. An old caretaker in a black cape with a hood to it locked it up with a whole bunch of keys . . . Do you, too, feel an infinite delight & value in *detail* – not for the sake of detail but for – the life *in* the life of it. I never can express myself (& you can laugh as much as you please.)

K.M. has frequently been dismissed as 'sensitive' or 'feminine' implying that she lapsed too frequently into precious, coy or sentimental descriptions. Although there was inevitably some exaggeration and over-writing in her letters and notes, for these after all were private papers not carefully crafted stories, she herself detested excessive sentimentality of any kind. After a dramatic description of her joy at the birth of her Swiss maid's nephew she noted drily, 'You ought to keep this my girl, just as a *warning* to show what an arch-wallower you *can* be!' At one point she took L.M. to task somewhat impatiently for her letter writing:

I shall destroy the other letter I have written. Perhaps Jack is right; I *am* a tyrant. But . . . look here (a) Will you please either date your letters or put the day on the top (b) Do you mind cutting out the descriptions as much as you *can* ? That kind of yearning sentimental writing about a virginia creeper and the small haigh voices of tainy children is more than I can stick . . . My advice is to 'concentrate more' & do not worry about the golden leaves so much. Fall they will! I am up. I am better and at work again. Cheer up!

Lady Ottoline Morrell felt that K.M. was continually searching for copy, and indeed her notebook and pen were seldom far from her, in a café or on a train she would note a brief incident or a fleeting idea that would be later developed into a story:

. . . and my sciatica! Put it on record in case it ever goes. What a pain it is. Remember to give to someone in a story one day.

Other writers such as Ivy Compton Burnett have been sceptical of this 'notebook habit', but frequently a hastily jotted phrase reappeared in a letter or a story – it may have been just a glimpsed image or an idea which would become the starting point of a story.

These notes and letters are particularly important for what they reveal of K.M.'s artistic development. As a writer she believed deeply in the importance of writing as an art, constantly discussing and explaining her ideas about her own work and others. She found herself increasingly bored by modern women novelists who 'reveal themselves as . . . sex maniacs', remarking:

I'm sure I've read 20 novels this autumn by *Lady* writers that might all be called *How I lost my Virginity!* If that wasn't bad enough they never tell the truth – they always tell *How I WISHED to lose my Virginity* – and in fact I don't believe they ever did lose it.

Of Lawrence's *The Lost Girl* she wrote:

Lawrence denies his humanity . . . he denies Life – I mean *human* life. His hero and heroine are non-human. They are animals on the prowl they do not feel: they scarcely speak . . .

Later, however, she described Lawrence as the only writer living for whom she profoundly cared. In 1922 she wrote of *Aaron's Rod*:

I do not want to be hard I hope to God I am not unsympathetic . . . Life is so short. The world is rich. There are so many adventures possible. Why do we not gather our strength together and LIVE? It all comes to much the same thing. In youth most of us are, for various reasons, slaves. And then, when we are able to throw off our chains, we prefer to keep them. Freedom is dangerous, is frightening. If only I can be a good enough writer to strike a blow for freedom! It is the one axe I want to grind. Be free – and you can afford to give yourself to life! Even to believe in life.

I do not go all the way with Lawrence. His ideas of sex mean nothing to me. But I feel nearer L. than anyone else. All these last months I have thought as he does about many things.

As for 'that great tome', *Ulysses*, she disliked the pervading atmosphere of 'wet linoleum and unemptied pails', but nevertheless admitted a rather begrudging admiration. On meeting Joyce she was overawed by his detailed classical knowledge:

About Joyce – Don't read it unless you are really going to really worry about it. It's no joke. It's fearfully difficult and obscure and one needs to have a really vivid memory of the Odyssey and of English Literature to make it out at all. It is wheels within wheels within wheels. Joyce certainly had not one grain of a desire that one should read it for the sake of the coarseness, though I confess I find many 'a ripple of laughter' in it. But that's because (although I don't *approve* of what he's done) I do think Marian Bloom and Bloom are superbly seen at times. Marian is the complete female. There's no denying it . . . she is also the night and the day, she is also an image of the teeming earth, full of seed, rolling round and round. And so on and so on.

Joyce was after all, she felt, after the truth and that was the most important thing. Her reading notes, discussed more fully in the next section, show the development of her reading habits; writers as widely different as Wilde and Chekhov she turned to for inspiration. Always poetry, not 'dumb-bell poetry', but Keats and Shakespeare, was one of her greatest pleasures. Rather surprisingly she considered herself old fashioned, which may explain her initial doubts about T. S. Eliot's poetry. At Garsington in June 1917 she had read his newly published 'Prufrock' to the guests. In an undated letter to Virginia Woolf she described it as being really a short story. To Sydney Waterlow she confided in 1921:

I think thats what I want modern poetry to be. I even have a feeling (this is private!) that Johnnie Keats would have admired it and written Elliot no end of a letter.

This was confirmed when she described it to Violet Schiff as:

the 1st modern poem. It stays in ones memory as a work of art, so different in that from Ulysses. The further I am away from it the less I think of it. As to reading it again or even opening that great tome – never!

Eliot-Virginia? The poems look delightful but . . . How one could write so absolutely without emotion – perhaps that's an achievement . . . These dark young men.
to Virginia Woolf

T.S. Eliot, Mark Gertler and Lady Ottoline Morrell, Garsington

Recently there has been considerable interest in K.M. as a feminist. Although she did not see herself as one, the role of women in society was a topic to which she frequently returned, albeit with rather contradictory comments.

During the 1880s and early 1890s many New Zealand women had agitated for the right to vote. Public notices had advised such 'epicene electioneering women' to 'go home, to look after their children, cook their husbands' dinners and generally attend to the domestic affairs for which Nature designed them.' They would thus win 'the respect of all right-minded people – an end not to

Drawing from letter to
J.M. Murry, March 1920

be attained by unsexing themselves and meddling in masculine
concerns of which they are profoundly ignorant'. Despite such
opinions the Suffrage Bill was passed by two votes in September
1893, long before women in Britain had won equal franchise.
Nevertheless women did not succeed in gaining full, social equality that the suffragists had hoped would follow.

In 1903 young Kass Beauchamp wrote an entertaining sketch
of a meeting in the Assembly Rooms. An enthusiastic eloquent
woman was addressing:

'great tall gaunt looking' women who 'seemed to be seized with a mania
to appear masculine . . . It seemed to be her great desire to squeeze out
all the tenderness . . . all the affectionate ways that should belong by rights
to every woman and to put in their places divided skirts.'

Writing to Garnet Trowell in 1908, she described going to
report on a Suffrage Meeting for an unidentified newspaper:

two women who looked like very badly upholstered chairs pounced on
me, and begged me to become a voluntary worker. There were over two
hundred present – all . . . in deadly earnest . . . they got up and talked and
argued until they were hoarse . . . I ran into the street – cool air and
starlight . . . And decided I could not be a suffragette – the world was too
full of laughter. Oh, I feel I could remedy the evils of this world so much
more easily – don't you?

This was one of her few references to the Society for the Pro-
motion of Women's Rights, whose members were so active during
her years in England. C. A. Hankin has also pointed out that Vera
Brittain records her as performing on stage at 'The Cave of Harmony', a lesbian club in London, after her return from France in
1916.

K.M. was in many ways as liberated in her life style and ideas
as any modern woman, as a letter from Edward Marsh to Rupert
Brooke in May 1913 emphasises:

She got turned out of an omnibus the other day for calling a woman a
whore. She really ought to remember she's a lidy. The provocation was
that the woman said that all suffragettes ought to be trampled to death
by horses. Katherine tho' not a suffragette protested and the woman said,
'You with your painted lips!'

Although not militant she was an independent free thinker who
understood completely the need for personal freedom and equality.
As such she was impatient of stereotyped sexual roles. In May
1908 she had described Elizabeth Robins as:

the first of a great never ending procession of splendid, strong women
writers. All this suffragist movement is *excellent* for our sex – kicked
policemen or not kicked policemen.

She had begun to glimpse:

. . . what women in the future will be capable of achieving. They truly, as
yet, have never had their chance. Talk of our enlightened days and our
emancipated country – pure nonsense we are firmly held with the self-
fashioned chains of slavery. Yes, now I see that they are self-fashioned,
and must be self-removed.

Here is a little summary of what I need – power, wealth and freedom.
It is the hopelessly insipid doctrine that love is the only thing in the world,
taught, hammered into women, from generation to generation, which
hampers us so cruelly. We must get rid of that bogey – and then, comes
the opportunity of happiness and freedom.

Her relationships with women were vitally important to that sense
of happiness and freedom; perhaps too an attempt to find the love
and affection she had wanted from her mother. Quite apart from
the physical nature of her early bisexual relationships, she gained
much of her support and nurturing from women. This was particularly true of her relationship with L.M., but also, at different
times from others: her cousin Sylvia Payne, Beatrice Hastings,
Anne Estelle Rice, Lady Ottoline Morrell, her cousin Countess
Elizabeth Russell and Dorothy Brett. Despite the moody fickle-

ness which often led her to criticise them, her letters to these last four and L.M. were often warmly affectionate with an almost underlying complicity – a sense of 'you and I against the world'. In her notebook story 'Juliet' she had written of the friendship between Pearl and Juliet:

Our friendship is unique . . . All the comforts of matrimony with none of its encumbrances . . . we are both individuals. We both ask from the other personal privacy, and we can be silent for hours when the desire seizes us! . . . Think of a man always with you. A woman cannot be wholly natural with a man – there is always a feeling that she must take care that she doesn't let him go.

Certainly in her stories there is a sense that men and women belonged to different, though connected worlds; that the men were less evolved emotionally, dominating, paternalistic and sometimes with a propensity for cruelty, coarseness and violence.

Clearly equality between loving individuals was the ideal basis for a relationship. In a gossipy letter to L.M. from Looe in 1918 about a fellow New Zealander and intimate friend from Queen's College days, Ruth Herrick, she suggested the wrongness of an unequal relationship:

Men dont like Ruth at all – that has made her very bitter (This is the news I glean for you) But the reason for it is that she is 'always in love with some woman' she becomes desperately infatuated with women just as she used to with Robin & Poppy Robinson – devotes herself to them, slaves for them – just as she did when she was a 'little girl' she sounds to me rather a tragic figure cant you try & see her.

She had, incidentally, one Christmas at school given Ruth Herrick a volume of Robert Herrick's poetry with a loving inscription. But that relationship, like so many others, seemed simply to disappear, to become irrelevant.

Like George Sand and Marie Bashkirtseff, whom she admired, she too was to attempt in many ways to throw off those chains which would bind her to the traditional woman's role – but it was not always as simple as she had envisaged:

Am I such a tyrant – Jack dear – or do you say it mainly to tease me? I suppose I'm a bad manager & the house seems to take up so much time if it isn't looked after with some sort of method. I mean – – when I have to clean up twice over or wash up extra unnecessary things I get frightfully impatient and want to be working. So often this week, Ive heard you and Gordon talking while I washed dishes. Well, someone's got to wash dishes & get food. Otherwise – 'Theres nothing in the house but eggs to eat'. Yes. I hate hate HATE doing these things that you accept just as all men

All this suffragist movement is excellent for our sex. to Vera, 12 June 1908

accept of their women. I can only play the servant with very bad grace indeed Its all very well for females who have nothing else to do – – & then you say I am a tyrant & wonder because I get tired at night! . . .

I loathe myself, today. I detest this woman who 'superintends' you and rushes about, slamming doors & slopping water – all untidy with her blouse out & her nails grimed. I am disgusted & repelled by the creature who shouts at you 'You might at least empty the pail & wash out the tea leaves!' Yes, no wonder you 'come over silent.'

Oh, Jack, I wish a miracle would happen – that you would take me in your arms & kiss my hands & my face & every bit of me & say 'its alright, you darling thing. I quite understand.'

All the fault of money, I suppose . . .

Years later in a lighter mood, K.M. described Murry's attempts to teach her chess.

If he wallops me absolutely he remarks, 'A good game. You're getting on.' If it is a draw he exclaims 'My God Im a complete idiot. Ive lost my head completely.' This strikes me as very male. The gentle female would never be so brutal.

She confessed to being a failure at some of the traditional feminine chores, 'no good at buttons, puddings,' and 'knitting turns me into an imbecile. It's the female tradition I suppose.'

In 1922 she looked forward to no longer living in hotels but still did not relish the thought of running a house: 'I haven't the domestic virtues.' Nevertheless one of her most characteristic qualities was a strong sense of fastidiousness:

. . . I have an old servant, a butter and sugar thief who is an *artist* in her way – a joy. Her feeling for hot plates & for what dear Henry James might call the real right gravy is supreme. These things are so important. I don't think I could love a person who liked gravylene or browno or whatever they call it.

In her work this fastidiousness resulted in fine precision, but in a domestic situation it could make life very trying – particularly for L.M., who could not always match her friend's exacting standards:

There is as usual a smell of onions & chop bones in the house. Perhaps L.M. is just frying something in the pan 'for the sake of the nice savoury smell,' while she washes up.

Her journals reveal that the same fastidious standards were also applied to others. In a moment of bitterness she reviled Dorothy Brett, one of her closest friends, for her 'bitten nails – the dirty neck – the film on the teeth!'

Hounded by her illness, by a cough that was 'like a big wild dog who followed me home one day & has taken a most unpleasant fancy to me', she moved restlessly from place to place in search of the final cure. Her letters and notes give vivid glimpses of lamp-stained evenings, blue windy days, greedy porters, 'ancient landla-dies', officious foreign bureaucrats and the less romantic aspects of travel:

Another thing I hate the french bourgeoisie for is their absorbed interest in evacuation. What is constipating or what not? That is a real *crite-rion* . . . At the end of this passage there is a W.C. Great Guns! they troop and flock there . . . and not only that. They are all victims of the most amazing Flatulence imaginable. Air Raids over London dont hold a can-dle to 'em. This, I suppose is caused by their violent purges and remedies, but it seems to me very 'unnecessary'.

Of the discomfort of French houses she dryly remarked

. . . what appalling furniture – and never one comfortable chair. If you want to talk the only possible thing to do is to go to bed. Its a case of either standing on your feet or lying in comfort under a puffed up eider-down. I quite understand the reason for what is called french moral laxity. You're simply forced into bed – no matter with whom – there's no other place for you . . . Supposing a *young* man comes to see about the electric light & will go on talking . . . or a friend drops in to tea and asks you if you believe in Absolute Evil. How can you give your mind to these things when youre sitting on four knobs and a square inch of cane. How much better to be snug and *give yourself up to it.*

Thinking of D. H. Lawrence's wide travels she wrote

It is a pity that Lawrence is driven so far. I am sure that Western Australia will not help. The desire to travel is a great, real temptation But does it do any good? It seems to me to correspond to the feelings of a sick man who thinks always, 'if only I can get away from here I shall be better.' However – there is nothing to be done. One must go through with it. No one can stop that sick man, either, from moving on and on . . .

Nevertheless it seems that she too, even without her illness, would also have been driven from place to place by her own demon of restlessness in search of the elusive peace and freedom she so desired. Some would have considered this, like her innate skill with words, to be an inheritance from past generations. Her par-ents had moved frequently and her grandfather Arthur's constant moves had become a family joke.

So often it seemed to her that her restless wandering had finally led her to the perfect place, but always for K.M. it took very little to shatter that perfection. On arranging to extend the lease of the Villa Isola Bella in Menton she exclaimed triumphantly, 'This little place is and always will be for me the one and only place, I feel'. Only five months later she wrote:

Here it is so cold that it might be November. . . . All our flags are pinned on Switzerland. Meadows, trees, mountings, and kind air. I hope we shall get there in time.

Reality seldom matched the dream and so the search went on. It was, as she wryly quoted, better to 'be imprudent moveables than prudent fixtures'.

Not only must the constant moving and travelling have been very wearying and bewildering for L.M. and Murry, but it was also extremely expensive. The question of Harold Beauchamp's generosity or parsimony has been debated so many times there seems little point in further discussion. Her private papers do, however, reveal much of her financial position and the constant haunting feeling that she would never have sufficient money. Harold Beauchamp made his daughter an allowance of £100 a year which many have considered generous, bearing in mind the cost of living at that time. K.M.'s flat at Clovelly Mansions, for example, was rented for £52 a year. In 1916 she wrote an effusive, presumably sincere letter to her father to thank him for increasing her allowance from £10 a month to £13:

I scarcely know how to thank you for yet another proof of your unexampled generosity to me, darling. It puts my finances on such a secure and easy footing at a time when so many are in want . . . Again, from my heart I thank you. I think of you every day . . .

Her accounts for 1920 show an allowance of £25 a month which was certainly not ungenerous from the father of a married daughter. Her allowance was also supplemented by occasional gifts from both parents and she had her father's assurance that she could, in an emergency, call on him for up to £50. She was confident enough of his support to assure Murry, 'I am sure I shall always have enough from Father to keep US in a cottage with penny packets of seed to feed us . . . ' At the end of 1919, sounding less optimistic, she told Murry that she would not get 'another sou' out of him – presumably the allowance had been under further discussion. Her father no doubt expected that she would be supported adequately after her marriage to Murry – by her own writing and by her husband, particularly when he became editor of the *Athenaeum*. Certainly K.M. would generally have been far too proud to admit to him that this was not always so, but in her notes and letters she returns time and again to the subject of money and her dread of poverty.

I have been very careful of my money here & everything is paid up to date.
to J.M. Murry, 12 February 1914

Page of accounts, Notebook

Her first husband George Bowden and many of her friends clearly had the impression that she was desperately short of money. The early years with Murry were certainly precarious and even by 1920 she could describe herself as 'poor as a mouse'. Her illness was responsible for many extra expenses and L.M. was bitter that K.M.'s father should come for an expensive lunch and leave his daughter nothing but five cigarettes.

A major crisis occurred when K.M. was in Switzerland in May 1921. She was alarmed by the suspicion that her London bank manager – who also acted for her father – had informed him of her uncharacteristically healthy account, and by her cousin's remark that Beauchamp begrudged her her £300 allowance. Her suspicion of the bank manager was correct, but to Beauchamp's credit the allowance continued. Not surprisingly K.M. opened a separate account elsewhere for her earnings. It was considerably more difficult, however, to write to her father. Her silence was broken four months later in a long letter to which he added his own comments:

I can emphatically say that in *thought, word* & *deed*, I have never be-grudged any of my children the amounts I have paid them . . .

There were some spasmodic attempts at accounting, even to the extreme of listing a safety pin bought for Murry; and some brave resolutions:

My precious, please don't ever send me a *penny* of extra money. That is very straight dinkum. Save it. Put it away. We shall want all our pockets full for later. I shall save all I can & faire des economies as far as I can. Trust me.

She could, nevertheless, also be very reckless. She once bought baby clothes for her maid's sister's child and remarked:

The butcher's bill on *red* slaughtered butcher's paper is quite unpaid and now I can't pay it. But you see that's what I am like about money, never to be pitied or helped!

Hotels, servants, travel, treatment and taxis – not to mention the many lengthy telegrams – all were a constant drain on her re-sources. Early in 1916 she determined:

This year I have to make money & get known – I want to make enough money to be able to give Lesley some. In fact I want to provide for her – thats my idea & to have enough so that Jack and I shall be able to pay our debts & live honourably.

Shortly after her marriage in 1918, however, she wrote to L.M. from Looe, 'Jones dear Have you any tea to spare? It is like this I have borrowed £8 from Jack this month & I don't dare to ask for any more – Yet it is not enough to see me through . . . '
Such requests were frequent as were her complaints in later years that it was financial necessity that forced her to continue her time-consuming and frustrating book reviewing – 'bound to journalism for bread'.
It was not that she wished 'to *live rich* – God forbid – but I must be free'. Even in 1922 while in Sierre she felt the need to borrow £100 from her cousin Elizabeth:

I will pay it back the moment my book is paid for. But that will not be before the late autumn . . . May I keep it as long as that? Of course, if in

Opposite:

Father darling, I must get over this fear . . .
to Harold Beauchamp,
1 November 1921 with his
note at the top

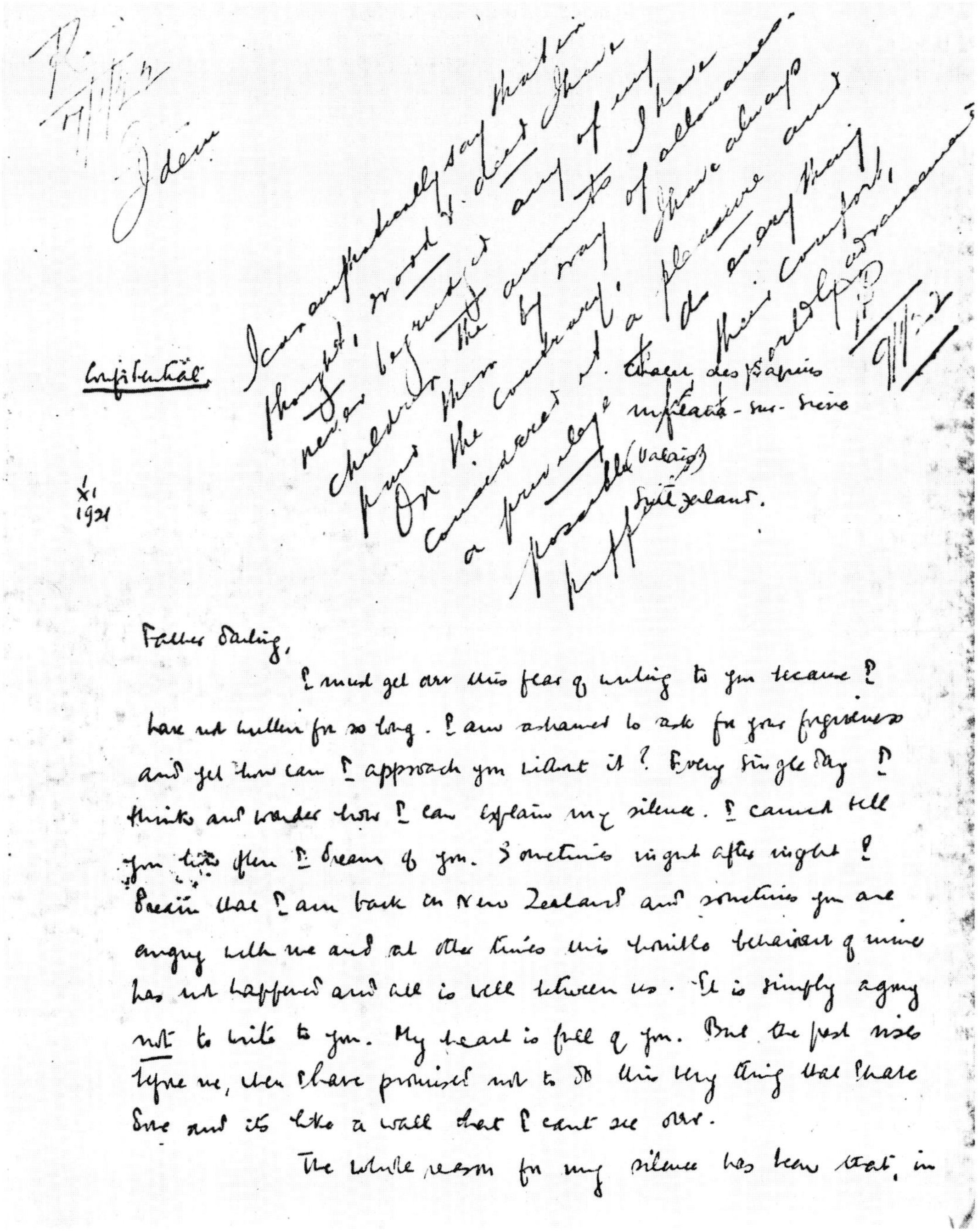

R
7/1/22

I can emphatically say that in thought, word & deed I have never begrudged any of my children the amounts of allowances I have made them by way of allowances. On the contrary it has always been a pleasure & considered it a privilege to do anything for their comfort & advancement.
9/1/22

Confidential.

XI
1921

Chalet des Sapins
Montana-sur-Sierre
(Valais)
Switzerland.

Father darling,

I must get over this fear of writing to you because I have not written for so long. I am ashamed to ask for your forgiveness and yet how can I approach you without it? Every single day I think and wonder how I can explain my silence. I cannot tell you how often I dream of you. Sometimes night after night I dream that I am back in New Zealand and sometimes you are angry with me and at other times this horrible behaviour of mine has not happened and all is well between us. It is simply agony not to write to you. My heart is full of you. But the fact rises before me, that I have promised not to do this very thing that I have done and it's like a wall that I can't see over.

The whole reason for my silence has been that, in

the meantime my Papa shakes a money bag at me – But it is far more likely to be a broomstick.

She was well aware of her own fallibility where money was concerned, 'I always feel sooner or later it will turn up . . . in the crown of ones hat or in the jam pot.'

Although she despised selfishness or lack of generosity, she was well able to rebuke L.M. for extravagance with the household money or for leniency in exacting too little rent from their tenants. Many of her bitterest misunderstandings with Murry were over money. In this as in so many other things K.M. was a creature of contradictions; at times she would gently decline his offers of assistance, at others she bemoaned his selfishness, pointing out in 1919, for example, that she received only £50 of his £800 salary. In a letter marked 'confidential' to L.M. she wrote:

I really must tell you this or jump out of bed or out of the window. You'll appreciate it so. I paid the surgeon on the nail yesterday. That was all right. I expected to (only 100) but Jack came down & paid the cocher. When I said I'd paid the surgeon he replied 'The *cocher* is mine. I agreed on the price 20 francs beforehand.' Just now – making out the weeks bills he asked me for 11 francs for the carriage – half – plus a 2 franc tip! I think its awful to have to say it. But fancy not paying for your wifes carriage to & from the surgery! Is that simply extraordinary or am I? I really am staggered. I think it is the meanest thing I ever heard of. It's not the fact which is so queer but the lack of fine feeling. I suppose if one fainted he would make one pay 3d for a 6d glass of sal volatile & 1d on the glass. That really does beat Father . . .

In a letter to Richard Murry enclosing a cheque as a present K.M. explained:

And never think any money I send you deprives Jack of anything. As you know we keep our money affairs quite separate. He doesn't give me a penny and never has.

Her accounts and her letters to Murry show that this was a rather unfair exaggeration, despite their misunderstandings.

In the last months of her life she sent L.M. money with the quiet admonition:

When I say I have no money I do not mean I have not always money for you when you need it. I have. You only have to ask – so ask *please*.

She had, she gently explained, finally lost her 'money complex'.

On her death her estate was valued for probate at £266.6.4. Some sixty years later a first edition of *Prelude,* or a single letter, can fetch over £1000.

World War I was at first seen by the British as a relatively simple matter of teaching the Germans a lesson. Like many others, K.M. did not initially realise its full implications:

Its the fault of the Prussians and not those simple warmhearted bavarians, after all. Of course I cannot understand why somebody doesn't shoot the Kaiser, but I suppose these deeds are more difficult than they appear to the female eye.

It was, however, to be unlike anything she or the rest of her generation had ever seen, it destroyed the world she knew. 'A black cloud', it poisoned everything and was a foreboding presence in her letters and journals for those years. She felt too that others did not always share her horror:

I spoke about the war to her [L.M.] tonight – about the meaning of it and . . . how it was at the back of my mind all the time – was a sort of sea, rising and falling – never never still . . . Said she, (knitting a grubby vest) 'Roger has got four teeth' . . .

Her brother and many of her closest friends were killed, but her feeling was not one of vituperative hatred for the German people. She did not in fact wish her first book *In a German Pension* to be republished to exploit the anti-German feeling in Britain. Even as the Armistice was celebrated she realised that the end of the war would not bring mankind a miracle:

These preparations for Festivity are too odious. In addition to my money complex I have a food complex. When I read of the preparations that are being made in all the workhouses throughout the land – when I think of all those toothless old jaws guzzling . . . and then of all that beautiful youth feeding the fields of France – Life is almost too ignoble to be borne. Truly one must hate humankind in the mass, hate them as passionately as one loves the few, the very few. Ticklers, squirts, portraits eight times as large as life of Lloyd George and Beatty blazing against the sky – and drunkenness and brawling and destruction. I keep seeing all these horrors, bathing in them again and again (God knows I don't want to) and then my mind fills with the wretched little picture I have of my brother's grave. What is the meaning of it all?

One ought to harden one's heart until it is all over. But Oh – Life might be so wonderful – There's the unforgettable rub! And we've only one life and I cannot believe in immortality. I wish I could. To arrive at the gates of Heaven, to hear some grim old angel cry, 'Consumptives to the right – up the airy mountain, past the flower field and the boronia trees – sufferers from gravel, stone and fatty degeneration to the left of the Eternal Restaurant smelling of Beef Eternal'. How one would skip through!

This is all too calorias !

So deep was her awareness of life's contradictions it was not surprising that her letters and notes show an increasing distaste for society:

You will think me a sad old frump – but of course, like everybody else I don't think I am. Gossip – tittle tattle – *spreading the news* – all that fills me with horror – were I perfectly sincere I'd have to confess that I was always acting a part in my old palmy days. And now I've thrown the palm away . . .

As she remarked to Virginia Woolf:

. . . all parties are cursed if one cannot remain invisible at them. *Then* they must be heavenly – But to be a body revolving round other bodies is very heavy work.

Even the great cities she once loved lost their magic, 'London, it is life' the young New Zealander had declared but it became a '. . . dangerous place – a plague spot and nothing would get me there. I think I hate everything about it.'

The woman revealed in the letters was not always courageous, pleasant or even likable, but she was very human. A comparison of letters and notes shows that she was quite capable of destructive criticism of someone to whom she had just written an affectionate letter. Truly, as she said of Chekhov, 'letters are deceptive at any rate.'

An actress of many parts, K.M. was not above the occasional imaginative fabrication when it seemed necessary. Frederick Goodyear went so far as to write:

The demand you used to make on life was prodigious . . . you boasted of nothing more wholeheartedly than your successful lies and cheats. You openly and avowedly despised human beings in their social compacts & considered them fair game.

Theirs had been a particularly close, frank relationship and he had seen her more clearly than most.

Others saw only what she wished to reveal, even if it necessitated lying. In the middle of December 1914, for example, she was wretchedly miserable at Rose Tree Cottage, planning to leave Murry for Carco. Yet on the fifteenth she wrote to her father that she felt 'chirpy' and outlined her plans:

I had hoped to get a small job not far from the fighting line last month, but now it has been postponed until January, when D.V. I shall go to France and write some human documents for a newspaper syndicate. I am very keen to do so.

Opposite:
This is all too laborious!
Notebook entry while
working on 'The Aloe', 1916

All, of course, she was really intending to do was to share a few days with Carco.

Reading her letters and journals it seems that such deviousness came to her quite naturally, it was as if she transferred her talent for acting onto paper. A comparison of some of her letters to Murry and L.M. shows that in her attempts to retain both of those essential relationships, she deceived each of them.

On 21 May 1918 she wrote to L.M.:

Do please go & see Jack as soon as you can & find out about his cold also how he looks & seems. It is anguish to be away from him but as my presence seems to positively torture him I suppose it's the better of two horrors.

The next day she wrote to Murry,

I had a nightmare about L.M. last night. You know she *does* terrify me. I have got a complex about her regard for me. I suppose I shall get over it. She isn't a werewolf – is it? Are *you* sure.

Similarly her duplicity is clear when on 19 June she cajoled Murry:

I don't want any money at all, thank you, Mr Millionaire. My finances are quite satisfactory, and you sent me £8 for this month, you know.

Less than a week later she asked L.M.:

Jones dear Have you any tea to spare? It is like this I have borrowed £8 from Jack this month & I dont dare to ask for any more – yet it is not enough to see me through . . . You understand – dont you?

At times her letters have a querulous impatience and her notes show even greater intolerance; in her apparent preoccupation with her own illness, pains and misfortunes, she seemed utterly insensitive to others' feelings or desires. Although she could clearly see the irrational aspects of her behaviour, she was often unable to control it:

I don't *want* to quarrel, though I believe you think I do. The truth is that for the time being my nature is quite changed by illness . . . I turn into a fiend.

In an address book kept in her last years she noted:

I think the only thing which is really serious about me, really 'bad' really incurable, is my temper.

Impatient and highly strung by nature, weakened and increasingly nervous through illness, even the ordinary noises of the household routine, not to mention L.M.'s well-meaning interruptions, became an abrasive irritant:

Doors that bang, voices raised, smells of cooking even steps on the stairs are nothing short of anguish to me at times. There is an inner calm necessary to writing, a sense of equilibrium which is impossible to reach if it hasn't its outward semblance.

The sense of loneliness, the prevailing fear of isolation are as much a part of her letters and notes as they are of her stories. The physical separation from the man she loved and the friends she cared for, and the activities she could not share, was painful enough:

Very strange my love for you to-night – don't have it psychoanalysed. I saw you suddenly lying in a hot bath, blinking up at me – your charming beautiful body half under the water – I sat on the edge of the bath in my vest waiting to come in – Everything in the room was wet with steam and it was night time and you were rather languid. 'Tig chuck me that sponge.' No, Ill *not* think of you like that – Ill shut my teeth and not listen to my heart.

But it was more than just physical isolation; she felt keenly the essential aloneness and separateness of the individual:

How strange talking is – what mists rise and fall – how one loses the other and then thinks to have found the other – then down comes another soft final curtain . . . But it is incredible – don't you feel – how mysterious and isolated we each of us are – at the last. I suppose one ought to make this discovery once and for all, but I seem to be always making it again.

It was at such moments of spiritual loneliness that she confided in her journal her desire for some kind of religious belief. After her flight from Ospedaletti she briefly contemplated Catholicism: 'I for the first time think I should like to join the Roman Catholic Church. I must have something!' Two months later she mentioned the idea again, this time to L.M. Probably these thoughts resulted from the influence of her cousin, Connie Beauchamp and her friend, Jinnie Fullerton, whom she was with at this time in Menton. Although there were many times throughout her life when K.M. felt the need for some kind of spiritual peace, it was not to be through conventional religion:

No, theres no God . . . I thought of *The Gods* but they are marble statues with broken noses. There is no God or Heaven or help of any kind but love.

A month later at a time of even greater spiritual crisis she wrote, 'Honesty (why?) is the only thing one seems to prize, beyond life love, death, everything.'

K.M. was not a philosopher but a wilful, impetuous, talented woman who, despite illness and frustration, loved life immensely and who, through reading and experience, acquired certain understandings of it:

We resist – we are terribly frightened. The little boat enters the dark fearful gulf and our only cry is to escape – 'put me on land again.' But its useless. Nobody listens. The shadowy figure rows on. One ought to sit still and uncover ones eyes. I believe the greatest failing of all is *to be frightened*. Perfect Love casteth out Fear. When I look back on my life all my mistakes have been because I was afraid . . . Was that why I had to look on death? Would nothing less cure me? You know, one can't help wondering, sometimes . . . No, not a personal God or any such nonsense. Much more likely – the souls desperate choice . . .

At times her search for some kind of harmony in a discordant world seemed hopeless. She was:

quite overcome . . . by the *horror of life* – the sense that something is almost hopelessly wrong. What might be so divine is out of tune – or the instruments are all silent and nobody is going to play again. There *is* no concert for us. Isn't there? Is it all over? Is our desire and longing and eagerness, quite all that's left? Shall we sit here for ever in this immense wretched hall – waiting for the lights to go up – which never will go up.

Yet there were moments when the world seemed beautiful after all:

God forbid that another should ever live the life I have known here [Ospedaletti] and yet there are *moments* you know, old Boy, when after a dark day there comes a sunset – such a glowing gorgeous marvellous sky that one forgets all in the beauty of it – these are the moments when I am *really writing* – Whatever happens I have had these blissful, perfect moments and they are worth living for.

But were such glimpses enough? Was there nothing else?

No, one can't believe in *God*. But I must believe in something more *nearly* than I do. As I was lying here today I suddenly remembered that: 'Oh ye of little faith!' Not faith in a God. No, thats impossible. But do I live as though I believed in *anything?* Dont I live in *glimpses* only? There is something wrong: there is something small in such a life. One must live more fully and one must have more POWER of loving and feeling. One must be true to ones vision of life – in every single particular – And I am not. The only thing to do is to try again from tonight to be stronger and better to be *whole*.

Those glimpses which had given meaning and joy in her life, even if only briefly, were not always profound or mystical. The letters and notebooks reveal K.M. as a woman who felt not only a deeply urgent need to live but also an enthusiasm for the less

I never had a lovelier letter from you. And it came on my birthday, wasn't that good fortune. Wasn't that like you, the billiard champion? I did love you for it! You have a real very rare gift for writing letters.
to Dorothy Brett,
15 October 1922

Dorothy Brett, K. M., L. M.
Chateau Belle Vue

serious things in life. 'The fillums' and Charlie Chaplin, the comedy of the music halls and the power of Beethoven's Hammerklavier were all important pleasures. So too was her interest in painting. Although she claimed to know little about art her comments were perceptive and lucid. Her preference for Monet and Van Gogh over Renoir was perhaps characteristic. Her response to birds and flowers was even more acute and sensitive – throughout her life they were a constant, spontaneous delight:

John brought me a bunch of daffodils yesterday, the little half wild kind that smell sweet – far lovelier than the others, I always think. Garden daffodils are so plump and self contained, rather like ducks . . . I still 'in vacant or in pensive mood' go over those bunches you brought last summer, disentangle the sweet peas . . . What joy it is that these cannot be taken away from us. Time seems to make them fairer than ever.

In moments of disillusionment, K.M. frequently mentioned in diaries and letters the need to 'eliminate the personal' from her life, and the desire to devote herself wholly to her work. Despite her protestations at such moments that she no longer cared for people or personal relationships, some at least of the many people in her life remained important. The desire to be alone frequently led only to devastating loneliness. Forced to live apart, remote from those she cared for, letters became a vital part of her life. The tone of the letters varied according to her mood and the person to whom she was writing. Some were warmly spontaneous and conversational, in others, every word, every nuance, every inflection was carefully weighed and chosen. Somehow she managed to keep the many strands of her different relationships separate, some were relatively superficial, others such as the bond with her father were far more complex.

By the end of her life she had made her peace – of a kind – with her family. Her sisters remarked years later that K.M.'s portrait of Annie Beauchamp, their mother, in many of her stories had been 'completely wrong', 'very hurtful' and 'most extraordinary'. They described their mother as having a 'marvellous gift' for letter writing – a characteristic inherited by K.M. herself – tolerant, with

Ah, Jeanne, anyone who says to me 'do you remember', simply has my heart . . . I remember everything.
to Jeanne, 14 October 1921

Back row from left: K.M., Vera
In front: Leslie, Chaddie, Jeanne

a glowing personality and intelligence, a close friend and confidante. For K.M. the situation was different, she appears to have longed for a closer, warmer, more loving relationship. One letter, written to her mother in December 1914, hints at the possibility of the kind of intimacy she desired:

How terrible that you should have been ill again, and so severely ill . . . Every evening when my work was done and I sat down by the fire I felt your nearness . . . I cannot bear to think that we are far away from each other, and that I cannot come in and ask you if you feel inclined for a little pow wow . . .

Not surprisingly she did not mention the difficulties she and Murry were experiencing at that time, when she was contemplating joining Carco. Such 'selective' writing was typical of her letters – certainly she seldom told her family about her problems keeping them, as her sisters remarked, 'in the dark'.

Where her family was concerned K.M. was an erratic correspondent. Her mother dryly remarked to Leslie in her last unposted letter to him:

Kathleen has certainly only dreamt she has written me since the 4th of last April, as letters from London to N.Z. do not go astray. Never mind, poor child has evidently imagined she has written & thought of her Mother and Father.

After Leslie's death Annie Beauchamp wrote a letter to a friend which showed little regard for K.M. in comparison with her two older sisters:

Poor old Vera & Chad will feel it so much so far apart from any of their own people. The dear [Leslie] stayed with Kathleen in London for a few days last August while attending some instruction classes in London.

Four months later she commented:

You will be glad our darling Leslie was the means of bringing poor old Kass *right* into the fold again, she writes to us all most loving letters, she *adored* Leslie.

Nevertheless Annie Beauchamp did not see this as sufficient reason to reinstate this more wayward daughter in her will. On her death in 1918 her final instructions to her solicitor bequeathed all her belongings to Jeanne, who could then 'give anything she may wish to her sisters'. It was hard always for her parents to accept K.M.'s unconventional life and her 'irregular' relationship with Murry. It must, therefore, have been with real pleasure that she wrote to Murry in 1918 that, 'I feel very strongly that Mother has come bang over to our side & loves us.' When Annie Beauchamp died a few months later K.M. grieved deeply; part of that grief was no doubt for the relationship that might have been, intermingled with some guilt for her own part in its failure to develop. She had fought hard to win her independence, to stand alone, but the ties and the needs remained:

I miss her so. I often long to lean against Mother & know she understands things . . . that can't be told . . . but what Mother hadnt is an *under*stand-ing of Work.

Much has been written about the particular relationship K.M. shared with her brother. Murry, who was undoubtedly bewildered by her agony of loss, felt that part of its importance derived from Leslie's association with the innocent, beautiful world of child-hood. C. A. Hankin suggests that in fact K.M. resented Leslie, envying his special place in the family. Hankin postulates that the 'guilt for the hostile feelings towards the men in her family prob-ably heightened enormously the natural grief' K.M. felt at his death. Her suggestion is that with the 'rival' removed, perhaps the tragedy allowed her to 'effect some kind of inner reconciliation with her father' and also that 'Leslie, dead, became a kind of imaginary companion and lover whom Katherine bound to her, and used against Murry.' So much of anyone's inner life must be uncertain and thus open to various interpretations but according to L.M., K.M.'s relationship with Leslie was vitally important.

Journal entries and several stories written even before Leslie's death reinforce this view. An unpublished typescript signed and dated by her in 1909 is clearly based on her affectionate recollec-tions of Leslie, whom she had last seen, as a schoolboy, in Wel-lington the previous year. In this strange little story the central character is a girl who 'was sick of existing'. On a train journey she remembers:

When I last saw him . . . he was thirteen – very young, you see, but tall and splendidly made, broad shouldered . . . through all the sadness of my girlhood that child brought me light and sweetness. He had a little habit of bringing me flowers . . . I have so many pictures of him . . . in my mind you know. He will be the finest man on earth . . . And then particularly after he had been playing cricket I could hear him stumbling up the stairs, hot, out of breath, his shirt collar unbuttoned, his hair on end, damp with perspiration, and mopping his face with an indescribable handkerchief . . . Then he used to stand on a chair and part his hair before my mirror, called it a 'bug-track' after he'd been to school. He read too, everything I gave him . . . I remember very well saying Good-bye to him.

Something of this is reflected in Leslie's concerned affectionate

Do you remember sitting on the pink garden seat . . . Sitting on the seat, swinging our legs & eating the pears.

From the left: Leslie, K.M., Jeanne, Chaddie, Marion Ruddick, Belle Dyer

remarks about 'Katie' and 'Kathleen' in letters from Oxford and Bournemouth to his family. She wrote to him frequently and they spent some happy times together that year. A letter written on Selfridge's notepaper and which he took to France speaks of what was apparently their last meeting:

Dearest, I have an odd moment to spare & I'll use it in sending you a line – Ever since last Sunday you are close in my thoughts. It meant a tremendous lot, seeing you and being with you again and I was so frightfully proud of you – you know that, but I like saying it. But the worst of it is that I want always to be far *more* with you and for a long enough time for us to get over the 'preliminaries' . . .

   This is not a letter. It is only my arms round you for a quick minute.
                                     Your
                                     Katie

But what of those remaining family members with whom she continued to correspond until her death? Sitting in front of the fire at Fontainebleau on New Year's Eve 1922, K.M. had begun two letters. One, unfinished, was to her sisters, Chaddie and Jeanne:

My dearest Marie & Jeanney,
I am seizing the last moments of the old year to write to you for I cannot let it depart without a letter from me. I have been such a very bad correspondent lately. I am only too painfully aware of it. But it was awfully difficult to write. There seemed nothing to say. Were I to attempt to describe my present surroundings and way of life it would all sound like a dream and I have for the moment no interests outside it.

and wit, and their vitality. Although they consistently failed to understand each other she seems to have glimpsed the inner man beneath the 'pa-man' exterior. In a letter written to him on the last New Year's Eve but received after her death she could joke:

the old year is at his last gasp and in the very act of turning up his toes! May the New Year be full of happiness for you. I wish I could imagine we might meet in it, but perhaps in the one after I shall be fortunate enough to turn towards home . . . It is a dream I would love to realise . . .

Christmas . . . is no fun far away from ones own people . . . I think of us all going to St. Paul's . . . darling Leslie still a child enjoying everything. Such memories do not make for gaiety. I do wish the English climate were more temperate, and that I could look forward to *settling down* there. But the idea of settling down is to me what it seemed to be to Grandpa Beauchamp, only I am driven there: he went willingly. . . .

Chaddie and Jeanne write very happily. I have no idea of what Charles does all day, though, of course, Jeanne will make the best of it and find happiness – but I don't think it can be much fun living in a hotel in South Kensington.

Chaddie sent me a handkerchief for Christmas (her invariable present) and little Wilfred a morsel of ribbon that looked like her doll's sash. I still cannot imagine her a married woman . . .

Forgive this handwriting, dearest Father. My constant plea! But as usual my letter case is balanced on my knee at a rather groggy angle.

The New Year is already here. I must leave the fire and go to bed. God bless you darling Father. May we meet again at not too distant a date.

Ever your devoted child,
Kass

Some of K.M.'s warmest letters were written to Murry's younger brother Arthur, known as Richard, a painter who admired her greatly. They had spent many happy evenings together at concerts and music halls, K.M. vivacious in her coloured waistcoats and little jackets with bright silver buttons. Despite earlier occasional derogatory remarks 'I dont like Jack's family', her letters to him are gay and gently affectionate:

I hope all goes well with you, my dear no longer little brother. Even if dragons come along don't forget that ten to one (the best dragons at any rate) they are the guardians of treasures.

Another important friend with whom she corresponded often was S. S. Koteliansky, who admitted to both Virginia Woolf and Mark Gertler that there were things in K.M. which he disliked. Virginia Woolf noted: 'Her lies & poses have proved too much for him'. Nevertheless he loved her, and her letters to him are the natural expression of her own deep feelings of friendship and respect:

You know Richard I feel this next year 1922 is going to be a good one. Better than the ones that went before . . . I want it to be good for all of us . . . rich in happiness, fat in blessings. Jack shall have a crown, you a small sceptre – What's left for me? There is sure to be something small going. Happy Xmas, dear old boy.
to Richard Murry, December 1921

K.M., J.M. Murry, Richard Murry, Portland Villas, Hampstead

Thank you for your letter, dear Koteliansky . . . I am glad that you criticised me. It is right that you should have hated much in me. I was false in many things and *careless* – untrue in many ways. But I would like you to know that I recognise this and for a long time I have been trying 'to squeeze the slave out of my soul'. You will understand that I do not tell you this to prove I am an angel now! No. But I need not go into the reasons; you know them.

C. A. Hankin has remarked that K.M. was in a sense 'emotionally married to two people'. She herself joked, 'Jones as usual is wife of both of us.' Certainly the triangular relationship shared by Murry, K.M. and L.M. was a most unusual one. She was fiercely independent yet they were both indispensable to her. Neither one alone could meet all her needs. Can any one person ever do so for another? She would reject each of them in turn, she would use each of them to manipulate the other. She hurt them both, yet she loved them both. In May 1919 K.M. wrote:

I do not care for 'people' – and the idea of fame – of being a success – thats nothing – less than nothing. I *love* my family, a few others, dearly, and I love, in the old – in the ancient way, through & through, my husband.

The hundreds of letters which she wrote to John Middleton Murry – 699 pages in the 1951 edition – tell their own story of two people who loved each other deeply but were frequently forced apart by circumstances and, at times, by choice. She often wrote

There is the inexplicable fact that I love my typical english husband for all the strangeness between us. I do lament that he is not warm, ardent, eager, full of quick response, careless, spendthrift of himself, vividly alive – high spirited *but it makes no difference to my love.*
'Journal', May 1919

J.M. Murry

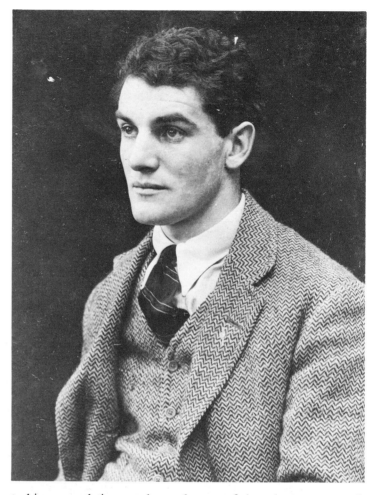

to him several times a day and some of these letters are surely among the most moving love letters ever written. At times they are alive with joy, at others perceptively witty and gay. Nor was she too proud to admit her deep need of him, 'Ah, but I wanted you today. Today I have longed for you. Have you known that? Can I long for you so and you not know?' At such moments she felt he was wholly necessary to her peace and happiness. 'If I was in bed with you I'd sleep . . . I *pine* when I am away from you just like ladies do in old songs . . . ' At the thought of seeing him after months of separation her letters are warm with love:

Perhaps all human activity is beautiful in the sunlight. Certainly these women lifting their arms, turning to the sun to shake out the wet clothes were supremely beautiful I couldn't help feeling – and after they have

lived they will die and it wont matter. It will be allright . . . Wander with me 10 years – will you, darling? Ten years in the sun. It's not long – only 10 springs.

You are coming quite soon now – aren't you, Boge?

You are you. I am I. We can only lead our own lives together.
to J.M. Murry, 7 November 1922

K.M. and J.M. Murry about 1920

Reality did not always hold such simple beauty. At times it seemed as if everything was against them '. . . We are the sport of circumstances . . . but how tired the dice get of being rattled & thrown!' Life became a kind of vicious conspiracy:

As I grew depressed he grew depressed but not *for* me. He began to write (1) about the suffering I caused him: *his* suffering *his* nerves . . . (2) a constant cry about money. He had none: he saw no chance of getting any – 'heavy debts' – 'as you know I am a bankrupt' . . . These letters, specially the letters about money cut like a knife through something that had grown up between us. They changed the situation for me, at least, for ever. We had been for 2 years drifting into a relationship, different to everything Id ever known – we'd been *children* to each other, openly confessed children, telling each other everything – & each *depending* equally upon the other. Before that Id been the man and he had been the woman & he had been called upon to make no real efforts. Hed never really 'supported' me. When we first met, in fact, it was I who kept him, and afterwards wed always acted (more or less) like men friends. Then the illness – getting worse & worse – & turning me into a woman and asking him to put himself away – & to *bear* things for me. He stood it marvellously. It helped very much because it was a 'romantic' disease . . . and also being 'children' together gave us a practically unlimited chance to play at life, not to live. It was child love . . . The letters – ended all of it.

Too often K.M. demanded from Murry more than he was able to give. So vital in spirit herself, she came reluctantly to realise that she demanded too much from their relationship:

. . . here's a woman who has been ill for over two years, who instead of 'looking after' the other has made demands upon a man who confesses he has very little vitality to spare and doesn't ultimately care for people except as symbols. Who finds that after all, he doesn't in the least desire her kind of Life but wants to be a scholar and live quietly, remotely . . .

Oh how well I understand this jealous passionate love of himself, this absorption and tenderness which comes from his wretched childhood & poor stifled youth . . .

It was not surprising that Murry should find life with K.M. trying and bewildering. Her highly-strung temperament and the peculiar nature of her disease resulted in rapid changes of attitude and mood. She could be utterly unreasoning, impatient, oversensitive and contrary. At times she was scornfully destructive, at others there was no scorn, simply an urgent cry for help: 'I've scarcely any time I feel. Arthur will draw posters 100 years. Praise him when I'm dead. Talk to ME I'm lonely. I havent ONE single soul . . . '

The many endearments, nicknames and abbreviations would seem sentimental to some readers but the letters were, after all, part of their private world – the conversation between two people escaping from a reality that could not always be easily endured. In this dream world their few possessions, such as K.M.'s Japanese doll Ribni and their successive cats, assumed what would normally be a disproportionate importance, becoming almost human participants. They dreamed too of an idyllic future, of children

You see, my love, the question is always 'Who am I?' and until that is discovered I don't see how one can really direct anything in ones self. 'Is there a Me?' one must be certain of that before one has a real unshakeable leg to stand on.
to J.M. Murry, 26 December 1922

K.M. 1920

*A symbol of liberation,
innovation and
unconventionality. Her life
was new, her manners and
dress were new, her art was
new.*
Margaret Drabble

K.M. 1916

and a fairytale farmhouse – the Heron in the country. They even bought a cottage, 'Broomies', on Chailey Common but were never to live in it. Even Murry recognised at times the emptiness of such a dream. In one of K.M.'s journals, not one of the many labelled 'private', is a short poem by him written during her stay in Bandol, entitled 'Ribni Speaks':

I think that she has been away too long
And you did wrong
Who let her go . . .
Foolish, headstrong
Self cheating children who have loved too long

A romantic idealist, K.M. was also enough of a realist at times to see herself – 'the most stupid woman I have ever met' – and their relationship clearly:

And you have got a terrific case against me which is: I am *over*-sensitive, *impossible* – Life being what it is. Also it is not within the bounds of possibility that we should be in quite the same worlds. I have hiding places – so have you. They are very different ones . . . We share *something* – not *all*. I think, by recognising that fully we shall cease hurting each other ever. What we share we prize enough to wish to share it: the rest is our own . . .

One of their greatest shared pleasures was their work. She saw them both as artists – members of a special tribe, set apart:

It seems to me – the more I read the papers & now from what you say, too – that you & I are in some way *really different* from other writers of our time. I mean it seems to us so natural & so easy to link up with Flaubert or another. It is part of our JOB . . . I mean it doesn't seem to me QUEER to be thinking about Othello at bregchick . . .

She respected his criticism of her work although not always agreeing with it. Her admiration for his work was genuine: 'Your review of Lewis is excellent – simply 1st chop.' To others she freely admitted her high regard ' . . . my money is on J.M.M. as THE English Critic . . . He's the man of the future I'm sure. He risks himself – T.S.E. never.' Nevertheless she did not hesitate to give him direct crisp advice on both writing and his editorial policy:

Your Hardy doesn't quite come off to my thinking. You seem to be hinting at a special understanding between yourself and the author. That's not fair: it puts me off . . . Now I'll be franker still. There are still traces of what I call your sham personality in this book & they mar it . . . I dont ask for false courage from anyone but I do think that even if you are shivering it is your duty as an artist and a man *not* to shiver . . . I must speak out plainly because your friends flatter you . . .

There you are. If you were to send me back my 1/9 wedding ring with this letter I should send the letter just the same & keep the ring in a matchbox & be very sorry.

I must risk being wrong. In my efforts to be clear I am crude. I must risk that. For as long as I live I never will be other than dead honest and dead sincere with you, as I would have you with me . . .

But I love you and believe in you Thats all.

Wig

Realising that her illness placed restrictions and frustrations on their relationship she resolved that they should be independent of each other. Discussing his reference to 'Madame la Princesse' she wrote:

I told you to be free – because I meant it. What happens in your personal life does NOT affect me. I have of you what I want – a relationship which is unique but it is not what the world understands by *marriage*. That is to say I do not in any way *depend* on you, neither can you shake me.

Nobody can. I do not know how it is, but I live withdrawn from my personal life. (This is hard to say) I am a writer first . . .

You are dearer than anyone in the world to me – but more than anything else . . . I want to write.

Yet despite such protestations her notes and letters reveal many times when she felt he failed her; when the man to whom she was married did not match up with the man she envisaged in her dreams and letters.

Do I make M. up? Is he thankful to sink into himself again? I feel relief in every line.

Similarly:

I realise how little Jack shares with me . . . He ought not to have married. There never was a creature less fitted by nature for life with a *woman.*

Yet there were times too when she felt the need to help him take life a little more lightly '. . . its not RIGHT to *LIVE* among mountains of gloom – or to sweat blood as one climbs them. One just must run on top and be careless.' Life for Murry would never be simple, and as she loved him this grieved her. 'You know, I am deeply sorry for Murry, he is like a man under a curse.'

   Towards the end of her life, K.M. tried to describe their relationship:

Looking back, my boat is almost swamped sometimes by seas of sentiment. 'Ah what I have missed. How sweet it was, how dear how warm, how simple, how precious!' And I think of the garden at the Isola Bella and the furry bees and the house wall so warm. But then I remember

From the other side of the world . . .
From a little land with no history,
(Making its own history, slowly and clumsily . . .
Like a child with a box of bricks)
I, a woman . . .
to Stanislaw Wyspianski, 1909

K.M. 1916

what we really felt there, the blanks, the silences, the anguish of continual misunderstanding. Were we positive, eager, real – alive? No, we were not. We were a nothingness shot with gleams of what might be. But no more. Well, I have to face everything as far as I can & see where I stand – what *remains* . . .

It was not that her love for him was less, but that it was different. Her last brief letter written to invite him to Fontainebleau is warm with affection and calmly happy in the knowledge that although their love had changed, as they themselves had changed, it had somehow survived 'in spite of all':

You get out of the train at Avon & take a cab here which costs 8 francs *with* tip. Ring the bell at the porters lodge and I'll open the gate. I hope you will decide to come, my dearest. Let me know as soon as you can – won't you? I hope Tchekhov's wife will be here. I have gone back to my big lovely room, too, so we should have plenty of space to ourselves. We can also sit & drink kiftir in the cowshed.

I cant write of other things in this letter. I hope to hear from you soon.
Your ever loving
Wig

The 1928 edition of K.M.'s letters does not include any of her letters to L.M., many of which have since been printed in L.M.'s own account of their relationship. L.M. was, of course:

not just an agency to which I apply for pills & cigarettes, free of charge – though your whole letter was concerned with trying to make me believe thats what I've brought our 'relationship' to. However if it pleases you to feel it, my dear, you must feel it – Lord knows I deserve it enough, according to the WORLD. I thought you were the person I flew to with bad tempers, worries, depressions, money troubles, wants, rages, silences, *everything,* enfin – but the little bottles, boxes & postal notes though God knows welcome, seemed to me to be only the trimmings – and not the feast. However, you think otherwise – which is humiliating to us both.

Take care of your wicked self
Katie

In L.M. she knew that she had a loyal friend in whom she could confide and whom she could trust absolutely so that her letters have an almost conversational quality:

It seems a mockery to be 29 and Mrs Honey says 'nought but a frame' when there is so much one longs to DO and BE and HAVE (I wish I didn't hear you saying in a small voice: But Katie you might be paralysed or pock marked or an amputé.) For it don't console me at all. I want to run; I want to jump; I want to scramble and rush and laugh.

Ah well – there you are. I don't know why I write to you so intimately.

Because of her temperament, the nature of her illness, her frustration and unhappiness at her separation from Murry and her unwillingness to surrender her own fragile independence, K.M. was frequently extraordinarily cruel to L.M. In her letters to Murry, Lady Ottoline Morrell, Virginia Woolf and others she mocked her as the 'Rhodesian Mountain', the 'Albatross'; poking fun at her awkwardness, her lack of intellect:

L.M. has made me perfectly *sick* today. Shes skittish 'dearie I'm very proud. I remembered the word for candle *bougie*. Thats right isn't it? I'm not really very stupid, you know. Its only when I am with you because you are so many million miles ahead of all the rest of mankind' – and so

The truth is friendship is to me every bit as sacred and eternal as marriage.
to L.M., September 1921

L.M. Rhodesia, 1914

In spite of what I have said and – and shall say – you have been a perfect friend to me.
to L.M.

on I *squirm,* try & hold my tongue – & then *bang* and again I shoot her dead – & up she comes again.

Her journals too reflect the ambivalent nature of her feelings. In an unposted draft of a letter from Montana she criticised others' demands on L.M.:

How can you have a *passion* for people to hold up their hands & tell you over & over & over that they need you!! Or are you simply insincere when you take a job? . . . You're just a kind of vacuum. I dont know. Its difficult! Its maddening. I suppose it gives you a trumpery sense of power. But no-one wants a slave you know. There's your mistake. One only wants to feel sure of another. Thats all . . . I like people to be 'gay' & to be happy but I cant bear *flirts.*

Was she perhaps aware of the irony of ascribing to others something of her own behaviour towards L.M.? The letter she finally posted, asking L.M. to return, contained many phrases from that draft but added:

Life never bores me . . . to arrive late at night in strange cities or to come into little harbours just at pink dawn when its cold with a high wind . . . to push through the heavy doors into small cafés and to watch the pattern people make among tables & bottles and glasses . . . to smell flowers and leaves . . .
to Bertrand Russell,
17 December 1916

K.M. about 1911

please dont make me have to protest. Accept! Take your place! Be my friend! Dont pay me out for what has been . . . you can, in spite of my rages, read as much love as you like into this letter. You won't read more than is there.

At times, undoubtedly, she felt suffocated and trapped by L.M.'s love:

She was sure I would be cold . . .

Are you sure you wont have your cape . . . etc etc etc? Her attitude made me quite sure. I went out. At the corner the flying, gay, eager wind ran at me. It was too much to bear. I went on for a yard or two, shivering – then I came home. I slipped the Yale key into the lock, like a thief – shut the door *dead* quiet. Up came old L.M. up the stairs

'So it WAS too cold, after all!' I couldn't answer or even look at her. I had to turn my back & pull off my gloves. Said she: 'I have a blouse pattern here I want to show you.' At that I crept upstairs, came into my room & shut the door. It was a miracle she did not follow . . . What is there in all this to make me HATE her so? What do you see? She has known me try & get in and out without anyone knowing it dozens of times – that is true. I have even *torn* my heart out & told her how it hurts my last little defences to be questioned, how it makes me feel just for the moment, an independent being, to be allowed to go & come unquestioned. But that is just Katie's 'funniness'. She doesn't mean it, of course . . .

She tried to explain her uncontrollable feelings:

*One afternoon she played . . .
for friends. One remarked 'I
do wish I could play the cello!'
'So do I.' was the response.*
Millie A. Parker

K.M., Queen's College

I am a kind of a person under a curse, and as I dont and can't let others know of my curse you get it all. But if you knew how tenderly I feel about you after one of my outbreaks. You do know I can't say nice things to you or touch you. In fact I behave like a fiend. But ignore all that. Remember that through it all I love you and understand.

Miraculously their friendship survived and K.M. gradually came to recognise and accept her feelings for L.M.:

. . . the old feeling is coming back – an ache, a longing – a feeling that I can't be satisfied unless I know you are *near*. Not on my account; not because I need you – but because in my horrid odious intolerable way I love you and am yours ever

K.M.

It seems incredible that L.M. persevered in what must so often have seemed a thankless task, but for her it had been a deliberate decision and one she did not regret. K.M.'s last gently affectionate letters from Fontainebleau to her friend go some way towards explaining the reasons behind that decision for they reveal something of the warmth, the nearness, and the brave spirit that L.M. had known and loved:

But you do see that our relationship was absolutely wrong now? You were identified with me. I prevented you from living at all. Now you have to learn & its terribly hard.

Forgive this paper. The parcels have arrived and are extremely satisfactory, thanks very much. Why are you still so awfully tragic? I feel you must be very ill physically. Tell me your *physical health.* I am not dead though you persist in pretending I am. And of course I shall not be here all my life. 'Connected' with this work & these ideas, yes, but that is different. As soon as I am cured I shall leave here and set up a little place in the South and grow something. You can come and talk over the fence if you like and are not too mournful. Come and stay with me if you promise to smile now & again. *Dear* Ida! Thank you for the tops and for everything. As I have said I'll write again at Christmas and provided you are a happy nature I shall beg you to join forces with me when I leave here, if you care to, of course, in some kind of farm. So learn all you can for goodness sake.

K.M.'s last unposted letter to her friend began with what must have seemed to L.M. a final bitter irony:

I have purposely not written to you before because I felt you wanted me to disappear –– for a little. I was right, wasn't I? But you have been in my mind to-day. How are you? How are your cows? As you see I am sending you 100 francs. Play with it. I don't want it . . . Write and tell me how you are will you? Dear Ida?

Although entries in each 'damning little notebook' were sporadic and fragmented, together with the letters they tell their own story. As a young girl she had demanded from life, 'power, wealth . . . the opportunity of happiness and freedom'. Happiness and freedom were not to be so easily achieved. The long search led her, rightly or wrongly, to Fontainebleau:

I mean to change my whole way of life entirely. I mean to learn to work in every possible way with my hands. The world as I know it is no joy to me and I am useless in it. People are almost non-existent. The world to me is a dream and the people in it are sleepers. I have known just instances of waking but that is all. I want to find a world in which these instances are united. Shall I succeed? I do not know. I scarcely care. What is important is to try & learn to live – really live – and in relation to everything – not isolated (this isolation is death to me).

This letter to Koteliansky finished with a rather characteristic postscript, 'All this sounds much too serious & dramatic. As a matter of fact there is absolutely no tragedy in it, of course.'

Arithmetic = Good,
Theology = Good, English
Reading = Very Good,
Geography = Good,
Ancient History = Good,
German = Excellent,
Drawing = Very Fair,
Cello = Good
K.M.'s Report, First Juniors,
Easter, 1903

K.M. Queen's College

*She is in danger of the worst
fate an artist can suffer – to be
overwhelmed by her own
legend.*
Katherine Anne Porter, 1937

K.M., Rottingdean 1910

Opposite:
*I am so keen upon all women having a
definite future, are not you? The idea of
sitting still and waiting for a husband is
absolutely revolting, and it really is the
attitude of a great many girls.*
to Sylvia Payne, 24 April 1906

K.M., Brussels 1906

Mes amitiés avec les vôtres

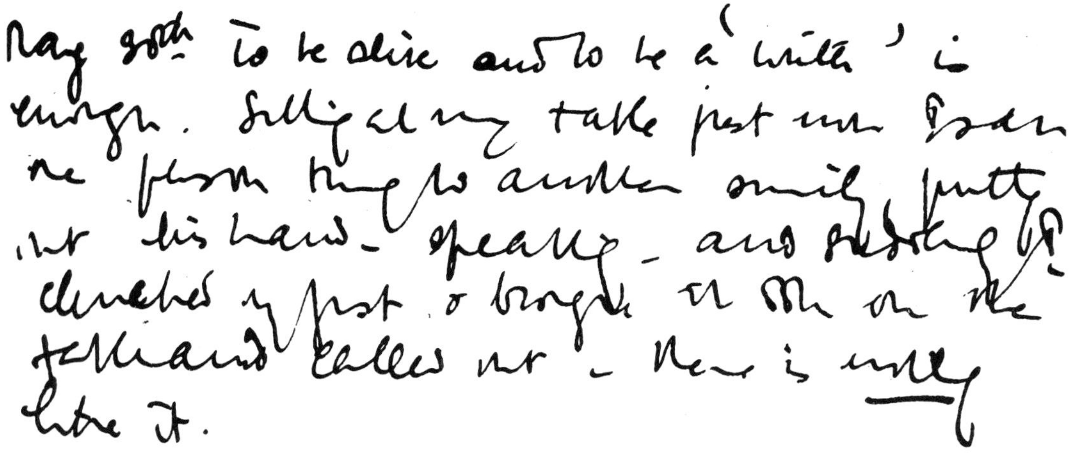

May 30th To be alive and to be a 'writer' is enough. Sitting at my table just now … there is nothing like it.

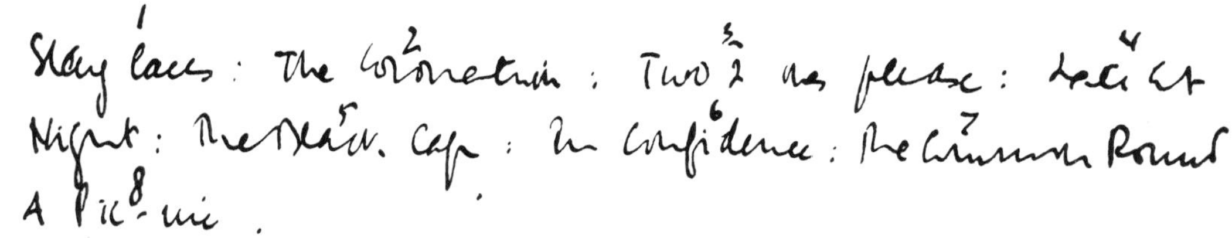

Stay-laces: The Coronation: Two Tuppenny Ones Please: Late at Night: The Black Cap: In Confidence: The Common Round: A Pic-nic.

Above:
To be alive and to be a 'writer' is enough.
Notebook, 30 May 1917

Part of a page showing a list of stories

All this week I have been most fearfully busy with a long story which was only finished late last night . . . It's called 'The Garden Party', and I have decided to call my new book by that title instead of the other.
to Dorothy Brett,
15 October 1921

3 *The short stories of K.M.*

A brief look at K.M.'s letters and journals shows that she was a compulsive writer. Her international reputation as one of the world's best-known short story writers, based on only eighty-eight collected stories, remains secure today. Nevertheless K.M. believed:

You know . . . I shall not be 'fashionable' long. They will find me out . . . I like such awfully unfashionable things – and people. I like sitting on doorsteps, and talking to the old woman who brings quinces, and going for picnics in a jolting little wagon, and listening to the kind of music they play in public gardens on warm evenings, and talking to captains of shabby little steamers, and in fact, to all kinds of people in all kinds of places. But what a fatal sentence to begin. It goes on for ever. In fact, one could spend a whole life finishing it. But you see I am not a highbrow. Sunday lunches and very intricate conversations on Sex and that 'fatigue' which is so essential and that awful 'brightness' which is even more essential – these things I flee from.

This was how she saw her work and her place in literature. It was, she knew, from life's 'tremendous trifles' that she created her stories. She chose ordinary people, everyday events: a charwoman, a child's dolls house. In this, the creation of something timeless from simple things, she was an innovator.

Three volumes of her stories appeared in her lifetime, only the last two of which were successful. The continuing interest in her life and work would undoubtedly have amazed her. Partly because of Middleton Murry's action in publishing her carefully edited letters and journals a legendary figure of K.M. emerged, adding to the already existing interest in her stories. In three months in 1923 there were three printings of *The Doves' Nest*. Middleton Murry produced some ten volumes of stories, letters and notes, many of which, she had never intended to be read by 'the impatient public'; her stories were collected and reprinted again and again and translated widely. By 1940 a single first edition copy of *In a German Pension,* the book she had so despised, was sold for $82.50 in New York. Her sole income from the book had been £15! Her work has been constantly debated, analysed, criticised. For some critics she was a writer's writer, to others a teller of tales. Others saw her work not as stories but as fragments or recollections. A more recent attempt to define the exact nature of her writing is Professor C.K. Stead's analysis of them as 'fictions' as opposed to narratives. At several stages in her life K.M. hoped to write a novel – these attempts included *Juliet, Young Country, The Aloe, Maata, Karori.* Even *The Aloe,* since published as a separate volume, was never truly completed. It seems very possible that her particular creative gift was for the short story alone; that her unique flashes of creativity could not be sustained. Perhaps she was right in saying that she could never write, 'a whole novel about anything'.

Three of her greatest stories, 'Prelude', 'The Daughters of the Late Colonel' and 'At the Bay' are similar to novels in that they are divided into twelve sections or episodes, an unusual device. Each episode has a different focus. They are also longer than the average short story. Many of her New Zealand stories also fall into two cycles: one, the larger, about the Burnell family, the second about the Sheridans. K.M. seems to have felt able to sustain her interest, and the reader's, in these characters. Indeed the stories most critics regard as her finest are from these two groups. Professor Ian Gordon's *Undiscovered Country* fits these together with other stories and journal entries in such a way as to suggest what a novel based on these might have been like. Did K.M. therefore do herself an injustice in saying she would not succeed in writing a novel? If not a novel, perhaps the novella, a piece of prose the length of Ernest Hemingway's *The Old Man and the Sea,* might have been a possible form?

Some of her comments about reviewing do suggest that she regarded contemporary novels 'as simply rubbish on the whole'. For her the short story was apparently the superior genre and the one at which she would have been content to excel.

K.M.'s earliest vignettes published in the *Native Companion,* and her 1908 story 'The Education of Audrey' show the unmistakable influence of Oscar Wilde in their subject matter, exotic mood and ornate style. From this she moved towards a more naturalistic type of story. Many of the early stories published in *In a German Pension* and *Something Childish But Very Natural* are immature, superficial, and technically often weak. She herself commented in February 1920:

I cannot have the German Pension republished under any circumstances.
It's far too *immature . . .* it's not good enough . . . It's positively juvenile
and besides that it's not what I mean: it's a lie.

*When the Kelvies were well
out of sight of Burnells . . .*
Draft of 'The Doll's House',
October 1921

Though they were often bitter, cynical and disillusioned satires,
those early stories foreshadowed her later ones in style, theme and

characterisation. There is wit, perception and some early, if un-even attempts at the interior monologue technique which she later developed so successfully. Often overlooked, they contain the pro-totypes of characters who would later fully develop 'in the round' – Frau Brechenmacher's husband was to evolve into the 'Boss' in 'The Fly' and the Binzer family became the Burnells.

Many of the *German Pension* stories focus on the situation of a young woman, often alone and vulnerable to avaricious, prying strangers. Her ambivalence about her own sexuality and women's traditional child-bearing role was also explored in them. The young bride in 'Frau Brechenmacher Attends a Wedding' had 'the appearance of an iced cake all ready to be cut and served in neat little pieces to the bridegroom.' Little Frau Brechenmacher lay waiting for her drunken chauvinistic husband, 'her arm across her face like a child expecting to be hurt'. Often the central rather ingenuous female figure was frequently forced to face reality when predatory, physically stronger men made unexpected crude advances.

Frequently the characters in these early stories are caricatured through exaggeration and oversimplification, even labelled as such – Herr Rat, the Young Man, the Coral Necklace. Others are more fully and skilfully developed. The skill with realistic dialogue is already evident, the setting and atmosphere are often clearly evoked. The sharp, sometimes cruel observation of human frailties and stupidities revealed through selected telling details is already fun-damental to her stories. The later subtlety is not yet a feature but certain techniques that mark her later writing are already part of her style. These include the compounding of words for effect as in 'a "fancy-not-recognising-that-at-her-first-glance" expression'; the skilful variation of sentence length, including the 'ungrammatical' minor sentence; the quick flash of colour; and the frequent use of simile and metaphor. The central character, often the same woman narrator, is already sometimes revealed through implication and symbolism rather than external description.

These early stories contain the embryonic treatment of the themes she would continue to explore – the essential aloneness and isolation of the human predicament; the conflict between love and disillusionment, between wistful childlike idealism and life's harsh reality, between beauty and ugliness, joy and suffering. For K.M., the juxtaposition of these themes seemed to illustrate life's inevitable paradoxes.

After the destruction of the war she wrote:

Now we know ourselves for what we are. In a way its a tragic knowledge. Its as though, even while we live again we face death. But *through Life:* thats the point. We see death in life as we see death in a flower that is fresh unfolded. Our hymn is to the flower's beauty – we would make that beauty immortal because we *know* . . .

Eventually she was to see beauty in the inevitability of life's paradoxes but in those early stories it only repelled and frightened her.

Two of her first adult stories set in New Zealand, 'The Education of Audrey' written in 1908, and 'Old Tar' have received little critical attention. Each is interesting for different reasons. Not only does 'The Education of Audrey' show the strong influence of Oscar Wilde, its atmosphere redolent with candles and gardenias, it is also the only one of her stories to combine New Zealand and London in setting. Like its predecessor, the unfinished *Juliet,* it is not great writing but rather quaintly contrived and pretentious, particularly in its philosophising about 'Art' and 'Life'. The heroine's capitulation in the last line is also uncharacteristic. Nevertheless it contains some vivid moments and, more importantly, the use of a phrase that was to become almost a talisman – 'Do you remember?' One passage in which Audrey reflects on her inappropriately childlike feelings of happiness is strikingly similar to the opening paragraphs of 'Bliss', written some ten years later. A comparison of the two suggests something of her development over those years.

'Old Tar', printed in the *Westminster Gazette* and the *New Zealand Times* in 1913, also offers some intriguing comparisons. The theme of disillusionment, of reality shattering a dream, was one she would rework more successfully many times. Nevertheless this is a stronger story, the touches of colour are painted with a surer brush: 'There was no wind; just a breeze rippled over the grass and shook the manuka flowers like tiny white stars down the yellow clay banks of the new road.' This surely is the world of 'The Aloe', 'Prelude' and 'The Doll's House'. In her description of Tar, 'a little pale freckled boy with a flop of black hair', K.M. gives us one of her first pictures of a 'real' child. Mrs Tar who:

turned into a fine lady and talked of nothing but the inconvenience she'd suffered living in the shop for the sake of her 'usband's father and his sentimentalness.

is one of many characters who would be epitomised through the humour of their speech. This and the phonetic spelling of Tar's speech were two devices she continued to use in order to create realistic dialogue. What is more significant is the strong presence in this early New Zealand story of the sea, and of the wind 'snuffling' around the big white house as it was to do later in 'The Aloe' and 'Prelude'.

A study of these stories and other early stories such as 'How

Pearl Button was Kidnapped', 'A Birthday', the haunting 'The Woman at the Store', 'Ole Underwood' and 'Millie' show that the New Zealand setting and memories which K.M. was to explore so effectively had already been recognised, valued and drawn upon. Thus her 'New Zealand' short stories were not, as was so often thought, the sudden, direct result of her brother Leslie's death in 1915. She returned to this storehouse of memories yet again, early in 1915. This time the results were to be far more significant.

In February 1915 K.M. met her brother briefly and accidentally in London. In Paris in March she began 'my first novel', now identified as *The Aloe*. She had in fact begun several 'novels' before: the adolescent *Juliet*, and *Maata* in August 1913, for which she had written a draft outline of thirty-two chapters but had finished only two by mid-November that year. A third had been begun in December that year, *Young Country*, set in Wellington, but only two chapters were again completed. Her ambitious calculations for '24 pages per day i.e. 5000 words – for 15 days 75,000 words' were not carried out.

The Aloe would be different. K.M. was still working on it during May 1915. During Leslie's visit to London that summer they revisited the past together. 'The Wind Blows' was written out of those memories and published in October, the month he died.

Ignoring the war and her own chaotic existence and deep unhappiness she turned again, in her grief, to New Zealand and tried to recreate those early days of their shared childhood:

I want to write about my own country until I simply exhaust my store – not only because it is 'a sacred debt' that I pay to my country because my brother & I were born there – but also because in my thoughts I range with him over all the remembered places. I am never far away from them. I long to renew them in writing.

Ah the people, the people we loved there – of them too I want to write – another 'debt of love'. Oh, I want for one moment to make our undiscovered country leap into the eyes of the old world. It must be mysterious, as though floating – it must take the breath. It must be 'one of those islands' . . . I shall tell everything – even of how the laundry basket squeaked at '75' – but all must be told with a sense of mystery – a radiance – an after glow because you my little sun of it, are set. You have dropped over the dazzling brim of the world. Now I must play my part . . .

It was not easy however to fulfil that sacred debt, to give shape to those memories until, on rediscovering *The Aloe* among her papers, she knew it was right and began work on it again.

In *The Aloe* and in later stories such as 'At The Bay' and 'The Doll's House' she showed her particular skill in creating the world of children, a world of light and shade, overshadowed by the prob-

Of daisies I will write. Of the dark. Of the wind & the sun & the mists . . . of all that you loved & that I too love and feel.
Notebook, 14 February 1916

Leslie Beauchamp

lems of the adult world. She captured the very sound of their voices, their moments of loneliness, fear and happiness. She was one of the first short story writers to evoke this childhood world so clearly, and to regard it as important enough to write about. We share their games of make believe, fantasies, important projects and adventures, their delights and guilt. Few knew better than K.M. the reality and value of the past within us:

I think the only way to live as a writer is to draw upon one's real, familiar life – to find the treasure . . . And the curious thing is that if we describe this which seems to us so intensely personal, other people take it to themselves and understand it as if it were their own.

There have been few writers whose life and work seem so inseparable, but there seems little point in debating whether it was her experiences in New Zealand or in England which had the greater influence on her work – she could not have written as she did without the particular combination of both those very different worlds, her own peculiar form of 'geographical schizophrenia'. Rebelling in her youth against the narrow, conventional bourgeois life of colonial New Zealand she had fled to London, Europe and 'Life'. Her experiences there provided her with the basis for many of her stories, including the German ones preferred by Leonard Woolf. Satirical, increasingly sophisticated, they had a quality of toughness in their clear-sighted depiction of society and its values. Increasingly disillusioned by that world, by her contemporaries and by the frequently unsatisfactory nature of her relationship with Murry; by her illness and increasing isolation; by the growing awareness that she had no certain future, she turned back increasingly to the past. Eventually she used those last pictures of childhood in what she acknowledged to be a 'dream' New Zealand, to reconcile the discordant elements in her European stories and many earlier New Zealand ones; and to attempt to resolve the conflicts in herself and in the world as she had known it. D. H. Lawrence remarked of his *Sons and Lovers* that, 'one sheds one's sicknesses in books'. For K.M., too, writing was a kind of therapy.

In her best stories K.M. created something beyond the limitations of time and place. They were the spontaneous but carefully crafted product of her experience of life:

Even if one does not acquire any fresh meat – one's vision of what one possesses is constantly changing into something rich and strange, isn't it? I feel mine is. 47 Fitzherbert Terrace, p.e., is colouring beautifully with the years and I polish it and examine it and only now is it ready to come out of the store room and into the uncommon light of day.

Frequently K.M. recognised the strong autobiographical element in her work even when she had not consciously intended it. She described it later to Murry, 'Funny thing is I think you'll always come walking into my stories . . . "The man she was in love with".' And, she warned him, 'You will recognise some of the people.' All too often, particularly in New Zealand, people were recognised and quite naturally did not always welcome that recognition. Even the names of many of her characters show the link between fact and fiction, as in Fairfield, the anglicised version of Beauchamp. To her father she wrote in 1922:

I meant to draw your attention, if I may, to one little sketch, 'The Voyage', which I wrote with dear little Grandma Beauchamp in mind. It is not in any way a likeness of her, but there are, it seems to me, traces of a resemblance.

To L.M., whose full name was Ida Constance Baker, she wrote from Cornwall about her story 'Carnation', 'I've even put you in as Connie Baker!' Later 'The Lady's Maid' was perhaps a kind of

Grandma made a small astonished face. Then she whispered primly to Fenella, 'What wickedness' And they sailed out . . .
'The Voyage'

Mrs Mary Elizabeth-Beauchamp (née Stanley)

recognition of L.M.'s selflessness. Certainly she was the model for the sympathetic, gently humorous portrayal of Constantia in 'The Daughters of the Late Colonel'. At times too K.M. felt she had actually brought 'the dead to life again'.

Interestingly, the first page of the manuscript of 'The Doll's House' begins, 'When dear old Mrs Hay went back to Wellington . . .' K.M. then crossed the name out, replacing it with the more anonymous town. Similarly, the early story 'A Birthday' is clearly set in Tinakori Road, despite the family's German names. At other times K.M. could not herself trace the origin of a particular story. It just evolved. After all,

When does one *really begin* a journey – or a friendship – or a love affair? It is those beginnings which are so fascinating and so misunderstood. There comes a moment when we realise we are already well on our way – déjà.

Certainly it is difficult to disentangle fact from fiction. K.M. deliberately chose at times to write about her own experiences, her own emotions and fantasies, but often she seems not to have fully understood them herself. They reveal far more of her, her attitudes and her complex personality than she intended. This adds to their fascination – and their relevance. In her intriguing, detailed study of the 'psychological basis' of K.M.'s stories, C. A. Hankin remarks: 'Regardless of what she might say in her letters, however, Katherine Mansfield's truest expression of what she felt for the people close to her appears in her stories.'

One fascinating example of the way in which K.M. used her own experiences deliberately as the basis for a story seems to have been overlooked. Readers and critics have all agreed that the story 'An Indiscreet Journey', is based on K.M.'s own journey to visit Carco in Gray in 1915, the four-day escapade Murry dismissed as a 'fiasco'. In the story the narrator has a letter written to 'My dear niece' asking her to visit her aunt in 'X'. Written by her soldier lover it was, in fact, a ruse intended to convince the Commissaire Militaire that her journey through wartime France was legitimate.

Among Murry's letters to K.M. is one small sheet in another handwriting. Dated 26 March 1915, this letter in French from Aix-les-Gray to 'Ma Chère amie' is signed 'Marguerite Bombard'. It thanks K.M. for her last letter from Paris, speaks of their meeting there again after the war as they had promised, but suggests that in the meantime she should visit Gray as 'Maman' has put a room at her disposal. The letter continues very affectionately then instructs K.M. to obtain a pass. Marguerite Bombard's letter was, like the lover's in the story, an 'unfamiliar letter in the familiar handwriting'. It is, in fact, the only known letter still in existence from Carco to K.M. K.M. had returned to Paris to stay in Carco's flat on 18 March. It would appear she had written to him and he felt sufficiently confident to reply in this way, suggesting another visit. Perhaps they had parted on better terms than Murry had imagined? Her reply, if there was one, is unknown. She returned to England on 31 March, revisiting Paris for twelve days in May. Like the original escapade, the idea of transforming Marguerite Bombard (alias Carco) into Julie Boiffard, Aix les Gray into 'X' and the inclusion of the letter in the story was the kind of game that K.M. would have enjoyed.

Her own experiences provided her with the raw material, but she did not seek merely to give a photographic reproduction. Perhaps too much emphasis has been placed on analysing precise autobiographical details; on discussing whether portraits of certain people were either fair or accurate or whether a certain place was really as she described. Like an impressionist painter she worked to convey the light and shade, the overall impression or mood; details were altered, outlines blurred and places, people or occasions merged into a composite picture. Art always transcended reality and real events or people were shaped and manipulated to fit the the impression she wished to create.

K.M. was a dedicated artist with 'a passion for technique', determined to find clarity, to 'write simply, fully, freely . . .' Truth, above all, came to be the aim of her writing:

You see for me – life and work are two things indivisible. It's only by being true to life that I can be true to art. And to be true to life is to be *good, sincere, simple, honest.*

She hoped in this way to enable others to see clearly. She felt eventually that neither her life nor her earlier work had been 'true'.

Throughout her life K.M. was constantly evaluating her style ('horrible expression!') and her craft, looking for greater discipline and clarity, altering and perfecting her method of narration, working to find that 'special prose' that was neither poetry nor prose. A comparison of *The Aloe* and the final version *Prelude* shows how stringent she was in her criticism of her own work.

Vincent O'Sullivan's elegant edition of *The Aloe* with its parallel printing of *Prelude* on the facing pages assists such a comparison and gives an accessible insight into K.M.'s creative process. She reworked the original story to tighten it in both structure and style in order to gain the particular effects she desired and, as a result, there is greater precision and coherence. A succession of adjectives is replaced by one precise word; extraneous details stripped away; interesting but superfluous characters, incidents and narrative passages are eliminated. Other incidents or details are added, particularly those which reveal more of the central characters.

A comparison of 'The Common Round' and 'Pictures' shows the same ruthless discipline. Some manuscripts show considerable alteration, revision affecting single words or whole passages. Others seem to have flowed spontaneously, requiring little change despite occasional marginal notes such as 'too much description!' Even 'The Daughters of the Late Colonel', written as it was at such a furious pace, was not greatly altered on a later reading, although the title was changed from 'Non-Compounders' – a reference to school days at Queen's College.

There is careful craftsmanship in her varied style, at times curt, terse, brittle, at others flowing, almost poetry, depending on the mood or situation she was describing. Her sentence construction reflected this care. She was well aware of the effect of a minor or simple sentence, in contrast to longer complex ones. To achieve the specific overall effect she desired she worked consciously at her technique. Even her use of dashes and dots was deliberate – it was not simply a matter of 'a feminine dash'. Of 'Miss Brill', her 'Insect Magnificat' she wrote:

I choose not only the length of every sentence, but even the sound of every sentence. I choose the rise and fall of every paragraph to fit her, and to fit

were my gratitude to equal my admiration

To Doctor Sorapure   May admiration would abide ant dep my gratitude.

Non-Compounders.

1.

The week after was one of the busiest weeks of their lives. Even when they went to bed it was only their bodies that lay down and rested; their minds went on, thinking things out, talking things over, wondering, deciding, trying to remember where —

Constanzia lay like a statue, her hands by her sides, her feet just overlapping each other, the sheet ~~up to~~ her chin. She stared at the ceiling.

"Do you think Father would mind if we gave his top-hat to the Porter?"

"The porter?" snapped Josephine. "Why ever the porter? What a very extraordinary idea."

"Because," said Constanzia, slowly, "he must often have to go to funerals. And I noticed at — at — the cemetery he only had a bowler." She paused. "I thought then how very much he'd appreciate a top-hat. We ought to give him a present, too. He was always very nice to Father."

"But," cried Josephine, flouncing round on her pillow and staring across the dark at Constanzia — "Father's head —!" And suddenly, for one awful moment, she nearly giggled. Not, of course, that she felt in the least like giggling. It must have been habit. Years ago, when they had stayed awake at night talking, their beds had simply heaved. And now — the porter's head, disappearing, popped out, like a candle, under Father's hat. The giggle mounted ~~mounted~~ ~~rising~~; she clenched her hands; she fought it down; she frowned fiercely at the dark and said "Remember" — terribly sternly.

"We can decide to-morrow," she said.

Constanzia had noticed nothing; she sighed.

"Do you think we ought to have our dressing-gowns dyed as well?"

"Black!" almost shrieked Josephine.

"Well, what else!" said Constanzia. "I was thinking — it doesn't

her on that day at that very moment. After I'd written it I read it aloud
. . . until it fitted her . . . If a thing has really come off it seems to me there
mustn't be one single word out of place, or one word that could be taken
out. That's how I AIM at writing. It will take some time to get anywhere
near there.

K.M. developed the ability to enter the very minds and souls of
her characters. The process of writing was 'a kind of *possession*'.
Describing her story 'The Voyage' she wrote:

I might have remained the grandma for ever after if the wind had changed
that moment. And that would have been a little bit embarrassing for
Middleton Murry.

As a result of this remarkable empathy, some of her finest characters are revealed through their own thoughts, memories and
feelings and not by external analysis or dissection so that the
reader too is able to identify with them as they meet her own
requirement that:

New people have appeared in that other world of ours, which sometimes
seems so much more real and satisfying than this one. That they have a
life and a being of their own we do not question; even that they 'go on'
long after the book is finished.

The reader slips without noticing from one character's mind to
another; there is no break or narrative comment necessary. We do
not need to be told at the beginning of 'The Doll's House' that
'perhaps the smell of paint would have gone off' is said in dis-
approving tones by an adult. We simply know.

   One word can reveal the point of view through which an incident
or character is seen, and simultaneously more about the character
whose vision we share. Through K.M.'s skill with dialogue the
characters become living, speaking people. The choice of words,
the catching of subtleties of contrasting pronunciation, intonation
and inflection convey so much. The children usually speak in short
sentences, simply, in 'children's language'. The adolescents and
adults speak quite differently depending on their mood. From this
we infer a great deal about the speakers. A skilled actress and
impersonator, she had a remarkable facility with dialogue, especially children's, which allows her stories to be successfully dra-
matised, not only for television and radio but in the classroom
and on stage. Her own dramatic pieces show how she herself
experimented in the area of drama. A sense of rhythm and timing,
an awareness of the nuances of speech characterise much of the
dialogue, in these and other stories. These dramatic experiments
also showed her how a story could progress without a narrator.

Opposite:
*That gentle caricature of her
cousin Sylvia Payne and me.*
L.M.

Manuscript page of 'The
Daughters of the Late Colonel'
with its original title, December
1920

She was to continue to work towards this elimination of the narrator in her writing, so having a profound influence on short story writing.

Moments of lethargy at times led to an almost physical inability to put pen to paper and consequent deep depression:

I do still lack application . . . There's so much to do and I do so little. Life would be almost perfect here if only when I was *pretending* to work I always was working . . . Look at all the stories that wait and wait just at the threshold. Why don't I let them in? . . . *Next day* Yet take this morning for instance. I dont want to write anything. Its grey, its heavy and dull and these stories seem unreal & not worth doing. I don't want to write; I want to *Live*.

Nevertheless she was determined always to become 'a better writer'. Writing to Murry, she condemned Virginia Woolf for ignoring the war in her novel *Night and Day* which seemed to her 'a lie in the soul . . . I feel in the *profoundest* sense that nothing can ever be the same – that as artists we are traitors if we feel otherwise; we have to take it into account and find new expressions new moulds for our new thoughts & feelings.' In her published review of the book she was more tactful, but Virginia Woolf was not deceived. K.M. felt the need to develop her own techniques, 'how are we going to convey these over tones, half tones, quarter tones, these hesitations, doubts, beginnings, if we go at them *directly?* . . . I do believe that there is a way . . . Its the truth we are after, no less (which, by the way, makes it so exciting)'.

Characteristically, she often felt she had failed. In the middle of the manuscript of 'Her First Ball' she wrote:

All that I write – all that I am – is on the border of the sea. It's a kind of playing. I want to put *all* my force behind it, but somehow, I *cannot!*

It was always the next story which would contain everything. In her search for 'the new word' she rejected the style and content of her early stories as well as many of the conventions of short story writing. Even at Fontainebleau, when her work was widely recognised, her idea of the short story was changing. Tired of her 'little stories like birds bred in cages', she hoped some new kind of writing would be the natural result of the spiritual rebirth she envisaged. She had always realised that carefully selected details were incredibly important, 'one can get only so *much* into a story; there is always a sacrifice.'

Inevitably it was her own attitudes which determined that selection. There was 'an infinite delight & value in detail' but it was not for detail's sake alone. Through the careful selection of detail she could *suggest*, and that should be enough. She could not tell anybody 'bang out' about the 'deserts of vast eternity' . . . They are my secret. I might write about a boy eating strawberries or a woman combing her hair on a windy morning & that is the only way I can ever mention them. But they *must* be there. Nothing less will do.

Therefore, instead of telling 'directly' she frequently worked obliquely through implication, suggestion and symbolism. The little lamp in 'The Doll's House' must surely be one of the most readily understood symbols in prose. A reader may know nothing of terms such as 'symbolism' but the little lamp will inevitably take on a deeper significance. Ordinary inanimate objects seem almost to take on a life of their own.

One of the most important techniques K.M. used in order to 'convey those over tones, half tones' was the use of contrast. At times the carefully developed contrasts provide the framework or structure for the story's events and also suggests the themes.

Frequently too the use of colour, light and shade are important in creating the atmosphere vital to the stories. In 'At the Bay', the morning sun streamed through the open window 'on to the yellow varnished walls and bare floor. Everything on the table flashed and glittered. In the middle there was an old salad bowl filled with yellow and red nasturtiums.' The beginning of 'The Woman at the Store', however, is very different: 'The white pumice dust swirled in our faces, settled and sifted over us . . . the sky was slate colour . . . There was nothing to be seen but wave after wave of tussock grass.' Another contrast is the setting of 'The Wind Blows' which is mainly an uncharacteristic monochrome.

Another of the characteristics of K.M.'s writing to which critics have paid much attention is her use of imagery. She seems to have been a writer who thought naturally in metaphor. Particularly apt images remain in the reader's mind. Our Else is 'a tiny wishbone of a child . . . a little white owl.' She and her sister are chased away from the doll's house 'like two little stray cats'. Sleek, insinuating, Mrs Harry Kember in 'At the Bay' swims away 'like a rat'. In 'The Woman at the Store' the narrator remarks:

there is no twilight in our New Zealand days, but a curious half-hour when everything appears grotesque – it frightens – as though the savage spirit of the country walked abroad and sneered at what it saw.

When writing about children the imagery is peculiar to their world and strikingly apt, so the doll's house, for example, is 'spinach green', its door like 'a little slab of toffee'. Frequently she used animal imagery and symbolism as a device for hinting at hidden layers of meaning. A striking example of this occurs in 'Bliss' when Bertha Young stands looking at the tall pear tree 'perfect . . . against the jade-green sky'. Below 'a grey cat, dragging its belly, crept across the lawn, and a black one, its shadow, trailed after. The sight of them, so intent and so quick, gave Bertha a curious shiver.'

The use of symbolism linking the concrete and the abstract, one of the most remarkable features of her work, was at times contrived, as she herself felt in 'Mr and Mrs Dove'. In other stories a single action or detail skilfully conveys an emotion, image and mood, the external and the internal become one. Certain images recur from her earliest sketches at Queen's College. Others like the wind, flowers and insects and particularly the metaphor of the fly occur constantly, both in her notes and letters as well as in her stories. Like the sun, sea and darkness, mist and trees, they were all an integral part of her vision of life and the fabric of her stories.

Impatient with those who specialised in 'cheap psycho-analysis' she herself was a perceptive writer of unusual psycholog-ical insight, so it is not surprising that much has been written about her symbolism and her imagery. One of the finest discus-sions of this aspect of her work is in Sylvia Berkman's critical study. Others have chosen to analyse specific images or symbols – the 'secret smile', sexual imagery, the father image, the dog image and even 'the ear as a symbol in Katherine Mansfield's work'! A more recent examination can be found in *The Life of Katherine Mansfield* by Antony Alpers and his new edition of the stories, and in C. A. Hankin's *Katherine Mansfield and Her Confessional Stories.*

Generally her symbols and images are skilfully woven into the vivid texture of the story; at other times one is selected as the centre of the total pattern, such as the lamp in 'The Doll's House', the pear tree in 'Bliss'. The use of natural elements in particular provides a central symbolism, a recurrent underlying motif linking many of her stories. These then were some of the methods that typified K.M.'s writing, enabling her to convey evanescent moods, to capture the essence of a fleeting moment. But what of the total pattern, the form of her stories?

Describing the form of *Prelude* to Dorothy Brett she remarked, 'It's more or less my own invention', and that form was to be gradually perfected and refined. Other important features of that form were the stream of consciousness technique, her use of flashbacks and her skill in conveying the multipersonal view-point. These are clearly illustrated in 'The Daughters of the Late Colonel' – 'a huge long story of a rather new kind. It's the outcome of the *Prelude* method – it just unfolds and opens . . . It's a queer tale though.' Past and present become fused as the story evolves through the characters' minds. The external narrator is almost eliminated. As so often in her work, the reader is dropped into the story and simply confronted by a particular situation. There is no preliminary establishing and identification of time and place. The reader is immediately involved; it is assumed that he or she has any necessary prerequisite knowledge and is, in a sense, part of the story too.

Some stories make use of interior monologue throughout, others combine some interior monologue or stream of consciousness with more conventional techniques. It is the multi-personal viewpoint, in particular, which has marked her writing. Often, although the story is told through a variety of viewpoints, the focus is most frequently on the central protagonist so that we share that character's experience in particular. At other times, characters or events are viewed through the eyes of different characters, being described in the language and syntax peculiar to that character. As a result of the multi-personal viewpoint we often see the characters from several angles, providing us with a constantly changing perspective.

Today K.M.'s 'episodic' or 'slice of life' technique is perhaps taken for granted but her stories were really the first of significance in English to be written without the conventional plot. The expected sequence of events: exposition, rising action, climax and conclusion have often been replaced by concentration on a moment or episode or loosely linked series of moments. The interest lies not so much in what *happens* but in *why* it happens.

The famous American short story writer, Edgar Allen Poe, had laid down clearly the principles of short story writing. English writers such as Kipling and H. G. Wells had continued to write stories with a carefully structured plot. Other writers, little known today had, however, been experimenting in a magazine, the *Yellow Book*, famous in the 1890s. There does not, however, appear any clear reference in her letters and journals to the *Yellow Book*, and she herself believed that what she was attempting was innovatory.

Sylvia Berkman, who like Marvin Magalaner and T. O. Beachcroft sees many similarities in her work to that of James Joyce, describes her stories as 'the swift, illuminated glimpse into a character or situation at a given moment.' By showing us a character at a particular moment so much more is disclosed. At times, it is as if by giving the reader that glimpse of a specific character at a specific moment, as if through an open doorway, she shows them making a gesture or speaking in a way that is typical of that character. That moment allows the reader's imagination to do the rest.

The conventions of time and tense become irrelevant. This flexible manipulation of time was something K.M. was still consciously trying to perfect in the last years of her life. 'What I feel it needs so peculiarly is a very subtle variation of "tense" from the present to the past & back again – and softness, lightness . . .'

There is no step-by-step development of plot but this does not mean, as one critic has suggested, that we are not moved by her stories because 'nothing happens' to her characters, or that they are merely 'incidents' not short stories. For her people, as for the rest of us, there are the moments of 'the soul's desperate choice'; the moment of crisis, external or internal, the discovery of 'the big snail under the leaf – the spot in the child's lung'. Her stories may appear formless but there is, in fact, a careful pattern of parts. They were tightly constructed, around that moment of crisis or turning point which in a way determined the pattern of the story. She explained this apparent lack of ordered events:

The diversity of life and how we try to fit in everything. Death included. That is bewildering . . . things ought to happen differently. First one and then another. But life isn't like that. We haven't the ordering of it . . .

Not surprisingly, she once showed great indignation about:

a stupid man . . . bringing out an anthology of short stories and he said the more 'plotty' a story I could give him the better. What about that for a word! It made my hair stand up in prongs. A nice 'plotty' story, please. People *are* funny.

This view did not lessen her admiration for Jane Austen's skill with plot. 'She makes modern episodic people like me, as far as I go, look very incompetent ninnies.' She and Jane Austen were, however, alike in their rather deliberately limited range of subject matter and their ironic pictures of sophisticated society's pretensions and conventions, for K.M. had gradually abandoned her early malicious, sometimes clumsily obvious satire for a more subtle and delicate irony.

Occasionally, too, like earlier writers such as Jane Austen, she addressed the reader in an intimate tone, inviting participation in the story and collusion with the narrator. K.M.'s last story, 'The Canary' – a monologue – involves the reader in such a way, 'there does seem to me something sad in life . . . I don't mean the sorrow that we all know . . .'

Often that sadness was juxtaposed with humour, an aspect that has been too often overlooked. She was a writer with an acute wit, a gift for mimicry and a true sense of the ridiculous. At times the humour was obvious and satirical, as in the German stories, with the caricature of the Norman Knights in 'Bliss'; at others it is more subtle, a delicate irony. 'The Daughters of the Late Colonel' illustrates a gentle compassionate humour in the portrayal of two spinster sisters who had dared to bury their bullying father 'without asking his permission'. 'At the Bay' is not only a superb evocation of mood and feeling, it is also a story with considerable humour.

The humour in her work was often gained from a single word, sometimes deliberately misspelled, mimicking the speaker's voice, even when it is a silent voice heard only in the character's mind. It is derived from exaggeration and caricature, from a careful contrasting of characters, the placing of a character in a particular situation; from the use of cleverly selected details, unconscious self revelation, word association.

H. E. Bates, while recognising a vivid clarity and a strangely personal quality, found her writing frequently immature and monotonous; the stories told in 'a kind of mental soliloquy, fluttering, gossipy, breathless' by her characters, 'all chattering overgrown schoolgirls busy asking and answering breathless facile questions about love and life and happiness.' This surely is a very narrow view which ignores many of her characters. Certainly some are weakly drawn types – particularly in the early stories – but others are truly alive, not drawn on a grand scale, but real people in a real world.

It is true that the majority of the characters in K.M.'s stories are female. She was frequently concerned with the particular relationships in which women were involved – with their children, with each other and with men. The role of women in society is central to much of her work, and most obviously so in the German stories.

It is therefore, as H. E. Bates and others have suggested, at times a 'female' world we are shown. In 'The Luftbad', which is set in a women's sunbathing enclosure in Wörishofen where the women are 'in their nakeds' there are, not surprisingly, no men. The point of view from which we view incidents, characters and relationships is frequently female and it is more often the female characters who win our sympathy. Some, like Beryl in 'At the Bay', are disillusioned by unexpected and coarse male advances. In others, the male characters' potential for seduction or physical violence is only hinted at.

Often too the worlds of male and female seem quite separate, only tenuously linked. The men seem quite alien at times to that world in which women are comfortable. One of K.M.'s most unattractive characters, Harry Young in 'Bliss', epitomises this. He 'loved doing things at high pressure', was an ambitious greedy poseur who dismissed his baby daughter with the words, 'My dear

Mrs Knight, don't ask me about my baby. I never see her. I shan't feel the slightest interest in her until she has a lover'. In 'At the Bay' Stanley leaves home feeling 'The heartlessness of women! The way they took it for granted it was your job to slave away for them while they didn't even take the trouble to see that your walking stick wasn't lost.' Meanwhile, without the irritant of his presence, even the women's voices changed, 'they sounded warm and loving as if they shared a secret.'

In the same story, however, Jonathan Trout is shown as an atypical male. He is more articulate than Stanley, willing to talk about 'cranky' ideas and dreams; happier talking in the garden than sitting in his 'jail' of an office. Through him K.M. gives a picture of what men might be if only they were allowed to be, and had the courage to break free from the role society has traditionally allotted them. Linda, who finds Jonathan attractive, is aware that even beneath Stanley's everyday exterior there is a more sensitive man.

The traditional role of women in society is also closely examined. Linda spends her time calming Stanley down, 'and what was left of her time was spent in the dread of having children'. The woman 'at the store' was once a barmaid 'pretty as a waxdoll' who 'knew one hundred and twenty-five different ways of kissing'. After six years of marriage and four miscarriages she has become a pathetic figure. 'Her front teeth were knocked out, she had red pulpy hands', she is driven to murder by loneliness and despair. Elsewhere, as in 'Pictures' and 'Miss Brill', K.M. explores the dilemma of older women, lonely, without family or support.

At times the male and female characters do achieve a kind of closeness and understanding, though it is rarely sexual but more akin to the kind of sympathetic bonding that often links the women in her stories. More often though the men are shown to be too inarticulate, uncommunicative and emotionally unevolved for this intimacy to take place. The boss in 'The Fly' who 'had arranged to weep' but 'no tears came' is perhaps the most frightening example of such men, and at the same time a plea for them to change. Clearly then her characters are not 'all chattering overgrown schoolgirls' as H. E. Bates would have us believe.

Even as the early influence of Oscar Wilde was waning she had realised the need to see:

a wider vision – a little Oscar, a little Symons . . . Ibsen, Tolstoi, Elizabeth Robins, Shaw . . . To weave the intricate tapestry of one's own life it is well to take a thread from many harmonious skeins – and to realise that there must be harmony. Not necessary to grow the sheep, comb the wool, colour and brand it – but joyfully take all that is ready, and with that saved time, go a great way further.

Among her favourite writers were D. H. Lawrence – when not obsessed by things physical; Shakespeare – in spite of *The Merchant of Venice*, a 'silly' play; and Dickens. In 1921 she turned to Proust '. . . at last. I have been pretending to read Proust for years . . . He is fascinating!' Tolstoy's *War and Peace* she considered 'great art . . . the real thing.' George Bernard Shaw on the other hand she dismissed as 'uninspired' and Ezra Pound was condemned for '*Chinese tub thumping!*'

Much has been written about the influence of Chekhov on K.M. His popularity reached its peak in England during the time her work was published. Contemporaries saw similarities in their work which made their short stories quite different from the genre as it had existed in England until that time in the hands of writers such as Kipling. The debate as to the degree of K.M.'s debt has continued since then. Was she in the words of one critic 'Plagiarist, Disciple or Ardent Admirer?' Was it that Chekhov's influence acted mainly to reinforce her existing feelings about the short story? Murry with considerable bias insisted that her method was wholly her own and her development would have been precisely the same if Chekhov had never existed. Charyanne Kurylo, using K.M.'s own heavily annotated 'small green Tchehovs', has traced Chekhov's influence on K.M.'s plots, themes and technique, citing almost parallel phrases and passages. These date from 'The-Child-Who-Was-Tired', one of her early stories, without doubt an adaptation of Chekhov's 'Sleepyhead', to the final stories. In this last period Ms Kurylo felt that K.M., pressured by commitments to publishers and lacking the vital inspiration of new experiences, borrowed heavily from Chekhov. She considers the idea for K.M.'s last great story, 'The Fly', which was completed in February, to have come from 'Small Fry' by Chekhov. Certainly there are similarities and K.M. had read the story. Her notebooks and letters show, however, that the image of the fly and its courageous, futile struggles had haunted K.M. for years and would inevitably have found artistic expression. Perhaps at times she took one aspect of a Chekhov story and then developed it in her own unique way – in this case Chekhov's clerk who tortures a cockroach. The conclusion of Kurylo's study is that 'While the sheer quantity of borrowing remains a disturbing problem, there is no question that Katherine Mansfield intended, and did finally make the "gift" she received from Chekhov her own.'

For those who know only a little of Chekhov, Conrad Aiken's review of *Bliss and Other Stories* probably sums up the situation, 'One has not read a page . . . before one has said "Chekhov": but one has not read two pages before Chekhov is forgotten.'

What after all is literary influence? Perhaps K.M.'s own comment to a young writer could apply equally to her own work:

'. . . your great admiration for Tchekhov has liberated you but you have
absorbed more of him than you are aware of and he's got in the way of
your individual expression . . .'

She herself, in her earliest days of writing, had expressed a
horror of plagiarism but nevertheless recognised:

we all, as writers, to a certain extent, absorb each other when we love . . .
Anatole France would say we eat each other, but perhaps nourish is the
better word.

Chekhov was, she admitted, her 'master'. From him she learned
a great deal, particularly her method of oblique narration. Like
him she realised that the plot of the story was of secondary importance to character and mood. As a result both did much to
narrow the range of the short story while at the same time deep-
ening the vision and sharpening the focus. Chekhov's range was
much greater as the sheer number of his stories alone indicates,
but like him she sought to write not of the superficial, external
things of life but of the hidden world – 'The form I would choose
has changed utterly. I feel no longer concerned with the same
appearance of things.' There are no great events, just ordinary
happenings in the lives of ordinary people. She herself frequently
acknowledged his influence on her and her work. In one little
doggerel verse on the fly leaf of the third volume of *The Tales of
Tchehov* she wrote:

By all the laws of M and P
This book is bound to belong to me
Besides I am sure that you agree
I am the English Anton T.

Later beside the same lines she noted 'God forgive me Tchehov,
for my impertinence (14 XII 1920)'
  She admired him intensely as man and writer. She felt too a
kind of kinship with him which increased as her illness advanced.
Until his death at forty-three, Chekhov had also spent much time
'chasing about in a desperate search after health'.
  Although K.M. did not speak, read or write Russian she made
a considerable contribution to the understanding of Chekhov's
work in Britain. Collaborating with Koteliansky in his translation,
she reworked his rather odd English so that it gained style, fluency
and coherence.

Comparisons have also been frequently made between the work
of K.M. and Virginia Woolf, despite Virginia Woolf's opinion of

'Bliss' and K.M's condemnation of Virginia Woolf's 'intellectual snobbery'. On the one hand there are those who find, 'Where Virginia Woolf is precious, Katherine Mansfield is priggish'. On the other there are those who might agree that 'if Virginia Woolf had written 'At the Bay' it might well have become the length of 'To the Lighthouse' '.

An interesting comparison can, however, be made between Virginia Woolf's *The Waves* and K.M.'s 'At the Bay'. What is important is not the specific example of phrase or image, but the attempt by both to reveal character through interior monologue or stream of consciousness. In their use of symbolism to link the concrete and the abstract; in their skill in exploring several levels of meaning simultaneously, moving backwards and forwards in time in their attempt to subordinate the narrative passages; and in their use of suggestion and telling detail both writers had a profound effect on English writing. They were, K.M. wrote to Virginia in 1917, 'after so very nearly the same thing', though several of her comments to Murry indicate that she did not always think so.

In her essay 'Modern Fiction', written in the spring of 1919 and admired by K.M., Virginia Woolf remarked, 'examine for a moment an ordinary mind on an ordinary day. The mind receives myriad impressions . . . Life is not a series of gig lamps symmetrically arranged . . .' K.M. too knew that 'life isn't like that'.

Many of K.M.'s opinions of contemporary writers were, of course, contained in her numerous book reviews. They have been condemned as 'negligible' by at least one critic, and she herself wearied of writing them, but like the comments in her letters and notes they indicated much about her, and the exacting standards she set for herself and others.

Even her reviews did not escape her own criticism. One scrapbook of cuttings of her reviews carried annotations – some terse; others rueful, wryly humorous. Beneath her review of 'Three Women Novelists' is the note, 'Not good enough. Uneven, shallow, forced . . . muslin handkerchief vocabulary! K.M.' Others she rejected as too facile or pompous, but occasionally they deserved faint approbation: 'Not bad. Touch of my gran'pa in it'.

For K.M. writing was an art. She scathingly rejected those who wrote for a pastime, without passion. She could admire a writer like Dostoevsky for setting up a 'mysterious relationship with the reader, this sense of *sharing*. We are never conscious that he is writing at us or for us . . .' In particular she brought her acerbic wit and withering scorn to bear on those who seemed in any way false. She believed that in writing, as in life – ideally at any rate – all should be 'dead true'. 'Why can't writers be warm, living,

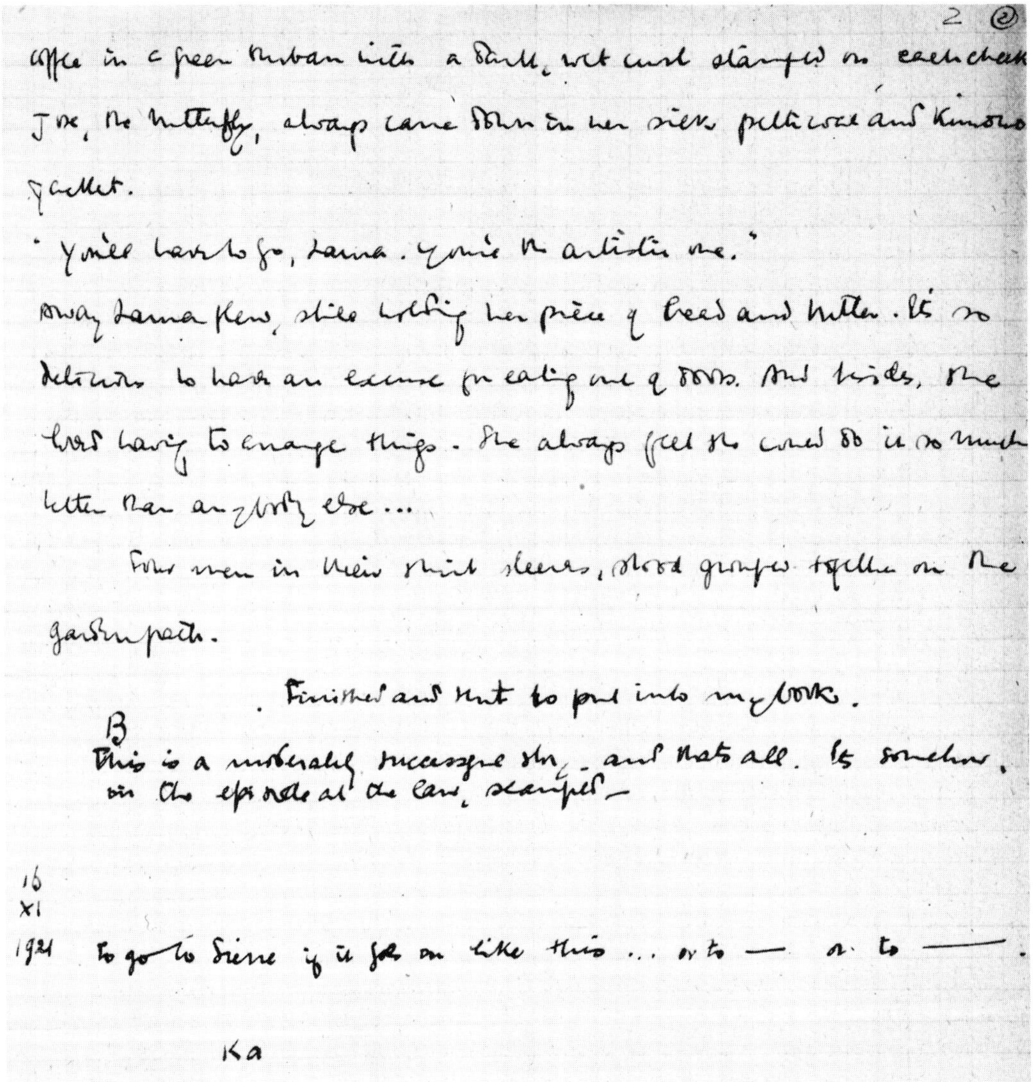

2

office in a green turban with a dark, wet curl stamped on each cheek.
Jose, the butterfly, always came down in her silk petticoat and kimono jacket.

'You'll have to go, Laura. You're the artistic one.'

Away Laura flew, still holding her piece of bread and butter. It's so delicious to have an excuse for eating out of doors. And besides, she loved having to arrange things. She always felt she could do it so much better than anybody else...

Four men in their shirt sleeves, stood grouped together on the garden path.

Finished and sent to put into my book.

B

This is a moderately successful story — and that's all. It's somehow, in the episode at the Lane, scamped —

16
XI
1921 To go to Sierre if it goes on like this ... or to — or to —.

Ka

This is a moderately successful story.
Draft of 'The Garden Party', November 1921

simple, merry or sad as it pleases them? All this falsity is so *boring*.' Discipline too was necessary. In one review she described the writer's 'passion for display. And this passion is so ungoverned that we cannot see the stars for fireworks.'

There was, she felt, a pervading tone of melancholy in contemporary novels, a lack of originality and freshness:

All roads lead to Calvary is another novel. It is not more; it is one of that enormous pile of novels . . . 'Are they fresh?' 'Yes, baked today, Madame'. But they are just the same as those that were baked yesterday and the day before – and the day before that. So much flour, a sprinkle of currants, a smear of sugar on the top.

At other times she wasted no words, her criticism was trenchant and forceful and annihilation politely complete. Taken publicly to task for her review of Compton MacKenzie's *The Vanity Girl* which she had described as a 'potboiler' and a betrayal of his art, she replied, haughtily unrepentant, '. . . we do not withdraw the word betrayal.'

In her journal she explained:

. . . It is not the business of the artist to grind an axe, to try and impose his vision of Life upon the existing world. *Art* is not an attempt to reconcile existence with his vision: it is an attempt to create his own world *in* this world. That which suggests the subject to the artist is the *unlikeness* to that we accept as reality. We single out – we bring into the light – we put up higher.

To avoid arrogance or inflexibility, in her opinion, art must also have tenderness – 'a dangerous word' – but a quality K.M. attempted to define:

Hang it all, Brett – a picture must have *charm* – or why look at it? It's the quality I call *tenderness* in writing, it's the tone one gets in a really first-chop musician.'

Too many modern writers also lacked 'continuity – they introduce their cooks, aunts, strange gentlemen, and so on, and once the pen is off them they are *gone* – dropped down a hole.'

She was particularly heated in her comments to Murry about some contemporary women writers. One published by Duckworth she denounces as:

a book for a rubber shop (mes excuses!) its a book about what she calls 'bedroom talk'. Its not downright lewd of course – not decent bawdy, but its a defence of female promiscuity by an hysterical underbred creature . . . Female writers discovering a freedom a frankness a license to speak their hearts, reveal themselves as – – sex maniacs. There's not a relationship between a man & woman that isn't the one sexual relationship – at its lowest. *Intimacy* is the sexual act.

Rebecca West was not beyond reproach either for a whole column review of *Sorel* and *Syndicalism*:

any-fresh-fish-to-gut-on-the-problem-of-marriage-is-to-be-welcomed, etc. She makes me feel a very old fashioned creature. I feel if I met her I should have to say: 'And are you . . . one of these *New Women*?'

These may seem surprising comments from a woman whose own life had frequently defied the sexual and social mores of conventional society, but K.M. seems to have examined her own behaviour, 'confronted myself as it were, looked squarely at the extraordinary conditions of my existence . . . It wasnt flattering or pleasant or easy.' Just as she now rejected 'all that horrible old twisted existence the weekends at Garsington, the *paralysis* of everybody the vanity and ugliness of so much', she condemned writers who saw the sexual act as the only way to achieve intimacy. Relationships for her, in both her writing and her life, were now to be achieved through a very different kind of intimacy.

Her attitude towards her own work was one of uncompromising criticism:

I do not think I am a good writer; I realise my faults better than anyone else could realise them. I know exactly where I fail. And yet, when I have finished a story & before I have begun another, I catch myself *preening* my feathers. It is disheartening. There seems to be some bad old pride in my heart . . . This interferes very much with work.

Some of her own work appears precious, sentimental and facile. She herself forbade the republication of 'Sixpence' because it was too sentimental. On a lazy day in Hampstead she wrote:

I ought to write something brief for the Nation today & earn a bit more money a little lunch at the Club . . . Its not difficult in fact it is too easy for me because if I do err more on one side than t'other – I'm over fluent.

She was, she judged at times, guilty of 'over writing and under-stating – its just carelessness.'

She saw all too clearly, 'It is most fearfully hard for me, as it is for you, not to be "intense". And whenever I am intense (really, this is so) I am a little bit false.'

Even when her work was at last recognised she felt:

I have done so little . . . There are these rows of stories, all waiting. All the same, I can't deny the praise is like a most lovely present . . . I've only begun. The only story that satisfies me to any extent is . . . 'The Daughters of the Late Col', and parts of Je ne parle pas. But heavens what a journey there is before one.

Of *The Garden Party and Other Stories* she wrote:

I have just finished the proofs of my new book. Its been like getting back into the skin one had sloughed off. Not at all the skin I thought it, either. But it cant be helped. I think one must risk being seen not at one's best. Its no good hiding the unfavourable photographs, though pride wants to. All the same I must take a deeper breath next time.

She knew though that there was 'so much to write, there is so little time.'

And won't the 'Intellectuals' just hate it. They'll think it's a New Primer for Infant Readers. Let 'em.
to Dorothy Brett, 12 May 1918

Cover for the first few copies of *Prelude*

Often it seemed her work had become the centre of her whole existence. 'It takes the place of religion – it *is* my religion – of people – I create my people – of 'life' – it is Life'. But what did others think of that world she had created?

In a letter to Murry she wrote, 'Tell me if anybody says they like it, will you? . . . Its just a queer feeling – after one has dropped a pebble in. Will there be a ripple or not?'

What really was her significance in the development of the short story? In Hugh Walpole's opinion, 'her talent was a *minor* one, but a lovely lasting and enriching one.' Was she then merely an important minor writer, or a writer of genius?

In moving away from the concept of the short story as a narrative and in suggesting through her work the immense possibilities of what could be done once the artificialities of conventional plot were eliminated, K.M. had a profound influence on the development of the modern short story – an influence freely acknowledged by Elizabeth Bowen and others. As T. Beachcroft states, she belongs with 'Eliot, Joyce and Virginia Woolf' as 'part of a new dawn'. Once K.M. and others had claimed the right to experiment others followed, frequently achieving a combination of the two methods.

It is particularly interesting to look at the views of her contemporaries. Thomas Hardy, John Galsworthy and H. G. Wells all regarded her very highly, whereas D. H. Lawrence had answered Catherine Carswell's enthusiasm for *Prelude* with the impatient reply, 'Yes, yes, but prelude to what?' She would, he felt, reject the stories that contained her unique combination of sentiment and charm and stop writing until she could find a different kind of story. It was a strangely accurate prediction. Although he saw similarities to Dickens in her vivid use of specific details and colour and her touches of humour, Lawrence felt that Murry was wrong about her, and wrong to try to promote her work so assiduously after her death:

She was *not* a great genius. She had a charming gift, and a finely cultivated one. But *not more*. And to try, as you do, to make it more is to do her no true service . . . she is delicate and touching – but not great! Why say great.

While dryly admitting her jealousy, Virginia Woolf felt that K.M. was one of the best women writers. *Prelude* was one of the first volumes published by the Hogarth Press because Virginia felt it to be, 'a good deal better than most stories'. In her diary she went further, recognising in it 'the living power, the detached existence of a work of art'.

Their relationship was a difficult one, however, and Virginia found little to admire in K.M.'s later stories. Shortly after her friend's death which, she said, had moved her greatly, she wrote to Jacques Raverat:

My theory is that while she possessed the most amazing *senses* of her generation so that she could actually reproduce this room for instance, with its fly, clock, dog, tortoise if need be, to the life, she was as weak as water, as insipid, and a great deal more commonplace, when she had to use her mind. That is, she can't put thoughts, or feelings, or subtleties of any kind into her characters, without at once becoming, where she's serious, hard, and where she's sympathetic, sentimental.

It is also possible to criticise the very restricted circumscribed range of her work, but like Jane Austen she chose to write only of what she had known and seen. 'The artist takes a *long look* at life. He says softly, "So this is what life is, is it?" And he proceeds to express that. All the rest he leaves.' Nevertheless she was well aware of the limitations imposed upon her by her illness and her isolation: 'I'm so *stale* – oh for a "weekend" or even a ciné or a theatre or the sound of music'.

Naturally K.M. was considerably disturbed when it was suggested to her that had she not been ill, she might never have been able to write as she had.

Her illness certainly led to a feeling of urgency, 'It's always a race to get in as much as one can before it disappears'. She seemed often to write in bursts, sudden moments of crystallisation. A particularly interesting example of this occurs in the manuscript of 'The Doll's House'. One page begins with the story's last few lines. Beneath an erratically drawn line is the preceding section about Willie Brent, 'he'd come to the front door . . .' Beneath that is a much earlier section, part of the scene at the school, 'Lil Kelvey's going to be a servant when she grows up . . .' An arrow indicates how these fragments were to be finally fitted together, like pieces in a jigsaw.

In spite of illness, unhappiness and bleak frustration K.M. retained a tremendous spontaneous enthusiasm for life. 'God! I'm *rooted* in Life. Even if I hate Life, I cant deny it. I spring from it and feed on it.' Often this enthusiasm had been for her vision of life, rather than for life's reality. Yet she knew she must learn to accept that reality: 'I don't believe a writer can ever do anything *worth* doing until he has – in the profoundest sense of the word – ACCEPTED Life.' Gradually she came to know herself; to gain the courage to accept life for what it really was:

But do you really feel all beauty is marred by ugliness and the lovely woman has bad teeth? I don't feel quite that . . . Beauty triumphs over ugliness in Life. That's what I feel. And that marvellous triumph is what I long to express . . . Life is, all at one and the same time, far more mysterious and far simpler than we know. It's like religion in that. If we want to have faith, and without faith we die, we must *learn* to accept.

Some of her finest stories are about that triumph, and that acceptance, and with her ability to capture fleeting moods and vibrant warm colours they have enduring relevance.

Some stories do not work, but at her best, K.M. succeeded in writing something between 'a poem and a reflection, a novel and an anecdote'. All readers will have those stories which for him or her epitomise the particular quality of her writing and which lead them to glimpse a moment of truth; the realisation of the inevitability of life and the 'beauty in that inevitability'.

Despite John Middleton Murry's efforts, the amount of work on which her worldwide reputation rests is comparatively slight. Her technical innovations and skill alone would have had an important influence on modern writing. Her finest stories are, however, far more than technical masterpieces. In speaking to that 'secret self we all have', they establish her place in literature. Through her we see the world we have always known – but we see it more clearly.

And now I'll be personal darling. Look here, you ought to have sent me that Corona! You really ought to have. Can't you possibly imagine what all this writing out has meant to a person as weak as I am damnably am? You can't, or a stone would have sent it. You knew what a help it was to me in London.
to J.M. Murry,
8 December 1920

4 Selected stories

*F*or K.M. life and art became indivisible. Her stories are the 'end product', the result of the coming together of the woman and the writer. I have therefore included a representative selection of her work as part of this introduction.

Some 118 of K.M.'s stories have been published, either in book form or periodicals, and even some of these were incomplete. Every reader, student or critic has his or her favourite. There have been a number of selected editions of her work and each has differed in its choice of stories. Similarly, anthologies of short stories frequently contain at least one story by K.M. but there is a wide variation of choice.

My selection has been governed partly by a desire to give a chronological idea of her development as a writer. Therefore they are arranged in order of publication rather than in the rather arbitrary order of most collected editions which place the early stories last. For that reason and for literary curiosity I have included two stories which have not appeared in the complete collected editions. I have also selected those stories which I have found appeal to readers meeting her work for the first time. They include several of which she herself, a relentless critic, approved and some which she rejected, though others have regarded them highly. They represent her 'two kick-offs in the writing game' – a protest against corruption and that feeling of being at peace. They also illustrate what I have described elsewhere as her 'geographical schizophrenia', illustrating the two very different worlds from which she created her stories.

With most I have included a short comment and brief notes from K.M. herself, either commenting on the story or illustrating its genesis. With some I have also included the opinion of at least one critic, with which the reader may disagree or agree!

The best

Page of signatures, Notebook
1904

that you did not live in the time that
Motoua did -

Kathleen

K

Kathleen M Beauchamp

Kathleen Beauchamp

K. M. Beauchamp

K. M. Beauchamp

K. M. Beauchamp

the best.

Katherine Mansfield Murry

Katherine Mansfield Murry

*Im a writer first & a woman
after. I can't give you* all *you
want.*
to J.M. Murry, 2 December
1920

The Education of Audrey

'Now, when, in the name of fortune, am I to see you? I have a thousand things to show you, and as many again to talk about, but not the slightest desire to come and interview you in a boarding house, or to take you out to tea. Come and see me this afternoon and give me your advice upon my wholly charming room. I have been in London a month, and twice we have met – once at a concert, where you looked daggers at me, once at a restaurant, where you did not look at me at all. Just wire me, dear. I'm hungry for you, here, this every minute with me. Are you coming? – Max.'

Audrey smiled. She stood by the open window, looking out upon the street, the note in her hand.

It was Saturday morning, and full of sunshine. She watched the fugue-like course of hansoms and four wheelers and automobiles. A man wheeling a barrow full of shining, waving palms in terra cotta jars, passed by. Just under her window a boy was singing:

Ladies fair, I bring to you
Sweet lavender with spikes of blue.

in a fresh, rough, vigorous voice. His basket was full of little bunches of the fragrant dainty blossom. Audrey felt she would like to buy it all, crush it in her hands, bury her face in it, absorb it.

At the corner pillar box a postman shovelled the collection of white envelopes into a canvas bag . . .

Again she read the note in her hand. A faint flush spread over her face. She walked over to the dressing table, leaned her elbows on the table, her chin in her hand, and nodded to the mirror face.

'We'll go, my dear, and enjoy ourselves, and wear our best clothes. But, first, kindly send a wire at the post office.' She pulled a fur cap, gloves and long soft coat from her wardrobe, and, as she stood buttoning her collar, the street sounds floating up, the autumn wind stirring the blinds, she laughed softly.

'I am the happiest woman on this earth,' said Audrey. 'I have youth – oh divine youth,' she beat her gloved hands together, 'and my beautiful voice, and freedom, absolute liberty.'

For days rain had been falling over London with a steady monotonous persistence. Now, in this sunshine, she felt intoxicated. It was sparkling and golden and enchanting, like champagne.

Lying in her bed that morning, she had felt all through her that wonderful sense of power, of complete confidence in herself, that happiness which always followed her successful concerts. And when

Do you remember . . . I walked down to the ferry with you . . .

The *Duchess* at Day's Bay wharf

she had come back from her bath, her hair, all wet, hanging round her face, she had run over to the piano and sung, 'Softly Awakes My Heart', and almost frightened herself with the golden sounds.

Now, a letter from Max, and the prospect of an adorable afternoon.

She almost ran down the street. A child, bowling a great hoop, skipped past her. 'It is an uncomfortable thing,' sighed Audrey, 'to possess a spirit that persists in hoop bowling at my mature age, when the flesh must plod the pavestones of convention.'

She wired to Max merely 'I come,' and went back to her rooms with her arms full of chrysanthemums, yellow and rusty red, with a flaming setting of Capegooseberry flower.

'What can I wear?' said Audrey, later, brushing her black silk like hair, and arranging it round her face in puffs and curls. 'Max is so intensely critical about clothes, and I mean to look beautiful.' She decided upon a Liberty dress of mauve face-cloth, trimmed with dull violet buttons, and a beaver hat of the same colour, with a long curled feather. She took a hansom to No. 9, East Square, and told the driver to call for her at 5.30; it was then a quarter after 4.

A sudden breeze in the Square caught the leaves of the plane trees, burnt a bright golden and a dull brown, and whirled them into the air like a flock of magic birds. Two floated on to her muff, and she held them against her cold face as she mounted the steep flight of stairs.

Max opened the door, and she gave him both her hands, and the two little golden leaves. 'See,' she said, 'I am bringing you summer.'

'Oh, Audrey, this is fine. Come along into the smoking room – this way.' He pushed aside the heavy purple portiere.

The room was full of gloom, but vivid yellow curtains hung straight and fine, before the three windows. Tall wrought-iron candlesticks stood in the corners. The intense whiteness of the candles suddenly brought back a memory of Saint Gudule at dusk, and Audrey caught her breath.

There were prints of beautiful women on the walls, and the graceful figure of a girl holding a green shell in her arms stood on one of the tables. There was a long low couch upholstered in dull purple, and quaint low chairs in the same colour. The air was full of the odour of chrysanthemums, the blossoms arranged in pewter bowls on the mantelshelf, and bookcases and tables. At the far corner of the room there was a great Bluthner piano.

Audrey gave Max her coat and furs and long gloves. She sat on the low lounge, her feet tucked under her, a big leather cushion at her back.

'Max, what a fascinating room!'

'I thought you'd like it,' he said, stirring the fire, and then flinging himself into a great chair facing her. 'Well, I've got you at last.'

'Silly boy, not to have hailed me before. I couldn't fly a flag out of my window to attract you.

Max leaned forward, impulsively – 'Do you realise how long it is since we have seen each other?'

'Oh, let me see – four years.'

'Yes, and I cannot realise that we have ever been apart.'

'Oh, Max. Do you remember our parting – that terrible place; you had to catch the evening boat. I walked down to the ferry with you along the road. I had no shoes and stockings on – do you remember? And the wind. You had proposed to me that afternoon with unqualified success on the back verandah, and we tried to kiss each other before the boat went, but the wind blew all my hair across my face.' Audrey flung back her head and laughed. 'Oh, what children!' she said. 'I watched that ship put out to sea; you stood by the rail, waving me a little friendly greeting. I was crying, without a handkerchief. I remember going back to my room, kneeling by the window, looking up at the fierce sky, and praying, 'Oh, God, keep him, keep him!' Audrey laughed again, this time a little bitterly. 'And this morning I got my first letter from you.'

Max got up and walked over to the fireplace. He stood looking into the glowing coals. 'Well,' he said, 'go on.'

'Are you enjoying it?' said Audrey, 'How very good and how very rare for a man to hear this! And after the absolute sense of my nearness had worn off, it was easy to put the whole episode away. You realised, and how wisely, that you must not be distracted. You thought of me in weak moments as 'poor little girl', or when your pictures failed you as 'dear little girl'. Oh, how much I owe you!' cried Audrey. 'Can it ever be repaid?'

Max faced her swiftly – 'What?'

'Yes,' she said, 'I owe you almost everything. You see, Max, for a little while I did worship you, lived in a strange passionate dream of you and of me, believed that love between man and woman was the only thing in the world, instead of a lion in the path I've conquered and walked over. Then grandfather died, and I kissed his dead face. I woke and came to Paris. I have all his money, you know, and slaved, and now' –

There was silence in the room. Then Audrey spoke again.

'Love', she said, 'is a means to the end. You must have gone through all the abandonment of love. You must have been bruised and scarred by his mighty fetters. You must have been tossed upon the very sea of passion, and if you can escape free in body and soul, there lies before you such a wide windswept waste of freedom, such promise of happiness in this freedom that you run forward, your arms outstretched to take the whole world into your embrace.'

Max took a green suede case from one of the tables. He sat down on the lounge beside Audrey. 'Do you think for a moment,' he said seriously, 'that I should question such philosophy. I am going to show you some of my work. – Want a cigarette?'

'Please.'

He handed her his case. Then he showed her a collection of sketches – 'This is where I spent last summer, Audrey, and a winter there. I call this "The Poet's House". Observe the great broken branch of the cedar trees that shadows half the picture. Can't you feel the mystery, the morbid imaginings, the exotic, feverish fancies, the long nights?'

'Oh, how good!' said Audrey.

'Here is "The Spirit of Music",' said Max. It was a portrait of herself, singing – wild rose tinted cheeks, shining eyes, her hair in two long braids.

'When did you do this?' she asked.

'Oh, about a year ago when I was a little "off colour", you know.'

Audrey pushed the sketch away from her.

'Do not laugh at me,' she cried.

'Oh, but why not? How can the laughter of a mere man disturb the freshness of your windswept spaces? But look, Audrey, here is my "Mystic Garden Scene" I wished to show you.'

Audrey stared at the picture in silence. Then – 'You are a genius, Max.'

'What arrests you immediately in my work?'

'Oh, of course a certain almost fierce concentration. Your touch is the very quintessence of power.'

'If you are to become an artist, Audrey, that is the secret. Art demands of her disciples absolute slavish obedience, complete surrender of everything in the years of their apprenticeship. But when those years are passed, we know that the time has come to realise one's nature perfectly – then to create. Do you understand me? You see, my dear girl,' he continued, lighting another cigarette, 'your experience of life is based upon – forgive me – a little literature and a great deal of morbid imaginings.' He crossed the room and lit the four candles upon the piano. 'Come and sing for me.'

Audrey felt intensely angry, also, that her splendid happiness was slipping from her. 'Oh, do not talk like this,' she said, seating herself at the piano, and looking up at Max: 'I have bought the experience that I possess with the very gold of my youth.'

Max laughed gently. 'Sing now,' he said, 'we can talk again afterwards.' He leaned across the piano and watched her. Her beautiful voice filled the room. She sang song after passionate song. And he thought: Could anything be more fascinating than to teach this beautiful child that she might so live her life, that each song she sang would be the crystallisation of a wonderful experience?

The music ceased. Audrey looked out of the window. 'Oh,' she said, 'it is pouring with rain, and quite late. Please bring me my coat and furs.' She drew on her gloves; he helped her into her coat. Her hands trembled so much that she could not fasten the collar.

'Here, let me,' said Max. He could feel that she was shivering, and, looking at her, he saw the pallor of her face. Her eyes were strangely bright, her underlip quivered.

'What is the matter, child?'

'Oh, I do not know,' she said, moving towards the door. The room had become quite dark now, the silver rain beat softly upon the windows.

'Audrey,' said Max, 'Audrey, you child, don't you know, dear, that you have not spent one atom of the gold of your youth, that you are still walking along the little white road of childhood, fighting lions with your fairy wand?'

'I have been happy.'

'Why are you crying?'

'Do you know how I feel?' she said painfully – 'as though my philosophy was a thing for sunshine and daylight – and, it is raining now. You have made me believe, Max, that I have been playing with life. Yet, I have been happy.'

'Yes, as a child is happy. Ah, there are heights and depths in Art and Life that you have never dreamed of, Audrey. If you could only realise what might belong to you! You are playing on the outskirts of a forest filled with beautiful scarlet flowers. One day, sooner or later, if you want to fulfil your destiny, some one will take you by the hand and lead you there, and you will learn.'

Silence again in the dark room . . . the silver rain beat against the window.

She suddenly turned towards him and stretched out her hands – 'Teach me, Max', said Audrey.

'The Education of Audrey' (the *Evening Post*, 30 January 1909)

'I have just written a sketch 'The Education of Audrey' – which I think you might like – of course it is London – but it is actually happy – and ends to begin – you understand?' (to Vera Mackintosh Bell, 17 January 1908)

Like the unfinished novel of her adolescence, *Juliet*, written in London and on her return to New Zealand, this story shows the dominant influence of Oscar Wilde. Certain phrases are repeated from *Juliet*:

Tall wrought iron candlesticks stood in the corners. The intense [dead] whiteness of the candles brought back a memory of Saint Gudule at dusk and Audrey [Juliet] caught her breath . . . The air [room] was full of the odour of chrysanthemums.

Contrived, pretentious? Yes, but written in Wellington, it shows already the careful selection of detail and colour, and a freshness in the Wellington section; the wind is already a strong presence. It is the only story in which she attempts to unite those disparate worlds in which she lived. It contains too for the first time the magical password to her youth – 'Do you remember?'

Frau Brechenmacher
Attends a Wedding

Getting ready was a terrible business. After supper Frau Brechenmacher packed four of the five babies to bed, allowing Rosa to stay with her and help to polish the buttons of Herr Brechenmacher's uniform. Then she ran over his best shirt with a hot iron, polished his boots, and put a stitch or two into his black satin necktie.

'Rosa,' she said, 'fetch my dress and hang it in front of the stove to get the creases out. Now, mind, you must look after the children and not sit up later than half-past eight, and not touch the lamp – you know what will happen if you do.'

'Yes, mamma,' said Rosa, who was nine and felt old enough to manage a thousand lamps. 'But let me stay up – the "Bub" may wake and want some milk.'

'Half-past eight!' said the Frau. 'I'll make the father tell you too.'

Rose drew down both corners of her mouth.

'But . . . but . . .'

'Here comes the father. You go into the bedroom and fetch my blue silk handkerchief. You can wear my black shawl while I'm out – there now!'

Rosa dragged it off her mother's shoulders and wound it carefully round her own, tying the two ends in a knot at the back. After

They walked home in silence. Herr Brechenmacher strode ahead, she stumbled after him. White and forsaken lay the road . . . suddenly she remembered how they had come home together the first night.

Bad Wörishofen

all, she reflected, if she had to go to bed at half-past eight she would keep the shawl on. Which resolution comforted her absolutely.

'Now, then, where are my clothes?' cried Herr Brechenmacher, hanging his empty letter-bag behind the door and stamping the snow out of his boots. 'Nothing ready, of course, and everybody at the wedding by this time. I heard the music as I passed. What are you doing? You're not dressed. You can't go like that.'

'Here they are – all ready for you on the table, and some warm water in the tin basin. Dip your head in. Rosa, give your father the towel. Everything ready except the trousers. I haven't had time to shorten them. You must tuck the ends into your boots until we get there.'

'Nu,' said the Herr, 'there isn't room to turn. I want the light. You go and dress in the passage.'

Dressing in the dark was nothing to Frau Brechenmacher. She hooked her skirt and bodice, fastened her handkerchief round her neck with a beautiful brooch that had four medals to the Virgin dangling from it, and then drew on her cloak and hood.

'Here, come and fasten this buckle,' called Herr Brechenmacher. He stood in the kitchen puffing himself out, the buttons on his blue uniform shining with an enthusiasm which nothing but official buttons could possibly possess. 'How do I look?'

'Wonderful,' replied the little Frau, straining at the waist buckle and giving him a little pull here, a little tug there. 'Rosa, come and look at your father.'

Herr Brechenmacher strode up and down the kitchen, was helped on with his coat, then waited while the Frau lighted the lantern.

'Now, then – finished at last! Come along.'

'The lamp, Rosa,' warned the Frau, slamming the front door behind them.

Snow had not fallen all day; the frozen ground was slippery as an icepond. She had not been out of the house for weeks past, and the day had so flurried her that she felt muddled and stupid – felt that Rosa had pushed her out of the house and her man was running away from her.

'Wait, wait!' she cried.

'No. I'll get my feet damp – you hurry.'

It was easier when they came into the village. There were fences to cling to, and leading from the railway station to the Gasthaus a little path of cinders had been strewn for the benefit of the wedding guests.

The Gasthaus was very festive. Lights shone out from every window, wreaths of fir twigs hung from the ledges. Branches decorated the front doors, which swung open, and in the hall the landlord voiced his superiority by bullying the waitresses, who ran about continually with glasses of beer, trays of cups and saucers, and bottles of wine.

'Up the stairs – up the stairs!' boomed the landlord. 'Leave your coats on the landing.'

Herr Brechenmacher, completely overawed by this grand manner, so far forgot his rights as a husband as to beg his wife's pardon for jostling her against the banisters in his efforts to get ahead of everybody else.

Herr Brechenmacher's colleagues greeted him with acclamation as he entered the door of the Festsaal, and the Frau straightened her brooch and folded her hands, assuming the air of dignity becoming to the wife of a postman and the mother of five children. Beautiful indeed was the Festsaal. Three long tables were grouped at one end, the remainder of the floor space cleared for dancing. Oil lamps, hanging from the ceiling, shed a warm, bright light on the walls decorated with paper flowers and garlands; shed a warmer, brighter light on the red faces of the guests in their best clothes.

At the head of the centre table sat the bride and bridegroom, she in a white dress trimmed with stripes and bows of coloured ribbon, giving her the appearance of an iced cake all ready to be cut and served in neat little pieces to the bridegroom beside her, who wore a suit of white clothes much too large for him and a white silk tie that rose half-way up his collar. Grouped about them, with a fine regard for dignity and precedence, sat their parents and relations; and perched on a stool at the bride's right hand a little girl in a crumpled muslin dress with a wreath of forget-me-nots hanging over one ear. Everybody was laughing and talking, shaking hands, clinking glasses, stamping on the floor –a stench of beer and perspiration filled the air.

Frau Brechenmacher, following her man down the room after greeting the bridal party, knew that she was going to enjoy herself. She seemed to fill out and become rosy and warm as she sniffed that familiar festive smell. Somebody pulled at her skirt, and, looking down, she saw Frau Rupp, the butcher's wife, who pulled out an empty chair and begged her to sit beside her.

'Fritz will get you some beer,' she said. 'My dear, your skirt is open at the back. We could not help laughing as you walked up the room with the white tape of your petticoat showing!'

'But how frightful!' said Frau Brechenmacher, collapsing into her chair and biting her lip.

'Na, it's over now,' said Frau Rupp, stretching her fat hands over the table and regarding her three mourning rings with intense enjoyment; 'but one must be careful, especially at a wedding.'

'And such a wedding as this,' cried Frau Ledermann, who sat

on the other side of Frau Brechenmacher. 'Fancy Theresa bringing
that child with her. It's her own child, you know, my dear, and it's
going to live with them. That's what I call a sin against the Church
for a free-born child to attend its own mother's wedding.'

The three women sat and stared at the bride, who remained
very still, with a little vacant smile on her lips, only her eyes
shifting uneasily from side to side.

'Beer they've given it, too,' whispered Frau Rupp, 'and white
wine and an ice. It never did have a stomach; she ought to have
left it at home.'

Frau Brechenmacher turned round and looked towards the
bride's mother. She never took her eyes off her daughter, but wrinkled her brown forehead like an old monkey, and nodded now
and again very solemnly. Her hands shook as she raised her beer
mug, and when she had drunk she spat on the floor and savagely
wiped her mouth with her sleeve. Then the music started and she
followed Theresa with her eyes, looking suspiciously at each man
who danced with her.

'Cheer up, old woman,' shouted her husband, digging her in the
ribs; 'this isn't Theresa's funeral.' He winked at the guests, who
broke into loud laughter.

'I *am* cheerful,' mumbled the old woman, and beat upon the
table with her fist, keeping time to the music, proving she was not
out of the festivities.

'She can't forget how wild Theresa has been,' said Frau Ledermann. 'Who could – with the child there? I heard that last Sunday
evening Theresa had hysterics and said that she would not marry
this man. They had to get the priest to her.'

'Where is the other one?' asked Frau Brechenmacher. 'Why
didn't he marry her?'

The woman shrugged her shoulders.

'Gone – disappeared. He was a traveller, and only stayed at their
house two nights. He was selling shirt buttons – I bought some
myself, and they were beautiful shirt buttons – but what a pig of
a fellow! I can't think what he saw in such a plain girl – but you
never know. Her mother says she's been like fire ever since she
was sixteen!'

Frau Brechenmacher looked down at her beer and blew a little
hole in the froth.

'That's not how a wedding should be,' she said; 'it's not religion
to love two men.'

'Nice time she'll have with this one,' Frau Rupp exclaimed. 'He
was lodging with me last summer and I had to get rid of him. He
never changed his clothes once in two months, and when I spoke
to him of the smell in his room he told me he was sure it floated

up from the shop. Ah, every wife has her cross. Isn't that true, my dear?'

Frau Brechenmacher saw her husband among his colleagues at the next table. He was drinking far too much, she knew – gesticulating wildly, the saliva spluttering out of his mouth as he talked.

'Yes,' she assented, 'that's true. Girls have a lot to learn.'

Wedged in between these two fat old women, the Frau had no hope of being asked to dance. She watched the couples going round and round; she forgot her five babies and her man and felt almost like a girl again. The music sounded sad and sweet. Her roughened hands clasped and unclasped themselves in the folds of her skirt. While the music went on she was afraid to look anybody in the face, and she smiled with a little nervous tremor round the mouth.

'But, my God,' Frau Rupp cried, 'they've given that child of Theresa's a piece of sausage. It's to keep her quiet. There's going to be a presentation now – your man has to speak.'

Frau Brechenmacher sat up stiffly. The music ceased, and the dancers took their places again at the tables.

Herr Brechenmacher alone remained standing – he held in his hands a big silver coffee-pot. Everybody laughed at his speech, except the Frau; everybody roared at his grimaces, and at the way he carried the coffee-pot to the bridal pair, as if it were a baby he was holding.

She lifted the lid, peeped in, then shut it down with a little scream and sat biting her lips. The bridegroom wrenched the pot away from her and drew forth a baby's bottle and two little cradles holding china dolls. As he dandled these treasures before Theresa the hot room seemed to heave and sway with laughter.

Frau Brechenmacher did not think it funny. She stared round at the laughing faces, and suddenly they all seemed strange to her. She wanted to go home and never come out again. She imagined that all these people were laughing at her, more people than there were in the room even – all laughing at her because they were so much stronger than she was.

They walked home in silence. Herr Brechenmacher strode ahead, she stumbled after him. White and forsaken lay the road from the railway station to their house – a cold rush of wind blew her hood from her face, and suddenly she remembered how they had come home together the first night. Now they had five babies and twice as much money; *but* –

'Na, what is it all for?' she muttered, and not until she had reached home and prepared a little supper of meat and bread for her man did she stop asking herself that silly question.

Herr Brechenmacher broke the bread into his plate, smeared it round with his fork and chewed greedily.

'Good?' she asked, leaning her arms on the table and pillowing her breast against them.

'But fine!'

He took a piece of the crumb, wiped it round his plate edge, and held it up to her mouth. She shook her head.

'Not hungry,' she said.

'But it is one of the best pieces, and full of the fat.'

He cleared the plate; then pulled off his boots and flung them into a corner.

'Not much of a wedding,' he said, stretching out his feet and wriggling his toes in the worsted socks.

'N – no,' she replied, taking up the discarded boots and placing them on the oven to dry.

Herr Brechenmacher yawned and stretched himself, and then looked up at her, grinning.

'Remember the night that we came home? You were an innocent one, you were.'

'Get along! Such a time ago I forget.' Well she remembered.

'Such a clout on the ear as you gave me . . . But I soon taught you.'

'Oh, don't start talking. You've too much beer. Come to bed.'

He tilted back in his chair, chuckling with laughter.

'That's not what you said to me that night. God, the trouble you gave me!'

But the little Frau seized the candle and went into the next room. The children were all soundly sleeping. She stripped the mattress off the baby's bed to see if he was still dry, then began unfastening her blouse and skirt.

'Always the same,' she said – 'all over the world the same; but, God in heaven – but *stupid*.'

Then even the memory of the wedding faded quite. She lay down on the bed and put her arm across her face like a child who expected to be hurt as Herr Brechenmacher lurched in.

'Frau Brechenmacher Attends a Wedding' (the *New Age*, 21 July 1910)

'Would you care for a copy of my wretched old book? It is young and bad, but I would like to send you one. It might amuse you a little.' (to Lady Ottoline Morrell, 14 January 1917, *The Collected Letters*)

'I cannot have the German Pension republished under any circumstances. It is far too immature . . . *It's not good enough* . . . It's positively juvenile, and besides that it's not what I mean: it's a lie.' (to J.M. Murry, 4 February 1920)

'. . . it's simply ridiculous to pretend there's anything to be ashamed of in the G.P. It was a splendid piece of work for 1911–12. Early work if you like. Write an introduction saying so if you like.' (J. M. Murry to K.M., 9 February 1920)

'It's *awfully* bad there's a kind of odious smartness about it which would make any decent critic or reader writhe. No amount of revision would make it presentable. I'd much rather sit tight on its grave.' (to Michael Sadleir, 25 March 1922)

'. . . youthful extravagance of expression and youthful disgust . . . I don't like ugliness for ugliness' sake.' (to Mr J. B. Pinker, 3 May 1922)

'. . . the most memorable of all stories in the volume'. (Sylvia Berkman, *Katherine Mansfield: A Critical Study*)

'an undisguised attack upon the sexually dominant male'. (C. A. Hankin, *Katherine Mansfield and Her Confessional Stories*)

Although Leonard Woolf preferred K.M.'s early stories for their wit and satire, feeling that she later became enmeshed in Murry's 'sticky sentimentality', most critics have regarded her early work, particularly *The German Pension*, as inferior. Recently it has been the subject of revived interest and reappraisal; many stories have been hailed as brave early examples of feminist literature, dealing with the now popular 'dame seule' theme.

In 'Frau Brechenmacher Attends a Wedding' K.M. sensitively explores a woman's silent pain and loneliness in a well-constructed, clever story.

The Woman at the Store

All that day the heat was terrible. The wind blew close to the ground; it rooted among the tussock grass, slithered along the road, so that the white pumice dust swirled in our faces, settled and sifted over us and was like a dry-skin itching for growth on our bodies. The horses stumbled along, coughing and chuffing. The pack-horse was sick – with a big open sore rubbed under the belly. Now and again she stopped short, threw back her head, looked at us as though she were going to cry, and whinnied. Hundreds of larks shrilled; the sky was slate colour, and the sound of the larks reminded me of slate pencils scraping over its surface. There was nothing to be seen but wave after wave of tussock grass, patched with purple orchids and manuka bushes covered with thick spider webs.

Jo rode ahead. He wore a blue galatea shirt, corduroy trousers and riding boots. A white handkerchief, spotted with red – it looked as though his nose had been bleeding on it – was knotted round his throat. Wisps of white hair straggled from under his wideawake – his moustache and eyebrows were called white – he slouched in the saddle, grunting. Not once that day had he sung

I don't care, for don't you see,
My wife's mother was in front of me!

It was the first day we had been without it for a month, and now there seemed something uncanny in his silence. Jim rode beside me, white as a clown; his black eyes glittered and he kept shooting out his tongue and moistening his lips. He was dressed in a Jaeger vest and a pair of blue duck trousers, fastened round the waist with a plaited leather belt. We had hardly spoken since dawn. At noon we had lunched off fly biscuits and apricots by the side of a swampy creek.

'My stomach feels like the crop of a hen,' said Jo. 'Now then, Jim, you're the bright boy of the party – where's this 'ere store you kep' on talking about. "Oh yes," you says, "I know a fine store, with a paddock for the horses and a creek runnin' through, owned by a friend of mine who'll give yer a bottle of whisky before'e shakes hands with yer". I'd like ter see that place – merely as a matter of curiosity – not that I'd ever doubt yer word – as yer know very well – *but . . .* '

Jim laughed. 'Don't forget there's a woman too, Jo, with blue

eyes and yellow hair, who'll promise you something else before she shakes hands with you. Put that in your pipe and smoke it.'

'The heat's making you balmy,' said Jo. But he dug his knees into the horse. We shambled on. I half fell asleep and had a sort of uneasy dream that the horses were not moving forward at all – then that I was on a rocking-horse, and my old mother was scolding me for raising such a fearful dust from the drawing-room carpet. 'You've entirely worn off the pattern of the carpet,' I heard her saying, and she gave the reins a tug. I snivelled and woke to find Jim leaning over me, maliciously smiling.

'That was a case of all but,' said he. 'I just caught you. What's up? Been bye-bye?'

'No!' I raised my head. 'Thank the Lord we're arriving somewhere.'

We were on the brow of the hill, and below us there was a whare roofed with corrugated iron. It stood in a garden, rather far back from the road – a big paddock opposite, and a creek and a clump of young willow trees. A thin line of blue smoke stood up straight from the chimney of the whare; and as I looked a woman came out, followed by a child and a sheep dog – the woman carrying what appeared to me a black stick. She made gestures at us. The horses put on a final spurt, Jo took off his wideawake, shouted, threw out his chest, and began singing 'I don't care, for don't you

We sleep tonight at the Rangitaiki and then the plains and the back blocks . . . Woman and daughter – the man . . .
Notebook, November 1907

The Rangitaiki Hotel

see . . . ' The sun pushed through the pale clouds and shed a vivid light over the scene. It gleamed on the woman's yellow hair, over her flapping pinafore and the rifle she was carrying. The child hid behind her, and the yellow dog, a mangy beast, scuttled back into the whare, his tail between his legs. We drew rein and dismounted.

'Hallo,' screamed the woman. 'I thought you was three 'awks. My kid comes runnin' in ter me. "Mumma", says she, "there's three brown things comin' over the 'ill," says she. An' I comes out smart, I can tell yer. "They'll be 'awks," I says to her. Oh, the 'awks about 'ere, yer wouldn't believe.'

The 'kid' gave us the benefit of one eye from behind the woman's pinafore – then retired again.

'Where's your old man?' asked Jim.

The woman blinked rapidly, screwing up her face.

'Away shearin'. Bin away a month. I suppose ye're not goin' to stop, are yer? There's a storm comin' up.'

'You bet we are,' said Jo. 'So you're on your lonely, missus?'

She stood, pleating the frills of her pinafore, and glancing from one to the other of us, like a hungry bird. I smiled at the thought of how Jim had pulled Jo's leg about her. Certainly her eyes were blue, and what hair she had was yellow, but ugly. She was a figure of fun. Looking at her, you felt there was nothing but sticks and wires under that pinafore—her front teeth were knocked out, she had red, pulpy hands and she wore on her feet a pair of dirty Bluchers.

'I'll go and turn out the horses,' said Jim. 'Got any embrocation? Poi's rubbed herself to hell!'

' 'Arf a mo!' The woman stood silent a moment, her nostrils expanding as she breathed. Then she shouted violently, 'I'd rather you didn't stop . . . You *can't*, and there's the end of it. I don't let out that paddock any more. You'll have to go on; I ain't got nothing!'

'Well, I'm blest!' said Jo heavily. He pulled me aside. 'Gone a bit off er dot', he whispered. 'Too much alone, *you know*', very significantly. 'Turn the sympathetic tap on 'er, she'll come round all right.'

But there was no need – she had come round by herself.

'Stop if yer like!' she muttered, shrugging her shoulders. To me – 'I'll give yer the embrocation if yer come along.'

'Right-o, I'll take it down to them.' We walked together up the garden path. It was planted on both sides with cabbages. They smelled like stale dish-water. Of flowers there were double poppies and sweet-williams. One little patch was divided off by pawa shells – presumably it belonged to the child – for she ran from her mother and began to grub in it with a broken clothes-peg. The yellow dog lay across the doorstep, biting fleas; the woman kicked him away.

'Gar-r, get away, you beast . . . the place ain't tidy. I 'aven't 'ad time ter fix things to-day – been ironing. Come right in.'

It was a large room, the walls plastered with old pages of English periodicals. Queen Victoria's Jubilee appeared to be the most recent number . A table with an ironing board and wash-tub on it, some wooden forms, a black horsehair sofa and some broken cane chairs pushed against the walls. The mantelpiece above the stove was draped in pink paper, further ornamented with dried grasses and ferns and a coloured print of Richard Seddon. There were four doors – one, judging from the smell, let into the 'Store', one on to the 'backyard,' through a third I saw the bedroom. Flies buzzed in circles round the ceiling, and treacle papers and bundles of dried clover were pinned to the window curtains.

I was alone in the room; she had gone into the store for the embrocation. I heard her stamping about and muttering to herself: 'I got some, now where did I put that bottle? . . . It's behind the pickles . . . no, it ain't.' I cleared a place on the table and sat there, swinging my legs. Down in the paddock I could hear Jo singing and the sound of hammer strokes as Jim drove in the tent pegs. It was sunset. There is no twilight in our New Zealand days, but a curious half-hour when everything appears grotesque – it frightens – as though the savage spirit of the country walked abroad and sneered at what it saw. Sitting alone in the hideous room I grew afraid. The woman next door was a long time finding that stuff. What was she doing in there? Once I thought I heard her bang her hands down on the counter, and once she half moaned, turning it into a cough and clearing her throat. I wanted to shout 'Buck up!' but I kept silent.

'Good Lord, what a life!' I thought. 'Imagine being here day in, day out, with that rat of a child and a mangy dog. Imagine bothering about ironing. *Mad*, of course she's mad! Wonder how long she's been here – wonder if I could get her to talk.'

At that moment she poked her head round the door.

'Wot was it yer wanted?' she asked.

'Embrocation.'

'Oh, I forgot. I got it, it was in front of the pickle jar.'

She handed me the bottle.

'My, you do look tired, you do! Shall I knock yer up a few scones for supper! There's some tongue in the store, too, and I'll cook yer a cabbage if you fancy it.'

'Right-o.' I smiled at her. 'Come down to the paddock and bring the kid for tea.'

She shook her head, pursing up her mouth.

'Oh no. I don't fancy it. I'll send the kid down with the things and a billy of milk. Shall I knock up a few extry scones to take with yer ter-morrow?'

'Thanks.'

She came and stood by the door.

'How old is the kid?'

'Six – come next Christmas. I 'ad a bit of trouble with 'er one way an' another. I 'adn't any milk till a month after she was born and she sickened like a cow.'

'She's not like you – takes after her father?' Just as the woman had shouted her refusal at us before, she shouted at me then.

'No, she don't! She's the dead spit of me. Any fool could see that. Come on in now, Else, you stop messing in the dirt.'

I met Jo climbing over the paddock fence.

'What's the old bitch got in the store?' he asked.

'Don't know – didn't look.'

'Well, of all the fools. Jim's slanging you. What have you been doing all the time?'

'She couldn't find this stuff. Oh, my shakes, you are smart!'

Jo had washed, combed his wet hair in a line across his forehead, and buttoned a coat over his shirt. He grinned.

Jim snatched the embrocation from me. I went to the end of the paddock where the willows grew and bathed in the creek. The water was clear and soft as oil. Along the edges held by the grass and rushes white foam tumbled and bubbled. I lay in the water and looked up at the trees that were still a moment, then quivered lightly and again were still. The air smelt of rain. I forgot about the woman and the kid until I came back to the tent. Jim lay by the fire watching the billy boil.

I asked where Jo was, and if the kid had brought our supper.

'Pooh,' said Jim, rolling over and looking up at the sky.

'Didn't you see how Jo had been titivating? He said to me before he went up to the whare, "Dang it! she'll look better by night light – at any rate, my buck, she's female flesh!" '

'You had Jo about her looks—you had me too.'

'No – look here. I can't make it out. It's four years since I came past this way and I stopped here two days. The husband was a pal of mine once, down the West Coast – a fine, big chap, with a voice on him like a trombone. She's been barmaid down the Coast – as pretty as a wax doll. The coach used to come this way then once a fortnight, that was before they opened the railway up Napier way, and she had no end of a time! Told me once in a confidential moment that she knew one hundred and twenty-five different ways of kissing!'

'Oh, go on, Jim! She isn't the same woman!'

''Course she is . . . I can't make it out. What I think is the old man's cleared out and left her: that's all my eye about shearing. Sweet life! The only people who come through now are Maoris and sundowners!'

Through the dark we saw the gleam of the kid's pinafore. She trailed over to us with a basket in her hand, the milk billy in the other. I unpacked the basket, the child standing by.

'Come over here,' said Jim, snapping his fingers at her.

She went, the lamp from the inside of the tent cast a bright light over her. A mean, undersized brat, with whitish hair and weak eyes. She stood, legs wide apart and her stomach protruding.

'What do you do all day?' asked Jim.

She scraped out one ear with her little finger, looked at the result and said, 'Draw.'

'Huh! What do you draw? Leave your ears alone!'

'Pictures.'

'What on?'

'Bits of butter paper an' a pencil of my Mumma's.'

'Boh! What a lot of words at one time!' Jim rolled his eyes at her. 'Baa-lambs and moo-cows?'

'No, everything. I'll draw all of you when you're gone, and your horses and the tent, and that one' – she pointed to me – 'with no clothes on in the creek. I looked at her where she couldn't see me from.'

'Thanks very much. How ripping of you,' said Jim. 'Where's Dad?'

The kid pouted. 'I won't tell you because I don't like yer face!' She started operations on the other ear.

'Here,' I said. 'Take the basket, get along home and tell the other man supper's ready.'

'I don't want to.'

'I'll give you a box on the ear if you don't,' said Jim savagely.

'Hie! I'll tell Mumma. I'll tell Mumma.' The kid fled.

We ate until we were full, and had arrived at the smoke stage before Jo came back, very flushed and jaunty, a whisky bottle in his hand.

' 'Ave a drink – you two!' he shouted, carrying off matters with a high hand. ' 'Ere, shove along the cups.'

'One hundred and twenty-five different ways,' I murmured to Jim.

'What's that? Oh! stow it!' said Jo. 'Why 'ave you always got your knife into me. You gas like a kid at a Sunday School beano. She wants us to go there to-night and have a comfortable chat. I' – he waved his hand airily – 'I got 'er round.'

'Trust you for that,' laughed Jim. 'But did she tell you where the old man's got to?'

Jo looked up. 'Shearing! You 'eard 'er, you fool!'

The woman had fixed up the room, even to a light bouquet of sweet-williams on the table. She and I sat one side of the table, Jo and Jim the other. An oil lamp was set between us, the whisky bottle and glasses, and a jug of water. The kid knelt against one of the forms, drawing on butter paper; I wondered, grimly, if she was attempting the creek episode. But Jo had been right about night time. The woman's hair was tumbled – two red spots burned in her cheeks – her eyes shone – and we knew that they were kissing feet under the table. She had changed the blue pinafore for a white calico dressing-jacket and a black skirt – the kid was decorated to the extent of a blue sateen hair ribbon. In the stifling room, with the flies buzzing against the ceiling and dropping on to the table, we got slowly drunk.

'Now listen to me,' shouted the woman, banging her fist on the table. 'It's six years since I was married, and four miscarriages. I says to 'im, I says, what do you think I'm doin' up 'ere? If you was back at the Coast I'd 'ave you lynched for child murder. Over and over I tells 'im – you've broken my spirit and spoiled my looks, and wot for – that's wot I'm driving at.' She clutched her head with her hands and stared round at us. Speaking rapidly, 'Oh, some days – an' months of them – I 'ear them two words knockin' inside me all the time – "Wot for!" but sometimes I'll be cooking the spuds an' I lifts the lid off to give 'em a prong and I 'ears, quite suddin again, "Wot for!" Oh! I don't mean only the spuds and the kid – I mean – I mean,' she hiccoughed – 'you know what I mean, Mr. Jo.'

'I know,' said Jo, scratching his head.

'Trouble with me is,' she leaned across the table, 'he left me too much alone. When the coach stopped coming, sometimes he'd go away days, sometimes he'd go away weeks, and leave me ter look after the store. Back 'e'd come – pleased as Punch. "Oh, 'allo," 'e'd say. " 'Ow are you gettin' on? Come and give us a kiss." Sometimes I'd turn a bit nasty, and then 'e'd go off again, and if I took it all right, 'e'd wait till 'e could twist me round 'is finger, then 'e'd say, "Well, so long, I'm off," and do you think I could keep 'im? – not me!'

'Mumma,' bleated the kid, 'I made a picture of them on the 'ill, an' you an' me an' the dog down below.'

'Shut your mouth!' said the woman.

A vivid flash of lightning played over the room – we heard the mutter of thunder.

'Good thing that's broke loose,' said Jo. 'I've 'ad it in me 'ead for three days.'

'Where's your old man now?' asked Jim slowly.

The woman blubbered and dropped her head on to the table. 'Jim, 'e's gone shearin' and left me alone again,' she wailed.

' 'Ere, look out for the glasses,' said Jo. 'Cheer-o, 'ave another drop. No good cryin' over spilt 'usbands! You, Jim, you blasted cuckoo!'

'Mr. Jo,' said the woman, drying her eyes on her jacket frill, 'you're a gent, an' if I was a secret woman I'd place any confidence in your 'ands. I don't mind if I do 'ave a glass on that.'

Every moment the lightning grew more vivid and the thunder sounded nearer. Jim and I were silent – the kid never moved from her bench. She poked her tongue out and blew on her paper as she drew.

'It's the loneliness,' said the woman, addressing Jo – he made sheep's eyes at her – 'and bein' shut up 'ere like a broody 'en.' He reached his hand across the table and held hers, and though the position looked most uncomfortable when they wanted to pass the water and whisky, their hands stuck together as though glued. I pushed back my chair and went over to the kid, who immediately sat flat down on her artistic achievements and made a face at me.

'You're not to look,' said she.

'Oh, come on, don't be nasty!' Jim came over to us, and we were just drunk enough to wheedle the kid into showing us. And those drawings of hers were extraordinary and repulsively vulgar. The creations of a lunatic with a lunatic's cleverness. There was no doubt about it, the kid's mind was diseased. While she showed them to us, she worked herself up into a mad excitement, laughing and trembling, and shooting out her arms.

'Mumma,' she yelled. 'Now I'm going to draw them what you told me I never was to – now I am.'

The woman rushed from the table and beat the child's head with the flat of her hand.

'I'll smack you with yer clothes turned up if yer dare say that again,' she bawled.

Jo was too drunk to notice, but Jim caught her by the arm. The kid did not utter a cry. She drifted over to the window and began picking flies from the treacle paper.

We returned to the table – Jim and I sitting one side, the woman and Jo, touching shoulders, the other. We listened to the thunder, saying stupidly, 'That was a near one,' 'There it goes again,' and Jo, at a heavy hit, 'Now we're off,' 'Steady on the brake,' until rain began to fall, sharp as cannon shot on the iron roof.

'You'd better doss here for the night,' said the woman.

'That's right,' assented Jo, evidently in the know about this move.

'Bring up yer things from the tent. You two can doss in the store along the kid – she's used to sleep in there and won't mind you.'

'Oh, Mumma, I never did,' interrupted the kid.

'Shut yer lies! An' Mr. Jo can 'ave this room.'

It sounded a ridiculous arrangement, but it was useless to attempt to cross them, they were too far gone. While the woman sketched the plan of action, Jo sat, abnormally solemn and red, his eyes bulging, and pulling at his moustache.

'Give us a lantern,' said Jim, 'I'll go down to the paddock.' We two went together. Rain whipped in our faces, the land was light as though a bush fire was raging. We behaved like two children let loose in the thick of an adventure, laughed and shouted to each other, and came back to the whare to find the kid already bedded in the counter of the store. The woman brought us a lamp. Jo took his bundle from Jim, the door was shut.

'Good night all,' shouted Jo.

Jim and I sat on two sacks of potatoes. For the life of us we could not stop laughing. Strings of onions and half-hams dangled from the ceiling – wherever we looked there were advertisements for 'Camp Coffee' and tinned meats. We pointed at them, tried to read them aloud – overcome with laughter and hiccoughs. The kid in the counter stared at us. She threw off her blanket and scrambled to the floor, where she stood in her grey flannel night-gown rubbing one leg against the other. We paid no attention to her.

'Wot are you laughing at?' she said uneasily.

'You!' shouted Jim. 'The red tribe of you, my child.'

She flew into a rage and beat herself with her hands. 'I won't be laughed at, you curs – you.' He swooped down upon the child and swung her on to the counter.

'Go to sleep, Miss Smarty – or make a drawing – here's a pencil – you can use Mumma's account book.'

Through the rain we heard Jo creak over the boarding of the next room – the sound of a door being opened – then shut to.

'It's the loneliness,' whispered Jim.

'One hundred and twenty-five different ways – alas! my poor brother!'

The kid tore out a page and flung it at me.

'There you are,' she said. 'Now I done it ter spite Mumma for shutting me up 'ere with you two. I done the one she told me I never ought to. I done the one she told me she'd shoot me if I did. Don't care! Don't care!'

The kid had drawn the picture of the woman shooting at a man with a rook rifle and then digging a hole to bury him in.

She jumped off the counter and squirmed about on the floor biting her nails.

Jim and I sat till dawn with the drawing beside us. The rain
ceased, the little kid fell asleep, breathing loudly. We got up, stole
out of the whare, down into the paddock. White clouds floated
over a pink sky – a chill wind blew; the air smelled of wet grass.
Just as we swung into the saddle Jo came out of the whare – he
motioned to us to ride on.

'I'll pick you up later,' he shouted.

A bend in the road, and the whole place disappeared.

'The Woman at the Store' (*Rhythm*, Spring 1912)

'A remarkable achievement . . . carefully wrought plot . . . The narrative
is given with scrupulous objectivity. The scene is set, the figures move
and speak, the plot unfolds, without a word or comment.' (Sylvia Berkman, *Katherine Mansfield: A Critical Study*)

'It ploughs the realistic sand with no single relief of wisdom or wit.'
(the *New Age*, 28 March 1912)

'I couldn't have "The Woman at the Store" reprinted.' (to J.M. Murry,
8 February 1920)

In 'The Woman at the Store', as in other stories, K.M. seems to
have combined two sources. While travelling on her camping tour
of the central North Island in 1907 the party stopped twice at the
Rangitaiki hotel and store where, on both occasions, K.M. seems
to have felt uneasy at the atmosphere between the 'woman and
daughter – the man'. On the return journey they travelled over
dry dusty pumice country through Rangitaiki to pitch camp not
far away at Runanga. The woman there, her child and the storm
that night became fused with the family at Rangitaiki in 'The
Woman at the Store'.

This is an unusual story for K.M., as it has a carefully structured
plot with a surprisingly twisted ending, and its haunting, strange
atmosphere gives it the quality of a mystery story. Like two others
also published in *Rhythm*, 'Millie' and 'Ole Underwood', it is a
starkly horrifying tale of murder. It captures too the powerful
brooding spirit of the land which is evoked so clearly in her notebook.

Old Tar

Old Tar must have begun building his house when he was about five years old. Every Sunday morning after church his father and he, hand in hand, went for a bit of a stroll while Mother got dinner, up the new road, through a barbed-wire fence, and on to the great green shoulders of Makra Hill. There they sat down on the blowing grass and pink 'fairy trumpets' or on the white and yellow daisies and dandelions, and while his father had a chew of tobacco, Old Tar (who was very young Tar indeed then) sat quiet and strained his little panting chest against his tight Sunday clothes. Far below, the sea ran with a crashing laugh up Makra beach and slipped back again, stealthy, quiet, and gathered together and came again, biting over the rocks and swallowing the sand. They could snuff it in their nostrils and taste it on their lips. There was nothing to be seen to left or right on them but other hill-tops bounded by dark, high masses of bush. Behind them there was the new road leading to Wadesville, and a further drop to the township, Karori; but all that was hidden, and might have been the length of days away. 'By gum!' the old man would mutter, lifting his worn head. 'It's a durn fine place ... it's a place to shake yer lungs out in – yer know, boy, my Pap bought this from the Maoris – he did. Ye-es! Got if off Ole Puhui for a suit of clothes an' a lookin'-glass of yer Granmaw's. My stars! He had an eye! Larst thing the ole man says to me was – "James," 'e says, "don't you be muckin' about with that bit of land top of Makra Hill. Don't you sell it. 'And it on," 'e says, "to you an' yours." ' 'Wot d'you mean?' asked the little boy one day, sitting, his legs straight out, making finger gloves of the fairy trumpets. 'Why, wot I mean is – when I'm put away it'll be yours. See?' 'Wot – all this?' cried the little boy, frightened, clutching the hill, as though he expected it to lump away with him on its back, like a great green camel. 'All this!' echoed the father, solemn. 'All yours – once you're through the fence.' Nothing more was said until dinner. He sat with his bib round his neck, drinking tinned soup with Worcester sauce. 'Pop,' he said, 'I'm goin' to build an 'ouse on my hill. Big as . . .' and he stretched his arms wide.

Tar was an only child. His father was fifty when he was born, and his mother forty-three. They were strict, upright people, owners of the Wadesville general store and post office. They did brisk business, and every Saturday night Tar helped his father fasten the wooden shutter on which was printed 'Closed in God's name. Those whom the Lord loveth He chasteneth.' He was brought up so severely that his animal spirits never bubbled at all, and he lived in a sober simmer, behind his mother's skirts and his father's counter. The first thing that he remembered was that Sunday morning when his father told him Makra Hill would be his, and the telling took such strange hold of him that there was no room in his mind for anything else. All his plans and plots, all his games and dreams were of what he would do when he had it, and of the fine house he'd build. Sometimes it would be bigger than Government House in Wellington, with its hundred bedrooms and fine red carpets, with palm trees growing out of them, and other times it would be a little house, just room enough to hold him and 'something to set'. Then it would be a farm with all animals on it – even white pigs. At fourteen his father put him behind the counter – a little, pale, freckled boy, with a flop of black hair falling into his eyebrows. After the shop was shut he'd pull off his apron and get a hunk of bread and jam and be off at a run, not stopping to take breath or to look this side or that until he reached the windy hill with the brimming sea below. Every stone of the hill he thought he knew; every pocket and cranny he marched over, lord and master. Swelled up with pride he'd dig with his heel: 'I'll have me front door here, and the rain tanks here, under the balcony scuppers.' And on winter nights in the iron chapel when the rain beat with a million hammers on the roof and walls, and the preacher with a stuck-out beard boomed, 'An' the mountains shall skip like r-rams and the little hills like young sheep,' something jumped in Tar, like a flare in the dark. He saw himself running away from the place and through the fence on the top of it. And the Day of Judgement was come and the hill leaping . . .

When Tar was twenty his mother died. She was chopping up a candle-box in the backyard, and suddenly the tomahawk fell from her hand and she dropped. Just like that. Not a word. He thought quick, 'If it'd been Pop I'd have had my hill – sure,' and hid away the money she left him and began to save every penny for the house. He married at thirty a quiet girl who bossed him. And the business grew and grew, and by-and-by they were well off. They had to add a room now and again at the back of the shop for the children. 'Oh, why can't you build a nice place somewhere, Father?' the wife used to scold. 'You wait, my girl,' said Tar, his eyes suddenly fierce. At last, when he was fifty, and his father ninety-five, the old man stretched out, creaked his bones, and died. That was on a Sunday night. Monday morning, Old Tar hitched the buggy and drove off to Karori, like a man drunk or to his wedding-feast. He wore his best black suit, he cut at the trees as he passed, and greeted people with a grin and a chuckle, and stopped at the builders. 'Look 'ere, Mr. Stubbs. Will you come back with me? There's a piece of ground I want to show you. I've decided to build.' Not until they were half-way home he remembered to tell Stubbs the old man had gone.

All Wadesville and Karori watched the building of Tar's house. Parties drove up to see it, and picnicked on the piles of yellow, sweet-smelling wood. The store brimmed over with customers, and Mrs. Tar, in black, with her troop of black alpaca children, turned into a fine lady, and talked of nothing but the hinconvenience she'd suffered living in the shop for the sake of her 'usband's father and his sentimentalness. Old Tar, after one day's burst of excitement, kept his grim joy to himself. But he was mad inside, so hot that he felt all the hard years in him melting away. He spent half the day with the workmen, and a great big barn began to grow out of the scooped and jagged hole dug in the side of the hill. It grew quickly. The stairs were up. The flooring was done upstairs. He could creep up at evening to the front room and look through the window-hole at the sea. He would go up and take a lantern and walk from room to room, silent as a cat, feeding his delight And at last it was finished. Old Tar's house, painted white with green 'pickings', reared up ready at the top of the hill. 'We'll make a party an' all go up this evening,' said his wife, 'an' have a fair look'. 'No you don't,' said Old Tar. 'I got to be there. Business. Measuring. I got to have my 'ead quiet. You kin go termorrow.' She shrugged and obeyed. Tar left the shop early. The setting sun was drawing from the earth the strong, sweet scents of day. There was no wind; just a breeze rippled over the grass and shook the manuka flowers, like tiny white stars down the yellow clay banks of the new road. He walked slowly. No need to get through the fence – the fence was down and carted away. Heavy ruts were carved in the side of the hill, and there was a path to the front door strewn already with a load of white shells. The big white house, with all its hollow eyes, glared at Old Tar.

'It's big,' he thought, and he said as though he prayed, 'Oh, Lord, it is big!' The builders had left the key under the verandah. He felt and found it, and let himself in. At first the house was very still, then it creaked a little, and he heard a tap drip. It smelt strongly of paint and varnish and fine ripe wood. A pencil ray of sun shone across the stairs. As he watched, it shifted and disappeared. The sun had set. Old Tar, tip-toe in his creaking boots, walked through his dream, up and down, in and out, prying like a woman, conscious as a lover, wondering and touching things, and knocking them with his knuckles to hear how thick they sounded. At last he felt a bit tired. He sat down on the stairs. It had begun to grow dusky. The shadows of the door lay across the front hall, sharp and long. He took off his hard hat and leaned his head with the boyish flop of hair against the stair-rail. In the quiet he heard the sea beat, beat up, and then he heard the wind, very slow, snuffling round the house like a lonely dog. 'Ooh Hee! Oooh Hee!' it sounded. 'A rare, sad noise', thought Old Tar, shaking his head to it. 'Sounds as if it'd lost something an' couldn't find it again.' 'Lost for evermore', and the sad words fell into his quiet heart and started strange, uneasy ripples. Sitting by himself like that, he felt queer and frightened, somehow. 'Ooh Hee! Ooh Hee!' sounded the wind, rattling the window sashes. ' 'Tain't like it used to sound up here', he thought. ' 'Tain't like it was in the old man's time.' 'Shake out yer lungs, me lad', he heard old Pop say. Clear as a dream Old Tar saw his Pop and himself sitting where the house stood now, he with the pink, sticky flowers in his fingers, the hill shining and the sea shining below. And then, like a man in a dream, he took off his boots, and stole down into the hall, out

My dear, I wrote a story called 'Old Tar' the other day, about Makra Hill, and sent it to the Westminster who accepted it. I'll send you a copy . . . Don't leave the paper on the Karori road or I shall be taken up for libel.
to Jeanne, October 1913

The house of Mr James Tarr, Makara Hill

of the house. It was getting darker every minute. Thin clouds flew over an ashen sky. The grass between his feet, Old Tar stepped back from the house and looked up at it. He saw in the dusky light the pits the workmen had dug in his hill. He saw the great trampled patches the timber piles had made, and he saw, between him and the sea, the white house perched, the big white nest for his wife and her brood on the top of his hill. As though he saw it for the first time, Old Tar muttered in a strange voice, 'Wot's it doing there – wot's it for?' and 'Oh, Lord, wot 'ave I done – wot 'ave I done, Lord?' A long time Old Tar stood there, while the dark sifted over him and the house paled and stretched up to the sky. His feet seemed to freeze into the cold grass of the hill, and dark thoughts flew across his mind, like clouds, never quiet, never breaking.

'Old Tar' (*Westminster Gazette*, October 1913, the *New Zealand Times*, December 1913.)

This story's interest lies in its early exploration of her memories of Wellington. Makara Hill overlooks Karori on one side, and a wild rugged stretch of coast on the other. The Karori Historical Society's *Stockade* revealed that a Mr J. Tarr, later the mayor, built a house on Makara Hill about 1870. K.M. must have remembered it and the Makara coastline vividly from her childhood. Ian Gordon has pointed out that in order to give the house its dramatic view she relocated the sea some 12 kilometres inland! In a less striking change the Wellington suburb of Wadestown, where Charlotte had been born, became Wadesville. The story foreshadows *Prelude* and 'The Doll's House' and, although K.M. herself cannot have thought it worth including in the collections published during her lifetime, it has some interest in its own right as well as making an intriguing comparison with her later work.

The Wind Blows

Suddenly – dreadfully – she wakes up. What has happened? Something dreadful has happened. No – nothing has happened. It is only the wind shaking the house, rattling the windows, banging a piece of iron on the roof and making her bed tremble. Leaves flutter past the window, up and away; down in the avenue a whole newspaper wags in the air like a lost kite and falls, spiked on a pine tree. It is cold. Summer is over – it is autumn – everything is ugly. The carts rattle by, swinging from side to side; two Chinamen lollop along under their wooden yokes with the straining vegetable baskets – their pigtails and blue blouses fly out in the wind. A white dog on three legs yelps past the gate. It is all over! What is? Oh, everything! And she begins to plait her hair with shaking fingers, not daring to look in the glass. Mother is talking to grandmother in the hall.

'A perfect idiot! Imagine leaving anything out on the line in weather like this . . . Now my best little Teneriffe-work teacloth is simply in ribbons. *What* is that extraordinary smell? It's the porridge burning. Oh, heavens – this wind!'

She has a music lesson at ten o'clock. At the thought the minor movement of the Beethoven begins to play in her head, the trills long and terrible like little rolling drums . . . Marie Swainson runs into the garden next door to pick the 'chrysanths' before they are ruined. Her skirt flies up above her waist; she tries to beat it down, to tuck it between her legs while she stoops, but it is no use – up it flies. All the trees and bushes beat about her. She picks as quickly as she can, but she is quite distracted. She doesn't mind what she does – she pulls the plants up by the roots and bends and twists them, stamping her foot and swearing.

'For heaven's sake keep the front door shut! Go round to the back,' shouts someone. And then she hears Bogey:

'Mother, you're wanted on the telephone. Telephone, Mother. It's the butcher.'

How hideous life is – revolting, simply revolting . . . And now her hat-elastic's snapped. Of course it would. She'll wear her old tam and slip out the back way. But Mother has seen.

'Matilda. Matilda. Come back im-me-diately! What on earth have you got on your head? It looks like a tea-cosy. And why have you got that mane of hair on your forehead?'

'I can't come back, Mother. I'll be late for my lesson.'

down the asphalt zigzag
where the fennel grows wild
and on to the esplanade.

The Zig Zag, Tinakori Road

'Come back immediately!'

She won't. She won't. She hates Mother. 'Go to hell,' she shouts, running down the road.

In waves, in clouds, in big round whirls the dust comes stinging, and with it little bits of straw and chaff and manure. There is a loud roaring sound from the trees in the gardens, and standing at the bottom of the road outside Mr. Bullen's gate she can hear the sea sob: 'Ah! . . . Ah! . . . Ah-h!' But Mr. Bullen's drawing-room is as quiet as a cave. The windows are closed, the blinds half pulled, and she is not late. The-girl-before-her has just started playing MacDowell's 'To an Iceberg'. Mr. Bullen looks over at her and half smiles.

'Sit down,' he says. 'Sit over there in the sofa corner, little lady.'

How funny he is. He doesn't exactly laugh at you . . . but there is just something . . . Oh, how peaceful it is here. She likes this room. It smells of art serge and stale smoke and chrysanthemums . . . there is a big vase of them on the mantelpiece behind the pale photograph of Rubinstein . . . *à mon ami Robert Bullen* . . . Over the black glittering piano hangs 'Solitude' – a dark tragic woman draped in white, sitting on a rock, her knees crossed, her chin on her hands.

'No, no!' says Mr. Bullen, and he leans over the other girl, puts his arms over her shoulders and plays the passage for her. The stupid – she's blushing! How ridiculous!

Now the-girl-before-her has gone; the front door slams. Mr. Bullen comes back and walks up and down, very softly, waiting for her. What an extraordinary thing. Her fingers tremble so that she can't undo the knot in the music satchel. It's the wind . . . And her heart beats so hard she feels it must lift her blouse up and down. Mr. Bullen does not say a word. The shabby red piano seat is long enough for two people to sit side by side. Mr. Bullen sits down by her.

'Shall I begin with scales', she asks, squeezing her hands together. 'I had some arpeggios, too.'

But he does not answer. She doesn't believe he even hears . . . and then suddenly his fresh hand with the ring on it reaches over and opens Beethoven.

'Let's have a little of the old master,' he says.

But why does he speak so kindly – so awfully kindly – and as though they had known each other for years and years and knew everything about each other.

He turns the page slowly. She watches his hand – it is a very nice hand and always looks as though it had just been washed.

'Here we are,' says Mr. Bullen.

Oh, that kind voice – Oh, that minor movement. Here come the little drums . . .

'Shall I take the repeat?'

'Yes, dear child.'

His voice is far, far too kind. The crotchets and quavers are dancing up and down the stave like little black boys on a fence. Why is he so . . . She will not cry – she has nothing to cry about . . .

'What is it, dear child?'

Mr. Bullen takes her hands. His shoulder is there – just by her head. She leans on it ever so little, her cheek against the springy tweed.

'Life is so dreadful,' she murmurs, but she does not feel it's dreadful at all. He says something about 'waiting' and 'marking time' and 'that rare thing, a woman,' but she does not hear. It is so comfortable . . . for ever . . .

Suddenly the door opens and in pops Marie Swainson, hours before her time.

'Take the allegretto a little faster,' says Mr. Bullen, and gets up and begins to walk up and down again.

'Sit in the sofa corner, little lady,' he says to Marie.

The wind, the wind. It's frightening to be here in her room by herself. The bed, the mirror, the white jug and basin gleam like the sky outside. It's the bed that is frightening. There it lies, sound asleep . . . Does Mother imagine for one moment that she is going to darn all those stockings knotted up on the quilt like a coil of snakes? She's not. No, Mother. I do not see why I should . . . The wind – the wind! There's a funny smell of soot blowing down the chimney. Hasn't anyone written poems to the wind? . . . 'I bring fresh flowers to the leaves and showers.' . . . What nonsense.

'Is that you, Bogey?'

'Come for a walk round the esplanade, Matilda. I can't stand this any longer.'

'Right-o. I'll put on my ulster. Isn't it an awful day!' Bogey's ulster is just like hers. Hooking the collar she looks at herself in the glass. Her face is white, they have the same excited eyes and hot lips. Ah, they know those two in the glass. Good-bye, dears; we shall be back soon.

'This is better, isn't it?'

'Hook on,' says Bogey.

They cannot walk fast enough. Their heads bent, their legs just touching, they stride like one eager person through the town, down the asphalt zigzag where the fennel grows wild and on to the esplanade. It is dusky – just getting dusky. The wind is so strong that they have to fight their way through it, rocking like two old drunkards. All the poor little pohutukawas on the esplanade are bent to the ground.

'Come on! Come on! Let's get near.'

Over by the breakwater the sea is very high. They pull off their hats and her hair blows across her mouth, tasting of salt. The sea is so high that the waves do not break at all; they thump against the rough stone wall and suck up the weedy, dripping steps. A fine spray skims from the water right across the esplanade. They are covered with drops; the inside of her mouth tastes wet and cold.

Bogey's voice is breaking. When he speaks he rushes up and down the scale. It's funny – it makes you laugh – and yet it just suits the day. The wind carries their voices – away fly the sentences like little narrow ribbons.

'Quicker! Quicker!'

It is getting very dark. In the harbour the coal hulks show two lights – one high on a mast and one from the stern.

'Look, Bogey. Look over there.'

A big black steamer with a long loop of smoke streaming, with the portholes lighted, with lights everywhere, is putting out to sea. The wind does not stop her; she cuts through the waves, making for the open gate between the pointed rocks that leads to . . . It's the light that makes her look so awfully beautiful and mysterious.

They are on board leaning over the rail arm in arm.

'... Who are they?'

'... Brother and sister.'

'Look, Bogey, there's the town. Doesn't it look small? There's the post-office clock chiming for the last time. There's the esplanade where we walked that windy day. Do you remember? I cried at my music lesson that day – how many years ago! Good-bye, little island, good-bye ...'

Now the dark stretches a wing over the tumbling water. They can't see those two any more. Good-bye, good-bye. Don't forget ... But the ship is gone, now.

The wind – the wind.

'The Wind Blows' (the *Signature*, 4 October 1915, as 'Autumn II')

'It's the only one worth reprinting.' (to J. M. Murry, 5 February 1920)

'I put that in because so many people admired it ... Virginia, Lytton & queer people like Mary Hamilton & Bertie all spoke so strongly about it ...' (to J. M. Murry, 6 April 1920)

'It's blowing guns today – a choppy sea – my favourite sea, brilliant blue with white lifting ...' (to J. M. Murry, 7 October 1920)

'... at dusk an old ancient wind sprang up and it is shaking and complaining. A terrible wind – a wind that one always mercifully forgets until it comes again ... It brings nothing but memories ... that one cannot without pain remember. It always carries my brother to me.' (to Dorothy Brett, 19 December 1921)

'Dust. Turning one's back on a high, tearing wind. Walking along the Esplanade when the wind carries the sea over. The wind of summer, so playful, that rocked and swung in the trees here. And wind moving through grass so that the grass quivers. This moves me with an emotion I don't ever understand'. (Montana, 23 January 1922)

'her hauntingly beautiful Wellington fragment' (Antony Alpers, *Katherine Mansfield*)

'. . . carrying in its staccato expression the emotional turmoil of an adolescent girl. The rough wind blows through the story, pushing, whirling, tearing and the girl's rebellious spirit beats equally. Here mood and external scene are admirably identified.' (Sylvia Berkman, *Katherine Mansfield: A Critical Study*)

'With its curious time shift or dream shift toward the end, it is touched by the numinous, as her best work later was.' (Antony Alpers, *The Life of Katherine Mansfield*)

'the most purely symbolist of her stories to this date . . . a highly sophisticated and modernist story . . . achieving a new intensity.' (Claire Hanson and Andrew Gurr, *Katherine Mansfield*)

Clearly based on the memories she had shared with Leslie during the summer of 1915, this story has a strange power. Matilda is K.M., she used the pseudonym Matilda Berry at this time, while Bogey was the family name for Leslie, which K.M. later transferred to Murry. It gives a hint, too, of the Trowells' house in Buller Street which must have been central to her artistic development. This presumably led her to the choice of the music teacher's name – Mr Bullen. Could her remarkable memory have failed her by one letter, was the change deliberate, or was there perhaps an error in transcribing the story from her handwriting? Is Mr Bullen another composite figure, based on Mr Trowell and her piano teacher Mr Robert Parker?

Anyone who has lived in Wellington will recognise immediately the relentless wind that drives inexorably through the story; not for nothing is K.M.'s birthplace nicknamed 'Windy Wellington'. It is also, with the sea, a dominant symbol in this story about a girl's transition into the adult world. It is a sharp contrast to 'The Woman at the Store'; some readers complain 'but it's not a *story*, nothing *happens*.' It is a story of a different kind, oblique, episodic, with its shift in time level, and the move into interior monologue at the beginning of the second part.

'Don't forget' – how ironic her own admonition in the closing lines must have seemed when her brother died only days after the story appeared.

Bliss

Although Bertha Young was thirty she still had moments like this when she wanted to run instead of walk, to take dancing steps on and off the pavement, to bowl a hoop, to throw something up in the air and catch it again, or to stand still and laugh at – nothing – at nothing, simply.

What can you do if you are thirty and, turning the corner of your own street, you are overcome, suddenly, by a feeling of bliss – absolute bliss! – as though you'd suddenly swallowed a bright piece of that late afternoon sun and it burned in your bosom, sending out a little shower of sparks into every particle, into every finger and toe? . . .

Oh, is there no way you can express it without being 'drunk and disorderly'? How idiotic civilisation is! Why be given a body if you have to keep it shut up in a case like a rare, rare fiddle?

'No, that about the fiddle is not quite what I mean,' she thought, running up the steps and feeling in her bag for the key – she'd forgotten it, as usual – and rattling the letter-box. 'It's not what I mean, because – Thank you, Mary' – she went into the hall. 'Is nurse back?'

'Yes, M'm.'

'And has the fruit come?'

'Yes, M'm. Everything's come.'

'Bring the fruit up to the dining-room, will you? I'll arrange it before I go upstairs.'

It was dusky in the dining-room and quite chilly. But all the same Bertha threw off her coat; she could not bear the tight clasp of it another moment, and the cold air fell on her arms.

But in her bosom there was still that bright glowing place – that shower of little sparks coming from it. It was almost unbearable. She hardly dared to breathe for fear of fanning it higher, and yet she breathed deeply, deeply. She hardly dared to look into the cold mirror – but she did look, and it gave her back a woman, radiant, with smiling, trembling lips, with big, dark eyes and an air of listening, waiting for something . . . divine to happen . . . that she knew must happen . . . infallibly.

Mary brought in the fruit on a tray and with it a glass bowl, and a blue dish, very lovely, with a strange sheen on it as though it had been dipped in milk.

'Shall I turn on the light, M'm?'

'No, thank you. I can see quite well.'

There were tangerines and apples stained with strawberry pink. Some yellow pears, smooth as silk, some white grapes covered with a silver bloom and a big cluster of purple ones. These last she had bought to tone in with the new dining-room carpet. Yes, that did sound rather far-fetched and absurd, but it was really why she had bought them. She had thought in the shop: 'I must have some purple ones to bring the carpet up to the table.' And it had seemed quite sense at the time.

When she had finished with them and had made two pyramids of these bright round shapes, she stood away from the table to get the effect – and it really was most curious. For the dark table seemed to melt into the dusky light and the glass dish and the blue bowl to float in the air. This, of course, in her present mood, was so incredibly beautiful . . . She began to laugh.

'No, no. I'm getting hysterical.' And she seized her bag and coat and ran upstairs to the nursery.

Nurse sat at a low table giving Little B her supper after her bath. The baby had on a white flannel gown and a blue woollen jacket, and her dark, fine hair was brushed up into a funny little peak. She looked up when she saw her mother and began to jump.

'Now, my lovey, eat it up like a good girl,' said nurse, setting her lips in a way that Bertha knew, and that meant she had come into the nursery at another wrong moment.

'Has she been good, Nanny?'

'She's been a little sweet all the afternoon,' whispered Nanny. 'We went to the park and I sat down on a chair and took her out of the pram and a big dog came along and put its head on my knee and she clutched its ear, tugged it. Oh, you should have seen her.'

Bertha wanted to ask if it wasn't rather dangerous to let her clutch at a strange dog's ear. But she did not dare to. She stood watching them, her hands by her side, like the poor little girl in front of the rich little girl with the doll.

The baby looked up at her again, stared, and then smiled so charmingly that Bertha couldn't help crying:

'Oh, Nanny, do let me finish giving her her supper while you put the bath things away.'

'Well, M'm, she oughtn't to be changed hands while she's eating,' said Nanny, still whispering. 'It unsettles her; it's very likely to upset her.'

How absurd it was. Why have a baby if it has to be kept – not in a case like a rare, rare fiddle – but in another woman's arms?

'Oh, I must!' said she.

Very offended, Nanny handed her over.

'Now, don't excite her after her supper. You know you do, M'm. And I have such a time with her after!'

Thank heaven! Nanny went out of the room with the bath towels.

'Now I've got you to myself, my little precious,' said Bertha, as the baby leaned against her.

She ate delightfully, holding up her lips for the spoon and then waving her hands. Sometimes she wouldn't let the spoon go; and sometimes, just as Bertha had filled it, she waved it away to the four winds.

When the soup was finished Bertha turned round to the fire.

'You're nice – you're very nice!' said she, kissing her warm baby. 'I'm fond of you. I like you.'

And, indeed, she loved Little B so much – her neck as she bent forward, her exquisite toes as they shone transparent in the fire-light – that all her feeling of bliss came back again, and again she didn't know how to express it – what to do with it.

'You're wanted on the telephone,' said Nanny, coming back in triumph and seizing *her* Little B.

Down she flew. It was Harry.

'Oh, is that you, Ber? Look here. I'll be late. I'll take a taxi and come along as quickly as I can, but get dinner put back ten minutes – will you? All right?'

'Yes, perfectly. Oh, Harry!'

'Yes?'

What had she to say? She'd nothing to say. She only wanted to get in touch with him for a moment. She couldn't absurdly cry: 'Hasn't it been a divine day!'

'What is it?' rapped out the little voice.

'Nothing. *Entendu*,' said Bertha, and hung up the receiver, thinking how much more than idiotic civilisation was.

They had people coming to dinner. The Norman Knights – a very sound couple – he was about to start a theatre, and she was awfully keen on interior decoration; a young man, Eddie Warren, who had just published a little book of poems and whom every-body was asking to dine, and a 'find' of Bertha's called Pearl Fulton. What Miss Fulton did, Bertha didn't know. They had met at the club and Bertha had fallen in love with her, as she always did fall in love with beautiful women who had something strange about them.

The provoking thing was that, though they had been about to-gether and met a number of times and really talked, Bertha couldn't make her out. Up to a certain point Miss Fulton was rarely, wonderfully frank, but the certain point was there, and beyond that she would not go.

Was there anything beyond it? Harry said 'No'. Voted her dullish, and 'cold like all blonde women, with a touch, perhaps, of anaemia of the brain.' But Bertha wouldn't agree with him; not yet, at any rate.

'No, the way she has of sitting with her head a little on one side, and smiling, has something behind it, Harry, and I must find out what that something is.'

'Most likely it's a good stomach,' answered Harry.

He made a point of catching Bertha's heels with replies of that kind . . . 'liver frozen, my dear girl,' or 'pure flatulence,' or 'kidney disease,' . . . and so on. For some strange reason Bertha liked this, and almost admired it in him very much.

She went into the drawing-room and lighted the fire; then, picking up the cushions, one by one, that Mary had disposed so carefully, she threw them back on to the chairs and the couches. That made all the difference; the room came alive at once. As she was about to throw the last one she surprised herself by suddenly hugging it to her, passionately, passionately. But it did not put out the fire in her bosom. Oh, on the contrary!

The windows of the drawing-room opened on to a balcony overlooking the garden. At the far end, against the wall, there was a tall, slender pear tree in fullest, richest bloom; it stood perfect, as though becalmed against the jade-green sky. Bertha couldn't help feeling, even from this distance, that it had not a single bud or a faded petal. Down below, in the garden beds, the red and yellow tulips, heavy with flowers, seemed to lean upon the dusk. A grey cat, dragging its belly, crept cross the lawn, and a black one, its shadow, trailed after. The sight of them, so intent and so quick, gave Bertha a curious shiver.

'What creepy things cats are!' she stammered, and she turned away from the window and began walking up and down . . .

How strong the jonquils smelled in the warm room. Too strong? Oh, no. And yet, as though overcome, she flung down on a couch and pressed her hands to her eyes.

'I'm too happy – too happy!' she murmured.

And she seemed to see on her eyelids the lovely pear tree with its wide open blossoms as a symbol of her own life.

Really – really – she had everything. She was young. Harry and she were as much in love as ever, and they got on together splendidly and were really good pals. She had an adorable baby. They didn't have to worry about money. They had this absolutely satisfactory house and garden. And friends – modern, thrilling friends, writers and painters and poets or people keen on social questions

– just the kind of friends they wanted. And then there were books, and there was music, and she had found a wonderful little dressmaker, and they were going abroad in the summer, and their new cook made the most superb omelettes . . .

'I'm absurd. Absurd!' She sat up; but she felt quite dizzy, quite drunk. It must have been the spring.

Yes, it was the spring. Now she was so tired she could not drag herself upstairs to dress.

A white dress, a string of jade beads, green shoes and stockings. It wasn't intentional. She had thought of this scheme hours before she stood at the drawing-room window.

Her petals rustled softly into the hall, and she kissed Mrs. Norman Knight, who was taking off the most amusing orange coat with a procession of black monkeys round the hem and up the fronts.

' . . . Why! Why! Why is the middle-class so stodgy – so utterly without a sense of humour! My dear, it's only by a fluke that I am here at all – Norman being the protective fluke. For my darling monkeys so upset the train that it rose to a man and simply ate me with its eyes. Didn't laugh – wasn't amused – that I should have loved. No, just stared – and bored me through and through.'

'But the cream of it was,' said Norman, pressing a large tortoiseshell-rimmed monocle into his eye, 'you don't mind me telling this, Face, do you?' (In their home and among their friends they called each other Face and Mug.) 'The cream of it was when she, being full fed, turned to the woman beside her and said: "Haven't you ever seen a monkey before?"'

'Oh yes!' Mrs. Norman Knight joined in the laughter. 'Wasn't that too absolutely creamy?'

And a funnier thing still was that now her coat was off she did look like a very intelligent monkey – who had even made that yellow silk dress out of scraped banana skins. And her amber earrings: they were like little dangling nuts.

'This is a sad, sad fall!' said Mug, pausing in front of Little B's perambulator. 'When the perambulator comes into the hall –' and he waved the rest of the quotation away.

The bell rang. It was lean, pale Eddie Warren (as usual) in a state of acute distress.

'It *is* the right house, *isn't* it?' he pleaded.

'Oh, I think so – I hope so,' said Bertha brightly.

'I have had such a *dreadful* experience with a taxi-man; he was *most* sinister. I couldn't get him to *stop*. The *more* I knocked and called the *faster* he went. And *in* the moonlight this *bizarre* figure with the *flattened* head *crouching* over the *lit-tle* wheel . . . '

He shuddered, taking off an immense white silk scarf. Bertha noticed that his socks were white, too – most charming.

'But how dreadful!' she cried.

'Yes, it really was,' said Eddie, following her into the drawing-room. 'I saw myself *driving* through Eternity in a *timeless* taxi.'

He knew the Norman Knights. In fact, he was going to write a play for N. K. when the theatre scheme came off.

'Well, Warren, how's the play?' said Norman Knight, dropping his monocle and giving his eye a moment in which to rise to the surface before it was screwed down again.

And Mrs. Norman Knight: 'Oh, Mr. Warren, what happy socks?'

'I *am* so glad you like them,' said he, staring at his feet. 'They seem to have got so *much* whiter since the moon rose.' And he turned his lean sorrowful young face to Bertha. 'There *is* a moon, you know.'

She wanted to cry: 'I am sure there is – often – often!'

He really was a most attractive person. But so was Face, crouched before the fire in her banana skins, and so was Mug, smoking a cigarette and saying as he flicked the ash: 'Why doth the bridegroom tarry?'

'There he is, now.'

Bang went the front door open and shut. Harry shouted: 'Hullo, you people. Down in five minutes.' And they heard him swarm up the stairs. Bertha couldn't help smiling; she knew how he loved doing things at high pressure. What, after all, did an extra five minutes matter? But he would pretend to himself that they mattered beyond measure. And then he would make a great point of coming into the drawing-room, extravagantly cool and collected.

Harry had such a zest for life. Oh, how she appreciated it in him. And his passion for fighting – for seeking in everything that came up against him another test of his power and of his courage – that, too, she understood. Even when it made him just occasionally, to other people, who didn't know him well, a little ridiculous perhaps . . . For there were moments when he rushed into battle where no battle was . . . She talked and laughed and positively forgot until he had come in (just as she had imagined) that Pearl Fulton had not turned up.

'I wonder if Miss Fulton has forgotten?'

'I expect so,' said Harry. 'Is she on the 'phone?'

'Ah! There's a taxi now.' And Bertha smiled with that little air of proprietorship that she always assumed while her women finds were new and mysterious. 'She lives in taxis.'

'She'll run to fat if she does,' said Harry coolly, ringing the bell for dinner. 'Frightful danger for blonde women.'

'Harry – don't,' warned Bertha, laughing up at him.   Came

another tiny moment, while they waited, laughing and talking, just a trifle too much at ease, a trifle too unaware. And then Miss Fulton, all in silver, with a silver fillet binding her pale blonde hair, came in smiling, her head a little on one side.

'Am I late?'

'No, not at all,' said Bertha. 'Come along.' And she took her arm and they moved into the dining-room.

What was there in the touch of that cool arm that could fan – fan – start blazing – the fire of bliss that Bertha did not know what to do with?

Miss Fulton did not look at her; but then she seldom did look at people directly. Her heavy eyelids lay upon her eyes and the strange half-smile came and went upon her lips as though she lived by listening rather than seeing. But Bertha knew, suddenly, as if the longest, most intimate look had passed between them – as if they had said to each other: 'You, too?' – that Pearl Fulton, stirring the beautiful red soup in the grey plate, was feeling just what she was feeling.

And the others? Face and Mug, Eddie and Harry, their spoons rising and falling – dabbing their lips with their napkins, crumbling bread, fiddling with the forks and glasses and talking.

'I met her at the Alpha show – the weirdest little person. She'd not only cut off her hair, but she seemed to have taken a dreadfully good snip off her legs and arms and her neck and her poor little nose as well.'

'Isn't she very *liée* with Michael Oat?'

'The man who wrote *Love in False Teeth*?'

'He wants to write a play for me. One act. One man. Decides to commit suicide. Gives all the reasons why he should and why he shouldn't. And just as he has made up his mind either to do it or not to do it – curtain. Not half a bad idea.'

'What's he going to call it – "Stomach Trouble"?'

'I *think* I've come across the *same* idea in a lit-tle French review, *quite* unknown in England.'

No, they didn't share it. They were dears – dears – and she loved having them there, at her table, and giving them delicious food and wine. In fact, she longed to tell them how delightful they were, and what a decorative group they made, how they seemed to set one another off and how they reminded her of a play by Tchekof!

Harry was enjoying his dinner. It was part of his – well, not his nature, exactly, and certainly not his pose – his – something or other – to talk about food and to glory in his 'shameless passion for the white flesh of the lobster' and 'the green of pistachio ices – green and cold like the eyelids of Egyptian dancers.'

When he looked up at her and said: 'Bertha, this is a very

admirable *soufflé*!' she almost could have wept with child-like pleasure.

Oh, why did she feel so tender towards the whole world to-night? Everything was good – was right. All that happened seemed to fill again her brimming cup of bliss.

And still, in the back of her mind, there was the pear tree. It would be silver now, in the light of poor dear Eddie's moon, silver as Miss Fulton, who sat there turning a tangerine in her slender fingers that were so pale a light seemed to come from them.

What she simply couldn't make out – what was miraculous – was how she should have guessed Miss Fulton's mood so exactly and so instantly. For she never doubted for a moment that she was right, and yet what had she to go on? Less than nothing.

'I believe this does happen very, very rarely between women. Never between men,' thought Bertha. 'But while I am making the coffee in the drawing-room perhaps she will "give a sign." '

What she meant by that she did not know, and what would happen after that she could not imagine.

While she thought like this she saw herself talking and laughing. She had to talk because of her desire to laugh.

'I must laugh or die.'

But when she noticed Face's funny little habit of tucking something down the front of her bodice – as if she kept a tiny, secret hoard of nuts there, too – Bertha had to dig her nails into her hands – so as not to laugh too much.

It was over at last. And: 'Come and see my new coffee machine,' said Bertha.

'We only have a new coffee machine once a fortnight,' said Harry. Face took her arm this time; Miss Fulton bent her head and followed after.

The fire had died down in the drawing-room to a red, flickering 'nest of baby phoenixes', said Face.

'Don't turn up the light for a moment. It is so lovely.' And down she crouched by the fire again. She was always cold ... 'without her little red flannel jacket, of course,' thought Bertha.

At that moment Miss Fulton 'gave the sign.'

'Have you a garden?' said the cool, sleepy voice.

This was so exquisite on her part that all Bertha could do was to obey. She crossed the room, pulled the curtains apart, and opened those long windows.

'There!' she breathed.

And the two women stood side by side looking at the slender, flowering tree. Although it was so still it seemed, like the flame of a candle, to stretch up, to point, to quiver in the bright air, to grow taller and taller as they *gazed* – almost to touch the rim of the round, silver moon.

How long did they stand there? Both, as it were, caught in that circle of unearthly light, understanding each other perfectly, creatures of another world, and wondering what they were to do in this one with all this blissful treasure that burned in their bosoms and dropped, in silver flowers, from their hair and hands?

For ever – for a moment? And did Miss Fulton murmur: 'Yes. Just *that*.' Or did Bertha dream it?

Then the light was snapped on and Face made the coffee and Harry said: 'My dear Mrs. Knight, don't ask me about my baby. I never see her. I shan't feel the slightest interest in her until she has a lover,' and Mug took his eye out of the conservatory for a moment and then put it under glass again and Eddie Warren drank his coffee and set down the cup with a face of anguish as though he had drunk and seen the spider.

'What I want to do is to give the young men a show. I believe London is simply teeming with first-chop, unwritten plays. What I want to say to 'em is: "Here's the theatre. Fire ahead." '

'You know, my dear, I am going to decorate a room for the Jacob Nathans. Oh, I am so tempted to do a fried-fish scheme, with the backs of the chairs shaped like frying-pans and lovely chip potatoes embroidered all over the curtains.'

'The trouble with our young writing men is that they are still too romantic. You can't put out to sea without being sea-sick and wanting a basin. Well, why won't they have the courage of those basins?'

'A *dreadful* poem about a *girl* who was *violated* by a beggar *without* a nose in a lit-tle wood . . . '

Miss Fulton sank into the lowest, deepest chair and Harry handed round the cigarettes.

From the way he stood in front of her shaking the silver box and saying abruptly: 'Egyptian? Turkish? Virginian? They're all mixed up,' Bertha realised that she not only bored him; he really disliked her. And she decided from the way Miss Fulton said: 'No, thank you, I won't smoke,' that she felt it, too, and was hurt.

'Oh, Harry, don't dislike her. You are quite wrong about her. She's wonderful, wonderful. And, besides, how can you feel so differently about someone who means so much to me. I shall try to tell you when we are in bed to-night what has been happening. What she and I have shared.'

At those last words something strange and almost terrifying darted into Bertha's mind. And this something blind and smiling whispered to her: 'Soon these people will go. The house will be quiet – quiet. The lights will be out. And you and he will be alone together in the dark room – the warm bed . . . '

She jumped up from her chair and ran over to the piano.

'What a pity someone does not play!' she cried. 'What a pity somebody does not play.'

For the first time in her life Bertha Young desired her husband.

Oh, she'd loved him – she'd been in love with him, of course, in every other way, but just not in that way. And equally, of course, she'd understood that he was different. They'd discussed it so often. It had worried her dreadfully at first to find that she was so cold, but after a time it had not seemed to matter. They were so frank with each other – such good pals. That was the best of being modern.

But now – ardently! The word ached in her ardent body! Was this what that feeling of bliss had been leading up to? But then, then –

'My dear,' said Mrs. Norman Knight, 'you know our shame. We are the victims of time and train. We live in Hampstead. It's been so nice.'

'I'll come with you into the hall,' said Bertha. 'I loved having you. But you must not miss the last train. That's so awful, isn't it?'

'Have a whisky, Knight, before you go?' called Harry.

'No, thanks, old chap.'

Bertha squeezed his hand for that as she took it.

'Good night, good-bye,' she cried from the top step, feeling that this self of hers was taking leave of them for ever.

When she got back into the drawing-room the others were on the move.

'. . . Then you can come part of the way in my taxi.'

'I shall be *so* thankful *not* to have to face *another* drive *alone* after my *dreadful* experience.'

'You can get a taxi at the rank just at the end of the street. You won't have to walk more than a few yards.'

'That's a comfort. I'll go and put on my coat.'

Miss Fulton moved towards the hall and Bertha was following when Harry almost pushed past.

'Let me help you.'

Bertha knew that he was repenting his rudeness – she let him go. What a boy he was in some ways – so impulsive – so simple.

And Eddie and she were left by the fire.

'I *wonder* if you have seen Bilks' *new* poem called *Table d' Hôte,*' said Eddie softly. 'It's *so* wonderful. In the last Anthology. Have you got a copy? I'd *so* like to *show* it to you. It begins with an *incredibly* beautiful line: "Why Must it Always be Tomato Soup?" '.

'Yes,' said Bertha. And she moved noiselessly to a table opposite the drawing-room door and Eddie glided noiselessly after her. She picked up the little book and gave it to him; they had not made a sound.

While he looked it up she turned her head towards the hall. And she saw . . . Harry with Miss Fulton's coat in his arms and Miss Fulton with her back turned to him and her head bent. He tossed the coat away, put his hands on her shoulders and turned her violently to him. His lips said: 'I adore you,' and Miss Fulton laid her moonbeam fingers on his cheeks and smiled her sleepy smile. Harry's nostrils quivered; his lips curled back in a hideous grin while he whispered: 'To-morrow,' and with her eyelids Miss Fulton said: 'Yes.'

'Here it is,' said Eddie. ' "Why Must it Always be Tomato Soup?" It's so *deeply* true, don't you feel? Tomato soup is so *dreadfully* eternal.'

'If you prefer,' said Harry's voice, very loud, from the hall, 'I can 'phone you a cab to come to the door.'

'Oh, no. It's not necessary,' said Miss Fulton, and she came up to Bertha and gave her the slender fingers to hold.

'Good-bye. Thank you so much.'

'Good-bye,' said Bertha.

Miss Fulton held her hand a moment longer.

'Your lovely pear tree!' she murmured.

And then she was gone, with Eddie following, like the black cat following the grey cat.

'I'll shut up shop,' said Harry, extravagantly cool and collected.

'Your lovely pear tree – pear tree – pear tree!'

Bertha simply ran over to the long windows.

'Oh, what is going to happen now?' she cried.

But the pear tree was as lovely as ever and as full of flower and as still.

'Bliss' (the *English Review*, August 1918)

'But though, God! I *have* enjoyed writing it, I am an absolute rag for the rest of the day . . . Please try and like it . . . You will "recognise" some of the people. *Eddie* of course is a fish out of the Garsington pond (which gives me joy) and Harry is touched with W.L.G. Miss Fulton is "my own invention". . .' (to J. M. Murry, 28 February 1918)

'Her next collection of stories won't have a trace of the cynicism that carried "Bliss" through the London drawing-rooms. They may possibly touch the larger public; but the clever intelligentsia will say: "How disap*point*ing!" ' (J. M. Murry to Sydney Waterlow, 11 July 1921)

'. . . the whole conception is poor, cheap, not the vision, however imperfect, of an interesting mind. She writes badly too. And the effect was as I say, to give me an impression of her callousness and hardness as a human being.' (*The Diary of Virginia Woolf*, 7 August 1918)

'a sophisticated failure . . . the discordant combination of caricature with emotional pathos.' (J. M. Murry in *Katherine Mansfield and other Literary Portraits*)

'The carefully rounded, highly plotted story . . . done superlatively well.' (*New York Times Book Review*, 5 August 1923)

'This story has been much admired, and its fame persists. I find it ultimately heartless, for while its women are human beings, the men are mere types . . . in the end we don't much care what happens to anyone. The satire of arty London drawing-rooms is as clever and thin as that of Aldous Huxley, himself the model for Eddie.' (Antony Alpers, *The Life of Katherine Mansfield*)

'one of Katherine Mansfield's most discussed and most controversial stories; and it is also among her most ambiguous . . . while critics have been unanimous about the effectiveness of her witty caricature of London's pseudo-bohemian "art set", they have been divided about the story's overall significance.' '. . . one of Katherine Mansfield's most horrifying psychological studies: a near surrealistic portrait of an immature woman caught up in a web of perversion.' (C.A. Hankin, *Katherine Mansfield and Her Confessional Stories*)

It is possible to read this story many times at different levels and on each reading to notice a new detail. It did much to establish K.M.'s reputation as a 'modern' writer. Although Virginia Woolf despised it, T. S. Eliot and others regarded it with considerable interest. There is clever satire in the grotesque caricature of the London/Garsington intelligentsia, yet there are moments of quite lyrical beauty and colour which impress themselves on the mind with vivid clarity. Through the character of Bertha, K.M. explores the nature of feminine friendship and female sexuality, both of which are recurring preoccupations in much of her work. Underneath the brittle sophistication the reader senses the underlying tension as it mounts to its disquieting climax. The abrupt ending leaves the reader wondering what will happen to Bertha now that she finally understands the irony of that bliss that earlier 'she did not know what to do with'. Will she finally grow up – or is she trapped in this deceptive world of polite pretence? The story works through symbolism, carefully selected detail and the clever unobtrusive fusing of the central character and narrator.

Pictures

Eight o'clock in the morning. Miss Ada Moss lay in a black iron bedstead, staring up at the ceiling. Her room, a Bloomsbury top-floor back, smelled of soot and face powder and the paper of fried potatoes she brought in for supper the night before.

'Oh, dear,' thought Miss Moss, 'I am cold. I wonder why it is that I always wake up so cold in the mornings now. My knees and feet and my back – especially my back; it's like a sheet of ice. And I always was such a one for being warm in the old days. It's not as if I was skinny – I'm just the same full figure that I used to be. No, it's because I don't have a good hot dinner in the evenings.'

A pageant of Good Hot Dinners passed across the ceiling, each of them accompanied by a bottle of Nourishing Stout . . .

'Even if I were to get up now,' she thought, 'and have a sensible substantial breakfast. . . ' A pageant of Sensible Substantial Breakfasts followed the dinners across the ceiling, shepherded by an enormous, white, uncut ham. Miss Moss shuddered and disappeared under the bedclothes. Suddenly, in bounced the landlady.

'There's a letter for you, Miss Moss.'

'Oh,' said Miss Moss, far too friendly, 'thank you very much, Mrs. Pine. It's very good of you, I'm sure, to take the trouble.'

'No trouble at all,' said the landlady. 'I thought perhaps it was the letter you'd been expecting.'

'Why,' said Miss Moss brightly, 'yes, perhaps it is.' She put her head on one side and smiled vaguely at the letter. 'I shouldn't be surprised.'

The landlady's eyes popped. 'Well, I should, Miss Moss,' said she, 'and that's how it is. And I'll trouble you to open it, if you please. Many is the lady in my place as would have done it for you and have been within her rights. For things can't go on like this, Miss Moss, no indeed they can't. What with week in week out and first you've got it and then you haven't, and then it's another letter lost in the post or another manager down at Brighton but will be back on Tuesday for certain – I'm fair sick and tired and I won't stand it no more. Why should I, Miss Moss, I ask you, at a time like this, with prices flying up in the air and my poor dear lad in France? My sister Eliza was only saying to me yesterday – "Minnie," she says, "you're too soft-hearted. You could have let that room time and time again," says she, "and if people won't look after themselves in times like these, nobody else will," she says.

"She may have had a College eddication and sung in West End concerts," says she, "but if your Lizzie says what's true," she says, "and she's washing her own wovens and drying them on the towel rail, it's easy to see where the finger's pointing. And it's high time you had done with it," says she.'

Miss Moss gave no sign of having heard this. She sat up in bed, tore open her letter and read:

'*Dear Madam*,

Yours to hand. Am not producing at present, but have filed photo for future ref.

Yours truly,
BACKWASH FILM CO.'

This letter seemed to afford her peculiar satisfaction; she read it through twice before replying to the landlady.

'Well, Mrs. Pine, I think you'll be sorry for what you said. This is from a manager, asking me to be there with evening dress at ten o'clock next Saturday morning.'

But the landlady was too quick for her. She pounced, secured the letter.

'Oh, is it! Is it indeed!' she cried.

'Give me back that letter. Give it back to me at once, you bad, wicked woman,' cried Miss Moss, who could not get out of bed because her nightdress was slit down the back. 'Give me back my private letter.' The landlady began slowly backing out of the room, holding the letter to her buttoned bodice.

'So it's come to this, has it?' said she. 'Well, Miss Moss, if I don't get my rent at eight o'clock to-night, we'll see who's a bad, wicked woman – that's all.' Here she nodded mysteriously. 'And I'll keep this letter.' Here her voice rose. 'It will be a pretty little bit of evidence!' And here it fell, sepulchral, '*My lady.*'

The door banged and Miss Moss was alone. She flung off the bedclothes, and sitting by the side of the bed, furious and shivering, she stared at her fat white legs with their great knots of greeny-blue veins.

'Cockroach! That's what she is. She's a cockroach!' said Miss Moss. 'I could have her up for snatching my letter – I'm sure I could.' Still keeping on her nightdress she began to drag on her clothes.

'Oh, if I could only pay that woman, I'd give her a piece of my mind that she wouldn't forget. I'd tell her off proper.' She went over to the chest of drawers for a safety-pin, and seeing herself in the glass she gave a vague smile and shook her head. 'Well, old girl,' she murmured, 'you're up against it this time, and no mistake.' But the person in the glass made an ugly face at her.

'You silly thing,' scolded Miss Moss. 'Now what's the good of crying: you'll only make your nose red. No, you get dressed and go out and try your luck – that's what you've got to do.'

She unhooked her vanity bag from the bedpost, rooted in it, shook it, turned it inside out.

'I'll have a nice cup of tea at an A B C to settle me before I go anywhere,' she decided. 'I've got one and thrippence – yes, just one and three.'

Ten minutes later, a stout lady in blue serge, with a bunch of artificial 'parmas' at her bosom, a black hat covered with purple pansies, white gloves, boots with white uppers, and a vanity bag containing one and three, sang in a low contralto voice:

'Sweet-heart, remember when days are forlorn
It al-ways is dar-kest before the dawn.'

But the person in the glass made a face at her, and Miss Moss went out. There were grey crabs all the way down the street slopping water over grey stone steps. With his strange, hawking cry and the jangle of the cans the milk-boy went his rounds. Outside Brittweiler's Swiss House he made a splash, and an old brown cat without a tail appeared from nowhere, and began greedily and silently drinking up the spill. It gave Miss Moss a queer feeling to watch – a sinking, as you might say.

But when she came to the A B C she found the door propped open; a man went in and out carrying trays of rolls, and there was nobody inside except a waitress doing her hair and the cashier unlocking the cash-boxes. She stood in the middle of the floor but neither of them saw her.

'My boy came home last night,' sang the waitress.

'Oh, I say – how topping for you!' gurgled the cashier.

'Yes, wasn't it,' sang the waitress. 'He brought me a sweet little brooch. Look, it's got "Dieppe" written on it.'

The cashier ran across to look and put her arm round the waitress's neck.

'Oh, I say – how topping for you.'

'Yes, isn't it,' said the waitress. 'O-oh, he is brahn. "Hullo," I said, "hullo, old mahogany." '

'Oh, I say,' gurgled the cashier, running back into her cage and nearly bumping into Miss Moss on the way. 'You are a *treat*!' Then the man with the rolls came in again, swerving past her.

'Can I have a cup of tea, Miss?' she asked.

But the waitress went on doing her hair. 'Oh,' she sang, 'we're not *open* yet.' She turned round and waved her comb at the cashier.

'*Are* we, dear?'

'Oh no,' said the cashier. Miss Moss went out.

'I'll go to Charing Cross. Yes, that's what I'll do,' she decided. 'But I won't have a cup of tea. No, I'll have a coffee. There's more of a tonic in coffee . . . Cheeky, those girls are! Her boy came home last night; he brought her a brooch with "Dieppe" written on it.' She began to cross the road . . .

'Look out, Fattie; don't go to sleep!' yelled a taxi-driver. She pretended not to hear.

'No, I won't go to Charing Cross,' she decided. 'I'll go straight to Kig and Kadgit. They're open at nine. If I get there early Mr. Kadgit may have something by the morning's post . . . I'm very glad you turned up so early, Miss Moss. I've just heard from a manager who wants a lady to play . . . I think you'll just suit him. I'll give you a card to go and see him. It's three pounds a week and all found. If I were you I'd hop round as fast as I could. Lucky you turned up so early . . . '

But there was nobody at Kig and Kadgit's except the char-woman wiping over the 'lino' in the passage.

'Nobody here yet, Miss,' said the char.

'Oh, isn't Mr. Kadgit here?' said Miss Moss, trying to dodge the pail and brush. 'Well, I'll just wait a moment, if I may.'

'You can't wait in the waiting-room, Miss. I 'aven't done it yet. Mr. Kadgit's never 'ere before 'leven-thirty Saturdays. Sometimes 'e don't come at all.' And the char began crawling towards her.

'Dear me – how silly of me,' said Miss Moss. 'I forgot it was Saturday.'

'Mind your feet, *please*, Miss,' said the char. And Miss Moss was outside again.

That was one thing about Beit and Bithems; it was lively. You walked into the waiting-room, into a great buzz of conversation, and there was everybody; you knew almost everybody. The early ones sat on chairs and the later ones sat on the early ones' laps, while the gentlemen leaned negligently against the walls or preened themselves in front of the admiring ladies.

'Hello,' said Miss Moss, very gay. 'Here we are again!'

And young Mr. Clayton, playing the banjo on his walking-stick, sang: 'Waiting for the Robert E. Lee.'

'Mr. Bithem here yet?' asked Miss Moss, taking out an old dead powder-puff and powdering her nose mauve.

'Oh yes, dear,' cried the chorus. 'He's been here for ages. We've all been waiting here for more than an hour.'

'Dear me!' said Miss Moss. 'Anything doing, do you think?'

'Oh, a few jobs going for South Africa,' said young Mr. Clayton. 'Hundred and fifty a week for two years, you know.'

'Oh!' cried the chorus. 'You *are* weird, Mr. Clayton. Isn't he a *cure*? Isn't he a *scream*, dear? Oh, Mr. Clayton, you do make me laugh. Isn't he a *comic*?'

A dark, mournful girl touched Miss Moss on the arm.

'I just missed a lovely job yesterday,' she said. 'Six weeks in the provinces and then the West End. The manager said I would have got it for certain if only I'd been robust enough. He said if my figure had been fuller, the part was made for me.' She stared at Miss Moss, and the dirty dark red rose under the brim of her hat looked, somehow, as though it shared the blow with her, and was crushed, too.

'Oh, dear, that was hard lines,' said Miss Moss, trying to appear indifferent. 'What was it – if I may ask?'

But the dark, mournful girl saw through her and a gleam of spite came into her heavy eyes.

'Oh, no good to you, my dear,' said she. 'He wanted someone young, you know – a dark Spanish type – my style, but more figure, that was all.'

The inner door opened and Mr. Bithem appeared in his shirt sleeves. He kept one hand on the door ready to whisk back again, and held up the other.

'Look here, ladies – ' and then he paused, grinned his famous grin before he said – ' *and bhoys.*' The waiting-room laughed so loudly as this that he had to hold both hands up. 'It's no good waiting this morning. Come back Monday; I'm expecting several calls on Monday.'

Miss Moss made a desperate rush forward. 'Mr. Bithem, I wonder if you've heard from . . . '

'Now let me see,' said Mr. Bithem slowly, staring; he had only seen Miss Moss four times a week for the past – how many weeks? 'Now, who are you?'

'Miss Ada Moss.'

'Oh yes, yes; of course, my dear. Not yet, my dear. Now I had a call for twenty-eight ladies to-day, but they had to be young and able to hop it a bit – see? And I had another call for sixteen – but they had to know something about sand-dancing. Look here, my dear, I'm up to the eyebrows this morning. Come back on Monday week; it's no good coming before that.' He gave her a whole grin to herself and patted her fat back. 'Hearts of oak, dear lady,' said Mr. Bithem, 'hearts of oak!'

At the North-East Film Company the crowd was all the way up the stairs. Miss Moss found herself next to a fair little baby thing about thirty in a white lace hat with cherries round it.

'What a crowd!' said she. 'Anything special on?'

'*Didn't* you know, dear?' said the baby, opening her immense pale eyes. 'There was a call at nine-thirty for *attractive* girls. We've all been waiting for *hours*. Have you played for this company before?' Miss Moss put her head on one side. 'No, I don't think I have.'

'They're a lovely company to play for,' said the baby. 'A friend of mine has a friend who gets thirty pounds a day . . . Have you *arcted* much for the *fil*-lums?'

'Well, I'm not an actress by profession,' confessed Miss Moss. 'I'm a contralto singer. But things have been so bad lately that I've been doing a little.'

'It's *like* that, isn't it, dear?' said the baby.

'I had a splendid education at the College of Music,' said Miss Moss, 'and I got my silver medal for singing. I've often sung at West End concerts. But I thought, for a change, I'd try my luck . . . '

'Yes, it's *like* that, isn't it, dear?' said the baby.

At that moment a beautiful typist appeared at the top of the stairs.

'Are you all waiting for the North-East call?'

'Yes!' cried the chorus.

'Well, it's off. I've just had a 'phone through.'

'But look here! What about our expenses?' shouted a voice.

The typist looked down at them, and she couldn't help laughing.

'Oh, you weren't to have been *paid*. The North-East never *pay* their crowds.'

There was only a little round window at the Bitter Orange Company. No waiting-room – nobody at all except a girl, who came to the window when Miss Moss knocked, and said: 'Well?'

'Can I see the producer, please?' said Miss Moss pleasantly. The girl leaned on the window-bar, half shut her eyes and seemed to go to sleep for a moment. Miss Moss smiled at her. The girl not only frowned; she seemed to smell something vaguely unpleasant; she sniffed. Suddenly she moved away, came back with a paper and thrust it at Miss Moss.

'Fill up the form!' said she. And banged the window down.

'Can you aviate – high-dive – drive a car – buck-jump – shoot?' read Miss Moss. She walked along the street asking herself those questions. There was a high, cold wind blowing; it tugged at her, slapped her face, jeered; it knew she could not answer them. In the Square Gardens she found a little wire basket to drop the form into. And then she sat down on one of the benches to powder her nose. But the person in the pocket mirror made a hideous face at her, and that was too much for Miss Moss; she had a good cry. It cheered her wonderfully.

'Well, that's over,' she sighed. 'It's one comfort to be off my feet.

And my nose will soon get cool in the air . . . It's very nice in here. Look at the sparrows. Cheep. Cheep. How close they come. I expect somebody feeds them. No, I've nothing for you, you cheeky little things . . . ' She looked away from them. What was the big building opposite – the Café de Madrid? My goodness, what a smack that little child came down! Poor little mite! Never mind – up again . . . By eight o'clock to-night . . . Café de Madrid. 'I could just go in and sit there and have a coffee, that's all,' thought Miss Moss. 'It's such a place for artists too. I might just have a stroke of luck . . . A dark handsome gentleman in a fur coat comes in with a friend, and sits at my table, perhaps. "No, old chap, I've searched London for a contralto and I can't find a soul. You see, the music is difficult; have a look at it." ' And Miss Moss heard herself saying: 'Excuse me, I happen to be a contralto, and I have sung that part many times . . . Extra-ordinary! "Come back to my studio and I'll try your voice now" . . . Ten pounds a week . . . Why should I feel nervous? It's not nervousness. Why shouldn't I go to the Café de Madrid? I'm a respectable woman – I'm a contralto singer. And I'm only trembling because I've had nothing to eat to-day . . ."A nice little piece of evidence, *my lady*" . . . Very well, Mrs. Pine. Café de Madrid. They have concerts there in the evenings . . . "Why don't they begin?" "The contralto has not arrived . . ." "Excuse me, I happen to be a contralto; I have sung that music many times." '

It was almost dark in the café. Men, palms, red plush seats, white marble tables, waiters in aprons, Miss Moss walked through them all. Hardly had she sat down when a very stout gentleman wearing a very small hat that floated on the top of his head like a little yacht flopped into the chair opposite hers.

'Good evening!' said he.

Miss Moss said, in her cheerful way: 'Good evening!'

'Fine evening,' said the stout gentleman.

'Yes, very fine. Quite a treat, isn't it?' said she.

He crooked a sausage finger at the waiter – 'Bring me a large whisky' – and turned to Miss Moss. 'What's yours?'

'Well, I think I'll take a brandy if it's all the same.'

Five minutes later the stout gentleman leaned across the table and blew a puff of cigar smoke full in her face.

'That's a tempting bit o' ribbon!' said he.

Miss Moss blushed until a pulse at the top of her head that she never had felt before pounded away.

'I always was one for pink,' said she.

The stout gentleman considered her, drumming with her fingers on the table.

'I like 'em firm and well covered,' said he.

Miss Moss, to her surprise, gave a loud snigger.

Five minutes later the stout gentleman heaved himself up.

'Well, am I goin' your way, or are you comin' mine?' he asked.

'I'll come with you, if it's all the same,' said Miss Moss. And she sailed after the little yacht out of the café.

'Pictures' (*Arts and Letters*, Autumn 1919 – first version 'The Common Round', the *New Age*, 31 May 1917)

'. . . met a woman who had been in the cinema with me – her old yellow teeth [?] and pink roses in her hat and hollow lovely [lonely?] eyes and battered hair. I shall not forget her. *No, no.* She was wonderful.' (27 January 1915, 119/27)

'. . . not a grain of sentiment . . . it is stark realism from first word to last and yet it gives an impression of infinite understanding and pity.' (*London Evening Standard*, 5 January 1921)

I have included this story partly because it has some humour in its association of ideas and images. It also provides a rare insight into the world of acting and films of which K.M. was for some time a part. The indomitable Ada Moss, drawn with humour and compassion, is one of the first of a remarkable line of middle-aged women that K.M. created and with whom the reader sympathises. Alone and embattled she soldiers on – though the solution to her problems was not to be followed by Miss Brill, Ma Parker or the Lady's Maid!

The Daughters of the Late Colonel

1

The week after was one of the busiest weeks of their lives. Even when they went to bed it was only their bodies that lay down and rested; their minds went on, thinking things out, talkings things over, wondering, deciding, trying to remember where . . .

Constantia lay like a statue, her hands by her sides, her feet just overlapping each other, the sheet up to her chin. She stared at the ceiling.

'Do you think father would mind if we gave his top-hat to the porter?'

'The porter?' snapped Josephine. 'Why ever the porter? What a very extraordinary idea!'

'Because,' said Constantia slowly, 'he must often have to go to funerals. And I noticed at – at the cemetery that he only had a bowler.' She paused. 'I thought then how very much he'd appreciate a top-hat. We ought to give him a present, too. He was always very nice to father.'

'But,' cried Josephine, flouncing on her pillow and staring across the dark at Constantia, 'father's head!' And suddenly, for one awful moment, she nearly giggled. Not, of course, that she felt in the least like giggling. It must have been habit. Years ago, when they had stayed awake at night talking, their beds had simply heaved. And now the porter's head, disappearing, popped out, like a candle, under father's hat . . . The giggle mounted, mounted; she clenched her hands; she fought it down; she frowned fiercely at the dark and said 'Remember' terribly sternly.

'We can decide to-morrow,' she said.

Constantia had noticed nothing; she sighed.

'Do you think we ought to have our dressing-gowns dyed as well?'

'Black?' almost shrieked Josephine.

'Well, what else?' said Constantia. 'I was thinking – it doesn't seem quite sincere, in a way, to wear black out of doors and when we're fully dressed, and then when we're at home – '

'But nobody sees us,' said Josephine. She gave the bed-clothes such a twitch that both her feet became uncovered and she had to

*If mother had lived, might
they have married?*

Avril Edgar (left) as Constantia
and Judy Parfitt as Josephine
from *A picture of Katherine
Mansfield*

creep up the pillows to get them well under again.

'Kate does,' said Constantia. 'And the postman very well might.'

Josephine thought of her dark-red slippers, which matched her dressing-gown, and of Constantia's favourite indefinite green ones which went with hers. Black! Two black dressing-gowns and two pairs of black woolly slippers, creeping off to the bathroom like black cats.

'I don't think it's absolutely necessary,' said she.

Silence. Then Constantia said, 'We shall have to post the papers with the notice in them to-morrow to catch the Ceylon mail . . . How many letters have we had up till now?'

'Twenty-three.'

Josephine had replied to them all, and twenty-three times when she came to 'We miss our dear father so much' she had broken down and had to use her handkerchief, and on some of them even to soak up a very light-blue tear with an edge of blotting-paper. Strange! She couldn't have put it on – but twenty-three times. Even now, though, when she said over to herself sadly 'We miss our dear father *so* much,' she could have cried if she'd wanted to.

'Have you got enough stamps?' came from Constantia.

'Oh, how can I tell?' said Josephine crossly. 'What's the good of asking me that now?'

'I was just wondering,' said Constantia mildly.

Silence again. There came a little rustle, a scurry, a hop.

'A mouse,' said Constantia.

'It can't be a mouse because there aren't any crumbs,' said Josephine.

'But it doesn't know there aren't,' said Constantia.

A spasm of pity squeezed her heart. Poor little thing! She wished she'd left a tiny piece of biscuit on the dressing-table. It was awful to think of it not finding anything. What would it do?

'I can't think how they manage to live at all,' she said slowly.

'Who?' demanded Josephine.

And Constantia said more loudly than she meant to, 'Mice.'

Josephine was furious. 'Oh, what nonsense, Con!' she said. 'What have mice got to do with it? You're asleep.'

'I don't think I am,' said Constantia. She shut her eyes to make sure. She was.

Josephine arched her spine, pulled up her knees, folded her arms so that her fists came under her ears, and pressed her cheek hard against the pillow.

2

Another thing which complicated matters was they had Nurse Andrews staying on with them that week. It was their own fault; they had asked her. It was Josephine's idea. On the morning – well, on the last morning, when the doctor had gone, Josephine had said to Constantia, 'Don't you think it would be rather nice if we asked Nurse Andrews to stay on for a week as our guest?'

'Very nice,' said Constantia.

'I thought,' went on Josephine quickly, 'I should just say this afternoon, after I've paid her, "My sister and I would be very pleased, after all you've done for us, Nurse Andrews, if you would stay on for a week as our guest." I'd have to put that in about being our guest in case –'

'Oh, but she could hardly expect to be paid!' cried Constantia.

'One never knows,' said Josephine sagely.

Nurse Andrews had, of course, jumped at the idea. But it was a bother. It meant they had to have regular sit-down meals at the proper times, whereas if they'd been alone they could just have asked Kate if she wouldn't have minded bringing them a tray wherever they were. And meal-times now that the strain was over were rather a trial.

Nurse Andrews was simply fearful about butter. Really they couldn't help feeling that about butter, at least, she took advantage of their kindness. And she had that maddening habit of asking for just an inch more bread to finish what she had on her plate, and then, at the last mouthful, absent-mindedly – of course it wasn't absent-mindedly – taking another helping. Josephine got very red when this happened, and she fastened her small, bead-like eyes on the tablecloth as if she saw a minute strange insect creeping through the web of it. But Constantia's long, pale face lengthened and set, and she gazed away – away – far over the desert, to where that line of camels unwound like a thread of wool . . .

'When I was with Lady Tukes,' said Nurse Andrews, 'she had such a dainty little contrayvance for the buttah. It was a silvah Cupid balanced on the – on the bordah of a glass dish, holding a tayny fork. And when you wanted some buttah you simply pressed his foot and he bent down and spread you a piece. It was quite a gayme.'

Josephine could hardly bear that. But 'I think those things are very extravagant' was all she said.

'But whey?' asked Nurse Andrews, beaming through her eyeglasses. 'No one, surely, would take more buttah than one wanted – would one?'

'Ring, Con,' cried Josephine. She couldn't trust herself to reply.

And proud young Kate, the enchanted princess, came in to see what the old tabbies wanted now. She snatched away their plates of mock something or other and slapped down a white, terrified blancmange.

'Jam, please, Kate,' said Josephine kindly.

Kate knelt and burst open the sideboard, lifted the lid of the jam-pot, saw it was empty, put it on the table, and stalked off.

'I'm afraid,' said Nurse Andrews a moment later, 'there isn't any.'

'Oh, what a bother!' said Josephine. She bit her lip. 'What had we better do?'

Constantia looked dubious. 'We can't disturb Kate again,' she said softly.

Nurse Andrews waited, smiling at them both. Her eyes wandered, spying at everything behind her eyeglasses. Constantia in despair went back to her camels. Josephine frowned heavily – concentrated. If it hadn't been for this idiotic woman she and Con would, of course, have eaten their blancmange without. Suddenly the idea came.

'I know,' she said. 'Marmalade. There's some marmalade in the sideboard. Get it, Con.'

'I hope,' laughed Nurse Andrews – and her laugh was like a spoon tinkling against a medicine-glass – 'I hope it's not very bittah marmalayde.'

3

But, after all, it was not long now, and then she'd be gone for good. And there was no getting over the fact that she had been very kind to father. She had nursed him day and night at the end. Indeed, both Constantia and Josephine felt privately she had rather overdone the not leaving him at the very last. For when they had gone in to say good-bye Nurse Andrews had sat beside his bed the whole time, holding his wrist and pretending to look at her watch. It couldn't have been necessary. It was so tactless, too. Supposing father had wanted to say something – something private to them. Not that he had. Oh, far from it! He lay there, purple, a dark, angry purple in the face, and never even looked at them when they came in. Then, as they were standing there, wondering what to do, he had suddenly opened one eye. Oh, what a difference it would have made, what a difference to their memory of him, how much easier to tell people about it, if he had only opened both! But no – one eye only. It glared at them a moment and then . . . went out.

4

It had made it very awkward for them when Mr. Farolles, of St. John's, called the same afternoon.

'The end was quite peaceful, I trust?' were the first words he said as he glided towards them through the dark drawing-room.

'Quite,' said Josephine faintly. They both hung their heads. Both of them felt certain that eye wasn't at all a peaceful eye.

'Won't you sit down?' said Josephine.

'Thank you, Miss Pinner,' said Mr. Farolles gratefully. He folded his coat-tails and began to lower himself into father's arm-chair, but just as he touched it he almost sprang up and slid into the next chair instead.

He coughed. Josephine clasped her hands; Constantia looked vague.

'I want you to feel, Miss Pinner,' said Mr. Farolles, 'and you, Miss Constantia, that I'm trying to be helpful. I want to be helpful to you both, if you will let me. These are the times,' said Mr. Farolles, very simply and earnestly, 'when God means us to be helpful to one another.'

'Thank you very much, Mr. Farolles,' said Josephine and Constantia.

'Not at all,' said Mr. Farolles gently. He drew his kid gloves through his fingers and leaned forward. 'And if either of you would like a little Communion, either or both of you, here *and* now, you have only to tell me. A little Communion is often very help – a great comfort,' he added tenderly.

But the idea of a little Communion terrified them. What! In the drawing-room by themselves – with no – no altar or anything! The piano would be much too high, thought Constantia, and Mr. Farolles could not possibly lean over it with the chalice. And Kate would be sure to come bursting in and interrupt them, thought Josephine. And supposing the bell rang in the middle? It might be somebody important – about their mourning. Would they get up reverently and go out, or would they have to wait . . . in torture?

'Perhaps you will send round a note by your good Kate if you would care for it later,' said Mr. Farolles.

'Oh yes, thank you very much!' they both said.

Mr. Farolles got up and took his black straw hat from the round table.

'And about the funeral,' he said softly. 'I may arrange that – as your dear father's old friend and yours, Miss Pinner – and Miss Constantia?'

Josephine and Constantia got up too.

'I should like it to be quite simple,' said Josephine firmly, 'and not too expensive. At the same time, I should like –'

'A good one that will last,' thought dreamy Constantia, as if Josephine were buying a night-gown. But, of course, Josephine didn't say that. 'One suitable to our father's position.' She was very nervous.

'I'll run round to our good friend Mr. Knight,' said Mr. Farolles soothingly. 'I will ask him to come and see you. I am sure you will find him very helpful indeed.'

5

Well, at any rate, all that part of it was over, though neither of them could possibly believe that father was never coming back. Josephine had had a moment of absolute terror at the cemetery, while the coffin was lowered, to think that she and Constantia had done this thing without asking his permission. What would father say when he found out? For he was bound to find out sooner or later. He always did. 'Buried. You two girls had me *buried*!' She heard his stick thumping. Oh, what would they say? What possible

excuse could they make? It sounded such an appallingly heartless
thing to do. Such a wicked advantage to take of a person because
he happened to be helpless at the moment. The other people seemed
to treat it all as a matter of course. They were strangers; they
couldn't be expected to understand that father was the very last
person for such a thing to happen to. No, the entire blame for it
all would fall on her and Constantia. And the expense, she thought,
stepping into the tight-buttoned cab. When she had to show him
the bills. What would he say then?

She heard him absolutely roaring. 'And do you expect me to pay
for this gimcrack excursion of yours?'

'Oh,' groaned poor Josephine aloud, 'we shouldn't have done it,
Con!'

And Constantia, pale as a lemon in all that blackness, said in a
frightened whisper, 'Done what, Jug?'

'Let them bu-ury father like that,' said Josephine, breaking down
and crying into her new, queer-smelling mourning handkerchief.

'But what else could we have done?' asked Constantia wonderingly. 'We couldn't have kept him, Jug – we couldn't have kept him
unburied. At any rate, not in a flat that size.'

Josephine blew her nose; the cab was dreadfully stuffy.

'I don't know,' she said forlornly. 'It is all so dreadful. I feel we
ought to have tried to, just for a time at least. To make perfectly
sure. One thing's certain' – and her tears sprang out again – 'father
will never forgive us for this – never!'

6

Father would never forgive them. That was what they felt more
than ever when, two mornings later, they went into his room to
go through his things. They had discussed it quite calmly. It was
even down on Josephine's list of things to be done. *Go through
father's things and settle about them.* But that was a very different
matter from saying after breakfast:

'Well, are you ready, Con?'

'Yes, Jug – when you are.'

'Then I think we'd better get it over.'

It was dark in the hall. It had been a rule for years never to
disturb father in the morning, whatever happened. And now they
were going to open the door without knocking even . . . Constantia's eyes were enormous at the idea; Josephine felt weak in the
knees.

'You – you go first,' she gasped, pushing Constantia.

But Constantia said, as she always had said on those occasions,
'No, Jug, that's not fair. You're eldest.'

Josephine was just going to say – what at other times she wouldn't have owned to for the world – what she kept for her very last weapon, 'But you're tallest,' when they noticed that the kitchen door was open, and there stood Kate . . .

'Very stiff,' said Josephine, grasping the door-handle and doing her best to turn it. As if anything ever deceived Kate!

It couldn't be helped. That girl was . . . Then the door was shut behind them, but they weren't in father's room at all. They might have suddenly walked through the wall by mistake into a different flat altogether. Was the door just behind them? They were too frightened to look. Josephine knew that if it was it was holding itself tight shut; Constantia felt that, like the doors in dreams, it hadn't any handle at all. It was the coldness which made it so awful. Or the whiteness – which? Everything was covered. The blinds were down, a cloth hung over the mirror, a sheet hid the bed; a huge fan of white paper filled the fire-place. Constantia timidly put out her hand; she almost expected a snowflake to fall. Josephine felt a queer tingling in her nose, as if her nose was freezing. Then a cab klop-klopped over the cobbles below, and the quiet seemed to shake into little pieces.

'I had better pull up a blind,' said Josephine bravely.

'Yes, it might be a good idea,' whispered Constantia.

They only gave the blind a touch, but it flew up and the cord flew after, rolling round the blind-stick, and the little tassel tapped as if trying to get free. That was too much for Constantia.

'Don't you think – don't you think we might put if off for another day?' she whispered.

'Why?' snapped Josephine, feeling, as usual, much better now that she knew for certain that Constantia was terrified. 'It's got to be done. But I do wish you wouldn't whisper, Con.'

'I didn't know I was whispering,' whispered Constantia.

'And why do you keep on staring at the bed?' said Josephine, raising her voice almost defiantly. 'There's nothing *on* the bed.'

'Oh, Jug, don't say so!' said poor Connie. 'At any rate, not so loudly.'

Josephine felt herself that she had gone too far. She took a wide swerve over to the chest of drawers, put out her hand, but quickly drew it back again.

'Connie!' she gasped, and she wheeled round and leaned with her back against the chest of drawers.

'Oh, Jug – what?'

Josephine could only glare. She had the most extraordinary feeling that she had just escaped something simply awful. But how could she explain to Constantia that father was in the chest of drawers? He was in the top drawer with his handkerchiefs and neckties, or in the next with his shirts and pyjamas, or in the lowest of all with his suits. He was watching there, hidden away – just behind the door-handle – ready to spring.

She pulled a funny old-fashioned face at Constantia, just as she used to in the old days when she was going to cry.

'I can't open,' she nearly wailed.

'No, don't, Jug,' whispered Constantia earnestly. 'It's much better not to. Don't let's open anything. At any rate, not for a long time.'

'But – but it seems so weak,' said Josephine, breaking down.

'But why not be weak for once, Jug?' argued Constantia, whispering quite fiercely. 'If it is weak.' And her pale stare flew from the locked writing-table – so safe – to the huge glittering wardrobe, and she began to breathe in a queer, panting way. 'Why shouldn't we be weak for once in our lives, Jug? It's quite excusable. Let's be weak – be weak, Jug. It's much nicer to be weak than to be strong.'

And then she did one of those amazingly bold things that she'd done about twice before in their lives: she marched over to the wardrobe, turned the key, and took it out of the lock. Took it out of the lock and held it up to Josephine, showing Josephine by her extraordinary smile that she knew what she'd done – she'd risked deliberately father being in there among his overcoats.

If the huge wardrobe had lurched forward, had crashed down on Constantia, Josephine wouldn't have been surprised. On the contrary, she would have thought it the only suitable thing to happen. But nothing happened. Only the room seemed quieter than ever, and bigger flakes of cold air fell on Josephine's shoulders and knees. She began to shiver.

'Come, Jug,' said Constantia, still with that awful callous smile; and Josephine followed just as she had that last time, when Constantia had pushed Benny into the round pond.

7

But the strain told on them when they were back in the dining-room. They sat down, very shaky, and looked at each other.

'I don't feel I can settle to anything,' said Josephine, 'until I've had something. Do you think we could ask Kate for two cups of hot water?'

'I really don't see why we shouldn't,' said Constantia carefully. She was quite normal again. 'I won't ring. I'll go to the kitchen door and ask her.'

'Yes, do,' said Josephine, sinking down into a chair. 'Tell her, just two cups, Con, nothing else – on a tray.'

'She needn't even put the jug on, need she?' said Constantia, as though Kate might very well complain if the jug had been there.

'Oh no, certainly not! The jug's not at all necessary. She can pour it direct out of the kettle,' cried Josephine, feeling that would be a labour-saving indeed.

Their cold lips quivered at the greenish brims. Josephine curved her small red hands round the cup; Constantia sat up and blew on the wavy steam, making it flutter from one side to the other.

'Speaking of Benny,' said Josephine.

And though Benny hadn't been mentioned Constantia immediately looked as though he had.

'He'll expect us to send him something of father's, of course. But it's so difficult to know what to send to Ceylon.'·

'You mean things get unstuck so on the voyage,' murmured Constantia.

'No, lost,' said Josephine sharply. 'You know there's no post. Only runners.'

Both paused to watch a black man in white linen drawers running through the pale fields for dear life, with a large brown-paper parcel in his hands. Josephine's black man was tiny; he scurried along glistening like an ant. But there was something blind and tireless about Constantia's tall, thin fellow, which made him, she decided, a very unpleasant person indeed . . . On the veranda, dressed all in white and wearing a cork helmet, stood Benny. His right hand shook up and down, as father's did when he was impatient. And behind him, not in the least interested, sat Hilda, the unknown sister-in-law. She swung in a cane rocker and flicked over the leaves of the *Tatler*.

'I think his watch would be the most suitable present,' said Josephine.

Constantia looked up; she seemed surprised.

'Oh, would you trust a gold watch to a native?'

'But, of course, I'd disguise it,' said Josephine. 'No one would know it was a watch.' She liked the idea of having to make a parcel such a curious shape that no one could possibly guess what it was. She even thought for a moment of hiding the watch in a narrow cardboard corset-box that she'd kept by her for a long time, waiting for it to come in for something. It was such beautiful, firm cardboard. But, no, it wouldn't be appropriate for this occasion. It had lettering on it: *Medium Women's 28. Extra Firm Busks*. It would be almost too much of a surprise for Benny to open that and find father's watch inside.

'And, of course, it isn't as though it would be going – ticking, I mean,' said Constantia, who was still thinking of the native love of jewellery. 'At least,' she added, 'it would be very strange if after all that time it was.'

8

Josephine made no reply. She had flown off on one of her tangents. She had suddenly thought of Cyril. Wasn't it more usual for the only grandson to have the watch? And then dear Cyril was so appreciative and a gold watch meant so much to a young man. Benny, in all probability, had quite got out of the habit of watches; men so seldom wore waistcoats in those hot climates. Whereas Cyril in London wore them from year's end to year's end. And it would be so nice for her and Constantia, when he came to tea, to know it was there. 'I see you've got on grandfather's watch, Cyril.' It would be somehow so satisfactory.

Dear boy! What a blow his sweet, sympathetic little note had been! Of course they quite understood; but it was most unfortunate.

'It would have been such a point, having him,' said Josephine.

'And he would have enjoyed it so,' said Constantia, not thinking what she was saying.

However, as soon as he got back he was coming to tea with his aunties. Cyril to tea was one of their rare treats.

'Now, Cyril, you mustn't be frightened of our cakes. Your Auntie Con and I bought them at Buszard's this morning. We know what a man's appetite is. So don't be ashamed of making a good tea.'

Josephine cut recklessly into the rich dark cake that stood for her winter gloves or the soling and heeling of Constantia's only respectable shoes. But Cyril was most unmanlike in appetite.

'I say, Aunt Josephine, I simply can't. I've only just had lunch, you know.'

'Oh, Cyril, that can't be true! It's after four,' cried Josephine. Constantia sat with her knife poised over the chocolate-roll.

'It is, all the same,' said Cyril. 'I had to meet a man at Victoria, and he kept me hanging about till . . . there was only time to get lunch and to come on here. And he gave me – phew' – Cyril put his hand to his forehead – 'a terrific blowout,' he said.

It was disappointing – to-day of all days. But still he couldn't be expected to know.

'But you'll have a meringue, won't you, Cyril?' said Aunt Josephine. 'These meringues were bought specially for you. Your dear father was so fond of them. We were sure you are, too.'

'I *am*, Aunt Josephine,' cried Cyril ardently. 'Do you mind if I take half to begin with?'

'Not at all, dear boy; but we mustn't let you off with that.'

'Is your dear father still so fond of meringues?' asked Auntie Con gently. She winced faintly as she broke through the shell of hers.

'Well, I don't quite know, Auntie Con,' said Cyril breezily.

At that they both looked up.

'Don't know?' almost snapped Josephine. 'Don't know a thing like that about your own father, Cyril?'

'Surely,' said Auntie Con softly.

Cyril tried to laugh it off. 'Oh, well,' he said, 'it's such a long time since –' He faltered. He stopped. Their faces were too much for him.

'Even *so*,' said Josephine.

And Auntie Con looked.

Cyril put down his teacup. 'Wait a bit,' he cried. 'Wait a bit, Aunt Josephine. What am I thinking of?'

He looked up. They were beginning to brighten. Cyril slapped his knee.

'Of course,' he said, 'it was meringues. How could I have forgotten? Yes, Aunt Josephine, you're perfectly right. Father's most frightfully keen on meringues.'

They didn't only beam. Aunt Josephine went scarlet with pleasure; Aunti Con gave a deep, deep sigh.

'And now, Cyril, you must come and see father,' said Josephine. 'He knows you were coming to-day.'

'Right,' said Cyril, very firmly and heartily. He got up from his chair; suddenly he glanced at the clock.

'I say, Auntie Con, isn't your clock a bit slow? I've got to meet a man at – at Paddington just after five. I'm afraid I shan't be able to stay very long with grandfather.'

'Oh, he won't expect you to stay *very* long!' said Aunt Josephine.

Constantia was still gazing at the clock. She couldn't make up her mind if it was fast or slow. It was one or the other, she felt almost certain of that. At any rate, it had been.

Cyril still lingered. 'Aren't you coming along, Auntie Con?'

'Of course,' said Josephine, 'we shall all go. Come on, Con.'

9

They knocked at the door, and Cyril followed his aunts into grandfather's hot, sweetish room.

'Come on,' said Grandfather Pinner. 'Don't hang about. What is it? What've you been up to?'

He was sitting in front of a roaring fire, clasping his stick. He had a thick rug over his knees. On his lap there lay a beautiful pale yellow silk handkerchief.

'It's Cyril, father,' said Josephine shyly. And she took Cyril's hand and led him forward.

'Good afternoon, grandfather,' said Cyril, trying to take his hand out of Aunt Josephine's. Grandfather Pinner shot his eyes at

Cyril in the way he was famous for. Where was Auntie Con? She
stood on the other side of Aunt Josephine; her long arms hung
down in front of her; her hands were clasped. She never took her
eyes off grandfather.

'Well,' said Grandfather Pinner, beginning to thump, 'what have
you got to tell me?'

What had he, what had he got to tell him? Cyril felt himself
smiling like a perfect imbecile. The room was stifling, too.

But Aunt Josephine came to his rescue. She cried brightly, 'Cyril
says his father is still very fond of meringues, father dear.'

'Eh?' said Grandfather Pinner, curving his hand like a purple
meringue-shell over one ear.

Josephine repeated, 'Cyril says his father is still very fond of
meringues.'

'Can't hear,' said old Colonel Pinner. And he waved Josephine
away with his stick, then pointed with his stick to Cyril. 'Tell me
what she's trying to say,' he said.

(My God!) 'Must I?' said Cyril, blushing and staring at Aunt
Josephine.

'Do, dear,' she smiled. 'It will please him so much.'

'Come on, out with it!' cried Colonel Pinner testily, beginning
to thump again.

And Cyril leaned forward and yelled, 'Father's still very fond of
meringues.'

At that Grandfather Pinner jumped as though he had been shot.

'Don't shout!' he cried. 'What's the matter with the boy? *Meringues*! What about 'em?'

'Oh, Aunt Josephine, must we go on?' groaned Cyril desperately.

'It's quite all right, dear boy,' said Aunt Josephine, as though
he and she were at the dentist's together. 'He'll understand in a
minute.' And she whispered to Cyril, 'He's getting a bit deaf, you
know.' Then she leaned forward and really bawled at Grandfather
Pinner, 'Cyril only wanted to tell you, father dear, that *his* father
is still very fond of meringues.'

Colonel Pinner heard that time, heard and brooded, looking
Cyril up and down.

'What an esstrordinary thing!' said old Grandfather Pinner.
'What an esstrordinary thing to come all this way here to tell me!'

And Cyril felt it *was*.

'Yes, I shall send Cyril the watch,' said Josephine.

'That would be very nice,' said Constantia. 'I seem to remember
last time he came there was some little trouble about the time.'

10

They were interrupted by Kate bursting through the door in her usual fashion, as though she had discovered some secret panel in the wall.

'Fried or boiled?' asked the bold voice.

Fried or boiled? Josephine and Constantia were quite bewildered for the moment. They could hardly take it in.

'Fried or boiled what, Kate?' asked Josephine, trying to begin to concentrate.

Kate gave a loud sniff. 'Fish.'

'Well, why didn't you say so immediately?' Josephine reproached her gently. 'How could you expect us to understand, Kate? There are a great many things in this world, you know, which are fried or boiled.' And after such a display of courage she said quite brightly to Constantia, 'Which do you prefer, Con?'

'I think it might be nice to have it fried,' said Constantia. 'On the other hand, of course, boiled fish is very nice. I think I prefer both equally well . . . Unless you . . . In that case –'

'I shall fry it,' said Kate, and she bounced back, leaving their door open and slamming the door of her kitchen.

Josephine gazed at Constantia; she raised her pale eyebrows until they rippled away into her pale hair. She got up. She said in a very lofty, imposing way, 'Do you mind following me into the drawing-room, Constantia? I've something of great importance to discuss with you.'

For it was always to the drawing-room they retired when they wanted to talk over Kate.

Josephine closed the door meaningly. 'Sit down, Constantia,' she said, still very grand. She might have been receiving Constantia for the first time. And Con looked round vaguely for a chair, as though she felt indeed quite a stranger.

'Now the question is,' said Josephine, bending forward, 'whether we shall keep her or not.'

'That is the question,' agreed Constantia.

'And this time,' said Josephine firmly, 'we must come to a definite decision.'

Constantia looked for a moment as though she might begin going over all the other times, but she pulled herself together and said, 'Yes, Jug.'

'You see, Con,' explained Josephine, 'everything is so changed now.' Constantia looked up quickly. 'I mean,' went on Josephine, 'we're not dependent on Kate as we were.' And she blushed faintly. 'There's not father to cook for.'

'That is perfectly true,' agreed Constantia. 'Father certainly doesn't want any cooking now whatever else –'

Josephine broke in sharply, 'You're not sleepy, are you, Con?'

'Sleepy, Jug?' Constantia was wide-eyed.

'Well, concentrate more,' said Josephine sharply, and she returned to the subject. 'What it comes to is, if we did' – and this she barely breathed, glancing at the door – 'give Kate notice' – she raised her voice again – 'we could manage our own food.'

'Why not?' cried Constantia. She couldn't help smiling. The idea was so exciting. She clasped her hands. 'What should we live on, Jug?'

'Oh, eggs in various forms!' said Jug, lofty again. 'And, besides, there are all the cooked foods.'

'But I've always heard,' said Constantia, 'they are considered so very expensive.'

'Not if one buys them in moderation,' said Josephine. But she tore herself away from this fascinating bypath and dragged Constantia after her.

'What we've got to decide now, however, is whether we really do trust Kate or not.'

Constantia leaned back. Her flat little laugh flew from her lips.

'Isn't it curious, Jug,' said she, 'that just on this one subject I've never been able to quite make up my mind?'

11

She never had. The whole difficulty was to prove anything. How did one prove things, how could one? Suppose Kate had stood in front of her and deliberately made a face. Mightn't she very well have been in pain? Wasn't it impossible, at any rate, to ask Kate if she was making a face at her? If Kate answered 'No' – and, of course, she would say 'No' – what a position! How undignified! Then, again, Constantia suspected, she was almost certain that Kate went to her chest of drawers when she and Josephine were out, not to take things but to spy. Many times she had come back to find her amethyst cross in the most unlikely places, under her lace ties or on top of her evening Bertha. More than once she had laid a trap for Kate. She had arranged things in a special order and then called Josephine to witness.

'You see, Jug?'

'Quite, Con.'

'Now we shall be able to tell.'

But, oh dear, when she did go to look, she was as far off from a proof as ever! If anything was displaced, it might so very well have happened as she closed the drawer; a jolt might have done it so easily.

'You come, Jug, and decide. I really can't. It's too difficult.'

But after a pause and a long glare Josephine would sigh. 'Now you've put the doubt into my mind, Con, I'm sure I can't tell myself.'

'Well, we can't postpone it again,' said Josephine. 'If we postpone it this time –'

12

But at that moment in the street below a barrel-organ struck up. Josephine and Constantia sprang to their feet together.

'Run, Con,' said Josephine. 'Run quickly. There's sixpence on the –'

Then they remembered. It didn't matter. They would never have to stop the organ-grinder again. Never again would she and Constantia be told to make that monkey take his noise somewhere else. Never would sound that loud, strange bellow when father thought they were not hurrying enough. The organ-grinder might play there all day and the stick would not thump.

It never will thump again,
It never will thump again,

played the barrel-organ.

What was Constantia thinking? She had such a strange smile; she looked different. She couldn't be going to cry.

'Jug, Jug,' said Constantia softly, pressing her hands together. 'Do you know what day it is? It's Saturday. It's a week to-day, a whole week.'

A week since father died,
A week since father died,

cried the barrel-organ. And Josephine, too, forgot to be practical and sensible; she smiled faintly, strangely. On the Indian carpet there fell a square of sunlight, pale red; it came and went and came – and stayed, deepened – until it shone almost golden.

'The sun's out,' said Josephine, as though it really mattered.

A perfect fountain of bubbling notes shook from the barrel-organ, round, bright notes, carelessly scattered.

Constantia lifted her big, cold hands as if to catch them, and then her hands fell again. She walked over to the mantelpiece to her favourite Buddha. And the stone and gilt image, whose smile always gave her such a queer feeling, almost a pain and yet a pleasant pain, seemed to-day to be more than smiling. He knew something; he had a secret. 'I know something that you don't know,' said her Buddha. Oh, what was it, what could it be? And yet she had always felt there was . . . something.

The sunlight pressed through the windows, thieved its way in, flashed its light over the furniture and the photographs. Josephine watched it. When it came to mother's photograph, the enlargement over the piano, it lingered as though puzzled to find so little remained of mother, except the ear-rings shaped like tiny pagodas and a black feather boa. Why did the photographs of dead people always fade so? wondered Josephine. As soon as a person was dead their photograph died too. But, of course, this one of mother was very old. It was thirty-five years old. Josephine remembered standing on a chair and pointing out that feather boa to Constantia and telling her that it was a snake that had killed their mother in Ceylon . . . Would everything have been different if mother hadn't died? She didn't see why. Aunt Florence had lived with them until they had left school, and they had moved three times and had their yearly holiday and . . . and there'd been changes of servants, of course.

Some little sparrows, young sparrows they sounded, chirped on the window-ledge. *Yeep-eyeep-yeep.* But Josephine felt they were not sparrows, not on the window-ledge. It was inside her, that queer little crying noise. *Yeep-eyeep-yeep.* Ah, what was it crying, so weak and forlorn?

If mother had lived, might they have married? But there had been nobody for them to marry. There had been father's Anglo-Indian friends before he quarrelled with them. But after that she and Constantia never met a single man except clergymen. How did one meet men? Or even if they'd met them, how could they have got to know men well enough to be more than strangers? One read of people having adventures, being followed, and so on. But nobody had ever followed Constantia and her. Oh yes, there had been one year at Eastbourne a mysterious man at their boarding-house who had put a note on the jug of hot water outside their bedroom door! But by the time Connie had found it the steam had made the writing too faint to read; they couldn't even make out to which of them it was addressed. And he had left next day. And that was all. The rest had been looking after father and at the same time keeping out of father's way. But now? But now? The thieving sun touched Josephine gently. She lifted her face. She was drawn over to the window by gentle beams . . .

Until the barrel-organ stopped playing Constantia stayed before the Buddha, wondering, but not as usual, not vaguely. This time her wonder was like longing. She remembered the times she had come in here, crept out of bed in her night-gown when the moon was full, and lain on the floor with her arms outstretched, as though she was crucified. Why? The big, pale moon had made her do it. The horrible dancing figures on the carved screen had leered at her and she hadn't minded. She remembered too how, whenever they were at the seaside, she had gone off by herself and got as close to the sea as she could, and sung something, something she had made up, while she gazed all over that restless water. There had been this other life, running out, bringing things home in bags, getting things on approval, discussing them with Jug, and taking them back to get more things on approval, and arranging father's trays and trying not to annoy father. But it all seemed to have happened in a kind of tunnel. It wasn't real. It was only when she came out of the tunnel into the moonlight or by the sea or into a thunderstorm that she really felt herself. What did it mean? What was it she was always wanting? What did it all lead to? Now? Now?

She turned away from the Buddha with one of her vague gestures. She went over to where Josephine was standing. She wanted to say something to Josephine, something frightfully important, about – about the future and what . . .

'Don't you think perhaps –' she began.

But Josephine interrupted her. 'I was wondering if now –' she murmured. They stopped; they waited for each other.

'Go on, Con,' said Josephine.

'No, no, Jug; after you,' said Constantia.

'No, say what you were going to say. You began,' said Josephine.

'I . . . I'd rather hear what you were going to say first,' said Constantia.

'Don't be absurd, Con.'

'Really, Jug.'

'Connie!'

'Oh, *Jug*!'

A pause. Then Constantia said faintly, 'I can't say what I was going to say, Jug, because I've forgotten what it was . . . that I was going to say.'

Josephine was silent for a moment. She stared at a big cloud where the sun had been. Then she replied shortly, 'I've forgotten too.'

'The Daughters of the Late Colonel' (the *London Mercury*, May 1921)

'The vicar called upon me yesterday and asked if he might come occasionally and administer a *little* Private Communion to me at any time . . . just a drain of wine I suppose, and a crumb of bread. Why a little? It puzzled me greatly.' (to Virginia Woolf, May 1919)

'Read this criticism. It takes the bisquito. But why a half brick at me? They do hate me those young men. The *Sat.Review* said my story was "a dismal transcript of inefficiency." What a bother! I suppose that, living alone as I do, I get all out of touch & what seems to me even *lively* is ghostly glee.' (to J. M. Murry, May 1921)

'While I was writing that story I lived for it but when it was finished, I confess I hoped very much that my readers would understand what I was trying to express. But very few did. They thought it was "cruel"; they thought I was sneering at Jug and Constantia; or they thought it was "drab". And in the last paragraph I was "poking fun at the poor old things." It's almost terrifying to be so misunderstood. There was a moment when I first had the idea when I saw the two sisters as *amusing*; but the moment I looked deeper (let me be quite frank) I bowed down to the beauty that was hidden in their lives . . . All was meant, of course, to lead up to that last paragraph, when my two flowerless ones turned with that timid gesture, to the sun. "Perhaps *now* . . ." And after that, it seemed to me, they died as surely as Father was dead.' (to William Gerhardi, 23 June 1921)

'I put my all into that story and hardly anyone saw what I was getting at. Even dear old Hardy told me to write more about those sisters. As if there was any more to say!' (to Dorothy Brett, 11 November 1921)

'The only occasion when I ever felt at leisure was while writing The Daughters of the Late Col. and then at the end I was so terribly unhappy that I wrote as fast as possible for fear of dying before the story was sent.' (*Journal*, 17 January 1922)

'The only story that satisfies me to any extent is the one you understand so well, *The Daughters of the Late Col.*, and parts of Je ne parle pas. But Heavens what a journey there is before one!' (to William Gerhardi, 8 February 1922)

'I'm 33. Yet I am only just beginning to see now what it is I want to do. It will take years of work to really bring it off. I've done one or two things like the Daughters of the Colonel which were the right kind. But *one* or *two*!' (to Richard Murry, March 1922, *Adam*)

'Katherine Mansfield's funniest story at the same time as it is thematically one of her most serious.' (C. A. Hankin, *Katherine Mansfield and Her Confessional Stories*)

'that masterpiece of love and pity – and of technique.' (Antony Alpers, *The Life of Katherine Mansfield*)

There is comedy and tragedy in the story of these sisters, free for the first time from their bullying, tyrannical father's dominating influence. Past and present are fused together for these two who, because of that past, can have no future. The story develops through association of ideas in an apparently random way – the multi-personal viewpoint gives the reader a constantly changing perspective and increasing involvement. The symbols integrate several layers of meaning simultaneously. Although there is a cleverly satirical caricature in the portrayal of Nurse Andrews it is a very different story from 'Bliss'. It leaves an impression of compassion; it is gentle comedy imbued with a sense of waste – and the wrongness of that waste.

At the Bay

Very early morning. The sun was not yet risen, and the whole of
Crescent Bay was hidden under a white sea-mist. The big bush-
covered hills at the back were smothered. You could not see where
they ended and the paddocks and bungalows began. The sandy
road was gone and the paddocks and bungalows the other side of
it; there were no white dunes covered with reddish grass beyond
them; there was nothing to mark which was beach and where was
the sea. A heavy dew had fallen. The grass was blue. Big drops
hung on the bushes and just did not fall; the silvery, fluffy toi-toi
was limp on its long stalks, and all the marigolds and the pinks
in the bungalow gardens were bowed to the earth with wetness.
Drenched were the cold fuchsias, round pearls of dew lay on the
flat nasturtium leaves. It looked as though the sea had beaten up
softly in the darkness, as though one immense wave had come
rippling, rippling – how far? Perhaps if you had waked up in the
middle of the night you might have seen a big fish flicking in at
the window and gone again . . .

Ah-Ah! sounded the sleepy sea. And from the bush there came

*As the morning lengthened
whole parties appeared over
the sandhills and came down
on the beach.*

the sound of little streams flowing, quickly, lightly, slipping between the smooth stones, gushing into ferny basins and out again; and there was the splashing of big drops on large leaves, and something else – what was it? – a faint stirring and shaking, the snapping of a twig and then such silence that it seemed someone was listening.

Round the corner of Crescent Bay, between the piled-up masses of broken rock, a flock of sheep came pattering. They were huddled together, a small, tossing, woolly mass, and their thin, stick-like legs trotted along quickly as if the cold and the quiet had frightened them. Behind them an old sheep-dog, his soaking paws covered with sand, ran along with his nose to the ground, but carelessly, as if thinking of something else. And then in the rocky gateway the shepherd himself appeared. He was a lean, upright old man, in a frieze coat that was covered with a web of tiny drops, velvet trousers tied under the knee, and a wideawake with a folded blue handkerchief round the brim. One hand was crammed into his belt, the other grasped a beautifully smooth yellow stick. And as he walked, taking his time, he kept up a very soft light whistling, an airy, far-away fluting that sounded mournful and tender. The old dog cut an ancient caper or two and then drew up sharp, ashamed of his levity, and walked a few dignified paces by his master's side. The sheep ran forward in little pattering rushes; they began to bleat, and ghostly flocks and herds answered them from under the sea. 'Baa! Baaa!' For a time they seemed to be always on the same piece of ground. There ahead was stretched the sandy road with shallow puddles; the same soaking bushes showed on either side the same shadowy palings. Then something immense came into view; an enormous shock-haired giant with his arms stretched out. It was the big gum tree outside Mrs. Stubb's shop, and as they passed by there was a strong whiff of eucalyptus. And now big spots of light gleamed in the mist. The shepherd stopped whistling; he rubbed his red rose and wet beard on his wet sleeve and, screwing up his eyes, glanced in the direction of the sea. The sun was rising. It was marvellous how quickly the mist thinned, sped away, dissolved from the shadow plain, rolled up from the bush and was gone as if in a hurry to escape; big twists and curls jostled and shouldered each other as the silvery beams broadened. The far-away sky – a bright, pure blue – was reflected in the puddles, and the drops, swimming along the telegraph poles, flashed into points of light. Now the leaping, glittering sea was so bright it made one's eyes ache to look at it. The shepherd drew a pipe, the bowl as small as an acorn, out of his breast-pocket, fumbled for a chunk of speckled tobacco, pared off a few shavings and stuffed the bowl. He was a grave, fine-looking old man. As he lit up and the blue smoke wreathed his head, the dog, watching, looked proud of him.

'Baa! Baaa!' The sheep spread out into a fan. They were just clear of the summer colony before the first sleeper turned over and lifted a drowsy head; their cry sounded in the dreams of little children . . . who lifted their arms to drag down, to cuddle the darling little woolly lambs of sleep. Then the first inhabitant appeared; it was the Burnells' cat Florrie, sitting on the gatepost, far too early as usual, looking for their milk-girl. When she saw the old sheep-dog she sprang up quickly, arched her back, drew in her tabby head, and seemed to give a little fastidious shiver. 'Ugh! What a coarse, revolting creature!' said Florrie. But the old sheep-dog, not looking up, waggled past, flinging out his legs from side to side. Only one of his ears twitched to prove that he saw, and thought her a silly young female.

The breeze of morning lifted in the bush and the smell of leaves and wet black earth mingled with the sharp smell of the sea. Myriads of birds were singing. A goldfinch flew over the shepherd's head and, perching on the tiptop of a spray, it turned to the sun, ruffling its small breast feathers. And now they had passed the fisherman's hut, passed the charred-looking little *whare* where Leila the milk-girl lived with her old Gran. The sheep strayed over a yellow swamp and Wag, the sheep-dog, padded after, rounded them up and headed them for the steeper, narrower rocky pass that led out of Crescent Bay and towards Daylight Cove. 'Baa! Baaa!' Faint the cry came as they rocked along the fast-drying road. The shepherd put away his pipe, dropping it into his breast-pocket so that the little bowl hung over. And straightway the soft airy whistling began again. Wag ran out along a ledge of rock after something that smelled, and ran back again disgusted. Then pushing, nudging, hurrying, the sheep rounded the bend and the shepherd followed after out of sight.

2

A few moments later the back door of one of the bungalows opened, and a figure in a broad-striped bathing-suit flung down their paddock, cleared the stile, rushed through the tussock grass into the hollow, staggered up the sandy hillock, and raced for dear life over the big porous stones, over the cold, wet pebbles, on to the hard sand that gleamed like oil. Splish-Splosh! Splish-Splosh! The water bubbled round his legs as Stanley Burnell waded out exulting. First man in as usual! He'd beaten them all again. And he swooped down to souse his head and neck.

'Hail, brother! All hail, Thou Mighty One!' A velvety bass voice came booming over the water.

Great Scott! Damnation take it! Stanley lifted up to see a dark head bobbing far out and an arm lifted. It was Jonathan Trout – there before him! 'Glorious morning!' sang the voice.

'Yes, very fine!' said Stanley briefly. Why the dickens didn't the fellow stick to his part of the sea? Why should he come barging over to this exact spot? Stanley gave a kick, a lunge and struck out, swimming overarm. But Jonathan was a match for him. Up he came, his black hair sleek on his forehead, his short beard sleek.

'I had an extraordinary dream last night!' he shouted.

What was the matter with the man? This mania for conversation irritated Stanley beyond words. And it was always the same – always some piffle about a dream he'd had, or some cranky idea he'd got hold of, or some rot he'd been reading. Stanley turned over on his back and kicked with his legs till he was a living water-spout. But even then . . . 'I dreamed I was hanging over a terrifically high cliff, shouting to someone below.' You would be! thought Stanley. He could stick no more of it. He stopped splashing. 'Look here, Trout,' he said, 'I'm in rather a hurry this morning.'

'You're WHAT?' Jonathan was so surprised – or pretended to be – that he sank under the water, then reappeared again blowing.

'All I mean is,' said Stanley, 'I've no time to – to – to fool about. I want to get this over. I'm in a hurry. I've work to do this morning – see?'

Jonathan was gone before Stanley had finished. 'Pass, friend!' said the bass voice gently, and he slid away through the water with scarcely a ripple . . . But curse the fellow! He'd ruined Stanley's bathe. What an unpractical idiot the man was! Stanley struck out to sea again, and then as quickly swam in again, and away he rushed up the beach. He felt cheated.

Jonathan stayed a little longer in the water. He floated, gently moving his hands like fins, and letting the sea rock his long, skinny body. It was curious, but in spite of everything he was fond of Stanley Burnell. True, he had a fiendish desire to tease him some-times, to poke fun at him, but at bottom he was sorry for the fellow. There was something pathetic in his determination to make a job of everything. You couldn't help feeling he'd be caught out one day, and then what an almighty cropper he'd come! At that moment an immense wave lifted Jonathan, rode past him, and broke along the beach with a joyful sound. What a beauty! And now there came another. That was the way to live – carelessly, recklessly, spending oneself. He got on to his feet and began to wade towards the shore, pressing his toes into the firm, wrinkled sand. To take things easy, not to fight against the ebb and flow of life, but to give way to it – that was what was needed. It was this tension that was all wrong. To live – to live! And the perfect morning, so fresh and fair, basking in the light, as though laughing at its own beauty, seemed to whisper, 'Why not?'

But now he was out of the water Jonathan turned blue with cold. He ached all over; it was as though someone was wringing the blood out of him. And stalking up the beach, shivering, all his muscles tight, he too felt his bathe was spoilt. He'd stayed in too long.

3

Beryl was alone in the living-room when Stanley appeared, wearing a blue serge suit, a stiff collar and a spotted tie. He looked almost uncannily clean and brushed; he was going to town for the day. Dropping into his chair, he pulled out his watch and put it beside his plate.

'I've just got twenty-five minutes,' he said. 'You might go and see if the porridge is ready, Beryl?'

'Mother's just gone for it,' said Beryl. She sat down at the table and poured out his tea.

'Thanks!' Stanley took a sip. 'Hallo!' he said in an astonished voice, 'you've forgotten the sugar.'

'Oh, sorry!' But even then Beryl didn't help him; she pushed the basin across. What did this mean? As Stanley helped himself his blue eyes widened; they seemed to quiver. He shot a quick glance at his sister-in-law and leaned back.

'Nothing wrong, is there?' he asked carelessly, fingering his collar.

Beryl's head was bent; she turned her plate in her fingers.

'Nothing,' said her light voice. Then she too looked up, and smiled at Stanley. 'Why should there be?'

'O-oh! No reason at all as far as I know. I thought you seemed rather –'

At that moment the door opened and the three little girls appeared, each carrying a porridge plate. They were dressed alike in blue jerseys and knickers; their brown legs were bare, and each had her hair plaited and pinned up in what was called a horse's tail. Behind them came Mrs. Fairfield with the tray.

'Carefully, children,' she warned. But they were taking the very greatest care. They loved being allowed to carry things. 'Have you said good-morning to your father?'

'Yes, grandma.' They settled themselves on the bench opposite Stanley and Beryl.

'Good morning, Stanley!' Old Mrs. Fairfield gave him his plate.

'Morning, mother! How's the boy?'

'Splendid! He only woke up once last night. What a perfect morning!' The old woman paused, her hand on the loaf of bread, to gaze out of the open door into the garden. The sea sounded. Through the wide-open window streamed the sun on to the yellow varnished walls and bare floor. Everything on the table flashed and glittered. In the middle there was an old salad bowl filled with yellow and red nasturtiums. She smiled, and a look of deep content shone in her eyes.

'You might *cut* me a slice of that bread, mother,' said Stanley. 'I've only twelve and a half minutes before the coach passes. Has anyone given my shoes to the servant girl?'

'Yes, they're ready for you.' Mrs. Fairfield was quite unruffled.

'Oh, Kezia! Why are you such a messy child!' cried Beryl despairingly.

'Me, Aunt Beryl?' Kezia stared at her. What had she done now? She had only dug a river down the middle of her porridge, filled it, and was eating the banks away. But she did that every single morning, and no one had said a word up till now.

'Why can't you eat your food properly like Isabel and Lottie?' How unfair grown-ups are!

'But Lottie always makes a floating island, don't you, Lottie?'

'I don't,' said Isabel smartly. 'I just sprinkle mine with sugar and put on the milk and finish it. Only babies play with their food.'

Stanley pushed back his chair and got up.

'Would you get me those shoes, mother? And, Beryl, if you've finished, I wish you'd cut down to. the gate and stop the coach. Run in to your mother, Isabel, and ask her where my bowler hat's been put. Wait a minute – have you children been playing with my stick?'

'No, father!'

'But I put it here,' Stanley began to bluster. 'I remember distinctly putting it in this corner. Now, who's had it? There's no time to lose. Look sharp! The stick's got to be found.'

Even Alice, the servant girl, was drawn into the chase. 'You haven't been using it to poke the kitchen fire with by any chance?'

Stanley dashed into the bedroom where Linda was lying. 'Most extraordinary thing. I can't keep a single possession to myself. They've made away with my stick, now!'

'Stick, dear? What stick?' Linda's vagueness on these occasions could not be real, Stanley decided. Would nobody sympathise with him?

'Coach! Coach, Stanley!' Beryl's voice cried from the gate.

Stanley waved his arm to Linda. 'No time to say good-bye!' he cried. And he meant that as a punishment to her.

He snatched his bowler hat, dashed out of the house, and swung down the garden path. Yes, the coach was there waiting, and Beryl, leaning over the open gate, was laughing up at somebody or other just as if nothing had happened. The heartlessness of women! The way they took it for granted it was your job to slave away for them while they didn't even take the trouble to see that your walking-stick wasn't lost. Kelly trailed his whip across the horses.

'Good-bye, Stanley,' called Beryl, sweetly and gaily. It was easy enough to say good-bye! And there she stood, idle, shading her eyes with her hand. The worst of it was Stanley had to shout good-bye too, for the sake of appearances. Then he saw her turn, give a little skip and run back to the house. She was glad to be rid of him!

Yes, she was thankful. Into the living-room she ran and called 'He's gone!' Linda cried from her room: 'Beryl! Has Stanley gone?' Old Mrs. Fairfield appeared, carrying the boy in his little flannel coatee.

'Gone?'

'Gone!'

Oh, the relief, the difference it made to have the man out of the house. Their very voices were changed as they called to one another; they sounded warm and loving and as if they shared a secret. Beryl went over to the table. 'Have another cup of tea, mother. It's still hot.' She wanted, somehow, to celebrate the fact that they could do what they liked now. There was no man to disturb them; the whole perfect day was theirs.

'No, thank you, child,' said old Mrs. Fairfield, but the way at that moment she tossed the boy up and said 'a-goos-a-goos-a-ga!' to him meant that she felt the same. The little girls ran into the paddock like chickens let out of a coop.

Even Alice, the servant girl, washing up the dishes in the kitchen, caught the infection and used the precious tank water in a perfectly reckless fashion.

'Oh, these men!' said she, and she plunged the teapot into the bowl and held it under the water even after it had stopped bubbling, as if it too was a man and drowning was too good for them.

4

'Wait for me, Isa-bel! Kezia, wait for me!'

There was poor little Lottie, left behind again, because she found it so fearfully hard to get over the stile by herself. When she stood on the first step her knees began to wobble; she grasped the post. Then you had to put one leg over. But which leg? She never could decide. And when she did finally put one leg over with a sort of stamp of despair – then the feeling was awful. She was half in the paddock still and half in the tussock grass. She clutched the post desperately and lifted up her voice. 'Wait for me!'

'No, don't you wait for her, Kezia!' said Isabel. 'She's such a little silly. She's always making a fuss. Come on!' And she tugged Kezia's jersey. 'You can use my bucket if you come with me,' she said kindly. 'It's bigger than yours.' But Kezia couldn't leave Lottie all by herself. She ran back to her. By this time Lottie was very red in the face and breathing heavily.

'Here, put your other foot over,' said Kezia.

'Where?'

Lottie looked down at Kezia as if from a mountain height.

'Here where my hand is.' Kezia patted the place.

'Oh, *there* do you mean?' Lottie gave a deep sigh and put the second foot over.

'Now – sort of turn round and sit down and slide,' said Kezia.

'But there's nothing to sit down *on*, Kezia,' said Lottie.

She managed it at last, and once it was over she shook herself and began to beam.

'I'm getting better at climbing over stiles, aren't I, Kezia?'

Lottie's was a very hopeful nature.

The pink and the blue sunbonnet followed Isabel's bright red sunbonnet up that sliding, slipping hill. At the top they paused to decide where to go and to have a good stare at who was there already. Seen from behind, standing against the sky-line, gesticulating largely with their spades, they looked like minute puzzled explorers.

The whole family of Samuel Josephs was there already with their lady-help, who sat on a camp-stool and kept order with a whistle that she wore tied round her neck, and a small cane with which she directed operations. The Samuel Josephs never played by themselves or managed their own game. If they did, it ended in the boys pouring water down the girls' necks or the girls trying to put little black crabs into the boys' pockets. So Mrs S. J. and the poor lady-help drew up what she called a 'brogramme' every morning to keep them 'abused and out of bischief.' It was all competitions or races or round games. Everything began with a piercing blast of the lady-help's whistle and ended with another. There were even prizes – large, rather dirty paper parcels which the lady-help with a sour little smile drew out of a bulging string kit. The Samuel Josephs fought fearfully for the prizes and cheated and pinched one another's arms – they were all expert pinchers. The only time the Burnell children ever played with them Kezia had got a prize, and when she undid three bits of paper she found a very small rusty button-hook. She couldn't understand why they made such a fuss . . . .

But they never played with the Samuel Josephs now or even went to their parties. The Samuel Josephs were always giving children's parties at the Bay and there was always the same food. A big washhand basin of very brown fruit salad, buns cut into four and a washhand jug full of something the lady-help called 'Limmonadear.' And you went away in the evening with half the frill torn off your frock or something spilled all down the front of your openwork pinafore, leaving the Samuel Josephs leaping like savages on their lawn. No! They were too awful.

On the other side of the beach, close down to the water, two little boys, their knickers rolled up, twinkled like spiders. One was digging, the other pattered in and out of the water, filling a small bucket. They were the Trout boys, Pip and Rags. But Pip was so busy digging and Rags was so busy helping that they didn't see their little cousins until they were quite close.

'Look!' said Pip. 'Look what I've discovered.' And he showed them an old, wet, squashed-looking boot. The three little girls stared.

'Whatever are you going to do with it? asked Kezia.

'Keep it, of course!' Pip was very scornful. 'It's a find – see?

Yes Kezia saw that. All the same . . .

'There's lots of things buried in the sand,' explained Pip. 'They get chucked up from wrecks. Treasure. Why – you might find –'

'But why does Rags have to keep on pouring water in?' asked Lottie.

'Oh, that's to moisten it,' said Pip, 'to make the work a bit easier. Keep it up, Rags.'

And good little Rags ran up and down, pouring in the water that turned brown like cocoa.

'Here, shall I show you what I found yesterday? said Pip mysteriously, and he stuck his spade into the sand. 'Promise not to tell.'

They promised.

'Say, cross my heart straight dinkum.'

The little girls said it.

Pip took something out of his pocket, rubbed it a long time on the front of his jersey, then breathed on it and rubbed it again.

'Now turn round!' he ordered.

They turned round.

'All look the same way! Keep still! Now!'

And his hand opened; he held up to the light something that

flashed, that winked, that was a most lovely green.

'It's a nemeral,' said Pip solemnly.

'It is really, Pip?' Even Isabel was impressed.

The lovely green thing seemed to dance in Pip's fingers. Aunt Beryl had a nemeral in a ring, but it was a very small one. This one was as big as a star and far more beautiful.

5

As the morning lengthened whole parties appeared over the sand-hills and came down on the beach to bathe. It was understood that at eleven o'clock the women and children of the summer colony had the sea to themselves. First the women undressed, pulled on their bathing dresses and covered their heads in hideous caps like sponge-bags; then the children were unbuttoned. The beach was strewn with little heaps of clothes and shoes; the big summer hats, with stones on them to keep them from blowing away, looked like immense shells. It was strange that even the sea seemed to sound differently when all those leaping, laughing figures ran into the waves. Old Mrs Fairfield, in a lilac cotton dress and a black hat tied under the chin, gathered her little brood and got them ready. The little Trout boys whipped their shirts over their heads, and away the five sped, while their grandma sat with one hand in her knitting-bag ready to draw out the ball of wool when she was satisfied they were safely in.

The firm, compact little girls were not half so brave as the tender, delicate-looking little boys. Pips and Rags, shivering, crouching down, slapping the water, never hesitated. But Isabel, who could swim twelve strokes, and Kezia, who could nearly swim eight, only followed on the strict understanding they were not to be splashed. As for Lottie, she didn't follow at all. She liked to be left to go in her own way, please. And that way was to sit down at the edge of the water, her legs straight, her knees pressed together, and to make vague motions with her arms as if she expected to be wafted out to sea. But when a bigger wave than usual, an old whiskery one, came lolloping along in her direction, she scrambled to her feet with a face of horror and flew up the beach again.

'Here, mother, keep these for me, will you?'

Two rings and a thin gold chain were dropped into Mrs Fairfield's lap.

'Yes, dear. But aren't you going to bathe here?'

'No-o,' Beryl drawled. She sounded vague. 'I'm undressing further along. I'm going to bathe with Mrs Harry Kember.'

'Very well.' But Mrs Fairfield's lips set. She disapproved of Mrs Harry Kember. Beryl knew it.

Poor old mother, she smiled, as she skimmed over the stones. Poor old mother! Old! Oh, what joy, what bliss it was to be young . . . .

'You looked very pleased,' said Mrs Harry Kember. She sat hunched up on the stones, her arms round her knees, smoking.

'It's such a lovely day,' said Beryl, smiling down at her.

'Oh, my *dear*!' Mrs Harry Kember's voice sounded as though she knew better than that. But then her voice always sounded as though she knew something more about you than you did yourself. She was a long, strange-looking woman with narrow hands and feet. Her face, too, was long and narrow and exhausted-looking; even her fair curled fringe looked burnt out and withered. She was the only woman at the Bay who smoked, and she smoked incessantly, keeping the cigarette between her lips while she talked, and only taking it out when the ash was so long you could not understand why it did not fall. When she was not playing bridge—she played bridge every day of her life—she spent her time lying in the full glare of the sun. She could stand any amount of it; she never had enough. All the same, it did not seem to warm her. Parched, withered, cold, she lay stretched on the stones like a piece of tossed-up driftwood. The women at the Bay thought she was very, very fast. Her lack of vanity, her slang, the way she treated men as though she was one of them, and the fact that she didn't care twopence about her house and called the servant Gladys 'Glad-eyes', was disgraceful. Standing on the veranda steps, Mrs Kember would call in her indifferent, tired voice, 'I say, Glad-eyes, you might heave me a handkerchief if I've got one, will you?' And Glad-eyes, a red bow in her hair instead of a cap, and white shoes, came running with an impudent smile. It was an absolute scandal! True, she had no children, and her husband . . . Here the voices were always raised; they became fervent. How can he have married her? How can he, how can he? It must have been money, of course, but even then!

Mrs Kember's husband was at least ten years younger than she was, and so incredibly handsome that he looked like a mask or a most perfect illustration in an American novel rather than a man. Black hair, dark blue eyes, red lips, a slow sleepy smile, a fine tennis player, a perfect dancer, and with it all a mystery. Harry Kember was like a man walking in his sleep. Men couldn't stand him, they couldn't get a word out of the chap; he ignored his wife just as she ignored him. How did he live? Of course there were stories, but such stories! They simply couldn't be told. The women he'd been seen with, the places he'd been seen in . . . but nothing was ever certain, nothing definite. Some of the women at the Bay privately thought he'd commit a murder one day. Yes, even while they talked to Mrs Kember and took in the awful concoction she was wearing, they saw her, stretched as she lay on the beach; but cold, bloody, and still with a cigarette stuck in the corner of her mouth.

Mrs Kember rose, yawned, unsnapped her belt buckle, and tugged at the tape of her blouse. And Beryl stepped out of her skirt and shed her jersey, and stood up in her short white petticoat, and her camisole with ribbon bows on the shoulders.

'Mercy on us,' said Mrs Harry Kember, 'what a little beauty you are!'

'Don't!' said Beryl softly; but drawing off one stocking and then the other, she felt a little beauty.

'My dear – why not?' said Mrs Harry Kember, stamping on her own petticoat. Really – her underclothes! A pair of blue cotton knickers and a linen bodice that reminded one somehow of a pillow-case . . . . 'And you don't wear stays, do you?' She touched Beryl's waist, and Beryl sprang away with a small affected cry. Then 'Never!' she said firmly.

'Lucky little creature,' sighed Mrs Kember, unfastening her own.

Beryl turned her back and began the complicated movements of someone who is trying to take off her clothes and to pull on her bathing-dress all at one and the same time.

'Oh, my dear – don't mind me,' said Mrs Harry Kember. 'Why be shy? I shan't eat you. I shan't be shocked like those other ninnies.' And she gave her strange neighing laugh and grimaced at the other women.

But Beryl was shy. She never undressed in front of anybody. Was that silly? Mrs Harry Kember made her feel it was silly, even something to be ashamed of. Why be shy indeed! She glanced quickly at her friend standing so boldly in her torn chemise and lighting a fresh cigarette; and a quick, bold, evil feeling started up in her breast. Laughing recklessly, she drew on the limp, sandy-feeling bathing-dress that was not quite dry and fastened the twisted buttons.

'That's better,' said Mrs Harry Kember. They began to go down the beach together. 'Really, it's a sin for you to wear clothes, my dear. Somebody's got to tell you some day.'

The water was quite warm. It was that marvellous transparent blue, flecked with silver, but the sand at the bottom looked gold; when you kicked with your toes there rose a little puff of gold-dust. Now the waves just reached her breast. Beryl stood, her arms outstretched, gazing out, and as each wave came she gave the slightest little jump, so that it seemed it was the wave which lifted her so gently.

'I believe in pretty girls having a good time,' said Mrs Harry

Kember. 'Why not? Don't you make a mistake, my dear. Enjoy yourself.' And suddenly she turned turtle, disappeared, and swam away quickly, quickly, like a rat. Then she flicked round and began swimming back. She was going to say something else. Beryl felt that she was being poisoned by this cold woman, but she longed to hear. But oh, how strange, how horrible! As Mrs Harry Kember came up close she looked, in her black waterproof bathing-cap, with her sleepy face lifted above the water, just her chin touching, like a horrible caricature of her husband.

6

In a steamer chair, under a manuka tree that grew in the middle of the front grass patch, Linda Burnell dreamed the morning away. She did nothing. She looked up at the dark, close, dry leaves of the manuka, at the chinks of blue between, and now and again a tiny yellowish flower dropped on her. Pretty – yes, if you held one of those flowers on the palm of your hand and looked at it closely, it was an exquisite small thing. Each pale yellow petal shone as if each was the careful work of a loving hand. The tiny tongue in the centre gave it the shape of a bell. And when you turned it over the outside was a deep bronze colour. But as soon as they flowered, they fell and were scattered. You brushed them off your frock as you talked; the horrid little things got caught in one's hair. Why, then, flower at all? Who takes the trouble – or the joy – to make all these things that are wasted, wasted. . . . It was uncanny.

On the grass beside her, lying between two pillows, was the boy. Sound asleep he lay, his head turned away from his mother. His fine dark hair looked more like a shadow than like real hair, but his ear was a bright, deep coral. Linda clasped her hands above her head and crossed her feet. It was very pleasant to know that all these bungalows were empty, that everybody was down on the beach, out of sight, out of hearing. She had the garden to herself; she was alone.

Dazzling white the picotees shone; the golden-eyed marigolds glittered; the nasturtiums wreathed the veranda poles in green and gold flame. If only one had time to look at these flowers long enough, time to get over the sense of novelty and strangeness, time to know them! But as soon as one paused to part the petals, to discover the under-side of the leaf, along came Life and one was swept away. And, lying in her cane chair, Linda felt so light; she felt like a leaf. Along came Life like a wind and she was seized and shaken; she had to go. Oh dear, would it always be so? Was there no escape?

. . . Now she sat on the veranda of their Tasmanian home,

leaning against her father's knee. And he promised, 'As soon as you and I are old enough, Linny, we'll cut off somewhere, we'll escape. Two boys together. I have a fancy I'd like to sail up a river in China.' Linda saw that river, very wide, covered with little rafts and boats. She saw the yellow hats of the boatmen and she heard their high, thin voices as they called . . .

'Yes, papa.'

But just then a very broad young man with bright ginger hair walked slowly past their house, and slowly, solemnly even, uncovered. Linda's father pulled her ear teasingly, in the way he had.

'Linny's beau,' he whispered.

'Oh, papa, fancy being married to Stanley Burnell!'

Why, she was married to him. And what was more she loved him. Not the Stanley whom every one saw, not the everyday one; but a timid, sensitive, innocent Stanley who knelt down every night to say his prayers, and who longed to be good. Stanley was simple. If he believed in people – as he believed in her, for instance – it was with his whole heart. He could not be disloyal; he could not tell a lie. And how terribly he suffered if he thought anyone – she – was not being dead straight, dead sincere with him! 'This is too subtle for me!' He flung out the words, but his open, quivering, distraught look was like the look of a trapped beast.

But the trouble was – here Linda felt almost inclined to laugh, though heaven knows it was no laughing matter – she saw *her* Stanley so seldom. There were glimpses, moments, breathing spaces of calm, but all the rest of the time it was like living in a house that couldn't be cured of the habit of catching fire, or a ship that got wrecked every day. And it was always Stanley who was in the thick of the danger. Her whole time was spent in rescuing him, and restoring him, and calming him down, and listening to his story. And what was left of her time was spent in the dread of having children.

Linda frowned: she sat up quickly in her steamer chair and clasped her ankles. Yes, that was her real grudge against life; that was what she could not understand. That was the question she asked and asked, and listened in vain for the answer. It was all very well to say it was the common lot of women to bear children. It wasn't true. She, for one, could prove that wrong. She was broken, made weak, her courage was gone, through child-bearing. And what made it doubly hard to bear was, she did not love her children. It was useless pretending. Even if she had had the strength she never would have nursed and played with the little girls. No, it was as though a cold breath had chilled her through and through on each of those awful journeys: she had no warmth left to give them. As to the boy – well, thank heaven, mother had taken him;

he was mother's, or Beryl's, or anybody's who wanted him. She had hardly held him in her arms. She was so indifferent about him, that as he lay there . . . Linda glanced down.

The boy had turned over. He lay facing her, and he was no longer asleep. His dark-blue, baby eyes were open; he looked as though he was peeping at his mother. And suddenly his face dimpled; it broke into a wide, toothless smile, a perfect beam, no less.

'I'm here!' that happy smile seemed to say. 'Why don't you like me?'

There was something so quaint, so unexpected about that smile that Linda smiled herself. But she checked herself and said to the boy coldly, 'I don't like babies.'

'Don't like babies?' The boy couldn't believe her. 'Don't like *me*?' He waved his arms foolishly at his mother.

Linda dropped off her chair on to the grass.

'Why do you keep on smiling?' she said severely. 'If you knew what I was thinking about, you wouldn't.'

But he only squeezed up his eyes, slyly, and rolled his head on the pillow. He didn't believe a word she said.

'We know all about that!' smiled the boy.

Linda was so astonished at the confidence of this little creature. . . . Ah no, be sincere. That was not what she felt; it was something far different, it was something so new, so . . . The tears danced in her eyes; she breathed in a small whisper to the boy, 'Hallo, my funny!'

But by now the boy had forgotten his mother. He was serious again. Something pink, something soft waved in front of him. He made a grab at it and it immediately disappeared. But when he lay back, another, like the first, appeared. This time he determined to catch it. He made a tremendous effort and rolled right over.

7

The tide was out; the beach was deserted; lazily flopped the warm sea. The sun beat down, beat down hot and fiery on the fine sand, baking the grey and blue and black and white-veined pebbles. It sucked up the little drop of water that lay in the hollow of the curved shells; it bleached the pink convolvulus that threaded through and through the sand-hills. Nothing seemed to move but the small sand-hoppers. Pit-pit-pit! They were never still.

Over there on the weed-hung rocks that looked at low tide like shaggy beasts come down to the water to drink, the sunlight seemed to spin like a silver coin dropped into each of the small rock pools. They danced, they quivered, and minute ripples laved the porous shores. Looking down, bending over, each pool was like a lake with pink and blue houses clustered on the shores; and oh! the vast mountainous country behind those houses – the ravines, the passes, the dangerous creeks and fearful tracks that led to the water's edge. Underneath waved the sea-forest – pink thread-like trees, velvet anemones, and orange berry-spotted weeds. Now a stone on the bottom moved, rocked, and there was a glimpse of a black feeler; now a thread-like creature wavered by and was lost. Something was happening to the pink, waving trees; they were changing to a cold moonlight blue. And now there sounded the faintest 'plop'. Who made that sound? What was going on down there? And how strong, how damp the seaweed smelt in the hot sun . . . .

The green blinds were drawn in the bungalows of the summer colony. Over the verandas, prone on the paddock, flung over the fences, there were exhausted-looking bathing-dresses and rough striped towels. Each back window seemed to have a pair of sand-shoes on the sill and some lumps of rock or a bucket or a collection of pawa shells. The bush quivered in a haze of heat; the sandy road was empty except for the Trouts' dog Snooker, who lay stretched in the very middle of it. His blue eye was turned up, his legs stuck out stiffly, and he gave an occasional desperate sounding puff, as much as to say he had decided to make an end of it and was only waiting for some kind cart to come along.

'What are you looking at, my grandma? Why do you keep stopping and sort of staring at the wall?'

Kezia and her grandmother were taking their siesta together. The little girl, wearing only her short drawers and her under-bodice, her arms and legs bare, lay on one of the puffed-up pillows of her grandma's bed, and the old woman, in a white ruffled dressing-gown, sat in a rocker at the window, with a long piece of pink knitting in her lap. This room that they shared, like the other rooms of the bungalow, was of light varnished wood and the floor was bare. The furniture was of the shabbiest, the simplest. The dressing-table, for instance, was a packing-case in a sprigged muslin petticoat, and the mirror above was very strange; it was as though a little piece of forked lightning was imprisoned in it. On the table there stood a jar of sea-pinks, pressed so tightly together they looked more like a velvet pin-cushion, and a special shell which Kezia had given her grandma for a pin-tray, and another even more special which she had thought would make a very nice place for a watch to curl up in.

'Tell me, grandma,' said Kezia.

The old woman sighed, whipped the wool twice round her thumb, and drew the bone needle through. She was casting on.

'I was thinking of your Uncle William, darling,' she said quietly.

'My Australian Uncle William?' said Kezia. She had another.

'Yes, of course.'

'The one I never saw?'

'That was the one.'

'Well, what happened to him?' Kezia knew perfectly well, but she wanted to be told again.

'He went to the mines, and he got a sunstroke there and died,' said old Mrs Fairfield.

Kezia blinked and considered the picture again. . . . A little man fallen over like a tin soldier by the side of a big black hole.

'Does it make you sad to think about him, grandma?' She hated her grandma to be sad.

It was the old woman's turn to consider. Did it make her sad? To look back, back. To stare down the years, as Kezia had seen her doing. To look after *them* as a woman does, long after *they* were out of sight. Did it make her sad? No, life was like that.

'No, Kezia.'

'But why?' asked Kezia. She lifted one bare arm and began to draw things in the air. 'Why did Uncle William have to die? He wasn't old.'

Mrs Fairfield began counting the stitches in threes. 'It just happened,' she said in an absorbed voice.

'Does everybody have to die? asked Kezia.

'Everybody!'

'*Me?*' Kezia sounded fearfully incredulous.

'Some day, my darling.'

'But, grandma.' Kezia waved her left leg and waggled the toes. They felt sandy. 'What if I just won't?'

The old woman sighed again and drew a long thread from the ball.

'We're not asked, Kezia,' she said sadly. 'It happens to all of us sooner or later.'

Kezia lay still thinking this over. She didn't want to die. It meant she would have to leave here, leave everywhere, for ever, leave – leave her grandma. She rolled over quickly.

'Grandma,' she said in a startled voice.

'What, my pet!'

'*You're* not to die.' Kezia was very decided.

'Ah, Kezia' – her grandma looked up and smiled and shook her head – 'don't let's talk about it.'

'But you're not to. You couldn't leave me. You couldn't not be there.' This was awful. 'Promise me you won't ever do it, grandma,' pleaded Kezia.

The old woman went on knitting.

'Promise me! Say never!'

... *the 'Mercury' is bringing out that very long seaweedy story of mine 'At the Bay'. I feel inclined to suggest to them to give away a spade an' bucket with each copy.*
to Dorothy Brett, 15 October 1921

But still her grandma was silent.

Kezia rolled off the bed; she couldn't bear it any longer, and lightly she leapt on to her grandma's knees, clasped her hands round the old woman's throat and began kissing her, under the chin, behind the ear, and blowing down her neck.

'Say never ... say never ... say never –' She gasped between the kisses. And then she began, very softly and lightly, to tickle her grandma.

'Kezia!' The old woman dropped her knitting. She swung back in the rocker. She began to tickle Kezia. 'Say never, say never, say never,' gurgled Kezia, while they lay there laughing in each other's arms. 'Come, that's enough, my squirrel! That's enough, my wild pony!' said old Mrs Fairfield, setting her cap straight. 'Pick up my knitting.'

Both of them had forgotten what the 'never' was about.

8

The sun was still full on the garden when the back door of the Burnells' shut with a bang and a very gay figure walked down the path to the gate. It was Alice, the servant girl, dressed for her afternoon out. She wore a white cotton dress with such large red spots on it, and so many that they made you shudder, white shoes and a leghorn turned up under the brim with poppies. Of course she wore gloves, white ones, stained at the fastenings with iron-mould, and in one hand she carried a very dashed-looking sun-shade which she referred to as her *perishall.*

Beryl, sitting in the window, fanning her freshly washed hair, thought she had never seen such a guy. If Alice had only blacked her face with a piece of cork before she started out the picture would have been complete. And where did a girl like that go in a place like this? The heart-shaped Fijian fan beat scornfully at that lovely bright mane. She supposed Alice had picked up some horrible common larrikin and they'd go off into the bush together. Pity to make herself so conspicuous; they'd have hard work to hide with Alice in that rig-out.

But no, Beryl was unfair. Alice was going to tea with Mrs Stubbs, who'd sent her an 'invite' by the little boy who called for orders. She had taken ever such a liking to Mrs Stubbs ever since the first time she went to the shop to get something for her mosquitoes.

'Dear heart!' Mrs Stubbs had clapped her hand to her side. 'I never seen anyone so eaten. You might have been attacked by canningbals.'

Alice did wish there'd been a bit of life on the road though. Made her feel so queer, having nobody behind her. Made her feel all weak in the spine. She couldn't believe that someone wasn't watching her. And yet it was silly to turn round; it gave you away. She pulled up her gloves, hummed to herself and said to the distant gum tree, 'Shan't be long now.' But that was hardly company.

Mrs Stubb's shop was perched on a little hillock just off the road. It had two big windows for eyes, a broad veranda for a hat, and the sign on the roof, scrawled MRS STUBBS'S, was like a little card stuck rakishly in the hat crown.

On the veranda there hung a long string of bathing-dresses, clinging together as though they'd just been rescued from the sea rather than waiting to go in, and beside them there hung a cluster of sand-shoes so extraordinarily mixed that to get at one pair you had to tear apart and forcibly separate at least fifty. Even then it was the rarest thing to find the left that belonged to the right. So many people had lost patience and gone off with one shoe that fitted and one that was a little too big. ... Mrs Stubbs prided herself on keeping something of everything. The two windows, arranged in the form of precarious pyramids, were crammed so tight, piled so high, that it seemed only a conjuror could prevent them from toppling over. In the left-hand corner of one window, glued to the pane by four gelatine lozenges, there was – and there had been from time immemorial – a notice:

> LOST! HANSOME GOLE BROOCH
> SOLID GOLD
> ON OR NEAR BEACH
> REWARD OFFERED

Alice pressed open the door. The bell jangled, the red serge curtains parted, and Mrs Stubbs appeared. With her broad smile and the long bacon knife in her hand she looked like a friendly brigand. Alice was welcomed so warmly that she found it quite difficult to keep up her 'manners.' They consisted of persistent little coughs and hems, pulls at her gloves, tweaks at her skirt, and a curious difficulty in seeing what was set before her or understanding what was said.

Tea was laid on the parlour table – ham, sardines, a whole pound of butter, and such a large johnny cake that it looked like an advertisement for somebody's baking powder. But the Primus stove roared so loudly that it was useless to try to talk above it. Alice sat down on the edge of a basket-chair while Mrs Stubbs pumped the stove still higher. Suddenly Mrs Stubbs whipped the cushion off a chair and disclosed a large brown paper parcel.

'I've just had some new photers taken, my dear,' she shouted cheerfully to Alice. 'Tell me what you think of them.'

In a very dainty, refined way Alice wet her finger and put the tissue back from the first one. Life! How many there were! There were three dozzing at least. And she held hers up to the light.

Mrs Stubbs sat in an arm-chair, leaning very much to one side. There was a look of mild astonishment on her large face, and well there might be. For through the arm-chair stood on a carpet, to the left of it, miraculously skirting the carpet border, there was a dashing waterfall. On her right stood a Grecian pillar with a giant fern tree on either side of it, and in the background towered a gaunt mountain, pale with snow.

'It is a nice style, isn't it?' shouted Mrs Stubbs; and Alice had just screamed 'Sweetly' when the roaring of the Primus stove died down, fizzled out, ceased, and she said 'Pretty' in a silence that was frightening.

'Draw up your chair, my dear,' said Mrs Stubbs, beginning to pour out. 'Yes,' she said thoughtfully as she handed the tea, 'but I don't care about the size. I'm having an enlargemint. All very well for Christmas cards, but I never was the one for small photers myself. You get no comfort out of them. To say the truth, I find them dis'eartening.'

Alice quite saw what she meant.

'Size,' said Mrs Stubbs. 'Give me size. That was what my poor dear husband was always saying. He couldn't stand anything small. Gave him the creeps. And, strange as it may seem, my dear' – here Mrs Stubbs creaked and seemed to expand herself at the memory – 'it was dropsy that carried him off at the larst. Many's the time they drawn one and a half pints from 'im at the 'ospital. . . . It seemed like a judgmint.'

Alice burned to know exactly what it was that was drawn from him. She ventured, 'I suppose it was water.'

But Mrs Stubbs fixed Alice with her eyes and replied meaningly, 'It was *liquid*, my dear.'

Liquid! Alice jumped away from the word like a cat and came back to it, nosing and wary.

'That's 'im!' said Mrs Stubbs, and she pointed dramatically to the life-size head and shoulders of a burly man with a dead white rose in the button-hole of his coat that made you think of a curl of cold mutton fat. Just below, in silver letters on a red cardboard ground, were the words, 'Be not afraid, it is I.'

'It's ever such a fine face,' said Alice faintly.

The pale-blue bow on the top of Mrs Stubbs's fair frizzy hair quivered. She arched her plump neck. What a neck she had! It was bright pink where it began and then it changed to warm apricot, and that faded to the colour of a brown egg and then to a deep creamy.

'All the same, my dear,' she said surprisingly, 'freedom's best!' Her soft, fat chuckle sounded like a purr. 'Freedom's best,' said Mrs Stubbs again.

Freedom! Alice gave a loud, silly little titter. She felt awkward. Her mind flew back to her own kitching. Ever so queer! She wanted to be back in it again.

9

A strange company assembled in the Burnell's washhouse after tea. Round the table there sat a bull, a rooster, a donkey that kept forgetting it was a donkey, a sheep and a bee. The washhouse was the perfect place for such a meeting because they could make as much noise as they liked and nobody ever interrupted. It was a small tin shed standing apart from the bungalow. Against the wall there was a deep trough and in the corner a copper with a basket of clothes-pegs on top of it. The little window, spun over with cobwebs, had a piece of candle and a mouse-trap on the dusty sill. There were clothes-lines criss-crossed overhead and, hanging from a peg on the wall, a very big, a huge, rusty horseshoe. The table was in the middle with a form at either side.

'You can't be a bee, Kezia. A bee's not an animal. It's a ninseck.'

'Oh, but I do want to be a bee frightfully,' wailed Kezia ... A tiny bee, all yellow-furry, with striped legs. She drew her legs up under her and leaned over the table. She felt she was a bee.

'A ninseck must be an animal,' she said stoutly. 'It makes a noise. It's not like a fish.'

'I'm a bull, I'm a bull!' cried Pip. And he gave such a tremendous bellow – how did he make that noise? – that Lottie looked quite alarmed.

'I'll be a sheep,' said little Rags. 'A whole lot of sheep went past this morning.'

'How do you know?'

'Dad heard them. Baa!' He sounded like the little lamb that trots behind and seems to wait to be carried.

'Cock-a-doodle-do!' shrilled Isabel. With her red cheeks and bright eyes she looked like a rooster.

'What'll I be?' Lottie asked everybody, and she sat there smiling, waiting for them to decide for her. It had to be an easy one.

'Be a donkey, Lottie.' It was Kezia's suggestion. 'Hee-haw! You can't forget that.'

'Hee-haw!' said Lottie solemnly. 'When do I have to say it?'

'I'll explain, I'll explain' said the bull. It was he who had the cards. He waved them round his head. 'All be quiet! All listen!' And he waited for them. 'Look here, Lottie.' He turned up a card. 'It's got two spots on it – see? Now if you put that card in the middle and somebody else has one with two spots as well, you say "Hee-haw", and the card's yours.'

'Mine?' Lottie was round-eyed. 'To keep?'

'No, silly. Just for the game, see? Just while we're playing.' The bull was very cross with her.

'Oh, Lottie, you *are* a little silly,' said the proud rooster.

Lottie looked at both of them. Then she hung her head; her lip quivered. 'I don't not want to play,' she whispered. The others glanced at one another like conspirators. All of them knew what that meant. She would go away and be discovered somewhere standing with her pinny thrown over her head, in a corner, or against a wall, or even behind a chair.

'Yes, you *do*, Lottie. It's quite easy,' said Kezia.

And Isabel, repentant, said exactly like a grown-up, 'Watch *me,* Lottie, and you'll soon learn.'

'Cheer up, Lot,' said Pip. 'There, I know what I'll do. I'll give you the first one. It's mine, really, but I'll give it to you. Here you are.' And he slammed the card down in front of Lottie.

Lottie revived at that. But now she was in another difficulty. 'I haven't got a hanky,' she said; 'I want one badly, too.'

'Here, Lottie, you can use mine.' Rags dipped into his sailor blouse and brought up a very wet-looking one, knotted together. 'Be very careful,' he warned her. 'Only use that corner. Don't undo it. I've got a little star-fish inside I'm going to try and tame.'

'Oh, come on, you girls,' said the bull. 'And mind – you're not to look at your cards. You've got to keep you hands under the table till I say "Go".'

Smack went the cards round the table. They tried with all their might to see, but Pip was too quick for them. It was very exciting, sitting there in the washhouse; it was all they could do not to burst into a little chorus of animals before Pip had finished dealing.

'Now, Lottie, you begin.'

Timidly Lottie stretched out a hand, took the top card off her pack, had a good look at it – it was plain she was counting the spots – and put it down.

'No, Lottie, you can't do that. You mustn't look first. You must turn it the other way over.'

'But then everybody will see it the same time as me,' said Lottie.

The game proceeded. Mooe-ooo-er! The bull was terrible. He charged over the table and seemed to eat the cards up.

Bss-ss! said the bee.

Cock-a-doodle-do! Isabel stood up in her excitement and moved her elbows like wings.

Baa! Little Rags put down the King of Diamonds and Lottie put down the one they called the King of Spain. She had hardly any cards left.

'Why don't you call out, Lottie?'

'I've forgotten what I am,' said the donkey woefully.

'Well, change! Be a dog instead! Bow-wow!'

'Oh yes. That's *much* easier.' Lottie smiled again. But when she and Kezia both had one Kezia waited on purpose. The others made signs to Lottie and pointed. Lottie turned very red; she looked bewildered, and at last she said, 'Hee-haw! Ke-zia.'

'Ss! Wait a minute!' They were in the very thick of it when the bull stopped them, holding up his hand. 'What's that? What's that noise?'

'What noise? What do you mean?' asked the rooster.

'Ss! Shut up! Listen!' They were mouse-still. 'I thought I heard a – a sort of knocking,' said the bull.

'What was it like?' asked the sheep faintly.

No answer.

The bee gave a shudder. 'Whatever did we shut the door for?' she said softly. Oh, why, why had they shut the door?

While they were playing, the day had faded; the gorgeous sunset had blazed and died. And now the quick dark came racing over the sea, over the sand-hills, up the paddock. You were frightened to look in the corners of the washhouse, and yet you had to look with all your might. And somewhere, far away, grandma was lighting a lamp. The blinds were being pulled down; the kitchen fire leapt in the tins on the mantelpiece.

'It would be awful now,' said the bull, 'if a spider was to fall from the ceiling on to the table, wouldn't it?'

'Spiders don't fall from ceilings.'

'Yes, they do. Our Min told us she'd seen a spider as big as a saucer, with long hairs on it like a gooseberry.'

Quickly all the little heads were jerked up; all the little bodies drew together, pressed together.

'Why doesn't somebody come and call us?' cried the rooster.

Oh, those grown-ups, laughing and snug, sitting in the lamp-light, drinking out of cups! They'd forgotten about them. No, not really forgotten. That was what their smile meant. They had decided to leave them there all by themselves.

Suddenly Lottie gave such a piercing scream that all of them jumped off the forms, all of them screamed too. 'A face – a face looking!' shrieked Lottie.

It was true, it was real. Pressed against the window was a pale face, black eyes, a black beard.

'Grandma! Mother! Somebody!'

But they had not got to the door, tumbling over one another, before it opened for Uncle Jonathan. He had come to take the little boys home.

10

He had meant to be there before, but in the front garden he had come upon Linda walking up and down the grass, stopping to pick off a dead pink or give a top-heavy carnation something to lean against, or to take a deep breath of something, and then walking on again, with her little air of remoteness. Over her white frock she wore a yellow, pink-fringed shawl from the Chinaman's shop.

'Hallo, Jonathan!' called Linda. And Jonathan whipped off his shabby panama, pressed it against his breast, dropped on one knee, and kissed Linda's hand.

'Greeting, my Fair One! Greeting, my Celestial Peach Blossom!' boomed the bass voice gently. 'Where are the other noble dames?'

'Beryl's out playing bridge and mother's giving the boy his bath . . . .Have you come to borrow something?'

The Trouts were for ever running out of things and sending across to the Burnells' at the last moment.

But Jonathan only answered, 'A little love, a little kindness;' and he walked by his sister-in-law's side.

Linda dropped into Beryl's hammock under the manuka tree and Jonathan stretched himself on the grass beside her, pulled a long stalk and began chewing it. They knew each other well. The voices of children cried from the other gardens. A fisherman's light cart shook along the sandy road, and from far away they heard a dog barking; it was muffled as though the dog had its head in a sack. If you listened you could just hear the soft swish of the sea at full tide sweeping the pebbles. The sun was sinking.

'And so you go back to the office on Monday, do you, Jonathan?' asked Linda.

'On Monday the cage door opens and clangs to upon the victim for another eleven months and a week,' answered Jonathan.

Linda swung a little. 'It must be awful,' she said slowly.

'Would ye have me laugh, my fair sister? Would ye have me weep?'

Linda was so accustomed to Jonathan's way of talking that she paid no attention to it.

'I suppose,' she said vaguely, 'one gets used to it. One gets used to anything.'

'Does one? Hum!' The 'Hum' was so deep it seemed to boom from underneath the ground. 'I wonder how it's done,' brooded Jonathan; 'I've never managed it.'

Looking at him as he lay there, Linda thought again how attractive he was. It was strange to think that he was only an ordinary clerk, that Stanley earned twice as much money as he. What was the matter with Jonathan? He had no ambition; she supposed that was it. And yet one felt he was gifted, exceptional. He was passionately fond of music; every spare penny he had went on books. He was always full of new ideas, schemes, plans. But nothing came of it all. The new fire blazed in Jonathan; you almost heard it roaring softly as he explained, described and dilated on the new thing; but a moment later it had fallen in and there was nothing but ashes, and Jonathan went about with a look like hunger in his black eyes. At these times he exaggerated his absurd manner of speaking, and he sang in church – he was the leader of the choir – with such fearful dramatic intensity that the meanest hymn put on an unholy splendour.

'It seems to me just as imbecile, just as infernal, to have to go to the office on Monday,' said Jonathan, 'as it always has done and always will do. To spend all the best years of one's life sitting on a stool from nine to five, scratching in somebody's ledger! It's a queer use to make of one's . . . one and only life, isn't it? Or do I fondly dream?' He rolled over on the grass and looked up at Linda. 'Tell me, what is the difference between my life and that of an ordinary prisoner. The only difference I can see is that I put myself in jail and nobody's ever going to let me out. That's a more intolerable situation than the other. For if I'd been – pushed in, against my will – kicking, even – once the door was locked, or at any rate in five years or so, I might have accepted the fact and begun to take an interest in the flight of flies or counting the warder's steps along the passage with particular attention to variations of tread and so on. But as it is, I'm like an insect that's flown into a room of its own accord. I dash against the walls, dash against the windows, flop against the ceiling, do everything on God's earth, in fact, except fly out again. And all the while I'm thinking, like that moth, or that butterfly, or whatever it is, 'The shortness of life! The shortness of life!' I've only one night or one day, and there's this vast dangerous garden, waiting out there, undiscovered, unexplored.'

'But, if you feel like that, why – ' began Linda quickly.

'*Ah!*' cried Jonathan. And that 'Ah!' was somehow almost exultant. 'There you have me. Why? Why indeed? There's the maddening, mysterious question. Why don't I fly out again? There's the window or the door or whatever it was I came in by. It's not hopelessly shut – is it? Why don't I find it and be off? Answer me that, little sister.' But he gave her no time to answer.

'I'm exactly like that insect again. For some reason' – Jonathan paused between the words – 'it's not allowed, it's forbidden, it's against the insect law, to stop banging and flopping and crawling up the pane even for an instant. Why don't I leave the office? Why don't I seriously consider, this moment, for instance, what it is that prevents me leaving? It's not as though I'm tremendously tied. I've two boys to provide for, but, after all, they're boys. I could cut off to sea, or get a job up-country, or –' Suddenly he smiled at Linda and said in a changed voice, as if he were confiding a secret, 'Weak . . . weak. No stamina. No anchor. No guiding principle, let us call it.' But then the dark velvety voice rolled out:

Would ye hear the story
How it unfolds itself . . .

and they were silent.

The sun had set. In the western sky there were great masses of crushed-up rose-coloured clouds. Broad beams of light shone through the clouds and beyond them as if they would cover the whole sky. Overhead the blue faded; it turned a pale gold, and the bush outlined against it gleamed dark and brilliant like metal. Sometimes when those beams of light show in the sky they are very awful. They remind you that up there sits Jehovah, the jealous God, the Almighty, Whose eye is upon you, ever watchful, never weary. You remember that at His coming the whole earth will shake into one ruined graveyard; the cold, bright angels will drive you this way and that, and there will be no time to explain what could be explained so simply. . . . But to-night it seemed to Linda there was something infinitely joyful and loving in those silver beams. And now no sound came from the sea. It breathed softly as if it would draw that tender, joyful beauty into its own bosom.

'It's all wrong, it's all wrong,' came the shadowy voice of Jonathan. 'It's not the scene, it's not the setting for. . .three stools, three desks, three inkpots and a wire blind.'

Linda knew that he would never change, but she said, 'Is it too late, even now?'

'I'm old – I'm old,' intoned Jonathan. He bent towards her, he passed his hand over his head. 'Look!' His black hair was speckled all over with silver, like the breast plumage of a black fowl.

Linda was surprised. She had no idea that he was grey. And yet, as he stood up beside her and sighed and stretched, she saw him, for the first time, not resolute, not gallant, not careless, but touched already with age. He looked very tall on the darkening grass, and the thought crossed her mind, 'He is like a weed.'

Jonathan stooped again and kissed her fingers.

'Heaven reward thy sweet patience, lady mine,' he murmured. 'I must go seek those heirs to my fame and fortune . . . .' He was gone.

11

Light shone in the windows of the bungalow. Two square patches of gold fell upon the pinks and the peaked marigolds. Florrie, the cat, came out on to the veranda and sat on the top step, her white paws close together, he tail curled round. She looked content, as though she had been waiting for this moment all day.

'Thank goodness, it's getting late,' said Florrie. 'Thank goodness, the long day is over.' Her greengage eyes opened.

Presently there sounded the rumble of the coach, the crack of Kelly's whip. It came near enough for one to hear the voices of the men from town, talking loudly together. It stopped at the Burnells' gate.

Stanley was half-way up the path before he saw Linda. 'Is that you, darling?'

'Yes, Stanley.'

He leapt across the flower-bed and seized her in his arms. She was enfolded in that familiar, eager, strong embrace.

'Forgive me, darling, forgive me,' stammered Stanley, and he put his hand under her chin and lifted her face to him.

'Forgive you?' smiled Linda. 'But whatever for?'

'Good God! You can't have forgotten,' cried Stanley Burnell. 'I've thought of nothing else all day. I've had the hell of a day. I made up my mind to dash out and telegraph, and then I thought the wire mightn't reach you before I did. I've been in tortures, Linda.'

'But, Stanley,' said Linda, 'what must I forgive you for?'

'Linda!' – Stanley was very hurt – 'didn't you realise – you must have realised – I went away without saying good-bye to you this morning? I can't imagine how I can have done such a thing. My confounded temper, of course. But – well' – and he sighed and took her in his arms again – 'I've suffered for it enough to-day.'

'What's that you've got in your hand?' asked Linda. 'New gloves? Let me see.'

Oh, just a cheap pair of wash-leather ones,' said Stanley humbly. 'I noticed Bell was wearing some in the coach this morning, so, as I was passing the shop, I dashed in and got myself a pair. What are you smiling at? You don't think it was wrong of me, do you?'

'On the *con*-trary, darling,' said Linda, 'I think it was most sensible.'

She pulled one of the large, pale gloves on her own fingers and looked at her hand, turning it this way and that. She was still smiling.

Stanley wanted to say, 'I was thinking of you the whole time I bought them.' It was true, but for some reason he couldn't say it. 'Let's go in,' said he.

12

Why does one feel so different at night? Why is it so exciting to be awake when everybody else is asleep? Late – it is very late! And yet every moment you feel more and more wakeful, as though you were slowly, almost with every breath, waking up into a new, wonderful, far more thrilling and exciting world than the daylight one. And what is this queer sensation, that you're a conspirator? Lightly, stealthily you move about your room. You take something off the dressing-table and put it down again without a sound. And everything, even the bedpost, knows you, responds, shares your secret. . . .

You're not very fond of your room by day. You never think about it. You're in and out, the door opens and slams, the cupboard creaks. You sit down on the side of your bed, change your shoes and dash out again. A dive down to the glass, two pins in your hair, powder your nose and off again. But now – it's suddenly dear to you. It's a darling little funny room. It's yours. Oh, what a joy it is to own things! Mine – my own!

'My very own for ever?'

'Yes.' Their lips met.

No, of course, that had nothing to do with it. That was all nonsense and rubbish. But, in spite of herself, Beryl saw so plainly two people standing in the middle of her room. Her arms were round his neck; he held her. And now he whispered, 'My beauty, my little beauty!' She jumped off her bed, ran over to the window and kneeled on the window-seat, with her elbows on the sill. But the beautiful night, the garden, every bush, every leaf, even the white palings, even the stars, were conspirators too. So bright was the moon that the flowers were bright as by day; the shadow of the nasturtiums, exquisite lily-like leaves and wide-open flowers, lay across the silvery veranda. The manuka tree, bent by the southerly winds, was like a bird on one leg stretching out a wing.

But when Beryl looked at the bush, it seemed to her the bush was sad.

"We are dumb trees, reaching up in the night, imploring we know not what,' said the sorrowful bush.

It is true when you are by yourself and you think about life, it is always sad. All that excitement and so on has a way of suddenly leaving you, and it's as though, in the silence, somebody called your name, and you heard your name for the first time. 'Beryl!'

'Yes, I'm here. I'm Beryl. Who wants me?'

'Beryl!'

'Let me come.'

It is lonely living by oneself. Of course, there are relations, friends, heaps of them; but that's not what she means. She wants someone who will find the Beryl they none of them know, who will expect her to be that Beryl always. She wants a lover.

'Take me away from all these other people, my love. Let us go far away. Let us live our life, all new, all ours, from the very beginning. Let us make our fire. Let us sit down to eat together. Let us have long talks at night.'

And the thought was almost, 'Save me, my love. Save me!'

. . . 'Oh, go on! Don't be a prude, my dear. You enjoy yourself while you're young. That's my advice.' And a high rush of silly laughter joined Mrs Harry Kember's loud, indifferent neigh.

You see, it's so frightfully difficult when you've nobody. You're so at the mercy of things. You can't just be rude. And you've always this horror of seeming inexperienced and stuffy like the other ninnies at the Bay. And – and it's fascinating to know you've power over people. Yes, that is fascinating . . . .

Oh why, oh why doesn't 'he' come soon?

If I go on living here, thought Beryl, anything may happen to me.

'But how do you know he is coming at all?' mocked a small voice within her.

But Beryl dismissed it. She couldn't be left. Other people, perhaps, but not she. It wasn't possible to think that Beryl Fairfield never married, that lovely, fascinating girl.

'Do you remember Beryl Fairfield?'

'Remember her! As if I could forget her! It was one summer at the Bay that I saw her. She was standing on the beach in a blue' – no, pink – 'muslin frock, holding on a big cream' – no, black – 'straw hat. But it's years ago now.'

'She's as lovely as ever, more so if anything.'

Beryl smiled, bit her lip, and gazed over the garden. As she gazed, she saw somebody, a man, leave the road, step along the paddock beside their palings as if he was coming straight towards her. Her heart beat. Who was it? Who could it be? It couldn't be a burglar, certainly not a burglar, for he was smoking and he strolled lightly. Beryl's heart leapt; it seemed to turn right over and then to stop. She recognised him.

'Good evening, Miss Beryl,' said the voice softly.

'Good evening.'

'Won't you come for a little walk?' it drawled.

Come for a walk – at that time of night! 'I couldn't. Everybody's in bed. Everybody's asleep.'

'Oh,' said the voice lightly, and a whiff of sweet smoke reached her. 'What does everybody matter? Do come! It's such a fine night. There's not a soul about.'

Beryl shook her head. But already something stirred in her, something reared its head.

The voice said, 'Frightened?' It mocked, 'Poor little girl!'

'Not in the least,' said she. As she spoke that weak thing within her seemed to uncoil, to grow suddenly tremendously strong; she longed to go!

And just as if this was quite understood by the other, the voice said, gently and softly, but finally, 'Come along!'

Beryl stepped over her low window, crossed the veranda, ran down the grass to the gate. He was there before her.

'That's right,' breathed the voice, and it teased, 'You're not frightened, are you? You're not frightened?'

She was; now she was here she was terrified, and it seemed to her everything was different. The moonlight stared and glittered; the shadows were like bars of iron. Her hand was taken.

'Not in the least,' she said lightly. 'Why should I be?'

Her hand was pulled gently, tugged. She held back.

'No, I'm not coming any farther,' said Beryl.

'Oh, rot!' Harry Kember didn't believe her. 'Come along! We'll just go as far as that fuchsia bush. Come along!'

The fuchsia bush was tall. It fell over the fence in a shower. There was a little pit of darkness beneath.

'No, really, I don't want to,' said Beryl.

For a moment Harry Kember didn't answer. Then he came close to her, turned to her, smiled and said quickly, 'Don't be silly! Don't be silly!'

His smile was something she'd never seen before. Was he drunk? That bright, blind, terrifying smile froze her with horror. What was she doing? How had she got here? The stern garden asked her as the gate pushed open, and quick as a cat Harry Kember came through and snatched her to him.

'Cold little devil! Cold little devil!' said the hateful voice. But Beryl was strong. She slipped, ducked, wrenched free.

'You are vile, vile,' said she.

'Then why in God's name did you come?' stammered Harry Kember.

Nobody answered him.

A cloud, small, serene, floated across the moon. In that moment of darkness the sea sounded deep, troubled. Then the cloud sailed away, and the sound of the sea was a vague murmur, as though it waked out of a dark dream. All was still.

'At the Bay' (the *London Mercury*, January 1922)

'*At the Bay* at last the milk white harbour catches the glitter and the gulls floating on the trembling water gleam like the shadows within a pearl.

The house dog comes out of his kennel dragging the heavy chain and kalop kalops at the water standing cold in the iron pan. The house cat emerges from nowhere bounds out to the kitchen window sill waiting for her spill of warm morning milk.' (*Journal*, December 1920)

'Finished "An Ideal Family" yesterday. It seems to me better . . . but still its not good enough . . . this kind of knowledge is too easy for me; its even a kind of trickery . . . I shall tackle something different – a long story – "At the Bay" with more *difficult* relationships. Thats the whole problem.' (*Journal*, 23 July 1921)

'I must stop this letter and get on with my new story. It's called "At the Bay" and it's (I hope) full of sand and seaweed, bathing dresses hanging over verandas and sandshoes on window sills, and little pink "sea" convolvulus, and rather gritty sandwiches, and the tide coming in. And it smells (oh, I *do* hope it smells) a little bit fishy.' (to Dorothy Brett, 8 August 1921)

' – a continuation of *Prelude* . . . I've been at it all night. My precious children have sat in here playing cards. I've wandered about all sorts of places – in and out – I hope it is good. It is as good as I can do, and all my heart and soul is in it . . . every single bit. Oh God, I hope it gives pleasure to someone . . . it is so strange to bring the dead to life again. There's my Grandmother, back in her chair with her pink knitting . . . And one feels *possessed*. And then the place where it all happens. I have tried to make it as familiar to "you" as it is to me. You know the marigolds . . . one tries to go deep – to speak to the secret self we all have.' (to Dorothy Brett, *Letters*, September 1921)

'It took me nearly a month to "recover" from "At the Bay" . . . I could not get away from the sound of the sea and Beryl fanning her hair at the window. These things would not *die down*. But now I am not at all sure about that story. It seems to me it's a little "wispy" – not what it might have been.' (*Journal*, 16 October 1921)

'As I reread At the Bay in proof, it seemed to me flat, dull, and not a success at all. I was very much ashamed of it. I am.' (*Journal*, 13 November 1921)

' "At the Bay" is a continuation of *Prelude* . . . a work of genius.' (Rebecca West, *New Statesman*, 18 March 1922)

'arguably her greatest story' (C. A. Hankin, *Katherine Mansfield and Her Confessional Stories*)

Despite her own harsh judgement 'At the Bay' has been highly praised by many readers and critics. If I were to choose one story to represent her work this would be that story. It appears so simple – a summer's day, from dawn to dark, in the life of a Wellington family. It is, of course, much more complex than this suggests. It brings together several of the themes she had explored throughout her life. It shows not just the moment of disillusionment on which so many of her early stories centred, but goes beyond in a mood of calm acceptance – ugliness, death, these are inevitable aspects of reality and must be accepted. Despite the moments of conflict and disillusionment the story ends as it began – at peace. The characters and their intricate relationships emerge clearly.

Technically it is a remarkable achievement. The slow lyrical descriptive opening is just one example of the way in which setting and atmosphere are evoked. Each word has been carefully selected. The dialogue ranges, for example, from the taut, brittle words of Mrs Kember to the warmer tones of the conversation between Kezia and her grandmother. There is humour and compassion; no longer is it a matter of 'ugliness for ugliness' sake' instead 'Beauty triumphs over ugliness in life, thats what I feel . . . and long to express.'

The Doll's House

When dear old Mrs Hay went back to town after staying with the Burnells she sent the children a doll's house. It was so big that the carter and Pat carried it into the courtyard, and there it stayed, propped up on two wooden boxes beside the feed-room door. No harm could come to it; it was summer. And perhaps the smell of paint would have gone off by the time it had to be taken in. For, really, the smell of paint coming from that doll's house ('Sweet of old Mrs Hay, of course; most sweet and generous!') – but the smell of paint was quite enough to make anyone seriously ill, in Aunt Beryl's opinion. Even before the sacking was taken off. And when it was . . .

There stood the doll's house, a dark, oily, spinach green, picked out with bright yellow. Its two solid little chimneys, glued on to the roof, were painted red and white, and the door, gleaming with yellow varnish, was like a little slab of toffee. Four windows, real windows, were divided into panes by a broad streak of green. There was actually a tiny porch, too, painted yellow, with big lumps of congealed paint hanging along the edge.

But perfect, perfect little house! Who could possibly mind the smell. It was part of the joy, part of the newness.

'Open it quickly, someone!'

The hook at the side was stuck fast. Pat prised it open with his penknife, and the whole house front swung back, and – there you were, gazing at one and the same moment into the drawing-room and dining-room, the kitchen and two bedrooms. That is the way for a house to open! Why don't all houses open like that? How much more exciting than peering through the slit of a door into a mean little hall with a hat-stand and two umbrellas! That is – isn't it? – what you long to know about a house when you put your hand on the knocker. Perhaps it is the way God opens houses at the dead of night when He is taking a quiet turn with an angel. . . .

'Oh-oh!' The Burnell children sounded as though they were in despair. It was too marvellous; it was too much for them. They had never seen anything like it in their lives. All the rooms were papered. There were pictures on the walls, painted on the paper, with gold frames complete. Red carpet covered all the floors except the kitchen; red plush chairs in the drawing-room, green in the dining-room; tables, beds with real bedclothes, a cradle, a stove,

The house. It was long and low built, with a pillared veranda and balcony all the way round. The soft white bulk of it lay stretched upon the green garden like a sleeping beast.
'Prelude'

Chesney Wolde, Karori

a dresser with tiny plates and one big jug. But what Kezia liked more than anything, what she liked frightfully, was the lamp. It stood in the middle of the dining-room table, an exquisite little amber lamp with a white globe. It was even filled all ready for lighting, though, of course, you couldn't light it. But there was something inside that looked like oil and moved when you shook it.

The father and mother dolls, who sprawled very stiff as though they had fainted in the drawing-room, and their two little children asleep upstairs, were really too big for the doll's house. They didn't look as though they belonged. But the lamp was perfect. It seemed to smile at Kezia, to say, 'I live here.' The lamp was real.

The Burnell children could hardly walk to school fast enough the next morning. They burned to tell everybody, to describe, to – well – to boast about their doll's house before the schoolbell rang.

'I'm to tell,' said Isabel, 'because I'm the eldest. And you can join in after. But I'm to tell first.'

There was nothing to answer. Isabel was bossy, but she was always right, and Lottie and Kezia knew too well the powers that went with being eldest. They brushed through the thick buttercups at the road edge and said nothing.

'And I'm to choose who's to come and see it first. Mother said I might.'

For it had been arranged that while the doll's house stood in the courtyard they might ask the girls at school, two at a time, to come and look. Not to stay to tea, of course, or to come traipsing through the house. But just to stand quietly in the courtyard while Isabel pointed out the beauties, and Lottie and Kezia looked pleased. . . .

But hurry as they might, by the time they had reached the tarred palings of the boys' playground the bell had begun to jangle. They only just had time to whip off their hats and fall into line before the roll was called. Never mind. Isabel tried to make up for it by looking very important and mysterious and by whispering behind her hand to the girls near her, 'Got something to tell you at play-time.'

Playtime came and Isabel was surrounded. The girls of her class nearly fought to put their arms round her, to walk away with her, to beam flatteringly, to be her special friend. She held quite a court under the huge pine trees at the side of the playground. Nudging, giggling together, the little girls pressed up close. And the only two who stayed outside the ring were the two who were always outside, the little Kelveys. They knew better than to come anywhere near the Burnells.

For the fact was, the school the Burnell children went to was not at all the kind of place their parents would have chosen if there had been any choice. But there was none. It was the only school for miles. And the consequence was all the children of the neighbourhood, the Judge's little girls, the doctor's daughters, the storekeeper's children, the milkman's, were forced to mix together. Not to speak of there being an equal number of rude, rough little boys as well. But the line had to be drawn somewhere. It was drawn at the Kelveys. Many of the children, including the Burnells, were not allowed even to speak to them. They walked past the Kelveys with their heads in the air, and as they set the fashion in all matters of behaviour, the Kelveys were shunned by everybody. Even the teacher had a special voice for them, and a special smile for the other children when Lil Kelvey came up to her desk with a bunch of dreadfully common-looking flowers.

They were the daughters of a spry, hard-working little washer-woman, who went about from house to house by the day. This was awful enough. But where was Mr Kelvey? Nobody knew for certain. But everybody said he was in prison. So they were the daughters of a washerwoman and a gaolbird. Very nice company for other people's children! And they looked it. Why Mrs Kelvey made them so conspicuous was hard to understand. The truth was they were dressed in 'bits' given to her by the people for whom she worked. Lil, for instance, who was a stout, plain child, with big freckles, came to school in a dress made from a green art-serge tablecloth of the Burnells', with red plush sleeves from the Logans' curtains. Her hat, perched on top of her high forehead, was a grown-up woman's hat, once the property of Miss Lecky, the postmistress. It was turned up at the back and trimmed with a large scarlet quill. What a little guy she looked! It was impossible not to laugh. And her little sister, our Else, wore a long white dress, rather like a nightgown, and a pair of little boy's boots. But whatever our Else wore she would have looked strange. She was a tiny wishbone of a child, with cropped hair and enormous solemn eyes – a little white owl. Nobody had ever seen her smile; she scarcely ever spoke. She went through life holding on to Lil, with a piece of Lil's skirt screwed up in her hand. Where Lil went, our Else followed. In the playground, on the road going to and from school, there was Lil marching in front and our Else holding on behind. Only when she wanted anything, or when she was out of breath, our Else gave Lil a tug, a twitch, and Lil stopped and turned round. The Kelveys never failed to understand each other.

Now they hovered at the edge; you couldn't stop them listening. When the little girls turned round and sneered, Lil, as usual, gave her silly, shamefaced smile, but our Else only looked.

And Isabel's voice, so very proud, went on telling. The carpet made a great sensation, but so did the beds with real bedclothes, and the stove with an oven door.

When she finished Kezia broke in. 'You've forgotten the lamp, Isabel.'

'Oh yes,' said Isabel, 'and there's a teeny little lamp, all made of yellow glass, with a white globe that stands on the dining-room table. You couldn't tell it from a real one.'

'The lamp's best of all,' cried Kezia. She thought Isabel wasn't making half enough of the little lamp. But nobody paid any attention. Isabel was choosing the two who were to come back with them that afternoon and see it. She chose Emmie Cole and Lena Logan. But when the others knew they were all to have a chance, they couldn't be nice enough to Isabel. One by one they put their arms round Isabel's waist and walked her off. They had something to whisper to her, a secret. 'Isabel's *my* friend.'

Only the little Kelveys moved away forgotten; there was nothing more for them to hear.

Days passed, and as more children saw the doll's house, the

fame of it spread. It became the one subject, the rage. The one question was, 'Have you seen Burnells' doll's house? Oh, ain't it lovely!' 'Haven't you seen it? Oh, I say!'

Even the dinner hour was given up to talking about it. The little girls sat under the pines eating their thick mutton sandwiches and big slabs of johnny cake spread with butter. While always, as near as they could get, sat the Kelveys, our Else holding on to Lil, listening too, while they chewed their jam sandwiches out of a newspaper soaked with large red blobs.

'Mother,' said Kezia, 'can't I ask the Kelveys just once?'

'Certainly not, Kezia.'

'But why not?'

'Run away, Kezia; you know quite well why not.'

At last everybody had seen it except them. On that day the subject rather flagged. It was the dinner hour. The children stood together under the pine trees, and suddenly, as they looked at the Kelveys eating out of their paper, always by themselves, always listening, they wanted to be horrid to them. Emmie Cole started the whisper.

'Lil Kelvey's going to be a servant when she grows up.'

'O-oh, how awful!' said Isabel Burnell, and she made eyes at Emmie.

Emmie swallowed in a very meaning way and nodded to Isabel as she'd seen her mother do on those occasions.

'It's true – it's true – it's true,' she said.

Then Lena Logan's little eyes snapped. 'Shall I ask her?' she whispered.

'Bet you don't,' said Jessie May.

'Pooh, I'm not frightened,' said Lena. Suddenly she gave a little squeal and danced in front of the other girls. 'Watch! Watch me! Watch me now!' said Lena. And sliding, gliding, dragging one foot, giggling behind her hand, Lena went over to the Kelveys.

Lil looked up from her dinner. She wrapped the rest quickly away. Our Else stopped chewing. What was coming now?

'Is it true you're going to be a servant when you grow up, Lil Kelvy?' shrilled Lena.

Dead silence. But instead of answering, Lil only gave her silly, shamefaced smile. She didn't seem to mind the question at all. What a sell for Lena! The girls began to titter.

Lena couldn't stand that. She put her hands on her hips; she shot forward. 'Yah, yer father's in prison!' she hissed spitefully.

This was such a marvellous thing to have said that the little girls rushed away in a body, deeply, deeply excited, wild with joy. Someone found a long rope, and they began skipping. And never did they skip so high, run in and out so fast, or do such daring things as on that morning.

In the afternoon Pat called for the Burnell children with the buggy and they drove home. There were visitors. Isabel and Lottie, who liked visitors, went upstairs to change their pinafores. But Kezia thieved out at the back. Nobody was about; she began to swing on the big white gates of the courtyard. Presently, looking along the road, she saw two little dots. They grew bigger, they were coming towards her. Now she could see that one was in front and one close behind. Now she could see that they were the Kelveys. Kezia stopped swinging. She slipped off the gate as if she was going to run away. Then she hesitated. The Kelveys came nearer, and beside them walked their shadows, very long, stretching right across the road with their heads in the buttercups. Kezia clambered back on the gate; she had made up her mind; she swung out.

'Hullo,' she said to the passing Kelveys.

They were so astounded that they stopped. Lil gave her silly smile. Our Else stared.

'You can come and see our doll's house if you want to,' said Kezia, and she dragged one toe on the ground. But at that Lil turned red and shook her head quickly.

'Why not?' asked Kezia.

Lil gasped, then said, 'Your ma told our ma you wasn't to speak to us.'

'Oh, well,' said Kezia. She didn't know what to reply. 'It doesn't matter. You can come and see our doll's house all the same. Come on. Nobody's looking.'

But Lil shook her head still harder.

'Don't you want to?' asked Kezia.

Suddenly there was a twitch, a tug at Lil's skirt. She turned round. Our Else was looking at her with big, imploring eyes; she was frowning; she wanted to go. For a moment Lil looked at our Else very doubtfully. But then our Else twitched her skirt again. She started forward. Kezia led the way. Like two little stray cats they followed across the courtyard to where the doll's house stood.

'There it is,' said Kezia.

There was a pause. Lil breathed loudly, almost snorted; our Else was still as stone.

'I'll open it for you,' said Kezia kindly. She undid the hook and they looked inside.

'There's the drawing-room and the dining-room, and that's the –'

'Kezia!'

It was Aunt Beryl's voice. They turned round. At the back door stood Aunt Beryl, staring as if she couldn't believe what she saw.

'How dare you ask the little Kelveys into the courtyard!' said her cold, furious voice. 'You know as well as I do, you're not allowed to talk to them. Run away, children, run away at once. And don't come back again,' said Aunt Beryl. And she stepped into the yard and shooed them out as if they were chickens.

'Off you go immediately!' she called, cold and proud.

They did not need telling twice. Burning with shame, shrinking together, Lil huddling along like her mother, our Else dazed, somehow they crossed the big courtyard and squeezed through the white gate.

'Wicked, disobedient little girl!' said Aunt Beryl bitterly to Kezia, and she slammed the doll's house to.

The afternoon had been awful. A letter had come from Willie Brent, a terrifying, threatening letter, saying if she did not meet him that evening in Pulman's Bush, he'd come to the front door and ask the reason why! But now that she had frightened those little rats of Kelveys and given Kezia a good scolding, her heart felt lighter. That ghastly pressure was gone. She went back to the house humming.

When the Kelveys were well out of sight of Burnells', they sat down to rest on a big red drainpipe by the side of the road. Lil's cheeks were still burning; she took off the hat with the quill and held it on her knee. Dreamily they looked over the hay paddocks, past the creek, to the group of wattles where Logan's cows stood waiting to be milked. What were their thoughts?

Presently our Else nudged up close to her sister. But now she had forgotten the cross lady. She put out a finger and stroked her sister's quill; she smiled her rare smile.

'I seen the little lamp,' she said softly.

Then both were silent once more.

'The Doll's House' (the *Nation*, 4 February 1922)

'Vera Margaret, Charlotte Mary & K.M. were cleaning out the doll's house. There were three dippers of water on the floor, three little pieces of real monkey brand and in their hands they held three little rags – of various degrees of dirtiness. They were being systematic thorough little souls and their cheeks were flaming, their heads aching with exertion. "It's the chimleys" said K.M. polishing these articles with tremendous verve. "All the dust seems to fly into them." "On them" corrected C.M. in her careful cool little voice . . .

Outside the nursery window the rain was falling in torrents. They peeked [peered?] through & saw the long wet garden, the paddocks and far away the bush covered hills . . .' (London, 1906)

'And yet one has these "glimpses" . . . in that moment (what *do* I mean?) the whole life of the soul contained. One is flung up – out of life – one is "held", and then down, bright, broken, glittering onto the rocks, tossed back – part of the ebb and flow.' (*Journal*, February 1920)

'27. x .1921 Stories for my new book . . .
N.Z. *At Karori*: The little lamp I seen it. and then they were silent. Finito.
30. x .21' (*Journal*, 27 October 1921)

'the emblem of ecstasy, paradise, the world's desire' (*Times Literary Supplement*, 29 January 1925)

This is perhaps K.M.'s best-known and most accessible story. Few who read it can forget the little lamp, the reality of the children's playground, Kezia's confusion at adult rules and consequent defiance, Beryl's anger and satisfaction and, finally, Our Else's rare smile. The story has an almost cinematic quality; at times we see characters and objects in close up, at other times at a distance. The various incidents have the clarity of a series of images, perfectly framed, on film. It is a story in which characters are created in merely a few words, yet they are alive and completely convincing. Again the focus changes. We slip from one point of view to another. The relationship of the three sisters is made subtly clear, the blind prejudice of society is clearly exposed, children are shown to be as cruel as the adults they copy, but the tone is no longer one of anger at life's injustice. The unfairness, pain, anxiety and ignorance are shown to be only a part of life, to be balanced against those qualities suggested by the little lamp which is so much more important to Kezia and Our Else than the stiff sprawling 'father and mother dolls' or even 'the cross lady'.

The Fly

'Y'are very snug in here,' piped old Mr Woodifield, and he peered out of the great, green-leather armchair by his friend the boss's desk as a baby peers out of its pram. His talk was over; it was time for him to be off. But he did not want to go. Since he had retired, since his . . . stroke, the wife and the girls kept him boxed up in the house every day of the week except Tuesday. On Tuesday he was dressed and brushed and allowed to cut back to the City for the day. Though what he did there the wife and girls couldn't imagine. Made a nuisance of himself to his friends, they supposed. . . . Well, perhaps so. All the same, we cling to our last pleasures as the tree clings to its last leaves. So there sat old Woodifield, smoking a cigar and staring almost greedily at the boss, who rolled in his office chair, stout, rosy, five years older than he, and still going strong, still at the helm. It did one good to see him.

Wistfully, admiringly, the old voice added, 'It's snug in here, upon my word!'

'Yes, it's comfortable enough,' agreed the boss, and he flipped the *Financial Times* with a paper-knife. As a matter of fact he was proud of his room; he liked to have it admired, especially by old Woodifield. It gave him a feeling of deep, solid satisfaction to be planted there in the midst of it in full view of that frail old figure in the muffler.

'I've had it done up lately,' he explained, as he had explained for the past – how many? – weeks. 'New carpet,' and he pointed to the bright red carpet with a pattern of large white rings. 'New furniture,' and he nodded towards the massive bookcase and the table with legs like twisted treacle. 'Electric heating!' He waved almost exultantly towards the five transparent, pearly sausages glowing so softly in the tilted copper pan.

But he did not draw old Woodifield's attention to the photograph over the table of a grave-looking boy in uniform standing in one of those spectral photographers' parks with photographers' storm-clouds behind him. It was not new. It had been there for over six years.

'There was something I wanted to tell you,' said old Woodifield, and his eyes grew dim remembering. 'Now what was it? I had it in my mind when I started out this morning.' His hands began to tremble, and patches of red showed above his beard.

Poor old chap, he's on his last pins, thought the boss. And, feeling kindly, he winked at the old man, and said jokingly, 'I tell you what. I've got a little drop of something here that'll do you good before you go out into the cold again. It's beautiful stuff. It wouldn't hurt a child.' He took a key off his watchchain, unlocked a cupboard below his desk, and drew forth a dark, squat bottle. 'That's the medicine,' said he. 'And the man from whom I got it told me on the strict Q.T. it came from the cellars at Windsor Castle.'

Old Woodifield's mouth fell open at the sight. He couldn't have looked more surprised if the boss had produced a rabbit.

'It's whisky, ain't it?' he piped feebly.

The boss turned the bottle and lovingly showed him the label. Whisky it was.

'D'you know,' said he, peering up at the boss wonderingly, 'they won't let me touch it at home.' And he looked as though he was going to cry.

'Ah, that's where we know a bit more than the ladies,' cried the boss, swooping across for two tumblers that stood on the table with the water-bottle, and pouring a generous finger into each. 'Drink it down. It'll do you good. And don't put any water with it. It's sacrilege to tamper with stuff like this. Ah!' He tossed off his, pulled out his handkerchief, hastily wiped his moustaches, and cocked an eye at old Woodifield, who was rolling his in his chaps.

The old man swallowed, was silent a moment, and then said faintly, 'It's nutty!'

But it warmed him; it crept into his chill old brain – he remembered.

'That was it,' he said, heaving himself out of his chair. 'I thought you'd like to know. The girls were in Belgium last week having a look at poor Reggie's grave, and they happened to come across your boy's. They're quite near each other, it seems.'

Old Woodifield paused, but the boss made no reply. Only a quiver in his eyelids showed that he heard.

'The girls were delighted with the way the place is kept,' piped the old voice. 'Beautifully looked after. Couldn't be better if they were at home. You've not been across, have yer?'

'No, no!' For various reasons the boss had not been across.

'There's miles of it,' quavered old Woodifield, 'and it's all as neat as a garden. Flowers growing on all the graves. Nice broad paths.' It was plain from his voice how much he liked a nice broad path.

The pause came again. Then the old man brightened wonderfully.

'D'you know what the hotel made the girls pay for a pot of jam?' he piped. 'Ten francs! Robbery, I call it. It was a little pot, so

Gertrude says, no bigger than a half-crown. And she hadn't taken more than a spoonful when they charged her ten francs. Gertrude brought the pot away with her to teach 'em a lesson. Quite right, too; it's trading on our feelings. They think because we're over there having a look round we're ready to pay anything. That's what it is.' And he turned towards the door.

'Quite right, quite right!' cried the boss, though what was quite right he hadn't the least idea. He came round by his desk, followed the shuffling footsteps to the door, and saw the old fellow out. Woodifield was gone.

For a long moment the boss stayed, staring at nothing, while the grey-haired office messenger, watching him, dodged in and out of his cubby-hole like a dog that expects to be taken for a run. Then: 'I'll see nobody for half an hour, Macey,' said the boss. 'Understand? Nobody at all.'

'Very good, sir.'

The door shut, the firm heavy steps recrossed the bright carpet, the fat body plumped down in the spring chair, and leaning forward, the boss covered his face with his hands. He wanted, he intended, he had arranged to weep . . . .

It had been a terrible shock to him when old Woodifield sprang that remark upon him about the boy's grave. It was exactly as though the earth had opened and he had seen the boy lying there with Woodifield's girls staring down at him. For it was strange. Although over six years had passed away, the boss never thought of the boy except as lying unchanged, unblemished in his uniform, asleep for ever. 'My son!' groaned the boss. But no tears came yet. In the past, in the first months and even years after the boy's death, he had only to say those words to be overcome by such grief that nothing short of a violent fit of weeping could relieve him. Time, he had declared then, he had told everybody, could make no difference. Other men perhaps might recover, might live their loss down, but not he. How was it possible? His boy was an only son. Ever since his birth the boss had worked at building up this business for him; it had no other meaning if it was not for the boy. Life itself had come to have no other meaning. How on earth could he have slaved, denied himself, kept going all those years without the promise for ever before him of the boy's stepping into his shoes and carrying on where he left off?

And that promise had been so near being fulfilled. The boy had been in the office learning the ropes for a year before the war. Every morning they had started off together; they had come back by the same train. And what congratulations he had received as the boy's father! No wonder; he had taken to it marvellously. As to his popularity with the staff, every man jack of them down to old Macey couldn't make enough of the boy. And he wasn't in the least spoilt. No, he was just his bright natural self, with the right word for everybody, with that boyish look and his habit of saying, 'Simply splendid!'

But all that was over and done with as though it never had been. The day had come when Macey had handed him the telegram that brought the whole place crashing about his head. 'Deeply regret to inform you . . . ' And he had left the office a broken man, with his life in ruins.

Six years ago, six years . . . . How quickly time passed! It might have happened yesterday. The boss took his hands from his face; he was puzzled. Something seemed to be wrong with him. He wasn't feeling as he wanted to feel. He decided to get up and have a look at the boy's photograph. But it wasn't a favourite photograph of his; the expression was unnatural. It was cold, even stern-looking. The boy had never looked like that.

At that moment the boss noticed that a fly had fallen into his broad inkpot, and was trying feebly but desperately to clamber out again. Help! help! said those struggling legs. But the sides of the inkpot were wet and slippery; it fell back again and began to swim. The boss took up a pen, picked the fly out of the ink, and shook it on to a piece of blotting-paper. For a fraction of a second it lay still on the dark patch that oozed round it. Then the front legs waved, took hold, and, pulling its small, sodden body up, it began the immense task of cleaning the ink from its wings. Over and under, over and under, went a leg along a wing as the stone goes over and under the scythe. Then there was a pause, while the fly, seeming to stand on the tips of its toes, tried to expand first one wing and then the other. It succeeded at last, and, sitting down, it began, like a minute cat, to clean its face. Now one could imagine that the little front legs rubbed against each other lightly, joyfully. The horrible danger was over; it had escaped; it was ready for life again.

But just then the boss had an idea. He plunged his pen back into the ink, leaned his thick wrist on the blotting-paper, and as the fly tried its wings down came a great heavy blot. What would it make of that? What indeed! The little beggar seemed absolutely cowed, stunned, and afraid to move because of what would happen next. But then, as if painfully, it dragged itself forward. The front legs waved, caught hold, and, move slowly this time, the task began from the beginning.

He's a plucky little devil, thought the boss, and he felt a real admiration for the fly's courage. That was the way to tackle things; that was the right spirit. Never say die; it was only a question of . . . But the fly had again finished its laborious task, and the boss

had just time to refill his pen, to shake fair and square on the new-
cleaned body yet another dark drop. What about it this time? A
painful moment of suspense followed. But behold, the front legs
were again waving; the boss felt a rush of relief. He leaned over
the fly and said to it tenderly, 'You artful little b . . . ' And he
actually had the brilliant notion of breathing on it to help the
drying process. All the same, there was something timid and weak
about its efforts now, and the boss decided that this time should
be the last, as he dipped the pen deep into the inkpot.

It was. The last blot fell on the soaked blotting-paper, and the
draggled fly lay in it and did not stir. The back legs were stuck to
the body; the front legs were not to be seen.

'Come on,' said the boss. 'Look sharp!' And he stirred it with
his pen – in vain. Nothing happened or was likely to happen. The
fly was dead.

The boss lifted the corpse on the end of the paper-knife and
flung it into the waste-paper basket. But such a grinding feeling of
wretchedness seized him that he felt positively frightened. He
started forward and pressed the bell for Macey.

'Bring me some fresh blotting-paper,' he said sternly, 'and look
sharp about it.' And while the old dog padded away he fell to
wondering what it was he had been thinking about before. What
was it? It was . . . He took out his handkerchief and passed it
inside his collar. For the life of him he could not remember.

'The Fly' (the *Nation*, 18 March 1922)

'I feel like a fly who had been dropped into the milk jug and fished out again, but is still too milky and drowned to start cleaning up yet.' (to J. M. Murry, 11 January 1918)

'*December 31st* [1918] 4.45 p.m. Fly: Oh the times when she had walked upside down on the ceiling, run up glittering panes, floated on a lake of light, flashed through a shining beam!'

'And God looked upon the fly fallen into the jug of milk and saw that it was good . . .' (*Journal*, 31 December 1918)

'How tired one becomes of all these surfaces. Why do not more people live through and through? . . . And if it is not this superficial nothingness, it is M au grand sérieux throwing himself bodily into the milk jug after the drowning fly!' (to Lady Ottoline Morrell, June 1919)

'How beautiful willows are . . . how the sun rains down upon them . . . Oh Sun, shine forever! I feel a little bit drunk – rather like an insect that has fallen into the cup of a magnolia.' (to Dorothy Brett, 18 July 1919)

'A little fly has dropped by mistake into the huge sweet strong cup of a magnolia.' (*Journal*, 31 May 1919)

'I feel like a fly who is *just* out of the milk jug.' (to J. M. Murry, 3 December 1919)

'Dark Bogey is a little inclined to jump into the milk jug to rescue the fly.' (n.d. possibly 1921)

' "Why don't I fly out again? There's the window or the door or whatever it was I came in by . . . For some reason" – Jonathan paused between the words – "it's not allowed, it's forbidden, it's against the insect law, to stop banging and flopping and crawling up the pane even for an instant".' ('At the Bay', August 1921)

'I have just finished a queer story called *The Fly*. About a fly that falls into an inkpot and a Bank Manager.' (to Dorothy Brett, 26 February 1922)

'I am sorry you did not like *The Fly* and glad you told me. I *hated* writing it.' (to William Gerhardi, 14 June 1922)

'A terrible indictment . . . and beyond the horror in it there is love and pity.' (H. M. Tomlinson, the *Nation and Athenaeum*, 20 January 1923)

'An image of human life. The struggle of the fly symbolises the tenacity of instinct and its final death indicates that fate at times inflicts more than can be endured.' (Anne Friis, *Katherine Mansfield*)

'Katherine Mansfield's starkest view, her bitterest and almost final cry against corruption.' (Saralyn Daly, *Katherine Mansfield*)

Would you not like to try all sorts of lives – one is so very small – but that is the satisfaction of writing – one can impersonate so many people.
to Sylvia Payne, 24 April 1906

Note on sources

When I began what was to be an even simpler introduction, my sources were: *The Letters of Katherine Mansfield,* Volumes 1 and 2 (1928); *Katherine Mansfield's Letters to John Middleton Murry,* (1951); *The Scrapbook of Katherine Mansfield* (1927); *The Journal of Katherine Mansfield* (1927 and 1954 editions); *Novels and Novelists* (1930) and *Poems* (1923). Details of these are included in the list of works consulted. As my interest grew these were no longer sufficient. I have since been fortunate enough to have access to the materials held by the British Museum, now the British Library, and the Alexander Turnbull Library, Wellington.

Where my only source has been the two-volume *Letters of Katherine Mansfield* (1928) I have indicated this in the reference as *Letters.* Similarly where the volume of letters to J. M. Murry is my only source I have shown this.

The majority of relevant material in the Alexander Turnbull Library is included in the collection, MS papers 119. These papers, including the notebooks formerly numbered 1 to 46 have been reclassified so that Notebook 1, for example, is now Folio 24. For brevity this would be shown in the reference as 119/24. I have also quoted from letters to Sydney Waterlow, MS papers 1157, the Beauchamp family papers, MS papers 2063, the letters of Mrs Annie Beauchamp Acc 78-41.

Where I have consulted the letters in the British Library, catalogued according to the year and addition number, to Ida Baker (49064); Countess Russell (50844); Mark Gertler (49597F); Sidney Schiff (52919) and S. S. Koteliansky (48970) I have indicated this source as B.L. I have also consulted those to Ida Baker in her autobiography, *The Memories of L.M.*

Although this is only an introduction I regret not being able to refer throughout to primary sources as certain errors in the printed texts are therefore inevitably repeated. For the majority of K.M.'s letters to Virginia Woolf and Bertrand Russell I have relied on *Adam International Review,* nos 370–5, 1972–3.

Where I have been able to check the printed version with the original text I have tried to reproduce the original as closely as possible. In the case of the notebooks I have indicated both sources in the hope that this will show how the many notebooks have been fitted together in a literary jigsaw to give us the published *Journal.*

The five-volume collection of Katherine Mansfield's letters

edited by Margaret Scott and Vincent O'Sullivan will correct any errors I may have made or perpetuated. Perhaps one day an intrepid scholar will do the same with a new definitive edition of her notebooks and journals.

Where I have quoted from other published material such as *The Letters of Virginia Woolf*, I have indicated the source with a short title in the list of references. 'The Education of Audrey', which is included as a curiosity rather than for its literary value, is taken from the *Evening Post*, 30 January 1909, and 'Old Tar' from *The N.Z. Times*, 11 December 1913. The full title of sources is included in the list of books consulted.

Certain anecdotes about the life of Katherine Mansfield which I have included cannot be confirmed but I have attempted to indicate the source. Other incidents in her varied life inevitably remain somewhat confused.

List of References

Abbreviations used
The form 119/- ATL represents the appropriate folder in the Alexander Turnbull Library from the Collection: MANSFIELD, Katherine. Papers. MS Papers 119
ATL: Alexander Turnbull Library
BEA MS 2063/- ATL: BEAUCHAMP. Family Papers 2063 Alexander Turnbull Library
BL: British Library
McMaster: Bertrand Russell Archives, Mills Memorial Library, McMaster University, Hamilton, Ontario
Newberry: Mansfield Collection, Newberry Library, Chicago. Katherine Mansfield Papers 1902-1922
PC: photocopy
Texas: Harry Ransom Humanities Research Centre, University of Texas at Austin
ts: typescript

For all titles which are abbreviated full details are found in the lists of Books and Articles consulted.

Most commonly used short titles
BTW: Between Two Worlds John Middleton Murry
Journal: The Journal of Katherine Mansfield (1954) edited by John Middleton Murry
D.H. Lawrence *Moore: The Collected Letters of D.H. Lawrence* edited by Harry T. Moore
F.A. Lea: *John Middleton Murry* by F.A. Lea
Letters: The Letters of Katherine Mansfield (1928) 2 volumes, edited by John Middleton Murry
Letters of J.M. Murry: The Letters of John Middleton Murry to Katherine Mansfield edited by C.A. Hankin
LJMM: Letters of Katherine Mansfield to John Middleton Murry (1951) edited by John Middleton Murry

Page
2 'father was . . .' 'The Apple Tree' *Journal* 1915
  'I'm the . . .' i.v. B Coster 1980
3 'In the days . . .' 'About Pat' 'The Queen's College Magazine' December 1905
  'Grandma's Birthday . . .' *Journal* 21 January 1922, 119/43 ATL
4 'Our house . . .' *Journal* 12 March 1916, 119/65 ATL
  'I think of . . .' *Journal* 19 May 1919, 119/71 ATL
5 'a surly sort . . .' *Marsden, The History of a New Zealand School for Girls* Tosti Murray p66
  'I've been . . .' Radio New Zealand Archives
  'a wooden . . .' Marion Ruddick
  'Incidents in the Life of Katherine Mansfield' MS Papers 1339 ATL
6 'Why can't I . . .' *Journal* March 1916, 119/68 ATL
7 'A rough sea . . .' n.d. 1909-10, 119/31 ATL
  'The longer I . . .' to Harold Beauchamp 18 March 1922, 119/12 ATL
  'Father is . . .' 119/47 ATL

8 'I have . . .' 119/12 ATL
  'Nobody saw . . .' *Journal* February/March 1916, 119/68 ATL
9 'walking shadow . . .' i.v. with Owen Leeming, Radio New Zealand Archives
  'If she wanted . . .' i.v. Ruth Herrick 1979
  'All the stalls . . .' 'The Queen's College Magazine' 1906
  'I need you . . .' to L.M. B.L. Add 49064
10 'very good . . .' Reports in Queen's College Archives
  'She had been . . .' 'Juliet' 119/24 ATL
  'Juliet looked . . .' 'Juliet' 199/24 ATL
11 September 1905 scrapbook of Vera Mackintosh Bell qMS BEA 17.12.1974 ATL
  'Father is . . .' to Sylvia Payne, 24 April 1906, 119/1 ATL
  'I love her . . .' to Sylvia Payne, 4 March 1908, 119/1 ATL
  'He must always . . .' 119/62 ATL
12 'When I am . . .' *Journal* November 1906, 119/62 ATL
  'prying and curious . . .' 119/62 ATL
  'His hands . . .' 119/62 ATL
  'My Grandmother . . .' to Sylvia Payne, 8 January 1907, 119/1 ATL
13 'I feel . . .' 119/1 ATL
  'Damn my family . . .' *Journal* 21 October 1907, 199/62 ATL
  'If I do . . .' 'Juliet' 119/24 ATL
14 'Rain beating . . .' *Journal* 20 August 1907, 119/39 ATL
  'They have been . . .' to Vera Mackintosh Bell 19 June 1908, 119/1 ATL
15 'Here is . . .' to Vera Mackintosh Bell 1908, 119/1 ATL
  'five men . . .' to Sylvia Payne, 4 March 1908, 119/1 ATL
  'because his figure . . .' *Journal* 25 June 1907, 119/62 ATL
  'surly, moody . . .' i.v. Mr John Parker 1982
  'a child . . .' i.v. Jeanne Renshaw
  'to have the . . .' *Journal* 1907, 119/62 ATL
16 'Realise your youth . . .' *Journal* 1907, 119/62 ATL
  'the odd man . . .' 'Juliet' 119/24 ATL
  'I am here . . .' June 1907, 119/62 ATL
17 'Somehow silently . . .' June 1907, 119/62 ATL
  'O Oscar . . .!' 119/62 ATL
  'Do no other people . . .' 119/62 ATL
  'We would meet . . .' i.v. 1981 and 1983
18 'To me you . . .' *Journal* 11 August 1907, 119/62 ATL
  'look ahead . . .' *Journal* 20 August 1907, 119/62 ATL
  'I do not care . . .' *Journal* 6 September 1907, 119/62 ATL
  'I am always . . .' *Journal* 21 October 1907, 119/62 ATL
19 'Sweetness', 'sexy writings' Tom Mills to Guy Morris, 30 October 1937
  K. Mansfield to E.J. Brady 11 October 1907 Mitchell Library, Sydney.
  'In a year . . .' to Sylvia Payne, 4 March 1908 119/1 ATL
  'The sea sounded . . .' 119/25 ATL
20 'During the journey . . .' i.v. Mr H. Cullerne
  'After brief snatches . . .' *Journal* November 1907, 119/25 ATL

21 'And across . . .' November 1907, 119/25 ATL
'A party of us . . .' Unposted letter to Annie Beauchamp, 119/25 ATL
22 'I confess . . .' ibid.
'In the train . . .' ibid.
'Castles have been . . .' to Mattie Putnam n.d. Sunday 1907 scrapbook qMS Putnam 1906-30 ATL
'mein lieber Freund . . .' 23 January 1908, 119/25 ATL
Another possible explanation i.v. with Tom Mills, Radio New Zealand Archives
23 'I shall end . . .' *Journal* 10 February 1908, 119/62 ATL
'I purchase . . .' *Journal* 18 March 1908, 119/62 ATL
'I try & make . . .' to Anne Estelle Rice (Drey), January 1921 119/11 ATL
24 'O, Kathleen . . .' *Journal* 17 May 1908, 119/62 ATL
'I do not . . .' to Vera, n.d. June 1908, 119/1 ATL
'There was a pig . . .' 'The New Zealand Freelance', 4 July 1908
'To continue . . .' 'New Zealand Freelance', 4 July 1908
Shipping Register New Zealand Shipping Company Inward Passenger Lists 1904-12 p160. Voyage from Lyttleton 6 July 1908
'We are . . .' K.M. *Novels and Novelists* 30 January 1920
25 Aleister Crowley *The Memories of L.M.* Ida Baker p 86
'Jesus Wept' 'Memories of Katherine Mansfield', *Adam* No 300 p 78 Anne Estelle Rice (Drey)
'I lived there . . .' to Dorothy Brett *Letters,* 13 December 1921
26 'drunken, bestial . . .' 'The Winter Fire' 4 November 1908 II 53, 34 Newberry
27 Vera married . . . qMS BEA 74/96/1 ATL
'would meet . . .' 'A biographical note on K.M.'
G Bowden qMS BOW 91076 ATL
28 'this man . . .' 119/25 ATL
'29 April . . .' *Journal* 29 April 1909, 119/25 ATL
'I cannot sleep . . .' *Journal* 12 January 1920, 119/45 ATL. The writing in this small red notebook is minute. The last word is, however, not Trowell as it appears in the *Journal*
30 'I was soaped . . .' 'Bains Turcs'
'spring-lilac-rain . . .' *Journal* 14 July 1921, 116 Notebook 7 Newberry
'I am ill . . .' any *Journal* June 1909, 119/69 ATL
31 'the surgeon . . .' *The Memories of L.M.* p54
32 The exact nature This operation is discussed in detail in *The Life of Katherine Mansfield* A. Alpers p115, 122-4
'She looked . . .' 'Juliet' 119/24 ATL
34 'I've *acted* my sins . . .' to J.M. Murry, 31 October 1920, 119/10 ATL
Beatrice Hastings . . . Pierre Sichel *Modigliani* p271
'a series of sketches . . .' the 'Spectator' 30 December 1911
In a 1933 article the 'Tablet' 6 September 1933 qMS BEA 74 96/2 ATL
35 'Michael came . . .' *The Last Romantic* William Orton p280-2
'Dear: the evening . . .' *The Last Romantic* p285-6
36 'This is your egg . . .' *Between Two Worlds* J.M. Murry
'to seek out . . .' 'Rhythm' No 1 Summer 1911
'I am more . . .' J.M. Murry to Sydney Waterlow, 11 July 1921, MS Papers 1157/4 ATL

37 'Why don't you . . .' *BTW* p208
George Bowden These events are discussed by George Bowden in letters to Antony Alpers and J.M. Murry MS Papers 27718/25: qMS BOW 91076, ATL
38 'Tell him I've *left* . . .' Enid Bagnold *An Autobiography,* p86
39 'Tea, the chemist & marmalade –' *Journal* 17 January 1914, 119/56 ATL
'To KMM & JMM . . . cry' 119/42 ATL, part of this is included in the *Journal* February 1914
'Everything is packed . . .' letter quoted by J.M. Murry, *BTW* p277
40 'Have I ruined . . .' *Journal* March 1914, 119/46 ATL
41 'far too absorbed . . .' *Journal* 1 April 1914, 119/41 ATL
'Nothing that isn't . . .' *Journal* 4 April 1914, 119/41 ATL
'pretty rooms, pretty people' *Journal* 26 March 1914, 119/46 ATL
'I have nothing . . .' *Journal* 26 March 1914, 119/41 ATL
42 'what we have . . .' *Journal* 18 December 1914
'The second party . . .' *Mark Gertler: Selected Letters*, to Lytton Strachey, 1 January 1915
'this year . . .' *Journal* 1 January 1915, 119/27 ATL
'It is a pity . . .' to Koteliansky, December 1921, BL
43 'we were lovers . . .' *Journal* 8 January 1915, 119/27 ATL
'Jack & I . . .' *Journal* 8 January 1915, 119/27 ATL
'Jack & I lay . . .' *Journal* 9 January 1915, 119/27 ATL
'It seemed . . .' *Journal* 16 November 1914, 119/41 ATL
'a terribly innocent lover . . .' J.M. Murry's journal quoted in *The Life of John Middleton Murry*: F.A. Lea p31
'Even now . . .' J.M. Murry to K.M., 29 March 1915, *Letters of John Middleton Murry*, ed. C.A. Hankin 119/15 ATL
'This sad place . . .' *Journal* 21 January 1915, 119/27 ATL
'I ran up . . .' Leslie Beauchamp to his parents, 11 February 1915, BEA MS Papers 2063/2ATL
44 'I don't really . . .' *Journal* 20 February 1915, 119/27 ATL
'vaguely uncomfortable . . .' J.M. Murry to K.M. *Letters of John Middleton Murry,* 119/15 ATL
'we lay like 2 old people . . .' *Journal* 20 February 1915, 119/27 ATL
45 'it is very cold . . .' to Koteliansky, 8 March 1915, BL
'Marguerite Bombard' Francis Carco to K.M., 26 March 1915, 119/15 ATL
'the detail of life . . .' May 1915, 119/57 ATL
'dismissed Dado . . .' to J.M. Murry, 21 March 1915, 119/2 ATL
'there arrived "du monde" . . .' to J.M. Murry, 22 March 1915, 119/2 ATL
46 'I walked on . . .' to J.M. Murry, 23 March 1915, 119/2 ATL
'I wish we were . . .' J.M. Murry to K.M., *Letters of John Middleton Murry*, 25 March 1915, 119/25 ATL
'I fell into . . .' to J.M. Murry, 25 March 1915, 119/2 ATL
47 'I want to . . .' J.M. Murry to K.M., *Letters of John Middleton Murry*, 5 May 1915, 199/15 ATL
'They are walking . . .' *Journal* October 1915, 119/70 ATL
'The "aspegs" . . .' J.M. Murry BTW p350
'I had a most . . .' Leslie Beauchamp to his parents, August 1915, BEA MS Papers 2063/3 ATL

'sitting on the sofa . . .' Dorothy Brett, *Lawrence and Brett A Friendship* p19

'He puts . . .' *Journal* October 1915, 119/70 ATL

48 'Do you remember . . .' *Journal* November 1915, 119/70 ATL

49 'Do not be sad . . .' D.H. Lawrence to K.M. 20 December 1915 *Moore*

50 'So, feeling extremely solitary . . .' *Journal* December 1915, 119/70 ATL

'On the mantelpiece . . .' to Koteliansky, Marseilles 19 November 1915, Add. 48970 BL

51 'I have loved . . .' to J.M. Murry, 29 December 1915, 119/3 ATL

'I have found . . .' to J.M. Murry, 29 December 1915, 119/3 ATL

52 'Now I am just . . .' to J.M. Murry, 29 December 1915, 119/3 ATL

'We might be . . .' 'Camomile Tea' 1916 *Poems* 119/73 ATL

'undiscovered country . . .' *Journal* 22 January 1916

'I cannot stand . . .' to Koteliansky, 11 May 1916, BL

'I should like . . .' to Sydney Schiff, January 1922, *Letters*

53 'Except for . . .' to Beatrice Campbell, May 1916, 119/76 ATL

'I call it . . .' D.H. Lawrence to K.M. and L.M. Murry, 8 March 1916, *Moore*

54 'I hate games . . .' to Beatrice Campbell, May 1916 PC 119/76 ATL

'I shall *never* . . .' ibid.

'We had great . . .' Frieda Lawrence *The Memoirs and Correspondence*

'the terrible gift . . .' Frieda Lawrence to Gordon Campbell *Today We Will Only Gossip*, p95

'But I do . . .' Frieda Lawrence *The Memoirs and Correspondence* 4 October 1916

55 'Of course I . . .' to Mark Gertler n.d. Add. 49597F BL

56 'I should love . . .' *Memoirs of Lady Ottoline Morrell* p149-50

'ugly little house . . .' to Lady Ottoline Morrell n.d. August 1916, Newberry

'she's a queer study . . .' to Violet Schiff, 4 November 1920 Add. 52919 BL

57 'Last night . . .' to J.M. Murry, *LJMM* 18 May 1917, 119/4 ATL

'have been here . . . counterpanes.' *Carrington* 6 September 1916

'I loved her . . .' S.S. Koteliansky to Sydney Waterlow 21 June 1927, MS Papers 1157/2 ATL

58 'We acted . . .' *Carrington* 8 September 1916

'An amusing Xmas . . .' Aldous Huxley to Julian Huxley, 29 December 1916 *The Letters of Aldous Huxley*

59 You have already . . .!' to Bertrand Russell, 24 February 1916, McMaster

'admirable until . . .' to Bertrand Russell, 24 February 1917 *Adam* 370-5 p41 McMaster

'over the brim . . .' ibid.

'My last day . . .' to Bertrand Russell, January 1917, *Adam* 370-5 McMaster

'a woman who . . .' *Journal* 27 January 1915, 119/27 ATL

'strangely different . . .' Anne Estelle Rice (Drey),

Memories of Katherine Mansfield, Adam No. 300 p79

60 'I hope to move . . .' to Bertrand Russell, January 1917, *Adam* 370-5 McMaster

'in a sad . . .' *Carrington* 10 Febraury 1917

'In these notes . . .' *Journal* 30 May 1917, 119/47 ATL

'To be alive . . .' *Journal* 30 May 1917, 119/47 ATL

61 ''Last Sunday . . .' *The Letters of Aldous Huxley* 11 December 1917

'We could both . . .' *The Diary of Virginia Woolf* Vol. 1, 11 October 1917

'small, her sleek dark hair . . .' *Lawrence and Brett A Friendship* p 17-18

62 'She had daring . . .' Dorothy Brett and John Manchester, *Reminiscences of Katherine, Adam* 370-5 p86

'She was . . .' *The Letters of Aldous Huxley* 27 January 1963

'By nature . . .' Leonard Woolf *Beginning Again* p204

'dont let THEM . . .' to Virginia Woolf *Letters* August 1917

'Although I am . . .' to J.M. Murry, 23 December 1917, 119/4 ATL

63 'a most hideous breakdown . . .' *The Letters of Aldous Huxley* 13 December 1917

'that six weeks . . .' to K.M. *Letters of JMM* 26 March 1920

'And then came . . .' to J.M. Murry, 13 January 1918, 119/5 ATL

64 'My work excites . . .' to J.M. Murry, 3 February 1918, *Letters to John Middleton Murry*

'bright red blood . . .' *Journal* 19 February 1918, 119/71 ATL

'Bogey, this is . . .' to J.M. Murry 19 February 1918, 119/5 ATL

'This has been . . .' to J.M. Murry 22 March 1918, 119/6 ATL

65 ' ''Home looked lovely . . . you know'' ' to L.M. 12 April 1918 BL

'If I had . . .' *Journal* 26 April 1918, 119/35 ATL

66 'Our marriage . . .' to J.M. Murry, *LJMM* 27 May 1918, 119/7 ATL

'A very dark . . .' to J.M. Murry. *LJMM* 8 June 1918, 119/7 ATL

'The man in . . .' *Journal* June 1918, 119/71 ATL

'Of course L.M. . . .' *Journal* 22 May 1918, 119/35 ATL

'I want nothing . . .' to J.M. Murry *LJMM* 8 June 1918, 119/7 ATL

'wandering eternally . . .' to Lady Ottoline Morrell *Letters* 24 May 1918

67 '11500 miles . . .' *Journal* 20 June 1918, 119/35 ATL

'I feel . . .' to Lady Ottoline Morrell *Letters* 1918

'She *lived* . . .' to Dorothy Brett *Letters* 14 August 1918

'This was a . . .' Annie Beauchamp on Clara Palmer 6 May 1918 Acc 78.41, MS Papers 2063/ATL

68 'Oh why . . .' to Lady Ottoline Morrell *Letters* 13 November 1918

'In spite of . . .' to Clara Palmer 30 December 1918, 119/7 ATL

69 'seemed to . . .' to Dorothy Brett *Letters* 1 January 1919

'I wanted . . .' ibid.

'Since then . . .' to Anne Estelle Rice (Drey) 13 January 1919, 119/8 ATL

'Yes, Brett is . . .' to Sydney Waterlow March 1921, 119/11 ATL

70 'an unpleasant . . .' *The Letters of VW* Vol II, to Vanessa Bell,11 February 1917
'to have gone . . .' *VW* to Vanessa Bell June 1917
'the very best . . .' *VW* to Duncan Grant 15 May 1918
'superficial smartness . . .' *The Diary of VW* Vol I 7 August 1918
'husky feeble . . .' *The Diary of VW* 9 November 1918
'was almost entirely . . .' *The Diary of VW* 18 February 1919
'You are immensely . . .' to Virginia Woolf n.d. *Adam* 370-5

71 'she gave me . . .' *VW* Vol III to Dorothy Brett 2 March 1923
'Did she care . . .' Leonard Woolf quoting VW's diary 16 January 1923 in *Beginning Again*
'How I envy . . .' to J.M. Murry 30 November 1919
'I wonder if . . .' to Virginia Woolf 27 December 1920 *Adam* 370-5

72 'A husband . . .' to Virginia Woolf *Letters* 26 April 1919
'that tall . . .' *Journal* May 1919, 119/39 ATL
'my plans are . . .' to Anne Estelle Rice (Drey) 13 August 1919, 119/8 ATL
'Portland Villas . . .!' to Lady Ottoline Morrell, 22 July 1918 *Letters*
Murry's return. A comparison of sources reveals an interesting discrepancy in the date of his return, before or after the move to the Casseta *The Memories of L.M.* p140, *Letters* Vol I p242-4, *The Letters of John Middleton Murry to Katherine Mansfield* ed. C. Hankin p179-87; A. Alpers *The Life of Katherine Mansfield* 1980 p298

73 'Father suggested . . .' to J.M. Murry *LJMM* 12 November 1919 119/8 ATL
'My black fit . . .' to J.M. Murry *LJMM* 12 November 1919 ATL

74 'madness to love . . .' to J.M. Murry *LJMM* 30 November 1919 119/8 ATL
'your wonderful body . . .' J.M. Murry to K.M. *Letters of J.M. Murry* 1 November 1919
'your Saturday letter . . .' to J.M. Murry *LJMM* 7 November 1919
'I dont fret . . .' to J.M. Murry *LJMM* 8 December 1919
'January 8 BLACK . . .' *Journal* 8-12 January 1920, 119/45 ATL

75 'I look back . . .' to J.M. Murry *LJMM* 13 January 1920
'an ass and an ass . . .' *Journal* 23 January 1920, 119/45 ATL
'Goodbye. I am . . .' to J.M. Murry *LJMM* 9 February 1920 119/9 ATL

76 'I loathe you" D.H. Lawrence to K.M. quoted by K.M. to J.M. Murry *LJMM* 9 February 1920
'*The Nation* said . . .' D.H. Lawrence to Mary Cannan, 12 February 1921, *Moore*
'Two mud-worms . . .' D.H. Lawrence to Koteliansky 2 March 1921, *Moore*
'I am longing . . .' to J.M. Murry March 1920, 119/9 ATL

77 'for the first . . .' J.M. Murry's Journal 12 July 1953, quoted in *John Middleton Murry* F.A. Lea p165
'I can't help . . .' to Richard Murry *Letters* February 1920

'Yesterday we went . . .' to J.M. Murry 4 March 1920 119/9 ATL

78 'I am writing . . .' to Sidney Schiff 1920 BL
'Mention is . . .' to Richard Murry *Letters* February 1920

79 'Brett in her letters . . .' n.d. between 12 & 19 August 1920, 119/48 ATL
'Was their relationship . . .' *Journal* 19 August 1920, 119/48 ATL

80 'I wouldn't mind . . .' December 1920, 119/48 ATL
'it seemed . . .' 119/48 ATL
'I cough and cough . . .' *Journal* 12 August 1920 119/4 ATL
'would give any . . .' to J.M. Murry *LJMM* 16 September 1920 119/10 ATL

81 'I am stuck . . .' to Richard Murry *Letters* November 1920
'Murry is here . . .' to Anne Estelle Rice (Drey) 26 December 1920, 119/10 ATL
'If you . . .' to J.M. Murry 22 October 1920, 119/10 ATL

82 'Champagne in this . . .' to Anne Estelle Rice (Drey) 26 December 1920, 119/10 ATL
'suffering must become . . .' *Journal* 19 December 1920, 119/71 ATL
'This little place . . .' to J.M. Murry *LJMM* 10 November 1920 PC 119/110 ATL (original in Menton)

83 'and please darling . . .' to J.M. Murry *LJMM* 12 December 1920, 119/10 ATL
'We are . . .' *Journal* 27 December 1920, 119/58 ATL
'Elizabeth Bibesco has . . .' to L.M. 20 March 1921, BL
'little love letters . . .' A. Alpers *The Life of Katherine Mansfield* p332 TS Texas
'starving for . . .' quoted by F.A. Lea p81

84 'pasty & podgy . . .' *The Diary of V.W.* Vol I 6 December 1919
'We are both . . .' to Dorothy Brett *Letters* 20 April 1921
'Menton seems . . .' to L.M. 7 March 1922, BL

85 'a person to consult . . .' to L.M. 10 March 1922, BL
'a lady with . . .' to J.M. Murry *LJMM* 7 May 1921, 119/11 ATL
'The cleanliness . . .' ibid.
'We have taken . . .' to Lady Ottoline Morrell *Letters* 24 July 1921

86 'I think I . . .' to Violet Schiff 26 October 1921, BL
'cold comfort . . .' to Sydney Waterlow 3 December 1921, MS Papers 1153/3 ATL
'I confess . . .' to Sylvia Lynd 24 September 1921, PC119/75
'permanently part . . .' to L.M. 7 November 1921, BL
'quite settled . . .' to Richard Murry *Letters* 22 September 1921
'It's all scenery . . .' to Anne Estelle Rice (Drey) *Letters* 24 December 1921
'I suppose . . .' to Lady Ottoline Morrell *Letters* January 1922

87 'I want to . . .' to Raymond Drey *Letters* 27 December 1921
'That regret . . .' to Lady Ottoline Morrell *Letters* January 1922
'After five doses . . .' to Countess Russell 6 March 1922 PC 119/76 ATL

'in a tight . . .' to William Gerhardi *Letters* 14 June 1922
'Cities are too . . .' to L.M. 4 June 1922, BL
88 'Good God!' to L.M. 4 June 1922, BL
'I want you . . .' to L.M. 7 June 1922, BL
'I am the . . .' to Koteliansky, 4 July 1922, BL
89 'perhaps the truth . . .' to Countess Russell June-July 1921, BL
'I *do* believe . . .' to J.M. Murry *LJMM* 19 May 1921
90 'A *private* house . . .' to Sylvia Lynd 29 September 1922 PC 119/75 ATL
'It frightens me . . .' to Sylvia Lynd n.d. PC 119/75 ATL
'For a long time . . .' *Journal* December 1920, 119/65 ATL
91 'You see . . .' to Lady Ottoline Morrell *Letters* June 1918
'I can see . . .' to Dorothy Brett *Letters* 31 October 1921
92 'These pages from . . .' *Journal* 14 October 1922, 119/53 ATL
93 'Last evening . . . Katherine' Ida Baker's Diary 1922, 119/93 ATL
'in the deepest sense . . .' to J.M Murry *LJMM* 18/21 October 1922, 119/13 ATL
'I have long . . .' P.D. Ouspensky *In Search of the Miraculous* p386
'I have long . . .' P.D. Ouspensky *In Search of the Miraculous* p386
'Mr Gurdjieff . . .' to J.M. Murry *LJMM* 14/18 October 1922, 119/13 ATL
94 'I am at an end . . .' to J.M. Murry *LJMM* 24 October 1922
'There is not . . .' A.R. Orage *Talks with Katherine Mansfield*
'I am learning . . .' to L.M. 10 November 1922, BL
'the whole difficulty . . .' to L.M. 22/25 December 1922, BL
'At 34 . . .' to J.M. Murry *LJMM* November 1922
95 "I am not dead . . .' to L.M. 15 December 1922, BL
'moods when I simply pine . . .' to L.M. January 1923, unposted and found in her blotter
'the dancing here . . .' to J.M. Murry *LJMM* 12 November 1922, 119/13 ATL
96 'We had been . . .' J.M. Murry to Sydney Waterlow 11 January 1923, 1157/4 ATL
'That Friday . . .' Chaddie to Vera, January 1923, 119/96 ATL
'Let me take . . .' *Journal* September 1922, 119/53 ATL moved from 149
98 'My precious darling . . .' to J.M. Murry *LJMM* 11 January 1921 119/11 ATL
99 'Looking back . . .' 1922, 119/26 ATL
'all manuscripts notebooks . . .' Will cited by A. Alpers *The Life of Katherine Mansfield* (1980) p366
'All my manuscripts . . .' to J.M. Murry 7 August 1922, 119/13 ATL
'& as soon . . .' letter from Chaddie to Vera, ATL
'In spite of . . .' to J.M. Murry 7 August 1922, 119/13 ATL
100 'Tidied all my papers . . .' *Journal* 24 January 1922, 119/43 ATL
'Her letters are . . .' J.M. Murry *Katherine Mansfield and Other Literary Studies* p71

'It is Katherine . . .' J.M. Murry's *Journal* 14 October 1942 quoted by F.A. Lea p300
101 'saintliest of women' Thomas Moult *The Bookman* February 1923
'quite shocking and . . .' *Lytton Strachey* Vol II p358
'a selective camera' A.R. Orage 'Talks with Katherine Mansfield' 'The Century Magazine' November 1904
'Last night, there . . .' to J.M. Murry *LJMM* 19 May 1917, 119/4 ATL
102 'are you fair . . .' to J.M. Murry *LJMM* 9 December 1919, 119/8 ATL
'PLEASE SEND ME MONEY' to J.M. Murry *LJMM* August 1916, 119/4 ATL
'Poor Brett! She . . .' to J.M. Murry *LJMM* 17 March 1920, 119/9 ATL
'Don't feel bitter . . .' to Dorothy Brett *Letters* 26 March 1920
'Thank you . . .' to J.M. Murry *LJMM* 10 October 1920, 119/10 ATL
'I don't like . . .' ibid.
103 'I liked Vanessa . . .' J.M. Murry to K.M. *Letters of JMM* 23 November 1919, 119/118 ATL
'Yes I agree . . .' to J.M. Murry *LJMM* 29 November 1919, 119/8
'a great fat . . .' to J.M. Murry *LJMM* 11 May 1915, 119/2
'millionaire husband . . .' to J.M. Murry *LJMM* 19 March 1920 119/9 ATL
104 'I hear he . . .' *DHL* to Maria Huxley 5 December 1928 *Moore*
'if one was . . .' 119/71
105 Mary Cannan remarked . . . *Today we will only gossip* p68
'a secretive creature . . .' to L.M. 21 March 1922, BL
'I can't write . . .' to J.M. Murry 21 May 1918
'It really is . . .' to Sylvia Lynd *Letters* 24 September 1921
'The more I . . .' to K.M. *Letters of JMM* 7 February 1920
'I can't think . . .' to K.M. *Letters of JMM* 15 March 1920
106 'It is of . . .' *Journal* October 1922, 119/53 ATL
'Tedious Brief Adventure . . .' *Journal* July 1919, 119/48 ATL
'you are always . . .' to J.M. Murry 3 November 1919, 119/8 ATL
'Light refreshments . . .' to Anne Estelle Rice (Drey) 13 January 1919, 119/8 ATL
107 'my heart is . . .' to Anne Estelle Rice (Drey) 2 March 1920, 119/8 ATL
'Frieda writes me . . .' to Koteliansky 7 April 1919, BL
'the symbol of . . .' to Lady Ottoline Morrell *Letters* June 1921
'If I were . . .' to J.M. Murry *LJMM* 2 November 1919
'was a New Zealand . . .' to L.M. 18 April 1918, BL
108 'Someone brings . . .' *Journal* 27 December 1920, 119/58 ATL
'the roses hang . . .' to J.M. Murry *LJMM* 25 November 1919, 119/8 ATL
'The wind died . . .' *Journal* November/December 1915, 119/70 ATL
'This evening I . . .' to Koteliansky 17 March 1915, BL
109 'You ought to . . .' *Journal* October 1921, 119/5 ATL

'I shall destroy . . .' to L.M. 29 August 1921, BL
'reveal themselves as . . .' to J.M. Murry 17 October 1920
'I'm sure I've . . .' to Sydney Schiff 4 November 1920, BL
'Lawrence denies . . .' to J.M. Murry *LJMM* December
1920
'I do not . . .' to Koteliansky *Letters* 17 July 1922
110 'wet linoleum . . .' to Sydney Schiff *Letters* 15 January
1922, BL
'About Joyce . . .' to Dorothy Brett *Letters* 1 May 1922
'I think that's . . .' to Sydney Waterlow March 1921
1157/3 ATL
'the 1st modern . . .' to Violet Schiff *Letters* 24 August
1922, BL
111 'epicine electioneering women . . .' notice authorised
by Henry Wright, 103 Main Street, Wellington, ATL
'Eliot-Virginia?' to Virginia Woolf n.d. *Adam* 370-5
112 'great tall gaunt . . .' 27 December 1903, 119/60 ATL
'two women . . .' A. Alpers *The Life of Katherine
Mansfield* (1980) p73, 328 quoting K.M. to Garnet Trowell
17 September 1908
113 'The Cave of Harmony' C.A. Hankin *Katherine
Mansfield and her Confessional Stories* p136 citing Vera
Brittain *Radcliffe Hall: A Case of Obscenity* p95
'She got turned . . .' Christopher Hassall *Edward Marsh:
A Biography* p226
'the first of a great . . .' to Vera 12 June 1908, 119/1 ATL
'what women in . . .' *Journal* May 1908, 119/62 ATL
114 'Our friendship is . . .' 'Juliet', 119/24 ATL
'Men dont . . .' to L.M. 27 June 1918, BL
'*Am* I such . . .' to J.M. Murry *LJMM* Summer 1913,
119/2 ATL
115 'All this suffragist . . .' to Vera 12 June 1908, 119/1
ATL
116 :'If he wallops . . .' to Countess Russell 21 February
1922, BL
'no good at . . .' to Vera November 1921, 119/11 ATL
'knitting turns me . . .' to Countess Russell *Letters*
October 1921
'a pleasant, decent . . .' to Annie Beauchamp
15 December 1914, ATL BEA MS Papers 2063
'I haven't . . .' to Violet Schiff 24 August 1922, BL
'I have an . . .' to Sydney Schiff 1 December 1020, BL
'There is as . . .' *Journal* 24 October 1918, 119/35 ATL
'bitten nails . . .' 119/48 ATL
117 'like a big . . .' to Koteliansky April 1919, BL
'Another thing I . . .' to J.M. Murry *LJMM* 6 February
1918, 119/5 ATL
'what appalling furniture . . .' *Journal* March 1916,
119/57 an unposted letter to Frederick Goodyear
'It is a pity . . .' to Koteliansky *Letters* 2 August 1922
118 'This little place . . .' to J.M. Murry *LJMM*
10 November 1920 PC 119/100 ATL
'Here it is . . .' to Dorothy Brett *Letters* 20 April 1921
'I scarcely know . . .' to Harold Beauchamp 6 March
1916, 119/4 ATL
'I am sure . . .' to J.M. Murry *LJMM* 16 February 1918
119 'poor as a . . .' to J.M. Murry *LJMM* 27 September
1920
'I have been . . .' to J.M. Murry *LJMM* 12 February 1914,

119/2 ATL
120 'I can emphatically . . .' Harold Beauchamp's note on
letter received 9 January 1922, 199/11 ATL
'My precious, please . . .' to J.M. Murry *LJMM*
19 January 1918, 199/5 ATL
'The butcher's bill . . .' to Dorothy Brett *Letters* 8 August
1921
'This year I . . .' *Journal* 13 February 1916, 119/57 ATL
'Jones dead Have . . .' to L.M. 25 June 1918, BL
'bound to journalism . . .' to J.M. Murry *LJMM*
6 December 1920
'to *live rich* . . .' to J.M. Murry *LJMM* 6 December 1920
'I will pay . . .' to Countess Russell n.d. July? 1922, PC
ATL
121 'Father darling . . .' to Harold Beauchamp 1 November
1921, 119/11 ATL
122 'I always feel . . .' to Anne Estelle Rice (Drey) *Letters*
1 May 1922 119/11, 119/12 ATL
'I really must . . .' to L.M. 13 March 1921, BL
'And never think . . .' to Richard Murry 1920 *Adam*
370-5 p25
'When I say . . .' to L.M. 13 November 1922, BL
123 'Its the fault . . .' to Annie Beauchamp 15 December
1914, BEA MS Papers 2063/7 ATL
'I spoke about . . .' to J.M. Murry 23 February 1918.
119/5 ATL
'Those preparations for . . .' to Lady Ottoline Morrell
Letters November 1918
124 'This is all to laborious' to Dorothy Brett *Letters* to
something
'You will think . . .' to Dorothy Brett *Letters* 10 June 1919
'all parties are . . .' to Virginia Woolf n.d. *Adam* 370-5
p22
'dangerous place . . .' to L.M. 21 March 1922, BL
'letters are deceptive . . .' to J.M. Murry *LJMM*
15 October 1922, 119/13 ATL
'The demand you . . .' Frederick Goodyear to K.M.
9 April 1916, 119/15 ATL
'I had hoped . . .' to Harold Beauchamp 15 December
1914, BEA MS Papers 2063/7 ATL
126 'Do please go . . .' to L.M. 21 May 1918, BL
'I had a . . .' to J.M. Murry *LJMM* 22 May 1918
'I don't want . . .' to J.M. Murry *LJMM* 19 June 1918
'Jones dear . . .' to L.M. 25 June 1918, BL
'I don't *want* . . .' to L.M. 1 August 1918, BL
'I think the . . .' 119/36 ATL
127 'Doors that bang . . .' to Sydney Schiff January 1922,
BL
'Very strange my . . .' to J.M. Murry *LJMM* 19/20 March
1915, 119/2 ATL
'How strange talking . . .' to Lady Ottoline Morrell
Letters 24 July 1921
'I for the first . . .' *Journal* 8 February 1920, 119/45 ATL
'No theres no God . . .' to J.M. Murry *LJMM*
8 November 1919 119/8 ATL
'Honesty (why) is . . .' *Journal* 15 December 1919, 119/46
ATL
128 'We resist . . .' to J.M. Murry *LJMM* 18 October 1920
'quite overcome . . .' to Lady Ottoline Morrell *Letters*
24 May 1918

'God forbid that . . .' to Richard Murry *Letters* January 1920

'No, one can't believe . . .' to J.M. Murry *LJMM* 23 May 1921, 119/11 ATL

129 'John brought me . . .' to Countess Russell 6 March 1922, 119/76 ATL

'I never had . . .' to Dorothy Brett *Letters* 15 October 1922

130 'completely wrong . . .' Radio New Zealand Archives

'Ah Jeanne . . .' to Jeanne Renshaw *Letters* 14 October 1921

131 'how terrible that . . .' to Annie Beauchamp 18 December 1914 BEA MS Papers 2063/7 ATL

'Kathleen has certainly . . .' Annie Beauchamp to Leslie Beauchamp 12 October 1915, BEA MS Papers 2063/5 ATL

'Poor old Vera . . .' Annie Beauchamp to Clara Palmer 10 November 1915, BEA MS Papers 2063/5 ATL

'You will be . . .' Annie Beauchamp to Clara Palmer 16 March 1916 BEA MS Papers 2063/5 ATL

'give anything . . .' Annie Beauchamp to Mr Neave solicitor 18 July1918 BEA MS Papers 2063/5 ATL

'I feel very strongly . . .' to J.M. Murry *LJMM* 1 March 1918, 119/9 ATL

132 'I miss her so . . .' to J.M. Murry *LJMM* 8 February 1920, 119/9 ATL

'guilt for the . . .' C.A. Hankin *Katherine Mansfield and her Confessional Stories* p110-12

'When I last . . .' ts 'His sister's keeper' 1909 Newberry

133 'Dearest, I have . . .' to Leslie Beauchamp, Sunday (n.d. August) 1915 MS Papers 2413 ATL

'My dearest Marie . . .' to Chaddie and Jeanne 31 December 1922 ts 119/13 ATL

'Do you remember . . .' *Journal* October 1915, 119/70 ATL

134 'Their continual . . .' J.M.M. to K.M. *Letters of J.M. Murry* 13 January 1920, 119/20 ATL

'I'm so angry . . .' to J.M. Murry *LJMM* 22 March 1920

'Don't blame . . .' *Letters* 1 March 1921

135 'I remember . . .' to Jeanne *Letters* 14 October 1921, 119/11 ATL

'Just a note . . .' to Harold Beauchamp *Letters* 22 August 1922

'under the table . . .' to Countess Russell 1922, BL

'Thank you for . . .' to J.M. Murry *LJMM* Summer 1913

136 'the old year . . .' to Harold Beauchamp 31 December 1922 ts 119/13 ATL

'I dont like . . .' September 1918, 119/35 ATL

'I hope all . . .' to Richard Murry 3 October 1922 *Adam* 370-5

'Her lies & poses . . .' *The Diary of V.W.* Vol. I 18 January 1918

137 'Thank you for . . .' to Koteliansky *Letters* 4 November 1921 BL

'emotionally married . . .' C.A. Hankin *Katherine Mansfield and her Confessional Stories*

'Jones as usual . . .' to Violet Schiff 26 October 1921, BL

'I do not . . .' *Journal* 19 May 1919, 119/71 ATL

'You know Richard . . .' to Richard Murry December 1921 *Adam* 300-75

138 'Ah, but I . . .' to J.M. Murry *LJMM* 12 December 1915

'If I was . . .' to J.M. Murry *LJMM* 20 February 1918, 119/5 ATL

'Perhaps all . . .' to J.M. Murry *LJMM* 28 November 1920, 119/10 ATL

'There is the . . .' *Journal* May 1919, 119/39 ATL

139 'We are the sport . . .' to J.M. Murry *LJMM* 30 November 1919

'As I grew . . .' *Journal* 15 December 1919, 119/49 ATL

'You are you . . .' to J.M. Murry *LJMM* 7 November 1922, 119/13 ATL

140 'here's a woman . . .' to Violet and Sydney Schiff May 1920 BL

'I've scarcely . . .' to J.M. Murry *LJMM* 17 November 1920, 119/10 ATL

141 'You see . . .' to J.M. Murry *LJMM* 26 December 1922, 119/13 ATL

142 'Ribni speaks' 26 March 1918, 119/40 ATL

'And you have . . .' to J.M. Murry *LJMM* 27 November 1920, 199/10 ATL

'It seems to me . . .' to J.M. Murry *LJMM* 25 May 1921, 119/11 ATL

'Your review of . . .' to J.M. Murry *LJMM* 18 November 1919, 199/8 ATL

'my money is . . .' to Violet and Sydney Schiff 26 September 1920, BL

'Your Hardy doesn't . . .' to J.M. Murry *LJMM* December 1920, 119/10 ATL

143 'I told you . . .' to J.M. Murry *LJMM* 12 December 1920

'Do I make M. up . . .' *Journal* 6 February 1922, 119/43 ATL

'I realise how . . .' *Journal* June 1919, 119/39 ATL

'It's not RIGHT . . .' to J.M. Murry 8 December 1920, 199/10 ATL

'You know, I . . .' to Koteliansky 23 August 1922, BL

'Looking back, my boat . . .' to J.M. Murry *LJMM* 11 October 1922, 119/13 ATL

144 'in spite of . . .' 7 September 1922 119/12 ATL

'You get out . . .' to J.M. Murry *LJMM* 31 December 1922, 119/13 ATL

'not just an agency . . .' to L.M. 12 June 1918, BL

'It seems a . . .' to L.M. 1 June 1918, BL

145 'L.M. has made . . .' to J.M. Murry 2 March 1918, 119/6 ATL

'The truth is . . .' to L.M. September 1921, BL

146 'How can you . . .' 29 September 1921, II4 notebook 5 Newberry

147 'please don't make . . .' to L.M. 29 September 1921, BL

'She was sure . . .' *Journal* May 1919, 119/39 ATL

'Life never bores . . .' to Bertrand Russell 17 December 1916 *Adam* 370-5 McMaster

148 'I am a kind . . .' to L.M. 16 February 1922, BL

'the old feeling . . .' to L.M. 27 May 1922, BL

'But you do . . .' 10 November 1922, BL

'Forgive this paper . . .' 15 December 1922, BL

'I have purposely . . .' January 1923, BL

'One afternoon . . .' Millie A. Parker 'Broken Strings' *New Zealand Herald* 3 February 1923

149 'power, wealth and . . .' *Journal* May 1908, 119/62 ATL

'I mean to . . .' to Koteliansky 19 October1922, BL

150 'I am so . . .' to Sylvia Payne 24 April 1906, 119/1 ATL
152 'To be alive . . .' *Journal* 30 May 1917 119/47 ATL
'All this week . . .' to Dorothy Brett *Letters* 15 October 1921
153 'You know . . .' to William Gerhardi *Letters* 21 March 1921
155 'I cannot have . . .' to J.M. Murry *LJMM* 4 February 1920
156 'Now we know . . .' to J.M. Murry *LJMM* 16 November 1919, 119/8 ATL
158 'Maata' and 'Young Country' 1913 II3 Notebook 2, Newberry
'24 pages per day . . .' ibid.
'I want to . . .' *Journal* 22 January 1916, 119/68 ATL
159 'I think the . . .' quoted by J.M. Murry and R.E. Mantz *The Life of Katherine Mansfield* p95, to S.M. from Cape Town, their dating is 1908, but the content and 'treasure' image suggest 1921-22
'Of daisies I . . .' *Journal* 14 February 1916, 119/57 ATL
160 'Even if one . . .' to J.M. Murry 2 April 1920
'Funny thing is . . .' to J.M. Murry 9 February 1918, 119/5 ATL
'I meant to . . .' to Harold Beauchamp received 30 August 1922 119/13
'I've even put . . .' to L.M. 3 June 1918, BL
161 'the dead to . . .' to Dorothy Brett *Letters* September 1921
'When does one . . .' to Sydney Schiff 5 December 1921, BL
162 'Regardless of what . . .' C.A. Hankin *Katherine Mansfield and her Confessional Stories* p198
163 'Ma cherie amie . . .' Francis Carco to K.M. 26 March 1915, 119/15 ATL
'write simply, fully . . .' *Journal* 13 November 1921 II25 Notebook 6 Newberry
'You see for me . . .' *Journal* January 1921 II25 Notebook 6 Newberry
'too much description . . .' 131 Newberry
'I choose not . . .' to Richard Murry *Letters* 17 January 1921
165 'I might have . . .' to William Gerhardi *Letters* 13 March 1922
'New people have . . .' *Novels & Novelists* p125, 12 December 1919
'That gentle caricature . . .' *The Memories of L.M.* p153
166 'I do still . . .' *Journal* 18 July 1921 II7 Notebook 7 Newberry
'a lie in . . .' to J.M. Murry, 10 November 1919, 119/8 ATL
'how are we . . .' to Arnold Gibbons 24 June 1922, 119/12 ATL
'All that I . . .' *Journal* 25 July 1921
'little stories like . . .' to Elizabeth Russell *Letters* 31 December 1922 BL
'one can get . . .' *Journal* 17 January 1922, 119/43 ATL
'an infinite delight . . .' to Koteliansky 17 May 1915, BL
167 'deserts of vast . . .' to J.M. Murry *LJMM* 16 November 1919, 119/8 ATL
'convey those . . .' ibid.
168 'It's more or . . .' *Letters* 11 October 1917
'a huge long . . .' to Richard Murry *Letters* 1 January 1921

169 'the swift, illuminated . . .' Sylvia Berkman *Katherine Mansfield A Critical Study* p150
170 'What I feel . . .' *Journal* 21 November 1921, 119/54 ATL
'the big snail . . .' to J.M. Murry 20 October 1919, 119/8 ATL
'The diversity of . . .' to William Gerhardi *Letters* 13 March 1922
'a stupid man . . .' to Dorothy Brett *Letters* 12 November 1921
'She makes modern . . .' to Elizabeth Russell *Letters* December 1921
171 'a kind of . . .' H.E. Bates *The Modern Short Story* p129-30
172 'a wider vision . . .' *Journal* May 1908, 119/62 ATL
173 'at last I . . .' to Lady Ottoline Morrell *Letters* December 1921
'great art . . .' *Journal* January 1921
'*Chinese tub thumping!*' to V & S Schiff 3 December 1921 BL
'Plagiarist, Disciple or Ardent Admirer?' Ronald Sutherland *Critique V* p58
'While the sheer . . .' C. Kurylo *Chekhov and Katherine Mansfield* p193
'One has not . . .' 'The Short Story as Poetry', *The Freeman* 11 May 1921
174 'your great admiration . . .' to Arnold Gibbons 24 June 1922, 119/12 ATL
'we all, as writers . . .' to Arnold Gibbons 13 July 1922, 119/12 ATL
'The form I . . .' *Journal* 22 January 1916, 119/68 ATL
'God forgive me . . .' *Journal* December 1920 quoted from inscription on flyleaf of K.M.'s copy of *The Tales of Tchehov* Vol III trans. C. Garnet
'chasing about . . .' to J.M. Murry *LJMM* 15 October 1922
175 'intellectual snobbery' to J.M. Murry *LJMM*
'Where Virginia Woolf . . .' *Katherine Mansfield and other literary portraits* p8, J.M. Murry quoting V.S. Pritchett.
'If Virginia Woolf . . .' T.O. Beachcroft *The Modest Art* p171
'after so very . . .' to Virginia Woolf *Letters* 17 August 1917
'examine for a . . .' 'Modern Fiction' Virginia Woolf
'Not good enough' 4 April 1919 Scrapbook 1919 MS P MAN 97174
'Not bad . . .' MS P MAN 97174
'mysterious relationship' *Novels & Novelists* p113 28 November 1919
'Why can't writers . . .' to Countess Russell *Letters* November 1921
176 'passion for display . . .' *Novels and Novelists* p140 26 January 1920
'All roads lead to . . .' *Novels and Novelists* p142
Draft of 'The Garden Party' 119/64 ATL
177 'we do not . . .' Compton Mackenzie *My Life and Times Octave V*
'it is not . . .' *Journal* November 1921, 119/67 ATL
'Hang it all . . .' to Dorothy Brett *Letters* 26 February 1922

'continuity – they also . . .' to J.M. Murry 25 September 1920, 119/10 ATL

'a book for . . .' to J.M. Murry *LJMM* 17 October 1920, 119/10 ATL

'Sorel' and *'Syndicalism'* to J.M. Murry *LJMM* 23 October 1920 119/10 ATL

178 'confronted myself as . . .' to J.M. Murry *LJMM* 31 October 1920, 119/10 ATL

'all that horrible . . .' to J.M. Murry *LJMM* 4 March 1920, 119/10 ATL

'I do not . . .' *Journal* October 1921, 119/64 ATL

'I ought to . . .' *Journal* October 1918, 119/35 ATL

'overwriting and . . .' 1913 II1 Notebook 2 Newberry

'It is most . . .' to J.M. Murry 2 November 1922, 119/13 ATL

'I have done . . .' to William Gerhardi *Letters* 8 February 1922

'I have just . . .' to Sydney Waterlow 3 December 1921 1157/3 ATL

'so much to write . . .' to Violet Schiff August 1920, BL

179 'It takes the . . .' *Journal* 31 May 1919, 119/39 ATL

'Tell me if . . .' to J.M. Murry 9 May 1921, 119/11 ATL

'her talent was . . .' Hugh Walpole 4 November 1939

'And won't the . . .' to Dorothy Brett *Letters* 12 May 1918

180 'Eliot, Joyce and Virginia . . .' T.O. Beachcroft *The Modest Art* p164

'Yes, yes, but . . .' Catherine Carswell *The Savage Pilgrimage* p198

'She is *not* . . .' ibid.

'She is delicate . . .' D.H. Lawrence to J.M. Murry 25 October 1923

'a good deal better . . .' *The Letters of V.W.* Vol II to Clive Bell 16 July 1918

'the living power . . .' *The Diary of V.W.* Vol 1 12 July 1918

'My theory is . . .' *The Letters of V.W.* Vol 3 30 July 1923

181 'The artist takes . . .' to Dorothy Brett *Letters* 11 November 1921

'I'm so stale . . .' to J.M. Murry 28 November 1919, 119/8 ATL

'It's always a . . .' *Journal* 17 January 1922

'a whole novel . . .' March 1921 119/30 cf. *Journal* December 1920

Draft of 'The Dolls House' October 1921, 119/64 ATL

'as simply rubbish . . .' to J.M. Murry *LJMM* 13 October 1920

'God! I'm rooted . . .' to J.M. Murry *LJMM* 21 November 1919

'I don't believe . . .' to Sylvia Lynd *Letters* 31 January 1920

'But do you . . .' to Dorothy Brett *Letters* 9 March 1922

'A poem and . . .' *New Zealand Short Stories* Joan Stevens p47

182 'And now . . .' to J.M. Murry *LJMM* 8 December 1920

184 Page of Signatures 119/63 ATL; II 25 Notebook 6 Newberry

'Im a writer . . .' to J.M. Murry *LJMM* 2 December 1920, 119/10 ATL

199 'We sleep tonight . . .' 119/25 ATL

207 'A remarkable achievement' Sylvia Berkman *Katherine Mansfield: A Critical Study* p41

211 'My dear, I . . .' to Jeanne *The Collected Letters* October 1913 Newberry

219 'her hauntingly beautiful . . .' A. Alpers *Katherine Mansfield* p208

'carrying in its . . .' Sylvia Berkman *Katherine Mansfield: A Critical Study* p77

'With its curious . . .' A. Alpers *Katherine Mansfield* p182

220 'the most purely . . .' Clare Hanson and Andrew Gurr *Katherine Mansfield* p45,49

230 'a sophisticated failure . . .' J.M. Murry *Katherine Mansfield and other Literary Portraits* p8

'This story has . . .' A. Alpers *Katherine Mansfield* p274

'one of . . .' C.A. Hankin *Katherine Mansfield and her Confessional Stories* p143,149

276 'the Mercury is . . .' to Dorothy Brett *Letters* 15 October 1921

289 'Finished . . .' *Journal* 23 July 1921 II6 26 Newberry

290 'arguably . . .' C.A. Hankin *Katherine Mansfield and her Confessional Stories* p221

304 'An image of . . .' Anne Friis *Katherine Mansfield* p180

'Katherine Mansfield's . . .' Saralyn Daly *Katherine Mansfield* p109

305 'Would you not . . .' to Sylvia Payne 24 April 1906, 119/1 ATL

Works consulted

Although not exhaustive these lists may be useful for those readers wishing to learn more about Katherine Mansfield, her contemporaries and her writing.

Books

Ackroyd, Peter. *T.S. Eliot.* London: Hamish Hamilton, 1984

Adams, Anthony & Jones, Esmor. *Katherine Mansfield – a study of themes.* London: Harrap, 1975

Alpers, Antony. *Katherine Mansfield – A Biography.* London: Jonathan Cape, 1954

Alpers, Antony. *The Life of Katherine Mansfield.* London: Jonathan Cape, 1980

Anderson, Margaret. *The Unknowable Gurdjieff.* London: Routledge & Kegan Paul, 1962

Angus, Barbara. *A Guide to Katherine Mansfield's Wellington.* Wellington Regional Committee of the Historic Places Trust, 1985

Bagnall, A.G. *Okiwi,* Wellington: Mahina Press, 1972

Bagnold, Enid. *Autobiography.* London: Heinemann, 1969

Baker, Ida. *Katherine Mansfield: The Memories of L.M.* London: Michael Joseph, 1971

Bates, H.E. *The Modern Short Story.* London: Michael Joseph Ltd, 1971

Beachcroft, T.O. *The Modest Art: A Survey of the Short Story.* London: Oxford University Press, 1968

Beauchamp, Ethel. *Life at Anakiwa: The first 100 years 1863-1963.* Nelson: 1963

Beauchamp, Sir Harold. *Reminiscences and Recollections.* New Plymouth: T. Avery & Sons, 1937

Bedford, Sybille. *Aldous Huxley: A Biography,* vol. 1, 1894-1939. London: Chatto & Windus, 1973

Bell, Quentin. *Bloomsbury.* London: Futura Publications, 1974

Bell, Quentin. *Virginia Woolf: A Biography,* vol. 2, 1912-1941. London: Hogarth Press, 1972

Berkman, Sylvia. *Katherine Mansfield: A Critical Study.* New Haven: Yale University Press, 1951

Benet, Mary Kathleen. *Writers in Love.* New York: Macmillan, 1977

Boudot-Lamotte, Emmanuel. *Paris.* Paris: Paul Hartmann, 1937

Brett, Dorothy. *Lawrence and Brett: A Friendship.* London: Martin Secker, 1933

Brooke, Rupert, ed. Sir Geoffrey Keynes. *The Letters of Rupert Brooke.* London: Faber & Faber, 1968

Brophy, Brigid. *Don't Never Forget.* London: Jonathan Cape, 1966

Burgess, Anthony. *Flame Into Being: The Life and Work of D.H. Lawrence.* London: Heinemann, 1985

Carrington, Dora, ed. David Garnett. *Carrington: Letters & Extracts from her Diaries.* London: Jonathan Cape, 1970

Carswell, Catherine. *The Savage Pilgrimage: A Narrative of D.H. Lawrence.* Secker & Warburg, 1932

Carswell, John. *Lives and Letters.* London: Faber & Faber, 1978

Clark, Ronald W. *The Life of Bertrand Russell.* London: Jonathan Cape & Weidenfeld & Nicolson, 1975

Clarke, Isabel. *Katherine Mansfield.* Wellington: The Beltane Book Bureau, 1944

Curnow, Heather. *Katherine Mansfield.* Wellington: A.H. & A.W. Reed, 1968

Daly, Saralyn R. *Katherine Mansfield.* New York: Twain Publishers, 1965

Davin, D.M. *Katherine Mansfield in her letters.* Wellington: School Publications Branch, 1959

Davin, D.M. ed. *Katherine Mansfield Selected Stories.* Oxford University Press, 1969

Delaney, Paul. *D.H. Lawrence's Nightmare: The writer and his circle in the years of the great war.* Sussex: The Harvester Press, 1979

Eustace, C.J. *An Infinity of Questions: A Study of the Religion of Art.* Dennis Dobson, 1946

Foot, John. *The Edwardianism of Katherine Mansfield.* Wellington: Brentwoods Press, 1969

Fothergill, Robert A. *Private Chronicles: A Study of English Diaries.* London: Oxford University Press, 1974

Friis, Ann. *Katherine Mansfield: Life and Stories.* Copenhagen: Erik Munkigaard, 1946

Fullbrook, Kate. *Katherine Mansfield.* Sussex: The Harvester Press, 1986

Gadd, David. *The Loving Friends: A portrait of Bloomsbury.* London: The Hogarth Press, 1974

Garnett, David. *The Golden Echo: The Flowers of the Forest.* London: Chatto and Windus, 1953, 1955

Gathorne-Hardy, Robert. *Ottoline: The early memoirs of Lady Ottoline Morrell.* London: Faber & Faber, 1963

Gathorne-Hardy, Robert. *Ottoline at Garsington.* London: Faber & Faber, 1974

Gertler, Mark, ed. Noel Carrington. *Mark Gertler: Selected Letters.* London: Rupert Hart-Davis, 1965

Glenavy, Lady Beatrice. *Today we will only gossip.* London: Constable & Co. 1964

Gordon, Ian A. *Katherine Mansfield.* London: Longman Green & Co., 1964

Gordon, Ian A. *Undiscovered Country: The New Zealand Stories of Katherine Mansfield.* London: Longman Group, 1974

Gordon, Lyndall. *Virginia Woolf: A Writers Life.* Oxford University Press, 1986

Gurr, Andrew. *Writers in Exile: The Identity of Home in Modern Literature.* Sussex: The Harvester Press, 1981

Hankin, C.A. *Katherine Mansfield and Her Confessional Stories.* London: Macmillan, 1983

Hankin, C.A., ed. *The Letters of John Middleton Murry to Katherine Mansfield.* Auckland: Hutchinson Group, 1983

Hanson, Clare, and Gurr, Andrew. *Katherine Mansfield.* London: Macmillan, 1981

de Hartmann, Thomas. *Our Life with Mr. Gurdjieff.* Harmondsworth: Penguin, 1972

Hassell, Christopher. *Edward Marsh.* London: Longman, 1959

Hayman, Ronald. *Katherine Mansfield & Virginia Woolf.* London: Covent Garden, Essays, 1973

Holroyd, Michael. *Lytton Strachey; A Critical Biography,* vol. 1: *The Unknown Years.* Vol. II: *The Years of Achievement.* London: Heinemann, 1967, 1968

Hormasji, Nairman. *Katherine Mansfield: An Appraisal.* London: William Collins & Sons, 1967

Huxley, Aldous. *Point Counter Point.* London: Chatto & Windus, 1963

Huxley, Aldous, ed. Grover Smith. *The Letters of Aldous Huxley.* London: Chatto & Windus, 1969

Isherwood, Christopher. *Exhumations.* London: Methuen, 1966

Johnson-Darroch, Sandra. *Ottoline.* London: Chatto & Windus, 1976

Kaye, Elaine. *A History of Queen's College.* London: Chatto & Windus, 1972

Kneipp, Sebastian. *My Water Cure.* Kempten: Joseph Koesel, 4th English edn, 1986

Kurylo, C. *Chekov and Katherine Mansfield: A study in literary influence.* Michigan: University Microfilms, Ann Arbor, 1974

Lawlor, Pat. *A Katherine Mansfield Enthusiast: The Work of Guy N. Morris.* Wellington: The Beltane Book Bureau, 1951

Lawlor, Pat. *Mansfieldiana – A Brief Katherine Mansfield Bibliography.* Wellington: The Beltane Book Bureau, 1948

Lawlor, Pat. *The Loneliness of Katherine Mansfield.* Wellington: The Beltane Book Bureau, 1950

Lawlor, Pat. *The Mystery of Maata.* Wellington: The Beltane Book Bureau, 1946

Lawrence, D.H., ed. Aldous Huxley. *The Letters of D.H. Lawrence.* London: Heinemann, 1932

Lawrence, D.H., ed. Harry T. Moore. *The Letters of D.H. Lawrence.* London: Heinemann, 1962

Lawrence, Frieda, ed. E.W. Tedlock. *Frieda Lawrence: The Memoirs and Correspondence.* London: Heinemann, 1961

Lea, F.A. *John Middleton Murry.* London: Methuen, 1959

Lee, Hermione, ed. *The Secret Self: Short Stories by Women.* J.M. Dent & Sons, 1985

Lehmann, John. *Virginia Woolf and her World.* London: Thames & Hudson, 1975

Lenoel, Odette. *La Vocation de Katherine Mansfield.* Paris: Editions Albin Michel, 1946

Lucas, Robert, trans. by Geoffrey Skelton. *Frieda Lawrence.* London: Secker & Warburg, 1973

McCormick, E.M. *New Zealand Literature: A Survey.* Oxford University Press, 1959

McNeish, Helen. *Passionate Pilgrimage: A Love Affair in Letters.* Auckland: Hodder & Stoughton, 1976

Magalaner, Marvin. *The Fiction of Katherine Mansfield.* Southern Illinois University Press, 1971

Majumdar, Robin and McLaurin, Allen, eds. *Virginia Woolf: The Critical Heritage.* London: Routledge and Kegan Paul, 1975

Mantz, Ruth E. & Murry, J. Middleton. *The Life of Katherine Mansfield.* London: Constable & Co, 1933

Marsh, Edward. *A Number of People.* London: William Heinemann in association with Hamish Hamilton, 1939

Meyers, Jeffrey. *Katherine Mansfield: A Biography.* London: Hamish Hamilton, 1978

Moore, Harry T. *The Intelligent Heart.* London: Heinemann, 1954

Moore, Harry T. *The Priest of Love: A Life of D.H. Lawrence.* London: Heinemann, 1974

Moore, James. *Gurdijeff and Mansfield.* London: Routledge & Kegan Paul, 1980

Mulgan, Alan. *Great Days in New Zealand Writing.* Wellington: A.H. & A.W. Reed, 1962

Murray, Tosti. *Marsden: The History of a New Zealand School for Girls.* Wellington: Marsden School Old Girls' Assoc., 1967

Murry, Colin Middleton. *With One Hand Clapping.* London: Victor Gollancz, 1975

Murry, John Middleton. *Between Two Worlds.* London: Jonathan Cape, 1935

Murry, John Middleton. *Katherine Mansfield and other literary portraits.* London: Peter Nevill, 1949

Murry, John Middleton, intro. by T.S. Eliot. *Katherine Mansfield and other literary studies.* London: Constable & Co., 1959

Murry, John Middleton, selected by. *Katherine Mansfield Stories: A Selection.* World Publishing Co., 1946

Murry, John Middleton. *Son of Woman.* London: Jonathan Cape, 1931

Murry, Katherine Middleton. *Beloved Quixote: The Unknown Life of John Middleton Murry.* London: Souvenir Press (E & A) Ltd, 1986

Murry, Mary Middleton. *To Keep Faith.* London: Constable & Co., 1959

Nehls, Edward. *D.H. Lawrence: A Composite Biography.* University of Wisconsin Press, 1958

Nott, C.S. *Teachings of Gurdjieff: The Journal of a Pupil.* London: Routledge & Kegan Paul, 1961

Orton, William. *The Last Romantic.* London: Cassell & Co., 1937

O'Sullivan, Vincent. *Katherine Mansfield's New Zealand.* Auckland: Golden Press, 1974

O'Sullivan, Vincent, ed. *The Aloe: with Prelude.* Wellington: Port Nicholson Press, 1982

Ouspensky, P. *In search of the Miraculous.* London: Routledge & Kegan Paul, 1956

Rosenbaum, S.P., ed. *The Bloomsbury Group.* University of Toronto Press, 1975

Russell, Bertrand. *The Autobiography of Bertrand Russell.* London: George Allen & Unwin, 1968

Showalter, Elaine. *A Literature of their Own: British Women Novelists from Brontë to Lessing.* London: Virago, 1978

Sichel, Pierre. *Modigliani: A Biography.* New York: E.P. Dutton, 1967

Spater, George and Parsons, Ian. *A Marriage of True*

Minds: An Intimate Portrait of Leonard and Virginia Woolf. London: Jonathan Cape and Hogarth Press, 1977

Sprigge, Elizabeth. *The Life of Ivy Compton Burnett.* London: Victor Gollancz, 1973

Squire, J.C. *Books Reviewed.* London: Heinemann, 1923

Stevens, Joan. *New Zealand Short Stories.* Wellington: Price Milburn, 1968

Tomalin, Claire, ed. *Katherine Mansfield: Short Stories.* London: Everyman, 1983

Walker, Kenneth. *A study of Gurdjieff's teaching.* London: Jonathan Cape, 1957

Walsh, William, ed. *Readings in Commonwealth Literature.* Oxford: Clarendon Press, 1973

Willey, Margaret. *Three Women Diarists.* London; Jonathan Cape, 1957

Wolf, Josef and Burghardt, Ludwig. *Ein Bauerndorf wird Weltbad: Sebastian Kneipp und sein Wörishofen.* Bad Wörishofen: Verlag Erwin Geyer, 1971

Woolf, Leonard. *Beginning Again. An Autobiography of the years 1911-1918.* London: Hogarth Press, 1964

Woolf, Virginia. *The Common Reader.* London: Hogarth Press, 1925

Woolf, Virginia, ed. Anne Olivier Bell. *The Diary of Virginia Woolf,* vol. 2: 1915-1919. London: Hogarth Press, 1977

Woolf, Virginia, ed. Nigel Nicolson. *The Question of Things Happening: The Letters of Virginia Woolf, 1912-1922.* London: Hogarth Press, 1976

Woolf, Virginia, ed. Nigel Nicolson. *A Change of Perspective: The Letters of Virginia Woolf,* vol. 3. London: Hogarth Press, 1977

Articles and reviews

Aiken, Conrad. 'The Short Story as Poetry'. *The Freeman* 11 May 1921

Aiken, Conrad. 'Your Obituary, Well Written'. *The Collected Short Stories of Conrad Aiken.* London: Heinemann, 1966 (based on the writer's meeting and correspondence with Katherine Mansfield.)

Alpers, Antony. 'Literary Biography (in New Zealand)'. *Biography in New Zealand,* Allen & Unwin/Port Nicholson Press, 1985

Angus, Barbara. 'Recalling the Wellington of Katherine Mansfield'. *Historic Places,* March 1987

Boddy, Gill. 'In the Steps of Katherine Mansfield'. *Insight,* vol. 2, March-April, 1982

Bowyer, E.C. 'New Life Cult'. *The Daily News,* 16 February 1923

Bowyer, E.C. 'Forest Philosophers'. *The Daily News,* 19 February 1923

Brett, Dorothy. 'Katherine'. *Adam International Review,* no. 300, 1963-65

Brett, Dorothy and Manchester, John. 'Reminiscences of Katherine.' *Adam International Review,* nos 370-5, 1972-73

Carco, Francis. 'Souvenirs sur Katherine Mansfield'. *Les Annales,* 27 January 1933

Cazamian, Louis. 'D.H. Lawrence and Katherine Mansfield as Letter Writers'. The Lamont Lecture at Yale University, 5 March 1934

Dowling, David. 'Aunt Beryl's Doll's House'. *Landfall,* no. 134, June 1980

Else, Anne. 'Katherine Mansfield: A Re-examination.' *Biography in New Zealand.* Allen & Unwin/Port Nicholson Press, 1985

Gordon, Ian. 'The Banker and the Banker's Daughter'. *The NZ Listener,* 27 November 1976

Gordon, Ian. 'The House that Katherine Built'. *The Evening Post,* 14 March 1981

Gordon, Ian. 'Warmth and Hydrangeas'. *The NZ Listener,* 8 May 1976

Grindea, Miron, ed. 'Katherine Mansfield – fifty years after'. *Adam International Review,* nos 370-5, 1972-73

Hudson, Stephen. 'First Meetings with Katherine Mansfield'. *The Cornhill Magazine,* no. 1017, Autumn, 1958

Kafian, Adele. 'The Last Days of Katherine Mansfield'. *The Adelphi,* October-December 1946

Leeming, Owen. 'Katherine Mansfield's Rebellion'. *The NZ Listener,* 29 March, 5 April, 11 April 1963

Locke, Terry. 'K.M. and "Bliss"'. *Landfall* 135, September 1980

Lynd, Sylvia, 'Katherine Mansfield'. *The Weekly Westminster Gazette,* 20 January 1923

McEldowney, Dennis. 'Recent Biographical Writing on Katherine Mansfield'. *Ariel: A Review of International English Literature,* vol. 16, no. 4, October 1985

Mandente, Floriana. 'Katherine Mansfield A Ospedaletti'. *Settimo Giorno,* 3 April 1962

Mills, Tom. 'Katherine Mansfield'. *New Zealand Railways Magazine,* 1 September 1933, October 1938

Moore, James. 'George Ivanovitch Gurdjieff'. *Resurgence*

New, W.H. 'Mansfield Collected'. *Journal of New Zealand Literature,* no. 3, 1985

O'Sullivan, Vincent. 'The Magnetic Chain: Notes and Approaches to K.M.' *Landfall* 114, June 1975

Orage, A.R. 'Talks with Katherine Mansfield'. *The Century,* May/November 1924

Parker, Millie. 'Broken Strings'. *The New Zealand Herald,* 3 February 1923

Rice, Anne Estelle. 'Memories of Katherine Mansfield'. *Adam,* no. 300, 1963-65

Ruddick, Marion. 'Incidents in the Life of Katherine Mansfield'. *Chicago Evening Post,* Saturday, 8 December 1928

Shadbolt, Maurice. 'Katherine Mansfield and the Miracle of Grief'. *The Reader's Digest,* March 1975

Shereshevskaya, Maria. 'Katherine Mansfield: The English Anton T.' *The Dominion,* 12 January 1974

Stead, C.K. 'Katherine Mansfield and the Art of Fiction'. *The New Review,* vol. 4, no. 42, September 1977

Sutherland, Ronald. 'Katherine Mansfield Plagiarist, Disciple or Ardent Admirer?' *Critique,* V 1962 (58-71)

Taylor, Moira. 'The marvel is she understands'. *The NZ Listener,* 27 April 1974

Taylor, Moira. 'A child with the children'. *The NZ Listener,* 4 May 1974

Taylor, Moira. 'It'll be all right'. *The NZ Listener*, 11 May 1974

Tomlinson, Sophie. 'Mansfield in Bookform.' *Landfall* 156

University of Texas, *Catalogue of Katherine Mansfield, An Exhibition.* Humanities Research Centre, 1975

Wattie, Nelson, 'A Bibliography of Katherine Mansfield References 1970-1984'. *Journal of New Zealand Literature*, no. 3, 1985

Webby, Elizabeth. 'Katherine Mansfield: Everything and Nothing'. *Meanjin*, vol. 41, no. 2, June 1982

West, Rebecca. 'Notes on Novels: The Garden Party'. *New Statesman*, 18 March 1922

Selected bibliography of works by Katherine Mansfield

In a German Pension. London: Stephen Swift, December 1911. New York: Knopf, 1926*

Prelude. Richmond: Hogarth Press, July 1918

Je ne parle pas français. Hampstead: Heron Press, February 1920

Bliss and Other Stories. London: Constable, December 1920. New York: Knopf, January 1921*

The Garden Party and Other Stories. London: Constable, February 1922. New York: Knopf, May 1922*

The Doves' Nest and Other Stories, ed. J.M. Murry. London: Constable, June 1923. New York: Knopf, August 1923*

Poems, ed. J.M. Murry. London: Constable, November 1923. New York: Knopf, February 1924

Something Childish and Other Stories, ed. J.M. Murry. London: Constable, August 1924;* *The Little Girl*, New York: Knopf, October 1924

The Journal of Katherine Mansfield, ed. J.M. Murry. London: Constable, 1927. New York: Knopf, 1927

The Letters of Katherine Mansfield, ed. J.M. Murry, 2 vols. London: Constable, 1928, 1 vol., New York: Knopf, 1929

Maxim Gorki, Reminiscences of Leonid Andreyev, translated from the Russian by Katherine Mansfield and S.S Koteliansky. New York: Crosby Gaige, 1928

The Aloe, ed. J.M. Murry. London: Constable 1930. New York: Knopf, 1930

Novels and Novelists, ed, J.M. Murry. London: Constable, 1930

The Scrapbook of Katherine Mansfield, ed, J.M. Murry. London: Constable, 1937

Collected Stories of Katherine Mansfield. London: Constable, 1945 (a collection of the five volumes marked *)

The Stories of Katherine Mansfield, ed. Antony Alpers. Auckland: Oxford University Press, 1984 (includes material not in the 1945 Constable edition, or other facsimile editions)

'Brave Love' transcribed by Margaret Scott in *Landfall* (Christchurch), XXVI, March 1972

'The Unpublished Manuscripts of Katherine Mansfield' transcribed and edited by Margaret Scott in the *Turnbull Library Record* (new series): vol. III, no. 1, March 1970, pp4-28; vol. III, no. 3, November 1970, pp128-33; vol. IV, no. 1, May 1971 pp4-20; vol. V, no. 1, May 1972, pp9-25; vol. VI, no. 2, October 1973, pp4-8; vol. VI, no. 1, May 1974, pp4-14; vol. XII, no. 1, May 1979, pp11-28

Katherine Mansfield: Publications in Australia 1907-9, Jean Stone. Sydney: Wentworth Books, 1977

Katherine Mansfield's Letters to John Middleton Murry, 1913-1922, ed. J.M. Murry. London: Constable, 1951

Journal of Katherine Mansfield, 'Definitive Edition', ed. J.M. Murry. London: Constable, 1954

The Letters and Journals of Katherine Mansfield: A Selection ed. C.K. Stead. London: Allen Lane, 1977 (includes 'To Stanislaw Wyspianski' a poem first printed in 1938)

The Collected Letters of Katherine Mansfield. Vol.1: 1903-1917, ed. Vincent O' Sullivan and Margaret Scott. Oxford: Clarendon, 1984; vol. 2: 1918-1919, 1987

The Urewera Notebook, ed. Ian Gordon. Oxford University Press, 1980 (the notebook kept by Katherine Mansfield during her 1907 North Island journey, transcribed and illustrated)

Index